Schooling the Nation

T0244181

WOMEN, GENDER, AND SEXUALITY
IN AMERICAN HISTORY

Editorial Advisors:
Susan K. Cahn
Wanda A. Hendricks
Deborah Gray White
Anne Firor Scott, Founding Editor Emerita

*For a list of books in the series, please see
our website at www.press.uillinois.edu.*

Schooling the Nation

The Success of the Canterbury Academy for Black Women

JENNIFER RYCENGA

With a Foreword by
KAZIMIERA KOZLOWSKI

UNIVERSITY OF ILLINOIS PRESS
Urbana, Chicago, and Springfield

Publication was supported by a grant from the
Howard D. and Marjorie I. Brooks Fund for
Progressive Thought. Many thanks to the Dean's
Office of the College of Humanities and the Arts at
San José State University for their support.

Cataloging data available from the Library of Congress

ISBN 978-0-252-04630-8 (hardcover)
ISBN 978-0-252-08837-7 (paperback)
ISBN 978-0-252-04758-9 (ebook)

To my mother, Dolores,
who thinks of all human beings with love and
equal consideration,
thank you for teaching me to do the same.

To the loyal, longsuffering first director of the
Prudence Crandall Museum,
Kaz Kozlowski,
who lost neither patience nor temper with me.

Our cause . . . I trust will be the means of arousing the nations to their duty with respect to the condition of our colored population, and be the means of allaying the prejudice of Americans.

—Sarah Harris, 1833

Contents

Foreword

I had the privilege of being the curator and site administrator of the Prudence Crandall Museum in Canterbury, Connecticut, for more than thirty-five years—from 1984 (when the State of Connecticut opened the museum to the public) until my retirement in 2018. As a Connecticut native, born, raised, and *educated*, I realized early in my tenure how unfamiliar I was with this educator, abolitionist, and radical thinker prior to becoming involved with the site. It became a goal to change this: to take every opportunity to share with the public what previous curators, I, my staff, museum volunteers, scholars, and researchers had and would uncover about this complex series of events. It seemed inexcusable that what took place in northeast Connecticut in the early nineteenth century was not common knowledge. It was obvious that there was so much more to this story, and the museum soon became a linchpin in sharing that story.

Once the Crandall Museum opened its doors, it became a destination for historians, authors, students, and visitors from across the nation and from around the globe who were eager to find out more about this group of amazing women. Women whose stories had, for far too long, been cast into history's shadows.

I met Jennifer Rycenga in 1997 when she visited the Prudence Crandall Museum for the first time. Even then it was obvious that what intrigued her most were the back stories of the Black and white women involved in the academy. In her I found a kindred spirit. A woman like me who was old enough to remember how important the 1972 passage of Title IX had been in expanding women's educational opportunities. Though our experiences as white female students pale in comparison to what nineteenth-century Black women experienced, I think both of us come to the Crandall story with the same appreciation for how education can drastically expand a young woman's worldview.

Though accounts of the events surrounding the Canterbury Female Boarding School have been told and retold, too often the importance of the contributions made by women, especially Black women, was either minimized at best or at worst completely ignored. Rycenga's meticulous and painstaking research raises all that may have been ignored to light, giving credit where credit is due.

The reality is that had Mariah Davis *not* supplied her employer, Prudence Crandall, with a copy of the *Liberator* newspaper while Davis worked as the academy's "household assistant," and had Sarah Harris *not* crossed the school's threshold in the fall of 1832 to ask, "Miss Crandall, I want to get a little more learning, if possible, enough to teach colored children," and had Prudence Crandall *not* weighed her options and determined, "As wealth was not mine, I saw no other means of benefiting them, than by imparting to those of my own sex that were anxious to learn, all the instruction I might be able to give, however small the amount," the school would have remained simply one of countless academies established to provide a private education to the daughters of wealthy white families during the early years of the republic.

The decisions Davis, Harris, and Crandall *do* choose to make is what sets them—and the Canterbury Female Boarding School—apart. It is these women's actions that serve as a catalyst for the events going forward. Three women, working within the constraints of society's imposed "women's sphere," doing all that they could to provide other women with an education. It's their determination and perseverance that create the first private academy for young Black women in the United States.

Schooling the Nation: The Success of the Canterbury Academy for Black Women also gives rightly deserved emphasis to the contributions and achievements the students of the second Canterbury Academy made once they were forced to leave the school. Rycenga gives an in-depth and comprehensive portrayal of what the students continued to achieve post-Canterbury. (Unlike a male lecturer at a program I attended a decade ago, who, when asked, "What happened to the students when the school closed?" responded with the simplistic and patronizing, "Well, they just left and went home.") The students may have been compelled to leave, but these young women were not leaving emptyhanded. They took with them the academic learning, life experiences, and friendships their time in Canterbury gave them. They went on to use these experiences to influence social change throughout the course of their lifetimes. It's as the author describes it—they used the opportunities education provided for not only their own benefit but also the benefit of others.

Rycenga, an educator herself, continues in this tradition. Her unique combination of academic interests and scholarly focus now adds this work to the list of publications that endeavor to view and understand our nation's complicated and often painful history through a variety of lenses. Lenses broad and clear enough to see the significance and value of the contributions of *all* those involved.

Schooling the Nation puts a spotlight on the lives and legacies of an amazing group of teachers and students. It shows how the events that took place over those seventeen months in the town of Canterbury, Connecticut, evolved from a local controversy to a flashpoint in the nation's struggle for civil rights. And, most important, it serves to remind us of the importance of doing the right thing.

Kazimiera Kozlowski
The Prudence Crandall Museum
Museum curator and site administrator (retired)
November 18, 2023

Preface

The educator must herself be educated.
—Karl Marx, *Theses on Feuerbach*
(gender modified)

A glance inside the Canterbury Female Academy in 1833 would reveal a surprising set of vignettes. Black women assiduously reading and heeding the moral messages of the most recent philosophic texts. African American clergymen vouching for the good intentions of a white woman teacher. White men using their privileged access to law, education, and publishing to fight for Black civil rights; a few even consciously expanding the meaning and practice of American democracy to white women, Black women, and Black men by respecting their intellectual contributions. Teenagers of color withstanding taunts, sexual innuendo, vigilante threats, and actual courtroom dramas to pursue their education. White and Black women living, working, and studying together despite openly hostile neighbors.

These unusual moments establish a beachhead for American intersectionality: the Canterbury Academy, in its second incarnation as a center of advanced learning for "Young Ladies and Little Misses of Color." More than two dozen Black women studied with Prudence Crandall (1803–90) over the eighteen months that her second academy flourished in eastern Connecticut. The idea for this school emerged from the initiative of Black women, who found in Crandall a receptive white woman. Her response was an early example of what we now term antiracism: the conscious perception that all people are equally entitled to share in human community, with no negative qualities inherent in social identities.[1]

Antiracism *should* be foundationally clear, the gist of it declared thus: "All men are created equal." Yet, that very Declaration of Independence seeds the contradictions: its author was an enslaver who compared Blacks to orangutans while fathering mixed-race children in an ipso facto exploitative sexual relationship with Sally Hemings (1773–1835), whom he enslaved. Arriving at and sustaining intersectional antiracism in an environment laced with presumptions of Black inferiority, female passivity, and denigration of the poor turn out to be very thorny practices. But not impossible.

This book tells America's Canterbury tale as Chaucer did his narrative, through human diversity. To achieve this, *Schooling the Nation* focuses on networks, alliances, and intersectional activism. These reveal the range and impact of the Canterbury Academy in African American, women's, and abolitionist history. The story encompasses race, gender, sexuality, class, citizenship, access to education, religious affiliation, spiritual seeking, nonviolence, and social justice. It is both an inspiring story and a cautionary tale. American feminist history has been haunted by rifts over race and class. This makes Canterbury, in its exceptionalism, both wondrous and maddening: exemplary for its success yet disappointing for not having become commonplace. Understanding it in its complexity can goad and guide us to more and better practices for social justice.

Education is the gateway to the shared inheritance and culture of humanity. Peoples' ability to preserve and convey vast accumulated storehouses of knowledge, from one generation to another, is nothing short of miraculous. This is true whether education is formal or informal, technical or speculative, culturally validated or stolen on the sly.[2]

The regrettably pervasive human impulse to bar access to our shared storehouse of knowledge is a less sanguine legacy. The Canterbury Academy stands as a preeminent example of both access gained and access denied, as teachers and students, allies and families struggled in the face of steady white opposition. This narrative does not lavish attention on the enemies of the school. Those white men are too representative of their time and place, too wedded to the limits of the given, and frankly too self-centered to be of much interest in an intersectional analysis. They are mentioned, but their names are not on the marquee.

The heroes of this retelling are Maria Davis, Sarah Harris Fayerweather, Eliza Glasko, Miranda Glasko, Julia Williams, Elizabeth Brown Smith, Mary Elizabeth Miles, Ann Eliza Hammond, Elizabeth Marshall and her daughters, Frederick Olney, Maria Stewart, Peter Williams Jr., Theodore Wright, Henry Highland Garnet, James Hayborn, David Walker, Prudence Crandall, Almira Crandall, Jonathan Dymond, Lydia Maria Child, Charles Burleigh and his siblings William Burleigh and Mary Burleigh, Samuel J. May, David Ruggles, William Lloyd Garrison, and many more. Together these people—Black and white, male and female—labored to change America. They did not succeed as completely as we (and they) might have wished, but neither did they fail.

Prudence Crandall's Academy marks a rare breach in white attitudes toward Black higher education in the antebellum north. Black women received in Canterbury the highest level of education open to women at the time, imbibing knowledge while in a perilous fishbowl. Despite constant harassment, the students stayed focused on their purpose. Never did they reveal each other's names to the hostile mobs. Never did they sway from the discipline of nonviolence that their teacher, their readings, and their own Christianity encouraged. Their lives after the school show they had been well prepared. By the end of the nineteenth century, the school was held dear in memory by Black men and women, from newspaper editors to humble soldiers.

The Canterbury school is often dismissed as a failure because of its closure following a devastating physical attack on the building in September 1834. Yet, one of the students, recording her bittersweet memory of the school's end, indicates that it was a success:

> I have found among them [my schoolmates] simple manners and intelligent minds; and there, if anywhere, love was without dissimulation. My teacher was ever kind: with him [William Burleigh] I saw religion, not merely adopted as an empty form, but a living, all-pervading principle of action. He lived like those who seek a better country.[3]

This student's testimony lauds the experiment that was the Canterbury Academy. The students, their families, teachers, supporters, and larger network had worked and struggled together not for individual achievement alone but always, as Kabria Baumgartner writes, "to a greater good and a broader purpose," a just and enlightened world.[4]

Acknowledgments

This project has spanned the entire twenty-first century, making the construction of a complete acknowledgment list daunting. I was introduced to the women of the abolitionist movement through a series of fortuitous meetings in the 1990s. I was inspired by the writings of Maria Stewart, which I had learned of through the personal mentorship of Sue Houchins and reading Raya Dunayevskaya. As I came to analyze race, gender, and sexuality, I benefitted from immersive intellectual discussions in southern California with Ruth Wilson Gilmore, Karen Barad, Michelle Gubbay, Benita Ramsey, and Zayn Kassam.

On a museum jaunt in 1997, my mother Dolores and I stopped at the Prudence Crandall Museum in Canterbury, and the die was cast. We were welcomed by the superb first curator Kazimiera Kozlowski. From this point, connections to museum interns, scholars, artists, and local historians pursuing further knowledge of Canterbury flourished. Especially helpful in this regard have been Lisa Joseph, Donna DuFresne, Gertrude Blanks, Arthur Marinelli, Lynne Pitman, Erica Ciallela, Paula Roswell, Vicki Sear, Nicole Chalfant, Jo Ann Hauck, Richard Hauck, Holly Fulton, and Bill Peebles. The current curator, Joan DiMartino, has understood the myriad ways to incorporate the work of scholars into the museum and is a fabulous working colleague.

The most dedicated promoter of Prudence Crandall's memory, Barry McGuire, recently passed away, but his memory is embedded in the vast acreage of the Elk Falls, Kansas, roadside history monument to Crandall that he conceived as a fitting way to celebrate her. He was invaluable to me in my research and became a dear friend. While in residence at the Five College Women's Center in Northampton, Massachusetts, Roanne Wilson,

Susan Edwards, and the late Richard Gassan provided material and emotional assistance.

The scholarly friends of Prudence Crandall form a geometrically expanding circle of talented thinkers and committed researchers. The preceding full-length studies and archival repositories created by David O. White, Rodney Davis, Marvis Welch, Susan Strane, Julie Winch, Philip Foner, Josephine Pacheco, Paul Goodman, and William Mayer form the bedrock of scholarship. More recently, that bedrock has been sculpted into a meticulous weave by Afua Cooper, Carla Peterson, Kabria Baumgartner, Peter Hinks, Donald Williams, Nancy Steenburg, Elizabeth Stevens, Kate Blankenship, Lois Brown, Robert Forbes, Kristin Waters, Tom Schuch, Dwight Brown and Anna Brown of Westerly, Rhode Island, Hudson River Film and Video, and Dale Plummer, to name a few. Descendants of the Crandall family and of the students have also been remarkably generous, from the late Jessica Nashold and her sons Barney and Hank to Joyce Mosely, Joyce Stevos, Judy Piper, and Chuck Piper.

My colleagues at San José State University were invaluable, offering feedback, new leads, and funding research trips and sabbaticals. Special thanks to my department chairs—Chris Jochim, Shannon Rose Riley, and Selma Burkom—and my colleagues with related interests: Ruma Chopra, Persis Karim, Maria Alaniz, Mira Amiras, J. Todd Ormsbee, Erik Johnson, Kenneth Peter, Jim Lindahl, Bob Rucker, Steve Millner, Ethel Walker, Daniel Lanza Rivers, Erica Colmenares, William Meredith, Rona Halualani, Lois Helmbold, Funie Hsu, Valerie Lo, Matthew Kapell, and deceased faculty Ruth Wilson, Richard Keady, and Ken Kramer. So many students added to this project with their responses, most notably, Vicki Robison and Tyson Amir. A sequence of intellectually minded deans aided my project, especially Shannon Miller, Carmen Sigler, and Lisa Vollendorf.

The librarians at the Martin Luther King Jr. Library, especially Nick Szyldowski, Peggy Cabrera, and Silke Higgins, are remarkable colleagues. Archival librarians have a remarkable job, entrusted with the protection of the past for the sake of the future. I have visited over seventy archives of all sizes, from the luxurious American Antiquarian Society to the sprawling treasures of the Kansas State Historical Society, to modest vertical files at public libraries. At every stop I have found capable professionals at work, excited to see materials they've protected being utilized, and unfailingly dedicated to the mission of sharing knowledge. I cannot thank them sufficiently.

Friends have come to my rescue many times by reading drafts, hearing talks and laughing and rejoicing with me. Thanks especially to Ruth Charloff, David Black, Louis Mazza, Ted Floyd, Greg Lawrence, Emily Culpepper, Linda Barufaldi, Arisika Razak, Laurie Green, Lou Turner, Leslie Flint, Donna Pomeroy, Michael Retter, Matt Hale, Julene Johnson, Merav Vonshak, Deb Kramer, and Cat Chang. I have also been privileged to be in an exceptional cohort that started in the Young Scholars in American Religion program, consisting of Deborah Dash Moore, Laura Levitt, Liza McAlister, Tracy Fessenden, Ava Chamberlain, Kate Joyce, David Watt, Judith Weisenfeld, and the late Leonard Primiano. We may no longer be exactly young, but we remain creative and mutually encouraging.

My editor at the University of Illinois Press, Dominique Moore, has been a joy to work with, as has her assistant Leigh Ann Cowan. I am doubly indebted to series editor Wanda Hendricks for her work on Fannie Barrier Williams, as well as her championing of my manuscript. Susanna Sturgis and Laura Helper guided me with gentle editorial hands. The anonymous readers offered strong suggestions that have improved this work.

My family has stood by me over the years, aiding in transcription projects and encouraging me when my spirits lagged. My sisters and their spouses— Clara and Rick Marchese, and Mary and John Shukie—always welcomed me with open arms when I would emerge bleary-eyed from research libraries, giving me love, advice, and victuals. My nieces and nephews have been stupendous, especially my longest-running research assistant, Miranda Marchese. My mother, Dolores, the guiding voice of moral suasion in my conscience, remains my biggest cheerleader and most consistent nag. My late mother-in-law, Millie Wagner, provided space and time and love. As to my wife, Peggy Macres, I cannot say enough. Her patience with a project that has lasted our entire partnership, as well as her trenchant critiques when I was about to err from overenthusiasm or her timely intervention to prevent groanworthy puns places every reader in her debt.

Schooling the Nation

INTRODUCTION

A Luminous Moment

> History is best figured not as an accurate
> record or transcript of the past but as a per-
> spectival discourse that seeks to articulate
> a living memory for the present and future.
> —Elizabeth Schussler-Fiorenza

The story of Prudence Crandall and her Canterbury Female Boarding School for Black women is replete with made-for-Hollywood heroes and villains, yet retains a stubborn marginality. This book seeks to center the story, because the efforts of Crandall and the students are sterling examples of cooperation, struggle, and success with resonance over the centuries.

Crandall—a white woman raised Quaker who converted to the Baptists—opened a select academy under the sponsorship of the white male leadership of the town of Canterbury, Connecticut, in 1831. In the fall of 1832, a Black woman, Sarah Harris, asked if she could enroll, in order to become a teacher herself. Harris risked this request because her future sister-in-law and Crandall's household assistant, Maria Davis, had been supplying the teacher with the abolitionist newspaper, the *Liberator*. After hearing Sarah's entreaty, Crandall deliberated and then agreed. White parents, scandalized by this novel interracial experiment, demanded Crandall dismiss Harris. Crandall, instead, chose to reconfigure her academy for Black women only. She sought and gained the support of William Lloyd Garrison, the *Liberator*'s editor. By April 1833, despite fierce opposition from white town leaders, this second academy opened. At least thirty-one students attended the second academy, despite the passage of a Black law attempting to forbid out-of-state Black students. Legal actions generated four trials, yet the school persisted until a devastating vigilante attack in September 1834. With the house uninhabitable and the students terrorized, Crandall and her allies closed the academy. Many, then and now, have declared the school a "failure," shunting the students and Crandall to obscurity.[1]

Others have recognized something of greater importance than just another "incident of racism."[2] Howard University opened Crandall Hall in 1931; the

University of Rhode Island named a residence hall for Sarah Harris Fayerweather in 1970. In 1959 early feminist scholar Eleanor Flexner extolled Crandall for belonging "not only to the antislavery movement, but also to that for woman's rights." Crandall literally gained monumental status when dubbed the official state heroine of Connecticut in 1995.[3]

Those who have heard and understood the story include the biographers of Crandall who have preceded me—most notably Susan Strane, Donald Williams, and Marvis Welch. Their excellent work, though, did not have the capability, made possible by advances in scholarship and the digitizing of newspapers, to fully reconstruct the Black dimensions of the story.

Despite such glimmers of recognition, Crandall and the school remain a footnote in most studies of abolition, race, and women's history. The Black students rarely merit even citational ciphers. The magnitude of what the Black community and Crandall were attempting and what she and her students accomplished has been oversimplified. This volume presents the story of Crandall and the students by embedding them as part of the currents—and a force altering those currents—in nineteenth-century America.

Agency—the ability to act—is central to this story, from both individuals and communities, especially when African American men and women and white women strategically exercise agency under structural constraints.[4] Canterbury saw contributions from four distinct groups: Black women, Black men, white women, and white men. Each group's social position dictated particular roles, generating a multipronged antiracist phalanx. This narrative spotlights instances of Black agency and female agency. It is also important to note how a cognitive minority of white men used their privilege to subvert racism. Any fight against imposed social stratifications generates novel interconnections among people—some structural, some serendipitous, some revelatory. In each chapter, Crandall and/or her Black students are placed at the hub of a wheel of connections that illuminates unexpected prismatic facets.

The Canterbury Academy aids in constructing a lineage for antiracism, facilitating a usable history around intersections of race and gender. This school for Black women provided significant—and sympathetic—visibility for immediate abolition. It arguably stands among the most successful abolitionist alliances—practically and ideologically—of white and Black, male and female. Inspired by Black women, carried into action by a white woman willing to disavow her privilege, endorsed and supported by the free Black male elite and the white male leaders of the incipient immediate abolition movement, the academy was not an act *by* whites *for* Blacks; it was *by* Black and white, female and male, *with* each other, *for* the participation of all. Furthermore, Canterbury focused national attention on northern racism.[5] At a time when most white abolitionists were afraid to be seen with their Black allies, Crandall spent two years in daily contact and cohabitation with African

Americans. While there were likely tense moments within that span, the experiences of Crandall and her other white teachers at the academy were less marked by the destructive aspects of American racism than most such interactions to that date. Everyone strove together, cherishing and learning from each other.

Young Ladies and Little Misses of Color:
Antiracist from Inception

Having been converted to abolitionist principles by Black women, Crandall vaulted to action. The phrase "Young Ladies and Little Misses of Color" in the advertisement for the second academy accorded honorific titles usually reserved for white women. Crandall used these terms without qualification, before the Black students had even arrived. She *presumed* their worthiness, without forcing them to prove their respectability first.

Black women and white women worked together to make the school a reality; Black men and white men worked together to sustain and promote it. But the vast majority of white people in the United States assumed white supremacy as a natural, God-given fact and consistently opposed the academy. A week before the reopening, this racist editorial pinpointed the school's nefarious intent: throwing down the gauntlet of full human equality:

> We must protest against carrying out the leveling principle to this extreme. We do not believe, that nature ever intended the sable race of Africa for our intimate associates. . . . It is unquestionably true, that every female, whatever may be the color of her skin, ought to have the advantage of a common school education; but all beyond this in the case of blacks, is a useless expenditure of time and money. . . . The notion that the blacks are our equals, and that by education and culture, they may be rendered proper subjects for the intimate connexions in life, with the whites, is preposterously absurd. . . . We ask in the name of common sense, if a young lady of the talents and acquirements of Miss Prudence Crandall, can descend so low, as to encourage the promiscuous herding of our amiable young ladies, with these "young ladies and little Misses of color," of which she speaks. We have long lamented the mental and moral darkness, in which the world is enveloped, but we were not aware that common sense, common propriety and even common decency, had taken their flight.[6]

In a classic reversal, the writer refers to social equality as "mental and moral darkness" lacking in "common sense . . . and even common decency." The editorialist highlights with pinpoint clarity the hierarchies that were challenged by the Canterbury venture: social order, respectability, the "intimate connexions" of sexuality, suitability of education to one's predetermined station.

Condescending attitudes, such as this infuriated editorialist's patronizing tone, were ubiquitous. To break through this seeming unanimity of white superiority was the necessary first step in creating an antiracist coalition. A few white abolitionists succeeded, though even they made missteps. It is hardly surprising that white abolitionists did not immediately grasp when they were being patronizing, monopolizing the agenda, or ignoring voices they had never been encouraged to hear. Scholars from Leon Litwack to Manisha Sinha have noted the ubiquity of racist attitudes among white abolitionists. Black activists at the time noted it, too, including Theodore Wright, Hosea Easton, and Martin Delany.[7] But while the vicissitudes of these early attempts at antiracism are easy to critique in their shortcomings or, in contrast, to iconize uncritically from their high points, neither approach is helpful. The trail out of the tangled brambles of racism has had many false starts and snags. This obviates neither the successes nor the errors of those who cut the earliest pathways.

Reconceptualizing the Canterbury Academy

"How long shall the fair daughters of Africa be compelled to bury their minds and talents beneath a load of iron pots and kettles?"[8] Maria Stewart prophetically demanded an answer, having seen her own life course impeded by the vise grips of racism and lack of access to education. Stewart knew—and had the courage to proclaim publicly—that women needed more opportunities for higher education. Her clarion call to establish a high school, made in 1831, chronologically preceded Crandall's acceptance of Sarah Harris by only a few months.[9] This salient fact and the sequence of events that led to Harris being admitted to the school are keen instances of Black community activism and initiative. Crandall's school fulfilled a need expressed by Blacks to have higher educational opportunities for women, enabling some in the free Black middle class to access professions such as teaching. Part of a strategy of uplift and respectability, the Canterbury Academy received public endorsements from eight Black and seven white male abolitionist leaders. The school imparted a foretaste of an America where cooperation across lines of race, gender, and class would be possible. Many of the Black students went on to be teachers and moved in middle-class circles where they assisted in struggles for citizenship, suffrage, and security in their lives, neighborhoods, and for their children.

New forces and new dimensions are unleashed at moments of change. The eighteen months of the Canterbury school included a unity of action and thought, creating a dynamic learning situation, from textbook choices to the rhetorical strategies and diversity found in the abolitionist literature the students read.

Legal harassment of the school produced four trials. These courtroom dramas are famed for the arguments Crandall's white male legal team made in defense of Black citizenship. The crucial role of the students in these legal proceedings, though, has been undertheorized. They were key witnesses and speakers in the courtroom. In each of the cases where we have testimony from students, their poise, presence, and clarity were decisive; the two trials where they testified were won by the abolitionists. The trials were significant social dramas through which young Black women protected their own education and publicly dispelled racist discourse about their unfitness for education.

Matters of class status and economic security also affected the school. There were some impoverished students who attended the academy, including one receiving financial assistance from a formerly enslaved woman, a pair of sisters whom Crandall herself subsidized, and one who performed household tasks to defray expenses.[10] Later in her life, Crandall taught literacy to adults who had self-liberated, and her alumnae taught across class lines, too.

The peace movement was a concern to white abolitionists in and around Canterbury, including Crandall. Debates over nonviolent resistance are likewise important in African American history. The structural impediments to women adopting wholesale violence have led to nonviolence being almost axiomatic for women.[11] But here there was a difference: the students were imbibing the latest theories of nonviolence, in the work of Jonathan Dymond, while living the practice of nonviolence as they pursued their education.

A few misconceptions about Crandall and her school haunt the historic record. The first is confusion about Crandall's religious identity. While she was a birthright Quaker and attended Quaker schools, she converted to the Baptists in 1830. Many accounts stress her Quaker identity, placing her comfortably within a well-worn paradigm. This leads, though, to a reduction in the perception of her agency that erodes her independence of mind, especially when her Baptist affiliation is linked to her marriage to Baptist minister Calvin Philleo. Although this is a subtle error, its exposes presumptions that dismiss women's religious decisions as derivative, following fathers and husbands.

Speculation that the second Canterbury Academy was a mere tool of white male abolitionists are insidious innuendos.[12] Contemporary enemies of the school referred to Crandall as "the mere nominal defendant, put forward by others, whose machinations would disturb the tranquility of this whole nation."[13] But far from being a white-hatched scheme, abundant evidence points to the involvement of Black women and men in the founding and sustenance of the academy. Attempts to deny or sidestep this Black and female agency maintain the patronizing rhetoric that referred to Crandall as a deluded female who had "imbibed the wild notions of Garrison," only changing her scholars to Black ones "at the instigation of Garrison."[14] Crandall never wavered in crediting Davis and Harris with bringing her to consciousness. In the decision to change the student body to Black women, Crandall affirmed she had been "wholly self-moved," which her correspondence with Garrison corroborates.[15] The very notion that Black families would risk the safety of their teenage daughters to further a publicity stunt is ludicrous. But glib assumptions follow when Black lives are not accorded full humanity.

Intersectionality is a theoretical perspective that consistently forefronts multiple factors involved in identities and social positioning. Canterbury can add appreciably to an understanding of intersectionality, since it involved six dimensions of identity: race, gender, class, age, religion, and sexuality. One of the students, Mary E. Miles, wrote of having to face "prejudice against poverty, prejudice against color" and "prejudice against her sex."[16] The students and their allies consciously combated the constant psychic drain of racism.[17]

Second, despite Flexner's recognition of Crandall's role in women's history, there are specific aspects of the school—the embrace of nonviolence, the constant "specter" of interracial marriage, the assumptions that threats of violence and legal action would intimidate the women—that point to the need for a more thorough feminist analysis. The academy, preceding the Grimké sisters and Seneca Falls, suggests that women's rights in the United States did not have to wreck on the shoals of racism as happened after the Civil War and in pockets of the Second Wave.

Third, the ages of the students and of their teachers interlock with the sexualization of young women. The average age of the students was around sixteen, making them sexually mature people. Their age, in fact, fomented much of the white opposition: the school's enemies believed the academy offered more education than Blacks or women needed and that having these Black women in the village would spark sexual liaisons. For most of the life of the school, Crandall herself was unmarried, provoking all manner of sexual innuendo about her husband-hunting among Black men. Picturing the students as adolescents casts their ordeals at the hands of bullies in the street and in the judge's seat especially uncomfortable to imagine. The white male presumption that they could exploit Black women sexually (whether in slavery or freedom) likely led to salacious taunting. Yet, through all this the students persisted.

Fourth, religion plays a variety of roles in the story of Canterbury. Crandall and her students were ecumenical toward intra-Protestant religious differences. The students represented Quaker, Congregational, Episcopal, Baptist, and likely other denominations. The white Canterburian foes focused on religion's social status: the students were shut out by the prestigious Congregational Church but accepted in Crandall's own Baptist congregation.

Fifth, the class dimensions of eastern Connecticut, impacted by industrialization, maritime activity, disestablishment, and more, provided significant upward mobility to local Blacks like Isaac Glasko, William Harris, David Ruggles, and Frederick Olney. The developing class stratification of free Blacks in the major cities of New York and Philadelphia affected the students from those areas and constrain our knowledge, centuries later, about their lives after the school's closure.

The gravest misreading holds that the school was a failure. Consider how the *minds* of these Black women were the contested battleground. The white opposition did not want these young women to be heirs to the legacy of humankind, to be respectable members of the middle class, to become professional educators. They did not want these young Black women to be equal to young white women as marriage prospects. They didn't even want these free Black women to remain in the United States! The white opposition yearned to stunt the students' intellectual potential. They are the ones who failed utterly. This book amplifies the life stories of the students as the measure of the school's success.

The Luminous Moment

When Davis trusted her employer with the *Liberator*, when Harris dared approach the white teacher, and when Crandall genuinely listened to Harris—these constitute moments when history changed decisively, through the agency of women "hearing each other into being."[18] The personal nature of this story matters. Crandall's actual human relationships with Davis and Harris launched the process of uprooting the racism that inheres in everyone born and raised in a racist society. Crandall cannot and does not want to imagine an America without her friend Sarah Harris. In an unflattering recapitulation of Solomon's baby, the white opposition and colonizationists were all too willing, even eager, to see Black people leave.

The leading white men of Connecticut who opposed the school are distressingly typical. White Americans anywhere would have reacted with virulence against an advanced school for African Americans; Canterbury "probably did no worse than any town in the state would have done in similar circumstance."[19] White people opposed to Black improvement and even Black citizenship were ubiquitous and still are.

The school's enemies couldn't prevent the students' success. The school at the center of Canterbury became a hub of learning and sisterhood, a place where the expansion of women's minds and Black minds went beyond attempts to constrict them. The luminous moment of the Canterbury Academy for Young Ladies and Little Misses of Color sheds sufficient light to illuminate our way.

CHAPTER 1

Crandall and Canterbury
The (Un)Steady State
of the Standing Order

Do not get lost in a sea of despair. Be hopeful, be
optimistic. Our struggle is not the struggle of a day,
a week, a month, or a year, it is the struggle of a
lifetime. Never, ever be afraid to make some noise
and get in good trouble, necessary trouble.
—John Lewis

Why was Prudence Crandall, of all white people, primed to take bold steps
against racial prejudice? Academics, trained to find precedents, must morph
into seismologists at moments of monumental change, tracing subterranean
roots for discontinuities after an earthquake reveals fault lines and rearranges
the visible landscape.

Connecticut imagined itself as the Land of Steady Habits, an idyll of
"church harmony, purity, and homogeneity of belief" with the "Standing
Order"—white, male, educated Congregational elites—in charge.[1] But this
was always fictive; fissures proliferated in the early nineteenth century.

Connecticut's disestablishment of the Congregational Church in 1818
marked an epoch in the state's history. The way had been prepared by a large
in-migration of Quakers and Baptists. Southeastern Connecticut, blessed
with riverine industrial power and a strong port in New London, experienced
growing manufacturing enterprises and religious diversity. The relatively
small Black community was as economically secure as any in New England,
while the Quaker presence produced white women with leadership skills.
White radicals from New London to Hampton would provide one of the
richest veins of activists and thinkers in the abolition movement.

Crandall was fortunate to be raised Quaker, giving her spiritual, political,
and educational opportunities unavailable to most American women of any
race at the time. Quaker women's education was not frivolous but substan-
tive.[2] Though not devoid of sexism, Quaker lifeways produced women more
independent than the norm.

Auspicious as these circumstances might be, they only prepare the way. This chapter uses multiple lenses in considering what makes Prudence Crandall possible: personal, social, and political. Her family, faith, and schooling shape her, but so does the famed antebellum "Benevolent Empire"—a virtual archipelago of volunteer associations for large moral projects. The pivotal year of 1831 saw the immediate-abolition movement integrate Black and white, male and female, in a common cause. Missing any of these factors, the Canterbury Academy that Crandall cocreated would not have happened.

A Heritage of Stubborn Resistance:
Crandall's Background

Prudence Crandall was born September 3, 1803, in Hopkinton, Rhode Island, the second of four children born to Pardon Crandall (1778–1838) and Esther Carpenter Crandall (1784–1872).[3] Prudence's parents were married in a Seventh-Day Baptist ceremony, but sometime early in their marriage they became Quakers by convincement.[4] Pardon and Esther Crandall took the external forms of the Quaker faith seriously: plain dress, plain language, abstention from drinking and gambling, and disdain for slavery.[5] Being a member of the Society of Friends did not shield young Prudence from socially common presumptions about gender. Once, as a young girl, Prudence insisted on listening to a business discussion between her father and a neighbor. This act of "childish insubordination" resulted in her being "ignominiously led by the ear into the house."[6]

Another anecdote discloses oppressively taut marital dynamics between Pardon and Esther. Esther wanted to attend a Quaker clambake; she "gently importuned Pardon to take her." Her husband interpreted her request as badgering; he but "gruffly assent[ed]." The next day he drove her, in total silence, to the event. When they arrived, he turned the cart around and said, "You wanted to go to the clambake,—I took ye, didn't I?" After this humiliating public disappointment, the couple rode back home, and Pardon was at work by the early afternoon.[7] Such icy cruelty can only issue from a marital structure that assumes absolute female subordination to male authority.

After the Crandalls moved to Connecticut in July 1813, Esther became active in the Plainfield Quaker meeting, and their children attended the nearby Black Hill Quaker School. Prudence's three siblings all contributed to the abolitionist movement (though with significant differences of perspective): her older brother, Hezekiah (1800–1881), younger brother, Reuben (1806–38), and younger sister, Hannah Almira (1813–37).

The decision to relocate to Connecticut was part of a larger migration of Friends from Rhode Island to Connecticut, lured by an increase in manufacturing among Quakers and Connecticut's rich river system to power the mills.[8]

An old saying holds that Quakers came to America to do good and ended up doing well. Despite their partial isolation from aspects of political and social life in the colonies and early republic—or, perhaps, because this isolation directed their energies into economic channels—Quaker communities prospered materially. For New England Friends, the world transformed when Samuel Slater introduced Arkwright's water frame to America in the 1790s, revolutionizing the textile industry along the Blackstone River in Pawtucket, Rhode Island.

Slater's achievement had been aided by one of Rhode Island's great merchants, Moses Brown (1738–1836).[9] In 1774 he became a Quaker through contact with educator and reformer Anthony Benezet (1713–84).[10] Finding resonance between Benezet's condemnations of slavery and reading he had done in the works of John Wesley and Granville Sharp, Brown's conversion led to the manumission of those he had enslaved, followed by sixty years of stalwart abolitionism.[11] Moses Brown became a living link between the revolutionary era and antebellum abolition: he witnessed both Benezet's and Crandall's schools for Blacks.[12]

Prudence Crandall received a Quaker education, first in eastern Connecticut at Rowland Greene's Black Hill Friends School and then, for higher education, the New England Yearly Meeting Boarding School (NEYMBS) in Providence, Rhode Island. Thus she would have had repeated exposure to the name, thought, and impact of Anthony Benezet. Born to a Huguenot family in France in 1713, Benezet became a Quaker by convincement after moving to North America.[13] He understood the inner light as encompassing social and spiritual equality.[14] Working with John Woolman, Benezet helped make slave-owning forbidden among Quakers. Unlike many whites, Benezet authentically listened to African Americans, hearing of the tribulations of enslavement and the effects of prejudice.[15] An innovative pedagogue, he was a leader in education for girls and for African Americans.[16] Benezet educated Black and white students together, vouching for their intellectual equality:

> I can with truth and sincerity declare, that I have found amongst the negroes as great variety of talents, as among a like number of whites; and I am bold to assert, that the notion entertained by some, that the blacks are inferior in their capacities, is a vulgar prejudice, founded on the pride or ignorance of their lordly masters.[17]

The African Free School he established in 1770 educated future leaders of Philadelphia's free Black community.[18]

Benezet remained an inspiration to antebellum abolitionists, especially among Blacks, Friends, and women. African American preacher Peter Williams Jr. praised Benezet as an "inestimable person, sensible of the equality of mankind, [who] rose superior to the illiberal opinions" of his era.[19] Quaker Elizabeth Margaret Chandler wrote a poem to Benezet's memory,

Lydia Maria Child and Mary Grew included him amongst the abolitionist pan-
theon, and Angelina Grimké praised him in her 1837 speech at the Women's
Anti-Slavery Convention.[20]

Moses Brown, an heir to Benezet's legacy, maintained a daunting moral
schedule. He helped found Rhode Island's Historical, Peace, and Bible Societies, as well as working for temperance and against capital punishment.[21]
Brown took issues that had traditionally been exclusive to the Society of
Friends—such as peace and abolition—and brought them into the reform
movements of the nineteenth century, where non-Quaker forces extended
and expanded them. Brown kept a campus office at the NEYMBS. He invited
students to his mansion, donated food from his garden to the students' fare,
and attended religious meetings with them.[22] Crandall certainly experienced
Brown's indefatigable spirit personally.[23]

There exists one furtive glimpse of Crandall as a student. "Beauty, as a
flowery blossom soon fades, but the divine excellencies of the mind, like
the medicinal values of the plant, remain in it when all those charms are
withered." Prudence inscribed this extract from Caleb Bingham's *American
Preceptor; Being a New Selection of Lessons, for Reading and Speaking* in the
autograph book of classmate Mary Peace Hazard (1814–74).[24] The thoughtful
philosophic tone of this maxim is at marked variance from other autograph
contributions. Crandall hinted that she underwent a shaping spiritual experience in her youth, consistent with the highly individual religious choices she
made across her life.[25] This epigram might reflect that, or perhaps constituted
sage advice from an older student to a girl eleven years her junior.

What is missing from Crandall's youth are identifiable voices of African
American people. Even exemplary Quakers like Benezet did not encourage
"intimate social contact between the races; Moses Brown likewise maintained
social distance between the races."[26] Blacks were objects of charity, even for
the best-intentioned white philanthropists, who rarely perceived Blacks as
thinkers or historical actors. Chapter 2 of the current volume examines when
this changed for Crandall, through her interactions with Maria Davis and
Sarah Harris.

Female Education and Women's
Minds in Shifting Times

Teaching was the principal career path open to Prudence Crandall upon her
return from Providence. She taught in the common schools of Plainfield and
Lisbon in Connecticut with good reports, such that in 1831 the selectmen of
Canterbury presented her with the opportunity to be head mistress of her
own academy.[27]

The selectmen's desire to have a female academy joined in a trend sweep-
ing New England. A quality academy brought prestige to a town, as well as

producing better-polished daughters for marriage. Women's education in the early republic and antebellum periods, while always secondary to that of men, was encouraged. Motherhood was understood to require at least a modicum of education—reading, writing, and figuring—to teach children wisely and to run the household when men were away at warfare or seafaring.

The key figures in the lineage of women teachers in the Northeast from the early republic to the Civil War include Sally Pierce, Lydia Sigourney, Emma Willard, Catharine Beecher, and Mary Lyon, who each established female schools that achieved renown. While these schools assuredly advanced women's education, they did not do so in an intersectional manner.[28] Eager to embrace social respectability, they refrained from challenging racial segregation or male supremacy.

Catharine Beecher (1800–1878) cast the longest shadow at the time of Crandall's Canterbury venture. Despite upholding socially proscribed roles for women, she herself never married.[29] The eldest child of the famed preacher Lyman Beecher, she shared the early ambivalence of her family toward abolition and Black rights, including publicly disdaining Crandall's second academy.[30]

In 1823 Catharine Beecher founded the Hartford Seminary for women, envisioning teaching as the preeminent public profession for her students. Women teachers would be arbiters of social rectitude and carriers of moral influence: "she may fasten durable and holy impressions that shall never be effaced or wear away."[31] Beecher believed women were morally purer than men and able to transform society without being in the public sphere.

Beecher's view of women's intellect is internally contradictory: she seeks to develop women's intelligence while insisting on constraining it beforehand. What she sought turned out to be like sand through the fingers: women's moral influence had to be simultaneously invisible and all pervasive. She did, however, create a safe place for women like herself—white, middle class, unmarried, intelligent but not rebellious.

While Beecher bristled at the notion of women intellectuals,[32] she included moral philosophy in her curriculum. In 1829 a male editorialist fumed, "I had rather my daughters would go to school and sit down and do nothing, than to study philosophy, etc. These branches fill young Misses with vanity to the degree that they are above attending to the more useful parts of an education." A woman who studied philosophy would be "a dandizette at eighteen, an old maid at thirty," threatening marriageability itself.[33] How education impacted women's marital prospects dominated discussions of women's education in a literally mind-numbing way.

In 1837 the public career of the Grimké sisters, Angelina and Sarah, provoked alarmed Congregational Church leaders to reassert in their infamous Pastoral Letter that women's weakness and dependence were decreed by God. The prelates declared that when a woman "assumes the place and tone of man as a public reformer . . . she yields the power which God has given her for protection, and her character becomes unnatural."[34]

Such false naturalizing had been rehearsed privately in 1831 between Prudence and her younger brother, Reuben. Like his sister, Reuben had abandoned the family's Quaker practices, aligning with the "Standing Order" Congregational Church. Prudence stayed unconventional by joining the Baptists.[35] Her church, Packerville Baptist, included some female public preaching. Reuben disapproved and drew on conventional wisdom (dressed in divine authority) for maintaining male supremacy:

> As soon as the female arises or kneels down to pray in the public audiences, in the presence of her teacher, her protector, man, that moment, she has started out from under the protection and instruction of the good apostle Paul, and set herself up as the superior, by thus doing. . . . For he again says, "But let your women keep silence in the churches for it is a shame and abomination for women to pray with her head uncovered."[36]

More abstract and less crude than his father Pardon's display of male authority at the clambake, Reuben's intellectualization of patriarchy carries the implicit threat of any protection racket: those protecting you could just as easily destroy you. There is little to differentiate between his epistle and the Congregationalists' Pastoral Letter. The visibility of the Grimké sisters' breach of male supremacy demanded a public patriarchal reprimand. Reuben's private letter affirms that the undergirding logic was ever present. But women increasingly chafed against these arbitrary limitations.

Prudence Crandall did not conform to her brother Reuben's views.[37] She remained a member of Packerville Baptist and continued to conduct her school as she saw fit. If Crandall had the wherewithal to *resist* listening to her brother, then the fact that she *did* listen to Maria Davis and Sarah Harris becomes all the more remarkable.

A Local Herald:
The Windham County Peace Society

George W. Benson Sr. (1752–1836) was already an accomplished figure when he and his large family moved from Rhode Island to Brooklyn, Connecticut, in 1824. A business associate and friend of Moses Brown,[38] Benson's opposition to slavery included cofounding the Providence Society for Promoting the Abolition of Slavery in 1790 and lobbying for the Slave Trade Act (1794) that restricted US ports from outfitting or shielding slave-trading ships.[39] After the reckless bloodshed of the War of 1812, Brown and Benson coestablished the Rhode Island Peace Society in 1818 as an ecumenical rather than sectarian benevolent project.[40] Incorporating mass tract distribution, they scattered 28,704 pamphlets in three years.[41]

Benson brought his experience—and his spirited family—to his Connecticut retirement.[42] He there befriended the most energetic of Connecticut's pacifists, the redoubtable Samuel Joseph May (1797–1871), who in 1823 became Connecticut's sole Unitarian minister, accepting the pulpit in Brooklyn. Benson's arrival provided May with a strong mentor and exemplar. The younger man was fascinated by the religious diversity in the Benson household. Benson agreed with Quakers on many issues but had not joined their society. But two of his daughters, Anna and Mary, became Quakers by convincement. His wife and other children joined the Unitarians.

The Windham County Peace Society was launched by May and Benson Sr. in 1826.[43] In their first year, the society printed two pamphlets and gave most of them away. Members editorialized in the Windham County *Advertiser* "to expose the wickedness and impolity of war."

One would think that the peace movement had a better chance of exciting Christian activism, based on Jesus's pacifist principles, than temperance, given their Lord's willingness to turn water to wine. Yet, the attempt to wean the world from war was always the most hopeless of moral reform causes, due to the necessarily universal scope required. David Dodge and Noah Worcester, the earliest peace advocates in the United States, encouraged a coalition between strict pacifists and those who would allow for defensive wars. This was especially important in a young country that had won its independence and secured its unprecedented form of government via armed rebellion.

But just as antislavery would become a battle between immediatists and gradualists in the 1830s, the peace movement would be riven by a radical challenge. The clearest articulation of a Christian peace philosophy emanated from the pen of an English Quaker linendraper, Jonathan Dymond (1796–1828), who wrote his comprehensive *Essays on the Principles of Morality, and on the Private and Political Rights and Obligations of Mankind* (1829) between serving customers at his shop.[44] From that humble location, his logic made an impact on an all-star cast of pacifists: Henry David Thoreau, Leo Tolstoy, Anthony Norris Groves (and the Plymouth Brethren), Alexander Campbell, Rufus Jones, Charles Sumner, and William Lloyd Garrison.[45] But the Windham County Peace Society can claim pride of place as the first to publish Dymond in the United States, with a thousand copies of *On the Applicability of the Pacific Principles of the New Testament to the Conduct of States: And on the Limitations Which Those Principles Impose on the Rights of Self-Defence* printed in the spring of 1832.[46]

Dymond's position on war was radical nonresistance. Taking as his ground the fact that Jesus prevented violence during his arrest at Gethsemane, Dymond asks, "If, in defence of himself from the hands of bloody ruffians, his religion did not allow the sword to be drawn, for what reason can it be lawful to draw it?"[47] Dymond further argues that "defensive war" was an empty concept, since "in the fury of slaughter soldiers do not attend, they cannot attend, to questions of aggression. Their business is destruction, and their business they will perform. If the army of defence obtains success, it soon becomes an army of aggression."[48] Dymond calls for Christians to renounce war and violence entirely: "Christianity . . . wants men who are willing to *suffer* for her principles."[49]

May and other Garrisonians grasped how Dymond's philosophy provides parallels between absolute renunciation of war and immediate abolition of slavery.[50] Radical abolitionists and nonresistant pacifists shared a staunch moral absolutism in their quest to perfect society. The antebellum peace movement, though, usually did *not* function as a meeting ground for people from different social locations, remaining largely the province of white, educated men. Dymond's systematic philosophy, however, touched directly on the status of women. Furthermore, due to the Windham County Peace Society, Crandall and other women participants in early abolitionism—including the Black students—had direct access to his writings. George Benson Sr.'s daughters—Frances, Mary, Sarah, Anna, Charlotte, and Helen (future wife of William Lloyd Garrison)—had concrete access to Dymond's thought: their father commissioned them to sew the pamphlets that the Windham County Peace Society circulated![51] Crandall, during the crisis of her school, sought the refuge of the Benson household.[52] The Benson daughters were her friends. Imagine these intelligent white women, in the very act of practicing nonresistance, discussing their rationale and its sources.

Historian Donald Yacovone suggests that May found Dymond congenial because of an inherent gender reversal in passive resistance: "Dymond's Liberalism emphasized pacifism, submission, and dependence, qualities that the culture assigned to women but that May would employ to reject the world his father's generation had created and to achieve radical social change."[53] Taken a step further, what would the effects be on women—and on marginalized Black women—reading philosophy that places feminine qualities in a morally elevated position for effecting "radical social change?" Feminist scholars of religion have noted many instances in religious history where piety toward the divine has required the seeker to be self-abnegating. Because women in male-dominated societies are already well versed at humbling themselves, valorization of passivity can enable women to earn social prestige. This can be documented in times and places as varied as early Christianity, the bhakti devotional movements in India, philosophic Taoism in China, and medieval Christian mysticism in Europe.[54] Dymond's thought provides a parallel in abolitionism.

The American Colonization Society

Benevolent organizations always had both social and political dimensions. In the case of the American Colonization Society (ACS), the agenda was largely political but often masked as social amelioration. Formally launched on New Year's Day, 1817, the ACS played a central role as the foil to Crandall's school.[55] The goal of the ACS was to "colonize" manumitted free Blacks to Africa, to establish Christianity among the natives in an American beachhead on that continent. Land "purchased" by coercion from the Indigenous people in 1821 formed the basis of what is now Liberia.[56]

The ACS was founded exclusively by property-owning white men, mostly from the middle states. Among the most visible proponents of sending free Blacks to Africa were Francis Scott Key, Charles Fenton Mercer, Henry Clay, and Andrew Jackson; James Monroe would bequeath the ACS the prestige and power of the US presidency (Monrovia is Liberia's capital).[57] Judge Bushrod Washington (1762–1829), nephew of George Washington and a sitting US Supreme Court Justice, was the organization's first president. The ACS commenced with sterling status-quo support, including many enslavers.[58] The intrinsic elitism of the ACS existed partially because the proposed project of relocating free Blacks required logistical support from the federal government.[59] As Paul Goodman stresses, it is emblematic that the initial annual meetings of the ACS were held in the US House of Representatives.[60]

Thomas Jefferson suggested the removal of freed Blacks in his (in)famous *Notes on the State of Virginia* (1784). All free Blacks, he maintains, "should be colonized" to wherever is most convenient, because America could never be integrated:

> Deep rooted prejudices entertained by the whites; ten thousand recollections, by the blacks, of the injuries they have sustained; new provocations; the real distinctions which nature has made; and many other circumstances, will divide us into parties, and produce convulsions which will probably never end but in the extermination of the one or the other race.[61]

Claims of intractable prejudice and unbridgeable natural differences between the races became rote logic among most white Americans.

Following Gabriel Prosser's thwarted slave revolt in 1800, various colonization schemes were floated in Virginia. Then-Governor James Monroe endorsed either setting aside a territory in the west or sending Blacks to Haiti or Latin America.[62] Thinking Haiti's successful slave-led revolution had inspired Prosser, then-President Jefferson preferred Africa, intending to attach American blacks to Britain's Sierra Leone, which had been partially populated by African Americans who fought for the British during the American Revolution in exchange for freedom.[63] Sierra Leone offered a ready solution to "the basic urge" of colonization: "not to get Negroes over to Africa but to get them out of America."[64]

The ACS's stated ideal called for transporting free Blacks who volunteered to go to the American-administered Liberia, establishing them as proselytizers for the United States and Christianity. The ACS presented itself as a reasonable middle path for resolving the contradictions of slavery. They wanted to be perceived (by whites) as sympathetic to Blacks but without impugning the morality of slave owners. This "great tent of ambiguity" attracted large numbers of white Protestant ministers.[65] When the Reverend Ralph R. Gurley became executive secretary in 1825, he imbued the ACS with the ethos of a benevolent project, garnering endorsements from ministers and legislatures.[66]

Many rationales for colonization coexisted. Northern supporters saw it encouraging gradual abolition. Southern enslavers wanted free Blacks gone, seeing them as antislavery agitators whose family and friendship networks afforded them unique access to enslaved persons.[67] Colonizationists shared a fervid desire to keep the growing nation racially "pure"; the ACS's plans for African American removal paralleled the strategy of Indian removal that dominated federal policy toward Native nations.[68] As scholar Lewis Perry so succinctly puts it, the ACS held both enslavers and moderate abolitionists in an organization "successfully blending dislike of slavery with fear of free Negroes."[69]

The very idea of a multiracial republic became unthinkable, even anathema, to white male political leaders. Henry Clay, with his considerable rhetorical and political gravitas, referred to free Blacks as a "moral evil threatening to contaminate all parts of society."[70] At the ACS's first meeting, Clay proclaimed that "unconquerable prejudices" toward free Blacks made it better "to drain them off" and "rid our country of a useless and pernicious, if not dangerous" people. Since they opposed integration intrinsically, the ACS elites fought Black education ferociously. Elias Caldwell, secretary of the ACS, bluntly states that "the more you cultivate their minds, the more miserable you make them."[71]

For all its bluster, the ACS could not hide its retarded rate of progress nor wish away the resistance of most free Blacks.[72] Over the first fourteen years of its existence (1817–31), the society (which kept detailed records) sent 1,842 colonists to Liberia, with income short of $160,000: less than $1 for every free Black in the United States.[73] Most unbiased observers knew that colonization would never fulfill its goal of "racially cleansing" the young republic.[74]

Many whites who later became luminaries of the abolitionist movement participated in the American Colonization Society in the 1820s and early 1830s. Benjamin Lundy (1789–1839), editor of the newspaper *Genius of Universal Emancipation*, admitted that colonization was impractical but remained in favor of any tactic that would lead to freeing the enslaved. Samuel J. May founded an ACS auxiliary, (in)appropriately enough on the Fourth of July, 1829, in Brooklyn.[75] Most famously, Garrison himself was a supporter of colonization until his Black friends in Baltimore—most notable, William Watkins (1803–58)—disabused him of the ACS's false promises and premises, whereupon Garrison publicly renounced and denounced colonization.[76]

Free Black Organizing and Opposition
to African Colonization

An independent American colonization plan gelled when the Black Quaker sea captain Paul Cuffee (1759–1817) suggested that Blacks might be better able to rise out of subjection if some *voluntarily* moved to Africa.[77] ACS officials appropriated this to make it appear as if Cuffee supported colonization, using Cuffee as a veritable fig leaf to conceal their coercive racial prejudice.[78] But Cuffee had his suspicions about the sincerity of his white allies, and so he reached out to other African American leaders. Free Blacks rejected colonization decisively. Therein lies a tale of Black self-definition that presages Crandall's school, involving two key figures from among her future endorsers.

Cuffee's hopes for colonization were markedly different in tone and emphasis from the ACS. Cuffee wanted a colony to demonstrate the intelligence of Africans; he sought willing quality immigrants, rather than a wholesale relocation of all free Blacks.[79] James Forten (1766–1842), an accomplished African American businessman in Philadelphia, and Reverend Peter Williams Jr. (1787–1840), a Black Episcopal priest, initially supported the idea, provided it was voluntary.[80]

The free Black *community*, however, was far more wary, placing no trust in the good intentions of white enslavers. A meeting to denounce the ACS was held at Mother Bethel Church of the recently formed African Methodist Episcopal Church (AME) in January 1817. Forten felt the tension of being caught between his community and his desire to gain respectability with white leaders. Faced with a crowd of three thousand free Blacks, Forten decided to support their demand that they not be deported.[81] The resolutions from this meeting stated forthrightly that enslaved Africans had been the first to till the soil of North America successfully and that their descendants would not leave this land against their will. The Black community's self-worth emerged in their resentment over the calumnies of Clay that laid an "unmerited stigma . . . upon the reputation of the free People of Colour."[82]

Despite the Black community's unified voice, a visit from the leadership of the ACS led to dithering by Forten.[83] Wavering by the Black elite did nothing to defuse the righteous fear and anger of the Black community. When the ACS hoped to form a Black male auxiliary in Philadelphia in August, another Black protest meeting occurred. The document they produced, *Address to the Humane and Benevolent Inhabitants of the City and County of Philadelphia*, is remarkable for containing a full range of arguments against colonization, including the salient fact that most free Blacks did not want to leave, and that far from ending slavery, colonization would leave it more entrenched because enslavers would purposely deport any Blacks "who feel that they should be free" while "the tame and submissive will be retained, and subjected to increased rigour." Colonization would prevent families from reuniting, make a mockery of free Black efforts to educate themselves and better their station and allow prejudice to flourish without being challenged.[84]

The effects on Black leaders from this strong and thorough example of Black mass protest proved long lasting. Forten never again cooperated with the ACS. Crandall's school, which Forten and Williams endorsed, delivered pivotal blows against colonization's viability, logic, and respectability.[85]

The only disappointing aspect of this forthright Black opposition to the idea of colonization—an organized opposition that arose *simultaneously* with the formation of the ACS—is how it remained unknown. Whites blithely ignored all evidence of African American loyalty to America and scoffed at Black efforts to gain education and economic success. African Americans combatted this by amplifying their message.

The first sustained Black independent newspaper started in 1827. Two future endorsers of Crandall's school—Williams and Samuel Cornish—joined with John Russwurm and William Hamilton to publish *Freedom's Journal*.[86] The paper expanded rapidly through Northern urban Black communities, with over a thousand subscribers by mid-1827.[87] It provided a necessary precondition for Black organizing by creating a conduit for ideas between communities. *Freedom's Journal* stood for immediate abolition, until readers started noticing a change in Russwurm's editorials. By 1829 he morphed into a partisan for colonization. The paper's readers were appalled, and *Freedom's Journal* ceased publication in March 1829. Two months later, Cornish led the short-lived *Rights of All*, inheriting most of *Freedom's Journal*'s subscribers.[88] But although scholars now pore over the pages of these newspapers, the existence of the Black press went unnoticed by most whites at the time.

This publishing initiative provided African Americans a platform from which to participate in the expanding political democratization of the time. The growing literacy rate among free Blacks resulted in some incisive writing. One essayist, identified only as "Matilda," presented a cogent feminist analysis of the position of free Black women:

> The influence that we have over the male sex demands, that our minds should be instructed and improved with the principles of education and religion, in order that this influence should be properly directed. Ignorant ourselves, how can we be expected to form the minds of our youth, and conduct them in the paths of knowledge? . . . It is their bounden duty to store their daughters' minds with useful learning. They should be made to devote their leisure time to reading books, whence they would derive valuable information, which could never be taken from them.[89]

"Matilda" is a touchstone for free Black women's minds in the late 1820s.[90]

No single piece of writing had a greater impact on free Black self-definition than David Walker's stirring *Appeal to the Coloured Citizens of the*

World, but in Particular, and Very Expressly, to Those of the United States of America, published in 1829.[91] A relentless jeremiad, the *Appeal* coupled the emotionalism of evangelical Christianity with the American political legacy of revolutionary struggles for freedom, enunciating the demand for civil and human rights for all African Americans. Walker condemned Jefferson's racism while calling on America to heed the idealistic rhetoric of the Declaration of Independence.[92] Most controversially, Walker encouraged those who were captives under the system of slavery to revolt, declaring they would be amply justified in doing so.

Walker (1785–1830) was born to an enslaved father and a free Black mother; his condition followed the maternal line, but growing up in North Carolina meant he knew slavery intimately. As a young man he traveled extensively around the country before settling in Boston. There he became increasingly active in the Black community, helping to form the Massachusetts General Colored Association and serving as an agent and author for *Freedom's Journal*.[93] Walker's fame spread among free Blacks in the Northeast when his *Appeal* was read aloud in free Black communities (Walker even sewed the pamphlets into Black sailors' coats, enabling Southern circulation).[94]

While Walker's clarion call for revolution is famed, his attention to education was equally fervent and politically perspicacious:

> I pray that the Lord may undeceive my ignorant brethren, and permit them to throw away pretensions, and seek after the substance of learning. I would crawl on my hands and knees through mud and mire, to the feet of a learned man, where I would sit and humbly supplicate him to instil into me, that which neither devils nor tyrants could remove, only with my life—for coloured people to acquire learning in this country, makes tyrants quake and tremble on their sandy foundation. Why, what is the matter? Why, they know that their infernal deeds of cruelty will be made known to the world.[95]

Walker knew whereof he spoke; at about the same time as the publication of the *Appeal*, the Boston School Committee *refused* a *bequest* to open a high school for Black youth. The reasons given included that Blacks did not need higher education and that the (white) "public" could not be reasonably expected to shoulder such an unnecessary burden. The committee termed the request "inexpedient."[96]

Walker's death in 1830, now demonstrated to be from natural causes but widely suspected at the time of being an assassination by poison, removed this clearsighted man from the scene too early. In 1831, though, Garrison published the *Appeal* in the pages of the newspaper *The Liberator*, enlarging the audience for this profound thinker.

All the Voices: 1831 and the New Haven
Manual Labor College

In a remarkable confluence of events, 1831 witnessed a fully voiced society, the first payment on what Martin Luther King Jr. would call America's promissory note: open participation by Black women and men and white women in political and intellectual life.[97] Groups shut out from the franchise—Black men, Black women, white women, Native American peoples, immigrants, and proletarians—simultaneously launched and sustained their political participation. Black men, Black women, and white women engaged the issues of their day, deploying public reasoning to make a direct impact on the polity of the nation.[98] A cognitive sliver of white men were learning how to listen to these emerging voices. Although it would be many decades, even a century and more before each of the marginalized groups attained anything even resembling full political rights, the coincidence of their emergence ushers in an unexpected intersectional aspect of Jacksonian democracy. The personnel and history of various liberatory causes overlapped. It is no accident that many women's rights activists had abolitionist backgrounds or that Mount Holyoke's Mary Lyon was lionized by Lowell, Massachusetts, factory girls, or that Margaret Fuller had such a clearsighted understanding of the plight of Native Americans.

The major events of 1831 began auspiciously on New Year's Day with the inaugural issue of the *Liberator*. Far more traumatic was Nat Turner's slave revolt in Virginia in August, which consolidated white defense of slavery. Not even a month later, the writings of Maria Stewart (1803–1879), a free Black woman in Boston, were published in Garrison's *Liberator*. Meanwhile, the celebrated white domestic guru and novelist Lydia Maria Child (1802–1880), committed her energies to immediate abolition after Garrison "got hold of the strings of my conscience."[99]

These four decisive moments—the *Liberator*, Turner's revolt, the visibility of the free Black community, and the prominence of women (both Black and white) as *thinkers* in the movement to end slavery—define 1831 as pivotal. Prior to this, even the best-intentioned white abolitionists established few real links between Black and white people. Crandall's academy grew from the networks, dialogues, and insights of 1831.

A plan for an institute of higher learning for Black men in New Haven was hatched by Simeon Smith Jocelyn (1799–1879). A future endorser of Crandall's school, Jocelyn was a white abolitionist who worked with his Black allies to address their needs. Earnest and talented but unable to afford formal higher education, Jocelyn went into the engraving business (with his brother Nathaniel) until he perceived a call to ministry.[100]

Jocelyn's Congregational minister, the famed Nathaniel Taylor, attempted to reconcile Calvinism with the optimism of the Second Great Awakening. The resulting New Haven Theology provided the intellectual fuel for the social activism that accompanied the evangelical revival (especially for Congregationalists and Presbyterians).[101] Jocelyn imbibed from him a call to action that Taylor (a rather staid academic) could only enunciate abstractly.[102] Jocelyn joined the African Improvement Society (AIS), founded in July 1825 by some leading white men of New Haven.[103] The AIS later hired Jocelyn to be the minister of the United African Congregational Church; his ministerial work was within New Haven's free Black community.[104] Like all white benevolent projects aimed at Blacks during the mid-1820s, the AIS endorsed colonization, but it was rare in being willing to consider "racial uplift" of New Haven's Blacks, decoupling education from (coerced) emigration to Liberia.[105] Furthermore, the AIS created conditions for whites and Blacks to work together within the organization; their "board of managers was to be formed of white and colored members, chosen in 'expedient' proportions."[106] By 1831 Jocelyn had converted to immediatism, becoming an early ally of Garrison and the *Liberator*. Despite his mentors being staunch advocates for the ACS, Jocelyn's ministry enabled his break from colonizationism and nurtured his budding antiracism.

Jocelyn encouraged Black education in New Haven, spearheading the idea of a Black Manual Labor College in New Haven.[107] Thus, he—along with the free Black community of New Haven—reaped a whirlwind of white opposition.

The New Haven Manual Labor College proposal created the first deep alliance between white male immediate abolitionists and free Black male leaders in the Northeast. A few white abolitionists asked permission to attend and address the first annual convention of the people of colour in Philadelphia.[108] This respect for the proceedings and opinions of Blacks by whites marked an incipient effort to shape the agenda mutually. The white abolitionists in attendance were aware that free Blacks had been launching educational projects for the past decade and more, but as white men they strategically sought to use their status and privilege to create durable institutions. This group of white male abolitionists in 1831 included Jocelyn, Garrison, Lundy, and Arthur Tappan.[109] The early success (especially among Black readers) of the *Liberator* presaged this new interracial abolitionism. Garrison published Black writings, including Walker's *Appeal*.[110] Tappan and his brother Lewis contributed substantial funds from their accumulated fortune in import and mercantile sales. These white men brought a combination of practical experience and egalitarian idealism with them, as well as respect for African Americans as actors on their own behalf.

The Black attendees at the first annual convention of the people of colour were equally impressive and could boast of extensive experience in fostering Black education and achievement. Cornish, Williams, Forten, William Miller, and Joseph Cassey were among the attendees; all of them would give aid to Crandall's school two years later.

The plan that Jocelyn hatched was elegant in its optimism. The Manual Labor College would utilize a pedagogic model that balanced mental and manual labor, thus giving Black men skills that would improve their intellectual culture while not leaving them unfit for areas where Blacks had been able to find employment (seafaring professions being particularly popular; properly rigging a sail or battening down the hatches tended to enable meritocracy over caste). Jocelyn extolled New Haven's advantages. The city was "healthy and beautiful," with a "literary and scientific character" imparted by the presence of Yale University. Its central location ensured cheap boarding and provisions, augmented by trade with the West Indies that might induce wealthy Caribbeans of color to "send their sons . . . to be educated."[111] Jocelyn's other rationales, though, proved disastrous miscalculations. He asserted that New Haven's "inhabitants are friendly, pious, generous, and humane," and the city's "laws are salutary and protecting . . . to all, without regard to complexion."[112]

The Black convention leaders were delighted that Jocelyn, Garrison, and Tappan had openly broken from colonization. Walker had prophesied this in his *Appeal*: "Our friends who have been imperceptibly drawn into the [ACS] plot I view with tenderness . . . and I have only hope for the future, that they will withdraw themselves from it."[113] But for the day to arrive so fortuitously, with substantial funds and plans for institution building, was most welcome. Black minister Theodore Wright recalled how the Garrisonian disruption of the seeming unanimity of white support for colonization came "like the voice of an angel of mercy! Hope, hope then cheered our path. The signs of the times began to indicate brighter days. [Garrison] thundered, and next we hear of a Jocelyn of New Haven, an Arthur Tappan at his side, pleading for the rights of the Colored American."[114] Jocelyn met before the convention with Williams, who had been developing plans for a Black male high school in New York City. They agreed to work together for the New Haven school.[115] As James Brewer Stewart analyzed, the New Haven Negro College was "the most visionary interracial project yet attempted in the nation's history" and thus marks "a crucial point of departure" for the future of abolitionism.[116]

Following the early June convention, Black and white supporters of the New Haven Negro College conducted fundraising and support. The formal announcement of the plan, though, took place at a fateful moment: September 5, in the immediate aftermath of Nat Turner's revolt. Proslavery apologists trumpeted the brutality of Turner's guerrilla attacks as affirmation of their caricatures of Blacks as savages. Those who detested the Black presence in America seized the opportunity to quash Black higher education utterly.[117]

The local *Columbian Register* edited its pages so that stories about the proposed Manual Labor College would appear alongside stories about the Southampton, Virginia, revolt.[118] James Watson Webb, the inflammatory editor of New York City's *Courier and Enquirer*, entered the lists:

> What possible good can arise from giving them a collegiate education . . . ? Will it give to them that equality which exists among white men? Certainly not. The very leaders who open their purses for such objects will not allow a learned Negro to sit at their table or marry their daughter. . . . What benefit can it be to a waiter or coachman to read Horace, or be a profound mathematician?[119]

Many of the arguments raised against Black education in New Haven—threats of amalgamation, making colonization less likely, educating Blacks above their station, and giving Blacks access to something that not even all privileged whites enjoyed—would be recycled by Crandall's opponents.

Amidst "a high effervescence of hostility to the proposed college," its opponents (led by future Crandall antagonist David Daggett) crushed the plan by a resounding 700-4 margin.[120] The defeat of the Manual Labor College was total: it was never built. Jocelyn may have had friendships with many esteemed white men, but none of them broke ties with the racial status quo.[121]

Many scholars have conflated the failed Manual Labor College with Crandall's academy. While they are related to each other—sharing personnel, networks, and promotion of education for social change—the differences are profound. Canterbury had deeper local roots in Black agency than the New Haven project. Furthermore, the Manual Labor College never got started, never built any institutional base, and generated no alumni. By contrast, Crandall's academy operated for eighteen months, and a significant number of the Black students went on to lifelong achievement.

The spectacular, overwhelming failure of the Black college meant that Canterbury's eighteen-month lifespan shines as a notable success by comparison. This is central to understanding Canterbury's impact on abolitionism. As Garrison fretted, a second failure in Connecticut would have been disastrous for the fledgling movement.[122] The defeat of the Manual Labor College may well be the highwater mark for colonizationism, making Crandall's school— along with Garrison's publication of Black writings in *Thoughts on African Colonization*—the signal turnaround events.

Gender, though, is the largest distinction between Jocelyn's aspirational effort and Crandall's accomplishment. There are almost no women's voices of any kind in the entire debate about the New Haven Negro College (except racist insinuations that Black males would make the city unattractive to white females).[123] The discourse is largely confined to men. Canterbury, by contrast, always had Black and white, male and female, engaged in the conception, construction, and sustenance of the school.

New Haven and Canterbury certainly demonstrated the deep-seated racism of the north. But lumping the two of them together as Connecticut-based failures disguises how they form a progression, one that is aided by the infusion of women's perspectives. Canterbury also produced significant jurisprudence on race, as opposed to the always reprehensible practice of voting on civil rights that New Haven conducted. James Brewer Stewart, in his otherwise excellent article on the Manual Labor College, writes how "Garrison next championed the ill-fated cause of Prudence Crandall, whose attempts to open a school for 'colored girls' . . . were thwarted by opponents much like those who had blocked the Negro College."[124] While Stewart is arguing that Garrison was losing touch with his African American colleagues and arrogating leadership to himself (a sustainable argument, though not one I fully agree with), this quick mischaracterization of Crandall's school ignores her greater success and deeper connections to eastern Connecticut Black communities.

Turner's 1831 revolt was the culminating slave uprising of the early nineteenth century. Unlike earlier plots by Gabriel Prosser and Denmark Vesey that were betrayed before they could start, Turner's revolt commenced into an open, armed struggle. In late August 1831, Turner and a few close friends launched their assault by killing all the whites on the plantation where Turner had been enslaved, then repeating this method on nearby plantations, growing their army and weaponry with each assault. Turner (1800–1831), who was a literate, apocalyptical preacher and enslaved man, had a specific goal: the county seat of Jerusalem. The revolt raged for three days before white militia forces routed the Black army. Then the reprisals began, with many enslaved and free Blacks being summarily executed, while other Blacks were tortured to death by marauding whites. While the statistics are horrific enough—over two hundred Blacks and fifty-five whites killed during the revolt and aftermath—the sense of terror felt in the white community led to greater restrictions against Black education. An open debate about the future of slavery in Virginia wound up reinforcing the status quo.

Instead of imputing Turner's spirit of revolt to its obvious sources—love of liberty kept alive across unjust multigenerational captivity—most white reaction centered on his literacy, learning, and religious faith. This led to new laws in Virginia that forbade Blacks from reading and attending "unsupervised" religious services.[125] These restrictions and fears echoed northward to the New Haven controversy. As Hilary Moss suggests, "The bondsmen's rampage in Virginia showed New Haveners the consequences of too much black enlightenment. . . . Turner's last casualty was to be the first African college."[126]

Turner's revolt, the repercussions from it, and the failure of the New Haven College mark 1831 as the year that immediate abolition moved from an inchoate possibility to a force in antebellum America. Proslavery and anti-Black forces sensed the rise of a new ideological opponent and determined to crush it before it gained prominence.[127] In November the ACS congratulated the "citizens of New Haven on their escape from the monstrous evil of the contemplated location in their city of a college for the classical education of the colored youth of the United States."[128] Virginia Governor John Floyd, convinced that Turner's revolt was part of a nationwide conspiracy by free Blacks and Garrisonian abolitionists, asked for printed evidence of this conspiracy. The Chief Justice of the United States John Marshall obliged Governor Floyd with the recently published *Minutes and Proceedings of the First Annual Convention of the People of Colour*.[129] Southern states tried to get Boston officials to move against Garrison and the *Liberator*; Mayor Harrison Gray Otis of Boston said he wasn't even aware of this paper, which he dismissed as appealing to "a very few insignificant persons of all colors."[130] The District of Columbia in October 1831 made it illegal for free Blacks to possess the *Liberator*.[131]

However, another key intersectional moment had been birthed in the crucible of time between Turner's revolt and his capture at the end of October, when Black Bostonians gained a strong new voice for Black pride *and* feminism with the emergence of Maria Stewart. Born a free Black woman in 1803 in Connecticut, Maria Miller was orphaned at a young age. She was raised in a clergyman's family as a servant and remained a domestic worker until her marriage. It is not known exactly when she moved to Boston, but there she became part of the active Black community in the 1820s. She married a Black veteran of the War of 1812, James Stewart, in 1826. Walker's *Appeal* exerted a potent intellectual influence on Maria Stewart. But a rapid sequence of tragedies struck when her husband died in December 1829, then Walker himself passed in June 1830. Dishonest white lawyers compounded Stewart's sorrows, cheating her of her late husband's pension, forcing her return to domestic labor.[132]

The vast majority of early subscribers to the *Liberator*—over 80 percent—were African Americans, and the content of the paper reflected this with news of Black success, forthright honesty about Northern racism, and notices of African American events, as well as letters, essays, and reports from Black authors.[133] Stewart was among the *Liberator*'s supporters when it commenced in 1831. Thus, she offered her first essay, "Religion and the Pure Principles of Morality, the Sure Foundation on Which We Must Build" to Garrison in September. Its significance resides in both its occasion and its content. Published soon after Turner's revolt, Stewart boldly extended Walker's analysis to new circumstances, adding gendered insights. Recognizing the singularity of Stewart's voice and perspective, Garrison became her outspoken supporter, publishing her essay as a freestanding pamphlet.[134]

This alliance with Stewart cements the reputation of the youthful Garrison as a man able to listen to women. He had made that leap racially, opening his ears and his mind to the perspectives and agendas of Black men, starting with Hezekiah Grice and William Watkins in Baltimore.[135] Garrison's response to Walker's *Appeal* provides a telling example. He found that he disagreed with its call to armed struggle but recognized the importance of its ideas and published it.[136] Admirable as the interracial cooperation of Blacks and whites was, extending such recognition to women, too, would prove more difficult and became a factionalizing issue within the abolitionist movement. But in 1831 those fissures were not yet visible.[137]

The *Liberator* of September 3, 1831, squarely faced the greatest challenge yet to the newborn immediatist movement: how to portray Turner's revolt without conceding anything to the reactionary forces that asserted it corroborated their low opinion of African American capabilities and humanity. To his credit, after working closely with African American colleagues for two-plus years, Garrison's editorial maintains a precise tone, message, and clarity:

> Ye accuse the pacific friends of emancipation of instigating the slaves to revolt. . . . The slaves need no incentive at our hands. They will find in their stripes—in their emaciated bodies—in their ceaseless toil—in their ignorant minds . . . in your speeches and conversations, your celebrations, your pamphlets, your newspapers—voices in the air, sounds from across the ocean, invitations to resistance above, below, around them! What more do they need.[138]

The white editor of the *Liberator* had come to understand what it meant to be antiracist and could thread the needle; Maria Stewart as a Black woman did the same in a manner that united religious, female, and Black experience.

That momentous September 3 issue of the *Liberator* contains a small item, likely unnoticed by most readers: an addition to the roster of agents. William Harris of Norwich, Connecticut, would undertake to spread the newspaper in eastern Connecticut. It radiated out through his children and his future daughter-in-law—the young Maria Davis—who would drop the *Liberator* into Prudence Crandall's well-prepared white female consciousness.

CHAPTER 2

The Women and the Issues Are Joined

Maria Davis, Prudence Crandall, and Sarah Harris

> The full tradition of the Abolitionist movement . . . concentrated every strand of the struggle for freedom—abolition of slavery, woman's suffrage, labor movement—and thus released new human dimensions.
>
> —Raya Dunayevskaya and Charles Denby

Three young women, each listening to the other two and reaching for a changed world, created the conditions for the Canterbury Female Academy's second, more famous, existence. Maria Davis was, like Maria Stewart, a bright young woman consigned by racism to manual labor. Prudence Crandall was a white woman successfully following the teaching career open to her. She had a future of likely regional prestige as an educator in front of her, but she also had nurtured a conscience that recognized injustice.[1] Sarah Harris was the oldest daughter of a relatively prosperous Black farming couple, William and Sally Prentice Harris. Sarah Harris thirsted for more education, specifically so she could educate others in her community. Her youthful ambition was constrained by pervasive structural racism and sexism. In 1832 New England, Harris was effectively shut out from education above the district school level because of her race and from all college-level education because of her gender.

These three women created social change and did so prior to any public scrutiny. Harris's "great anxiety to improve in learning" fell on the sympathetic heart and mind of the white teacher. Crandall had been rendered receptive to Harris's request by Maria Davis, a Black woman employed as a "household helper," who cultivated the teacher's sympathy by plying her with copies of the *Liberator*, thus opening the world of Black thinkers and writers—including Black women like Maria Stewart—to Crandall. This trio of women—Harris, Davis and Crandall—broke silences between women of different races, different class statuses, and different levels of educational privilege. In so doing, they made the Academy possible, bequeathing to our time an example of intersectional agency. There are four separate moments that led from Crandall's first school to the famed second Academy: Maria Davis bringing Crandall the *Liberator*, Sarah Harris asking permission to attend the academy, Crandall admitting Harris, and Crandall seeking allies among the Immediate Abolitionists. This sequence of moments in 1832 birthed the academy for Black women in 1833. Black women's agency awakened white antiracism, bringing the school to life.

Jacksonian democracy was boisterously contradictory in creating conditions for new human relations between Black and white, male and female, and across classes. Race functioned as a veritable caste system;[2] entrenched racial prejudice was ubiquitous. Colonizationists proclaimed that whites and Blacks could never live together as equal citizens in the United States. This assumption seemed so natural to most whites that it was stated as self-evident fact.

Thus, white people who adopted an immediatist position—maintaining that Blacks and whites could and should live together in the United States—were challenging a vast system of presumptive white supremacy. It is important to consider the enormity of the task—philosophical, external, psychological, internal, and even unconscious—that white abolitionists faced. It is equally crucial to acknowledge that not all white abolitionists would rid themselves of prejudice at the same pace; different individuals followed idiosyncratic tempi. Each person had to examine their consciousness and conscience around race, a process thorny to induce, impossible to coerce. For white abolitionists in the early 1830s—when slavery was still legal in many Northern states, predominant in all Southern states, and permeated all commerce—the degree of consciousness necessary to overcome internalized racism was daunting. Most buckled under the pressure; even the famed white abolitionist leader Theodore Weld counseled caution against ostentatious displays of social intimacy and equivocated about the differences "between civil rights and social equality."[3] Given that prominent white abolitionists blanched in the glare from omnipresent racism, the success of Crandall in listening to Black women is admirable.

While it is crucial to acknowledge the incomplete nature of many white abolitionists' antiracism, their shortcomings are as nothing compared to the "pervasive" anti-abolitionism fueled by "violent antipathy toward the free Negro."[4] Racist anti-abolitionist white civic leaders orchestrated the disgraceful resistance to the academy, cheered on by the vast majority of the white population. From the highest ranks of the ruling class to the youngest ruffians, those who tormented Crandall and her Black students were white, cooperating to sustain overt white supremacy.

A force existed, though, that would reveal the weak spot in this seemingly tight weave of disdain. A well-networked free Black community snagged the attention of and then knit an alliance with a handful of white abolitionists. White supremacy had held together and even looked to bolster itself following the dawn of the *Liberator,* the Nat Turner revolt, the Virginia debate over slavery, and the failed New Haven Manual Labor College. Canterbury would mark a perceptible unraveling of this cloak of racism, precisely because of its thorough intersectionality. The agency of Black and white women ensured this rift in the fabric of racism would snag the skirt of sexism, too.

Crandall's First Academy:
Social Approval, High Academic Standards

When the white civic leaders of Canterbury approached Crandall to become the head mistress of a new female academy, they were clearly eager for its success. The acquisition of a prominent building at the main crossroads of Canterbury signaled that they wanted this academy to be a visible marker of their town's sophisticated prosperity.

The first official advertisement for the school appeared in the *Windham (Brooklyn, CT) Advertiser* on November 9, 1831, noteworthy for its academic tone, with no mention of sewing or other genteel arts often featured at schools.[5] The inclusion of chemistry and "natural and moral philosophy" parallels the intellectual rigor that Crandall had experienced at NEYMBS.[6] While any advertisement sings the praises of what it is promoting, the description of "the assiduity and attention which [Crandall] devotes to the health and morals of her pupils" rings true, vouched for by students over her lifespan. There is an acknowledgement of Christian religious diversity in the requirement that students attend a Sunday service somewhere,[7] corroborating Alexis de Tocqueville's observation that Americans were not jealously guarding the boundaries of denominationalism but "provided the citizens profess a religion, the peculiar tenets of that religion are of very little importance."[8]

The students started arriving in November 1831, most as day students from Canterbury itself. Almost all were from elite families of the area. Pleased with initial reports from the school, the board of visitors dropped by in January 1832. Their laudatory evaluation, published in March, carries an even-longer list of subjects taught.[9] The curriculum had expanded to include more "finishing" touches, but the academic tone remained high (with anatomy replacing chemistry).

Prudence was not alone in leading the school. Her younger sister, Almira, was there with her from the start as a coteacher, despite being just eighteen years old. There was a third woman in the house. Maria Davis, the "household helper," was an African American woman who had recently moved to

Canterbury from Boston to be close to her fiancé Charles Harris. She would sit in on classes when her work was done; like Almira, she was young but at seventeen older than most of the students.

Little is known about day-to-day life in this first incarnation of the academy. Amy Baldwin, one of the white students, reminisced about the "many pleasant noons we have spent together under the chestnut tree studying our definitions."[10] The reaction of the townspeople to the change of students would indicate that the first school had been a socially validated venture.

The First Moment:
Maria Davis and Prudence Crandall

Those who succeed in conventional ways leave visible marks. Finding facts on the white male leaders of Canterbury is easy: formal committees, elected offices, and membership in prestigious organizations leave ciphers in the historic record. But all who have researched women's history know that such external markers are scanty for women. The women most marginalized by race and class have the fewest records. Reconstructing the lives of individual women can be frustratingly piecemeal, disjunctions overwhelming any sense of continuity.

Many records exist for Prudence Crandall, since she was born into an active Quaker family that nurtured its legacy. She attended a Quaker educational institution. She was endorsed by town leaders. Compared to most women, this is a cornucopia. Similarly, there is more documentary evidence for Sarah Harris Fayerweather than for most Black women of the nineteenth century.[11] For Maria Davis, though, the usual dearth of data prevails.

Given the rarity of a strong documentary trail on any woman, understanding the discourse and dynamics between groups of women necessarily becomes even more fragile. Lesbian-feminist theorist Emily Culpepper coined the term "philosophia" for the active construction of a female train of thought.[12] Defining her neologism as "love of the wisdom of women," Culpepper suggests that scholars look for moments when women are developing ideas and taking actions among themselves. She adds that this is not a negative methodology nor one intended to be exclusive but one choice among many. Given that "wisdom formulated by women . . . has so often in history been distorted, denied, erased, suppressed, ridiculed, and cast into second place," a responsibility devolves upon scholars to highlight it now.[13]

From early 1832 to the beginning of the second academy for students of color in early 1833, a progression of *philosophiac* pivots occur. It is one of the liveliest examples of women inspiring women in the rich annals of American abolitionism. Sparks among four different women occur to set the school in motion. Maria Davis, Sarah Harris, Prudence Crandall, and Maria Stewart form a constellation of women learning from each other. They each bring something to the exchange, shine differently, their light sometimes bright, sometimes diffuse.

Everyone who has written about Crandall has noted these interactions, but the focus, pace, and detail of the story inevitably accelerate when famous men appear.[14] The narrative of how Prudence Crandall changed her academy from an all-white student body to a modestly integrated one and then to Black students exclusively, dwells on myriad newspaper articles, legal cases, and the organizing efforts of her allies and her enemies. This deflects attention from the women who molded the staying power and human legacy of Crandall's school. To understand Canterbury as part of antiracist history, feminist history, and Black intellectual history, women must remain central.

The person who serves as the linchpin to the existence of Crandall's second school, who sensed the possibilities latent in Prudence Crandall and whose own intelligence propelled her to share what she was learning from the *Liberator* with "the teacher"—is Maria Davis (ca. 1814–April 1, 1872). She was a free Black woman (described as an "octoroon . . . only slightly dark in color") who had been living in Boston.[15] With her engagement to Charles Harris, whose family lived in Canterbury, Maria moved to Connecticut and took the job as "family help" at Crandall's school.[16]

Charles Harris's father, William Harris, had become the Norwich, Connecticut, agent for the *Liberator* in the wake of Turner's rebellion in 1831.[17] Once Maria started working at Crandall's house, she had plenty of opportunities to observe the young teacher, taking the measure of Crandall's character. She furnished Crandall with copies of the *Liberator* until Maria felt confident in encouraging Sarah Harris, her future sister-in-law, to formally approach the white woman teacher. Maria Davis thus wove Prudence Crandall into five important radical sources: the abolitionist press, the radical intellectual currents of the free Black community of Boston, the local free Black community in eastern Connecticut, Maria's own manifest intellect, and Sarah Harris's desire for learning.[18]

Though Boston's Black community in the 1820s and early 1830s was small, (approximately two thousand people), they had capable organizers, highlighted by an active Freemason chapter, the presence of David Walker, the charismatic spiritual-political power of two major Black preachers, Samuel Snowden and Thomas Paul,[19] and the alliance between Black and white abolitionists that nurtured Garrison's *Liberator*.

This political acumen was not limited to men: women were involved in Black political life. Elizabeth Riley and Bathsheba Fowler spearheaded a committee to raise prepublication support for the *Liberator* in December 1830.[20] The early years of that paper included Black women's voices in letters, such as "Zelmire," who pointedly interrogated Christian hypocrisy in white churches "where our feelings are injured by this 'most foul, strange, and unnatural' prejudice, which exists among many white Christians towards us."[21]

Because not everyone in the Black community had full literacy skills, news was often read aloud—increasing the chance that women were imbibing ideas. The *Boston Evening Transcript* confirms widespread knowledge of Walker's work:

> Since the publication of that flagitious pamphlet, Walker's Appeal, for the consequences of which, if we mistake not, some fanatical white man will have to answer, we have noticed a marked difference in the deportment of our colored population. It is evident they have read this pamphlet, nay, *we know* that the larger portion of them have read it, or *heard* it read, and that they glory in its principles, as if it were a star in the east, guiding them to freedom and emancipation.[22]

Amos Beman, a Black abolitionist minister and son of Crandall endorser Jehiel Beman of Middletown, Connecticut, described how the Connecticut Black community would hear newspapers read by literate individuals. These ranged from the informal—a man generating much furor by reading a procolonizationist piece by Henry Clay—to repeated readings and recitations of the *Liberator*, Walker's *Appeal*, and Garrison's *Thoughts on African Colonization* "until their words were stamped in letters of fire upon our soul."[23]

Maria Stewart commenced her writing under the auspices of the *Liberator* in the fall of 1831, and her speeches were reprinted there through 1834 when she ceased public oratory and moved to New York to become a teacher.[24] Her ideas and forceful tone had to impress Crandall, who seemed awed, at this time in her life especially, by strong speakers—her Baptist minister Levi Kneeland, her future husband Calvin Philleo, and Garrison as examples. Stewart's vigorous rhetoric targeted the vileness of racial prejudice.[25] The time when Davis would have been supplying the *Liberator* would have been between November 1831 and September 1832 (without precluding the possibility of back issues and Stewart's pamphlet). During that time span, Stewart suggests that education and abolition will work in concert:

> The daystar from on high is beginning to dawn upon us. . . . These Antislavery societies, in my opinion, will cause many grateful tears to flow, and many desponding hearts to bound and leap for joy. . . . Many bright and intelligent ones are in the midst of us; but because they are not calculated to display a classical education, they hide their talents behind a napkin.[26]

Even more explicit was Stewart's call for education in "Religion and the Pure Principles of Morality":

> Shall it any longer be said of the daughters of Africa, they have no ambition, they have no force? By no means. Let every female heart become united,

and . . . we might be able to lay the cornerstone for the building of a High School, that the higher branches of knowledge might be enjoyed by us; and God would raise us up, and enough to aid us in our laudable designs.[27]

Stewart's combination of political activism and jeremiad-toned piety was revelatory from the pen of a Black woman. While she imbibed this style from Walker, voicing it through a woman giving public addresses, to audiences that were "promiscuous"—meaning all genders and races—marks her as distinctive. Given Garrison's endorsement of her writing, perhaps he had her in mind when he proffered women readers a rationale for becoming active in issues of slavery and race. He termed reticence a "misconception of duty" rather than "proper" female humility and self-erasure, adding that "the cause of bleeding humanity is always, legitimately, the cause of WOMAN."[28]

While we cannot know what particular articles Crandall read from the *Liberator*, the paper jolted her comprehension of how "the prejudice of the whites against color was deep and inveterate."[29] Here Maria Davis's influence on Crandall can be discerned; Davis's Boston background ensured she had heard intensive debates over the interlocking chains of racism and slavery. Davis embedded and reinforced a resolute conviction in Crandall that racial prejudice and segregation in the North needed eradication as much as slavery.

Valid inferences can be made concerning Davis. Until she moved to Windham County, Connecticut, sometime around 1831, she lived in Boston when Walker was having his greatest impact. The renewed and energetic movement in Black Boston was national (even international) in its scope, calling for solidarity among Blacks everywhere, linking slavery and racism, and endorsing moral uplift and education. Black Boston was the hub of a "growing interconnectedness among the educated elite of free blacks in the North and the simultaneous maturation of settled, self-aware free black communities."[30] Davis's association with the Harris family meant that her move to Connecticut did not remove her from these currents.

Crandall made two public statements about how she became acquainted with the *Liberator*. The first came during the crisis, in May 1833, and does not name Davis explicitly; this probably has to do with protecting a vulnerable friend and employee rather than being an attempt to suppress Davis's role:

> Previous to any excitement respecting her [Sarah Harris], there *fell in my way*, several publications that contained many facts relative to the people of color, of which I was entirely ignorant.
>
> My feelings began to awaken. I saw that the prejudice of the whites against color was deep and inveterate. In my humble opinion it was the strongest, if not the only chain that bound those heavy burdens on the wretched slaves, which we ourselves are not willing to touch with one of our fingers.[31]

Post–Civil War, Crandall acknowledged Maria's role quite explicitly:

> The reason for changing my school of white pupils for colored pupils is as follows: I had a nice colored girl, now Mrs. Charles Harris, as help in my family, and her intended husband regularly received the *Liberator*. The girl *took the paper from the offices and loaned it to me*. In that the condition of the colored people, both slaves and free, was truthfully portrayed, the double-dealing and manifest deception of the colonization society were faithfully exposed, and the question of immediate emancipation . . . boldly advanced.[32]

Crandall was not familiar with organized abolition before reading the *Liberator*, so Davis's role in shepherding the newspaper to her becomes pivotal. Davis is essential to the existence of the second academy. Without her intervention, it does not happen. Certainly, it is possible that Crandall could have become an antislavery partisan at some point. But the imagination necessary to attempt a high school for Black women required an unbendable spirit—which Crandall gained because of *how* the *Liberator* reached her: through a Black woman whom she knew as a person.

The two accounts of how Davis got the *Liberator* to Crandall make it clear that Crandall did not initiate obtaining the paper. Whether Davis was passive, simply putting the paper somewhere that Crandall would notice ("fell in my way") or took a direct and active approach ("took the paper from the offices and loaned it to me"), I argue that Davis knew what she was doing. It stretches credulity to postulate that Sarah Harris—the twenty-year-old daughter of a *Liberator* agent whose family knew of the New Haven Manual Labor College failure the previous year—would naïvely approach a white woman to ask permission to obtain higher learning. Indeed, the manner in which Canterbury's reaction to the question of Black education paralleled that of New Haven would only have confirmed what free Blacks in the North already knew: that (minimally) 99 percent of whites would respond negatively to such a request. Therefore, before any conversation between Crandall and Harris, Crandall had to *be vetted*; the person in a position to do that was Davis. She gauged Crandall's reaction to the paper, to establish whether Harris should attempt her request for education. Fortunately, for Harris, for the cause of abolition and for women's lives, Davis discerned Crandall's character accurately.

Davis was not acting selflessly in these interactions with Crandall; she, too, was gaining an education. Crandall recognized Davis's own curiosity: "Knowing her to be bright, she allowed her, when her work was done, to sit in a class room where she might absorb what was being taught."[33] Maria likely had plentiful opportunities to put reading, writing, and arithmetical skills to work later, when raising her children and helping run a restaurant.

This situation called for considerable bravery from Davis. She brought an incendiary newspaper to her place of employment, left it with the teacher, and took opportunities to engage with her employer, a white woman a decade older than herself. No matter how certain Davis was of the righteousness of the views expressed in the *Liberator*, an eighteen-year-old under the constraints of race, gender, class, and employment pressures must have been nervous, yet she calmed whatever butterflies danced through her frame.

The Second Moment:
Sarah Harris and Prudence Crandall

The celebrated Rosa Parks (1913–2005)—first Black woman to lie in state in the US Capitol—gained renown in the Montgomery bus boycotts.[34] She boarded a segregated bus and took her seat before the bus driver insisted that she move to make room for white passengers who were standing. If her claim to fame rested on one day too many of humiliation and oppression, she would not have received the honors of a nation upon her demise. Parks *was* tired that day but not physically; as she said, "The only tired I was, was tired of giving in."[35] Rosa Parks was not an isolated individual but part of a movement for social change: she was secretary of the local National Association for the Advancement of Colored People (NAACP) chapter and a recent attendee at the Highlander Folk School for activist training. A protest of some type had been in the discussion stages for months. The small step Parks took had years of organization (and exhaustion) behind it and would extend years beyond that moment. Parks seized the moment as a *conscious agent* of change.[36]

The idea of a humble but intellectually hungry Sarah Harris shyly emerging from segregated silence to ask for "a little more learning" carries a romantic sheen. But her request was informed by political acumen from her family, her own reading of the *Liberator*, and her perceptive trepidation that Crandall could be hurt by accepting her as a pupil. As Kaitlyn Greenidge describes it, "the carefulness of the words" reflect a further vetting of Crandall, using "the tone you adopt when you are unsure if the person you are talking to has the ability to see you as a fellow human." Harris intended to be a conscious agent of change, if Prudence Crandall could respond as a person and a sister.[37]

Sarah Harris (1812–1878) was the oldest daughter and second child of a prosperous couple, William Monteflora Harris (1783–1859) and Sally Prentice Harris (1794–1857). Her father was from the West Indies, most likely Haiti. While his own educational opportunities had been limited, he strove to obtain better futures for his children.[38] When Sarah was born in 1812, the family was based in Norwich, Connecticut, a medium-sized town with a growing African-American population. The Harrises were Congregationalists; Sarah Harris was accepted as a church member at sixteen.[39]

In January 1832 the ever-growing Harris family (William and Sally had twelve children) moved to Canterbury to take up farming. They purchased a large parcel of land (in Sally's name) and did well enough to expand their holdings twice in the coming years.[40] The Harris family was living an antebellum American dream. Their hard work and family cooperation brought increased material success and a measure of respectability rarely accorded to Blacks.

This idea—*respectability*—had particular meaning in the antebellum North, distinguishing those who deserved "important" people's attention (whom one was *able* to *respect*) from those who did not matter (the disreputable, the poor, the destitute). Most whites believed that all Blacks fell outside the parameters of respectability. The Harrises were living proof that people of color could reach the economic and moral bar to gain the perks of respectability: property ownership and access to education. Sarah Harris's church membership was frequently cited to reinforce her respectability.

The primary sources concerning Harris's request contain some variation. In the *Windham County Advertiser* letter, written within a year after Harris approached her, Crandall states:

> A colored girl of respectability—a professor of religion—and daughter of honorable parents, called on me sometime during the month of September last, and said in a very earnest manner, "Miss Crandall, I want to get a little more learning, enough if possible to teach colored children, and if you will admit me into your school I shall forever be under the greatest obligation to you. If you think it will be the means of injuring you, I will not insist on the favor." I did not answer her immediately, as I thought perhaps, if I gave her permission, some of my scholars might be disturbed. In further conversation with her, however, I found she had a great anxiety to improve in learning.
>
> Her repeated solicitations were more than my feelings could resist, and I told her if I was injured on her account I would bear it—she might enter as one of my pupils.[41]

This account, the closest in time to the events, indicates that Harris came to Crandall with a specific goal: becoming a teacher herself. She also provides Crandall with a reasonable rationale for refusing: the harm it might bring to the academy and Crandall's own ability to keep her fledgling institution open. Maria Stewart closely echoes this logic in one of her contemporaneous speeches:

> I have asked several individuals of my sex, who transact business for themselves, if providing our girls were to give them the most satisfactory references, they would not be willing to grant them an equal opportunity with others? Their reply has been—for their own part, they had no objection;

but as it was not the custom, were they to take them into their employ, they would be in danger of losing the public patronage.

And such is the powerful force of prejudice.[42]

Whether Harris had read this speech or simply knew the logic, it is clear that the ubiquity of racism called for white women to break the cycle of racial exclusion.

By choosing not to answer immediately, Crandall conceded that Harris's concern that harm could happen to the school was not unfounded. What is often overlooked is how Harris persisted past the original request with "repeated solicitations." This is confirmed in the later account of the school that Crandall wrote, except that the "repeated solicitations" become part of a normal social intercourse:

> Sarah Harris, a respectable young woman and a member of the church . . . called often to see her friend Maria, my family assistant. In some of her calls I ascertained that she wished to attend my school and board at her own father's house at some little distance from the village. I allowed her to enter as one of my pupils. By this act I gave great offence.[43]

Davis and Harris were in direct and frequent conversation, and Harris's visits to Davis provided occasions for Harris to approach Crandall. Much as Davis took the measure of Crandall's character, Harris was, likewise, evaluating Crandall's response and the appropriateness of reiterating her request (likely walking the fine line between admirable persistence and unwanted nagging).

Ultimately, it worked. Both Davis and Harris read Crandall accurately. The fact that they were right in their hunch about Crandall's character is now such a fait accompli that it is easy to overlook the gamble that Davis and Harris took. As aforementioned, Davis had brought a partisan newspaper into the home of her employer and presumed to speak to Crandall about it. These actions were hazardous for a young Black woman. When Harris took the initiative with this white authority figure and asked to join the school, it was not intended to flatter the teacher; on the contrary, because of the power relations and logic of race, the risk was all on Harris.

The deep reaches of Crandall's Quaker upbringing and schooling and the particular strain of Arminian Second Great Awakening piety with which she had aligned herself at Packerville Baptist made her receptive to Davis and Harris. Crandall's language echoes both evangelical Christianity and Quaker antislavery rhetoric. She said she had "been taught from early childhood the sin of Slavery."[44] Considering slavery a "sin" called for its repudiation, rendering gradualism morally impossible. Crandall's blended piety aided her now, when she talismanically took the advice of the Bible:

I felt in my heart to adopt the language of the Sacred Teacher when he said—"So I turned, and considered all the oppressions that are done under the sun: and, behold the tears of such as were oppressed, and they had no comforter; and on the side of the oppressors there was power, but they had no comforter."[45]

This text comes from within the most realistic, gloomy, even cynical book of the Bible: Ecclesiastes 4:1. Crandall's boldly puts racists squarely in the position of those who subjugate the oppressed. She interprets this text not according to the world-weary assessment of the original but as a structural analysis: the oppressed have tears, and the oppressors have power. She chooses to side with the oppressed when she decides to take action against the inequities, thus breaking from the narrator of Ecclesiastes who seems content to be passive ("So I turned, and considered").[46]

Crandall also uses a language that bridges her Quaker upbringing and her evangelistic conversion when she claims that her convictions came from her heart:

I said in mine heart here are my convictions. What shall I do? Shall I be inactive and permit "prejudice, the mother of abominations," to remain undisturbed? Or should I venture to enlist into the rank of those who with the *Sword of Truth* dare hold combat with prevailing iniquity.

Crandall's analysis unified emotion and accuracy, when she named racism the "mother of abominations." Crandall attacked racial prejudice at home rather than spitting invective at distant Southern enslavers. Crandall and Stewart were correct in their emphasis on racism, which has proven more intractable than slavery.[47]

Men were not directing this interchange: the idea for Harris to attend Crandall's school and Crandall's later decision to reopen the school for Black women were female-generated resolves.[48] This impulse for equal rights and mutual human recognition passes like a baton from Davis and her Boston-infused intellect and politics, to Harris's family background and educational aspirations, to Crandall's moral character.[49]

Given that the local Black community knew nothing of Crandall before this, her tenacious determination likely came as a pleasant surprise. But Harris and Davis knew that Crandall's radicalization had come through personal relations.

Reflecting upon this moment accords us a rare glimpse of the world palpably changing through the agency of women. Crandall's commitment to equal rights was never an abstraction: it was launched and mediated by contact with Black women whom she knew as people, neighbors, students, employees, and finally as friends. These three women experienced a moment of connection that transposed the moral drive for equality from abstraction to reality, from white paternalism to something more like human—in this case, *philosophiac*—collaboration.

The Third Moment: "By This Act I Gave Great Offence"

The precise date when Harris started attending classes at Crandall's first academy is not recorded but likely was mid-October 1832. Events unfolded slowly; white students, in particular, have been assumed to be accepting, since some of them had attended common schools with Harris or knew her from church.[50] As rumors began to circulate about a Black student, white parents condemned the change. Some did so furtively in veiled comments to Crandall's family.[51] The village's response coalesced into a two-pronged strategy: officially sanctioned disapproval and constant harassment.

White women led the first delegation to Crandall. There are numerous accounts of this meeting, but only one identifiable member of the group, Mary White (1785–1861), wife of Episcopal minister George S. White, who did *not* have a daughter at the school. This meeting took place sometime in the fall of 1832, long before Crandall conceived her plan to reconstitute the academy for Black women. Crandall was still working independently, with (and in support of) Davis and Harris. Crandall biographer Susan Strane imaginatively (and likely accurately) places Davis serving tea at this encounter. Once challenged, Crandall proclaimed that she would not break her commitment to Harris, even if it meant the school's ruination.[52] Unitarian minister and abolitionist Samuel J. May recalled how Crandall stressed Harris's respectability but to

> no avail. Prejudice blinds the eyes, closes the ears, hardens the heart. "Sarah belonged to the proscribed, despised class, and therefore must not be admitted into a private school with their daughters." This was the gist of all they had to say. Reasons were thrown away, appeals to their sense of right, to their compassion for injured fellow-beings, made no impression. "They would not have it said that their daughters went to school with a nigger girl." Miss Crandall was assured that, if she did not dismiss Sarah Harris, her white pupils would be withdrawn from her.[53]

Crandall highlighted qualities that should have made Harris "respectable," most crucially her church membership. These arguments were rejected—Blacks could never be respectable enough to attend a privileged "private school." The white women visitors did not emphasize colonizationist notions of sending Harris to Liberia, nor did they argue racial intellectual limitations. The objections they lodged were based on the *perceived function and prestige* of the school.[54]

Female academies were intended to prepare women to be cultured partners to their husbands and to teach skills for self-sufficiency should they
remain single or be widowed. Crandall's academically demanding curriculum
raised no known local objections. However, with the admission of Harris,
the gap between Crandall's academic goals and the perceived status of a
female academy became obvious. The mothers who objected express no fear
that their daughters might receive a lower quality of academic instruction.
Their fear was social. While these white women were almost certainly wives
of colonizationists, their focus was on their daughters' marriage prospects
rather than exporting free Blacks. Whether or not Sarah Harris stayed in the
country or the neighborhood was irrelevant to these white mothers, who
simply wanted her gone from *this* school.

Parents willing to pay the tuition for their daughters to get learning beyond
the common school level "expected their daughters to benefit from the presence of other young ladies as well as from formal instruction," including
emulating each other in manners and reinforcing each other's piety. Friendships formed at school would become the basis of social networks for young
women.[55] This included marriage prospects, wherein a young woman's female
friends would provide an entrée to meeting their brothers and cousins. Canterbury's fears of intermarriage stemmed partially from this presumed function of female academies. The transformation of Crandall's academy from a
female boarding school to a social experiment in integration was a far more
explicit challenge to social norms than lectures on chemistry.

Crandall's response to the threat of her school being ruined by student
defection was unwavering; her opponents dubbed her stubborn and "stiff-
necked."[56] She had accepted the shared humanity of all people and saw no
reason to backtrack on that realization. She also had formed a bond with
Harris and would cleave to that commitment in solidarity. Crandall aligned
herself and the academy with the egalitarian premises inherent in both Christianity and American thought.

Crandall had already made an interesting strategic decision: when she
accepted Sarah Harris, Crandall did not announce that change but waited
for the news to filter out at its own pace. There are many potential reasons
why she did this, starting with trepidations about possible responses.

Another reason can be found in Crandall's own Quaker heritage, preferring passive resistance to inflaming opposition. The example of Anthony
Benezet would have given Crandall a specific parallel. Benezet's Quakerism
extrapolated from the doctrine of the inner light to the radical social equality
of all people.[57] When Benezet accepted African American students, he, too,
kept quiet in a desire to avoid controversy and conflict and to observe how
the students performed.[58]

A personal/political reason why Crandall may have refrained from announcing Sarah's entrance has to do with "unlearning" her own racism. The Immediate Abolitionists, especially in the early years of the 1830s, constitute the first identifiable group of white Americans to consciously cultivate an antiracist consciousness.[59] Unlike abolitionists who joined the movement through hearing a public speech or attending an antislavery society, Crandall underwent this process intuitively, guided by Black women.

When the school was open, May wrote an account of the dynamics of overcoming prejudice.

> Some may here wish to ask why Miss Crandall did not first consult her patrons, the parents of those, who were already in her school? Her answer is, *She foresaw that there would be the same kind of opposition in their bosoms, which she had quelled in her own.* Their opinions and feelings could not help her to decide what was her duty. She thought it quite as likely that they would acquiesce, if nothing was said to them on the subject, as most of them were acquainted with the character of the girl, and knew it to be unexceptionable. At all events, she determined to act as she was persuaded was right, and meet the consequences, whatever they might be.[60]

Crandall knew what she had had to overcome when she acceded to Sarah's request. It makes her introspection more impressive that she deduced not everyone would be able to overcome this prejudice, or, at the very least, not everyone would be able to overcome it at the same rate as she had. Crandall's psychological insight proved correct: those with social power in Canterbury did not look at race through the moral lens that she had adopted.

Whites active in the antislavery movement did examine themselves for remnants of prejudice. Crandall's journey, spurred by Davis and Harris, stands as an independent verification of the process others were undergoing, particularly, in Boston around Garrison and in Cincinnati around Theodore Weld.[61] The *Liberator* inspired Crandall, but she didn't yet have a white abolitionist community. Aside from the support of her family (and their own conscious struggles with internalized racism varied), it is not clear if Crandall had any other white people around her with whom she could discuss the changes in her own heart between September 1832 and January 1833. Yet, it is during these months that she made the decisions and took the actions that make her an early exemplar of white solidarity against racism: admitting Sarah Harris, standing by her when challenged by whites, then hatching the idea of reopening her academy for Black women.

Readers familiar with Paul Goodman's *Of One Blood: Abolitionism and the Origins of Racial Equality* will recognize that my analysis of Crandall parallels his thesis that free Blacks played a central role in "converting whites to

racial equality and immediatism."[62] In their concerted opposition to colonization, initiating the Black press, and circulating works like Walker's *Appeal*,
Northern Blacks were prepared to assist at the birth of a white abolitionist
movement that would honor the worth of all people.

Crandall's relationships with Davis and Harris made her part of the growing list of "conversions" of white abolitionists to a lived understanding of
equality and shared humanity. Garrison's repudiation of colonization in 1830
serves as a marker for the commencement of this trend, due to the transformative impact he had on others. "Conversion" is no mere metaphor: these
lifechanging insights into human equality were spiritual moments for white
abolitionists, at once reinforcing their existing Christian understandings of
the equality of all souls before God and expanding such cosmological ideas
into a critique of political, social, and religious institutions. In this, white
abolitionists made a specific contribution to the growth of religious plural-
ism, launching an activist form of faith that escaped partisan denominational
confines and shared energies with individualist movements like American
transcendentalism.[63] Lydia Maria Child captured the fervid enthusiasm of the
early 1830s: "The Holy Spirit did actually descend upon men and women in
tongues of flame," infusing them "in a glow of faith."[64] Accomplished historian
David Brion Davis labeled abolitionism as a "surrogate" religious impulse,
which, in turn, reinvigorated a hoary theme in Christianity—spirit-versus-
letter.[65] Abolitionists—Black and white—were living out what they held as
Christian principles, rather than adhering to biblical literalism as colonizationists and opponents of abolition often did.

The white abolitionists also rekindled the age-old battle between deco-
rum and enthusiasm in religion, now replicated in the political realm. In this
they were well-placed between the free Black community, which had never
eschewed more demonstrative forms of worship, and the evangelical emotionalism of the Second Great Awakening. Furthermore, the Black church
(and Black preachers under slavery) consistently merged multiple functions
of religion—personal, communal, and political. In Walker's *Appeal*, one can
sense "a fierce religious impulse to destroy the social structures upholding
degradation and submission and replace them with institutions based on
Christian love and justice."[66] While not adopting this Black style wholesale
into their religiosity, white abolitionists withdrew their energy from institutions that refused to reckon with slavery and racial injustice. This later led to
Garrisonian nonresistance and the Come-Outer movement, in which abolitionists would lead people out of churches that refused to condemn slavery.

Crandall knew this tension between expressive and decorous religion. Her
Quaker upbringing and education had given her strong roots in the idea of
spiritual equality, but the expressive element of emotionalism was lacking
until her Baptist immersion and participation in the revivalism of Packerville

Baptist Church. While Davis and Harris were connected to the staid Congregational tradition, the writings in the *Liberator* they shared with Crandall conflated piety and politics: "I am a strong advocate for the cause of God, and for the cause of freedom," Maria Stewart unashamedly declared.[67]

Crandall's abolitionist faith is impressively self-assured from the start. Already used to the language of conversion, now with added militancy from the *Liberator*, Crandall's abolitionism did not need additional white corroboration. In the letter where she introduces herself to Garrison, she writes, "I have been for some months past determined if possible during the remaining part of my life to benefit the people of color."[68]

The antiracist impulse among white abolitionists was strong in the early 1830s, especially among white women. Lydia Maria Child's *Appeal in Favor of That Class of Americans Called Africans* focused half of its argument on questions of racial prejudice. Unfortunately, the coupling of antislavery and antiracist views that marked white abolition in these early years dissipated enough that by the organizational split at the end of the decade, the importance of a strongly articulated antiracism within the movement was much diluted.

In 1837 the Reverend Theodore Wright, one of Crandall's endorsers, gave a major speech that he called "Progress of the Antislavery Cause." Tracing the spirit of abolition from the American Revolution forward, he was alarmed by a lack of conviction from new converts to the cause in the late 1830s:

> Three years ago, when a man professed to be an abolitionist, we knew where he was. He was an individual who recognized the identity of the human family. Now a man may call himself an abolitionist and we know not where to find him. . . . Many throw themselves in, without understanding the breadth and depth of the principles of emancipation. . . . Unless men come out and take their stand on the principles of recognizing man as man, I tremble for the ark. . . . It is an easy thing to ask about the vileness of slavery at the South, but to call the dark man a brother. . . . to treat the man of color in all circumstances as a man and brother—that is the test.
>
> Every man who comes into this society ought to be *catechized*. . . . Abolitionists must annihilate in their own bosoms the cord of caste. . . . Every abolitionist would do well to spend a day in fasting and prayer over it and looking at his own heart.[69]

Wright's rhetoric invokes conversion: "catechized," "annihilate in their own bosoms." Despite Wright's worried tone, he provides retrospective confirmation of the earlier antiracism of white allies in the movement.

No white abolitionists of the nineteenth century can be said to have entirely "annihilate(d) in their own bosoms the cord of caste," Garrison's patronizing underestimation of Frederick Douglass being the unsettling prime example. But I agree with Goodman's assessment that "white abolitionists in the movement's first decade wrestled with racial prejudice" and in the process unfurled a series of "unprecedented challenges . . . again white supremacist ideas, behavior, customs, and laws."[70] Crandall's resistance against the same white people who had helped establish her first school was one of those "unprecedented challenges."[71]

The Fourth Moment:
Crandall's Decision to Find Allies

The first academy was likely doomed by December 1832. Crandall being immovable on Harris's enrollment, white parents intensified their threat to withdraw their daughters.[72] By the dawn of 1833, Crandall birthed a new plan. Perhaps, she conceived this from reading Stewart's call to "lay the corner-stone for the building of a High School" for Black women.[73] Stewart herself had long thirsted after education, decrying how Black women's intellects were condemned to disappear under a never-receding tide of manual labor.[74] Perhaps, Crandall could see in Stewart's description of minds buried beneath "a load of iron pots" the situation of Davis and Harris—two young women who had introduced her to the discourse of the *Liberator,* thereby teaching her something she had not known. Coincidentally or not, almost one and a half years to the date from Stewart's publishing her initial essay, Crandall's high school for Black women *did* open.

On January 18, 1833, Crandall wrote an unsolicited letter to William Lloyd Garrison. Admitting that they were strangers to each other "save through the medium of the public print," she mentions her academy.

> Now I will tell you why I write to you and the object is this: I wish to know your opinion respecting changing white scholars for colored ones. I have been for some months determined, if possible, during the remaining part of my life to benefit the people of color. I do not dare tell any of my neighbors anything about the contemplated change in my school and I beg you, Sir, that you will not expose it to anyone, or it would ruin my present school. Will you be so kind as to write me by the next mail and give me your opinion on the subject and if you consider it possible to obtain 20–25 young ladies of color to enter this school for the term of one year at the rate of $25 per quarter, including board, washing and tuition. I will come to Boston in a few days and make some arrangements about it. I do not suppose the number can be obtained from Boston alone; but from all the large cities in several states I thought they might be gathered.[75]

As she announces her impending visit, consider that both she and Garrison were unmarried and that he was notorious enough that sexual innuendoes (mainly interracial) were already circulating. Crandall invited herself, unbidden, to meet him. Furthermore, the *idea* of a school for Black women came from her—it is not Garrison or any other male abolitionist leader who made the initial suggestion. She also used her knowledge of the *Liberator* to consider the practical aspects of her plan, namely, that students would likely be drawn from a regional rather than a local base and that the *Liberator* would assist by virtue of its circulation among Northern free Blacks (knowledge gained though Davis and Harris).[76] The letter conveys a sense of urgency—"write me by the next mail"—as she resolved to head to Boston. Crandall uses a Second Great Awakening language of dedicating her entire life to the improvement of the world; significantly, she dates this dedication as being a few months old. Stewart similarly expressed a unity of religious piety and action, writing that she "felt a strong desire . . . to devote the remainder of my days to piety and virtue, and now possess that spirit of independence, that, were I called upon, I would willingly sacrifice my life for the cause of God and my brethren."[77] Piety and political action are seamlessly blended.

Crandall may not even have waited for a reply from Garrison before traveling to Boston.[78] Arriving on January 29, 1833, she sent a note over to his office, asking to meet him in the lobby of Mr. Barker's temperance hotel.[79] As Garrison's biographer Henry Mayer puts it, "William Lloyd Garrison had never kept a political tryst before, and Prudence Crandall had never made one, but the high cause quieted whatever misgivings they might have entertained."[80] This remarkable woman-initiated meeting, far from being considered in its own right, seems to have generated more attention around Crandall's secrecy with her erstwhile Canterbury supporters than for her perspicacity in conceiving this plan.[81] According to a later affidavit from storekeeper Richard Fenner, Crandall claimed to be headed to Boston to buy supplies for an "infant school."[82] This became a source of bitterness between Crandall and the townspeople, something that her enemies bruited about to besmirch her character. Some scholars have followed the townspeople in this, notably Edmund Fuller, who dwells on the incident to impugn Crandall as "a difficult person" who "did dissemble," acting rashly with "(o)bstinacy and anger . . . considering the aid and support her townsmen had given her."[83] This misplaced focus (and judgment) erase women's history by neglecting the structural reasons why Crandall felt she could not be open. It also personalizes the flaws of the person working for justice rather than the cosmological pettiness of her enemies. It was uncommon for women to propose independent institutional-organizing plans. While women had to ask male permission for their organizing efforts, men never had to formally ask women for permission. Crandall's bold self-initiated decision reveals a protofeminist disruption of the realpolitik of gender.

The results of the meeting between Garrison and Crandall are pivotal.[84] Garrison agreed to support her and gave her names of potential allies and Black families that might have daughters interested in the school. These contacts included Simeon Jocelyn, Arthur Tappan, and the Benson brothers in Providence, George and Henry. It seems likely that Garrison raised the specter of the New Haven Manual Labor College failure, especially given that he was recommending her to Jocelyn and Tappan.[85] Crandall followed up on Garrison's recommendations and thus activated the *Liberator* network in a genuinely interracial way. If her new high school for Black women were to succeed, a full alliance of Black and white, male and female, would have to occur. The marvel is that it did.

When Crandall parted from Garrison, she consciously built on the trail-blazing started when Davis carried the *Liberator* into the schoolhouse. That edifice itself would now become a focal point in the pages of the *Liberator* and across the network the paper had built. But these precious final four months of the first academy, from the moment Harris asked in the early fall, to Crandall's meeting with Garrison, merit sustained attention. The rest of the history hinges on these women. Their *philosophia* changed the trajectory of abolition, racial, and gender history.

CHAPTER 3

Activating the
Abolitionist Networks

What a happy country this will be,
if the whites will listen.
—David Walker

February 1833 was eventful for Prudence Crandall. She started the month visiting Black families in Providence, Rhode Island. Next she traveled alone to New York City, meeting with the city's most prominent Black ministers. These hectic peregrinations had ceased by month's end, when Crandall found herself in an increasingly hostile Canterbury whose leading citizens were determined to destroy her new academy.

The interpersonal initiative among Maria Davis, Sarah Harris, and Prudence Crandall highlights the intersection of gender and race. The birth of the school from shared ideas among women is literally momentous: it marked a discernible *moment* in the trajectory of full political and intellectual engagement of white women and free Black women in the chorus of American voices. This chapter turns to the next moment: the roles played by men, white and Black, in making the school possible. The time frame encompasses the two months preliminary to the academy for Black women, from Crandall's announcement of the change in the school in February to the opposition of Canterbury's whites. The drama in this brief time, marked by infuriate meetings and threats of violence, was exciting and patently dangerous. Far more significant than the histrionics, though, was the ingathering of the growing abolitionist movement as it morphed into a regional coalition of Black and white, male and female, amplifying and extending what Davis, Harris, and Crandall had started.

Crandall's Travels for Students and Contacts

Crandall's journeys are particularly noteworthy in the context of Black-white social interaction. The references from Garrison—mainly to Blacks involved

in the distribution of the *Liberator*—placed her in contact with a large portion
of the free Black leadership of the Northeast and with parents of potential
students. She apparently negotiated the interracial social terrain adroitly,
gaining credibility in the Black community. She also reconstituted the plan-
ning committee from the New Haven Manual Labor School by meeting with
Peter Williams Jr., Arthur Tappan, and Simeon Jocelyn. These strategic
meetings with powerful men, both Black and white, being initiated by a till-
then-unknown unmarried white woman, indicate how radically and swiftly
abolitionism was remaking the contours of political engagement. The pace
of these meetings also suggests Crandall's desire to have her new school succeed. She did not cede organizational efforts to the powerful men she met:
she directed the enterprise and decided the timing of her announcements
to Canterbury and the world.

Her meeting with Garrison in Boston had been on a Tuesday; by Friday,
February 1, she was in Providence. Here she met at least twice with Elizabeth Hammond. Hammond had been running a boardinghouse since her
husband's death in 1826; she knew everyone in Providence's African American neighborhoods.[1] She introduced Crandall to two white abolitionists,
the young Benson brothers, George Jr. and Henry, thus initiating the crucial
alliance between the Benson family and Crandall.

On Saturday morning, Hammond took Crandall to meet other Black parents; Crandall felt that half a dozen young women here could become students
in her new academy.[2] She also found in these families the same earnest thirst
for knowledge that she had observed in Davis and Harris: "They seemed
to feel much for the education of their children."[3] Hammond sent her two
daughters to the school; at least three other students came from Providence.

After this successful visit, Crandall returned to Canterbury. Here she took
one person into her confidence about her plans—Daniel Packer, a manufac-
turer and patron of the Packerville Baptist Church. He was circumspect,
cautioning her of the high chance of failure in gaining students, but he did not
foresee the ferocious opposition of the village (or refrained from speculating).
He would remain ambivalent through the life of the school, torn between his
business interests and personal impulses. For now, he recognized Crandall's
goal of educating Black women as "praiseworthy."[4]

A week after this meeting with Packer, Crandall's impatience materialized
in a February 12 letter to Garrison. After updating him on her progress, she
indicated that she was headed to New York City very soon and needed letters
of introduction from him. One connection she had already obtained, from
a member of the Harris family, or possibly from Packer, was with Reverend
William Miller, a maverick Black clergyman in New York City.[5]

Undertaking an unchaperoned trip to New York City to meet primarily
with Black men is astonishing proof of Crandall's boldness. "New England

disapproved of anyone—especially a single woman—going to New York City, that barbarous center of corruption and commercialism," let alone to meet with free African Americans in the service of cultivating interracial trust.[6] She arrived in the city on Friday, February 15. Her success there can be inferred from the fact that seven of her fifteen endorsers and at least nine students hailed from New York. In addition to Miller (who is not among her endorsers), she likely met with Williams, Theodore Wright, Samuel Cornish, and two Baptists, J. T. Raymond and James Hayborn: an all-star cast of activist Black clergymen engaged in educational initiatives, the Black press, and the convention movement. Much like Davis, Harris, and Hammond, these men had to evaluate the character of Prudence Crandall quickly and accurately. Given the failure of the New Haven Manual Labor College and the vast distance between New York City and Canterbury (geographically and culturally), they had to gain considerable confidence in her to endorse the academy. It would be the daughters of their parishioners at risk if another failure occurred. No students had been in jeopardy in New Haven, since the vote squashed the project on the drawing board. But with Crandall's school opening on April 1, 1833, the strategy had to be more immediate. She apparently impressed those with whom she conversed.[7] Receptive to listening and learning from free Blacks, Crandall likely imbibed much from these ministers. Williams, Cornish, and Wright, all excellent preacher-orators, impressed many white abolitionists, including Lydia Maria Child and Angelina Grimké.[8]

Enroute to New Haven, Crandall met the wealthy white abolitionist Arthur Tappan, who put his support—moral and financial—behind the proposed school, even offering to be present when the students arrived.[9] Having seen the opposition to the Manual Labor College, Tappan was wary of Canterbury's possible reaction but duly impressed with Crandall's character and plan.

Tappan's conversion to immediate abolition sprang from religious principles. Colonization's claim that racial prejudice was immutable constituted a "slander against the religion of Jesus" for claiming that a sin could not be overcome.[10] Tappan appreciated Crandall's deep religiosity; he knew she was a Baptist and appreciated her testifying that Harris was a pious church member, too.[11] His enthusiastic support buoyed Crandall, because she assumed (incorrectly) that his name and reputation would quell any fears Canterburians might have about her school.[12]

In New Haven she met with Jocelyn.[13] Though still optimistic about social change, he had been chastened by the Black college vote, warning Crandall of the pitfalls ahead.[14]

Back in Canterbury by February 22, she informed her family of her proposed new academy. If they were surprised, they remained doggedly on her side throughout the crisis; her opponents tried to drag her family into the conflict numerous times (as tyrants do), and (except for her brother Reuben's

reluctance) her family gave no succor to the enemy. Prudence wrote to Jocelyn that her family "pretty cordially received" the news. Likewise, she
spoke with some neighbors, who "to my astonishment . . . exhibited but
little opposition."[15]

Next it was time to face the white students who remained in the first
academy. This would, in essence, be the announcement to the world, as the
young women would tell their parents of this dramatic disruption in their
education. It was Monday, February 25, when she revealed that her school
was closing and reopening for the exclusive reception of "Young Ladies and
Little Misses of Color." As the girls took this news home to their parents—
many of whom had objected to the presence of Harris—anger smoldered in
Canterbury. Ellen D. Larned's account sets their reaction in context:

> Had she also consulted her generous friends and patrons in Canterbury,
> or even given them notice of her intentions, they would have had less
> ground of complaint, but their indignation when the proposed change in
> the complexion of the school was suddenly announced to them was greatly
> heightened by what they deemed an inexcusable breach of good faith in
> one they had so encouraged and befriended. . . . The people of Canterbury
> saw to their supreme horror and consternation that this popular school in
> which they had taken so much pride was to be superseded by something
> so anomalous and phenomenal that it could hardly be comprehended.[16]

A committee of her first academy's supporters visited her the next day: Rufus
Adams, David Frost Jr., Richard Fenner, and Dr. Andrew Harris. They pointedly presented the village's (white) perspective. In her report of this meeting,
conveyed in an urgent letter to Jocelyn, Crandall sounds isolated, asking for
an immediate reply.

Crandall's fears were not unjustified, since the committee of four came
"resolved to do everything in their power to destroy my undertaking and that
they could do it and should do it and what will be the result of this commotion
I cannot tell." But even under these trying circumstances, where the power
clearly lay in the hands of these embodiments of wealth, prestige, privilege
and the Standing Order, Crandall was not tongue-tied. She dropped Tappan's
name repeatedly, which informed her visitors that she had support and that
their hostility could have financial costs. Just as she had stood up to the wives
and mothers who wanted her to dismiss Harris, she remained firm in her
decision to "change the complexion" of her academy. Perhaps in her mind's
eye, she was able to contrast the sincerity of Elizabeth Hammond or Peter
Williams, in their encouragement of education for Black youth who had been
denied privilege, with the overweening sense of entitlement emanating from
the delegation. Rankled by possible caste violations at church, the committee
voiced concern that Crandall intended for her Black students to worship at

First Congregational, to which she replied that she would hold services with preachers at the school.[17]

Is there any reason to see things as the villagers did, with a sense of offense at Crandall's sudden change in the school's student body? The village's reputation was about to change. Academies were private schools but understood as public assets, much like private universities today. Crandall's decision meant that Canterbury would assume an importance in the national debate over the status of free Blacks that the town had neither invited nor sanctioned. This line of reasoning, though, erases the particularity of the change. Consider the reaction if Crandall had changed her school for wealthier white students (say, by raising tuition precipitously)? Or, as Richard Fenner allegedly heard, if she had decided to teach an elementary infant school instead of a high school? If she had blocked Blacks from ever attending, denied access to Catholics—any number of other conceivable restrictions would have been met gladly or caused only a minimum of grumbling by the few local whites thus excluded. The racial dimension of the change drove the outrage, not the propriety of Crandall keeping it a secret from them.

Samuel J. May addressed her precipitous change forthrightly in his published debate with Andrew Judson.

> You complain, and have elsewhere complained that Miss C[randall] made the change in her school abruptly—that she did it without asking the consent or even the advice of her former patrons. I apprehend that the blame for this must attach to yourselves rather than to her. If you had ever evinced that interest in the education and freedom and happiness of our colored brethren, which you now profess to feel, there can be little doubt that she would have disclosed to you her feelings and her purposes; and gladly have availed herself of your assistance. But she perceived that you, like most of our white brethren, regarded the colored children of our Heavenly Father as doomed to degradation, and not to be admitted to equal privileges even in this land of boasted liberty. Therefore she did not reveal her plan until it was matured. She anticipated that you would oppose it. The event has proved that she judged correctly.[18]

Any vestige of naïveté in Crandall dissipated after this visit from the officials that morning. Maintaining her academy for Black women was going to demand a two-front struggle: conducting the school itself and waging a public battle alongside her abolitionist allies.

Polarization in Canterbury: March 1833

White Canterbury's opposition to Crandall's second academy adopted a two-pronged approach: legal and extralegal. Threats of violence (veiled and explicit) shadowed every legal discussion, town meeting, and interpersonal contact. From the moment students started to arrive, regular harassment, crescendoing to vigilante violence, plagued the school. Because the perpetrators of this vigilantism were neither named nor prosecuted, we can only speculate on their identities. But many other instances in the 1830s attest that white "gentlemen of property and standing" were not above fomenting and participating in such disturbances.[19] This presents a reversal, typical of structures of oppression, in which the characteristics that the oppressors accuse their victims of holding are actually possessed by the accusers themselves, projected onto their targets. The threatened violence from free Blacks never emerged, least of all from the young women attending Crandall's school. But riotous destructive violence was frequently visited on free Blacks by whites, playing a decisive role in the academy's eventual closure.

Looming threats were gathering even prior to students being present. In March the academy was out of session pending its April 1 reopening. The opposition explicitly sought to block the proposed second academy from ever opening, and while they preferred civil means for doing so, they hinted that their anger might not be restrained.

The first gambit of the town leaders was a repeat visit by the committee to Crandall on March 1, where "every argumentative effort was made to convince her of the impropriety and injustice of her proposed measure . . . in a kind and affecting manner."[20] It is unlikely their patronizing approach seemed "kind" to Crandall. Although they tried to rankle the proud teacher, she maintained her composure under this predictable "mansplaining." The committee warned that educating Black women would lead the local Black community to "look up and claim an equality with the whites, and if they were all placed upon an equal footing property and life would no longer be safe."[21] Since it was the property and lives of free Blacks that were almost always at stake in racial disturbances, this was another reversal. Social equality was what the townsmen feared at root (seen in their concern over mixed-race seating in church). They also made their colonizationist loyalties clear: they said that educating Blacks was fine but not in their town.[22]

The village emissaries claimed one dubious rhetorical victory, though, when they steered the discussion to "amalgamation." When the dangers of "the leveling principles, and intermarriage between the white and blacks" were raised, Crandall bluntly responded, "Moses had a black wife."[23] Crandall's enemies could now paint the school with the broad brush (and flammable oil paint) of interracial marriage.[24]

Some scholars have considered this a strategic error by Crandall. Strane refers to this comment as "didactic and politically ruinous." Williams mentions that Crandall's supporters never repeated this in their version of events, while her enemies used the quip to fan "the flames of racial fear and

prejudice" and to change the subject from equality in education to "amalgamation" and interracial marriage.[25] But issues of educational equality, agency
for free Blacks in social dealings, citizenship, and the right to marry whom
one wishes are not unrelated. In Massachusetts the abolitionists *were* bold
enough to openly champion interracial marriage.[26]

The discussion of amalgamation became central to the school's purpose
and history. This is because both sides knew that social equality between
Blacks and whites would ultimately have to include all aspects of equality, including freedom to marry. Anti-abolitionists played on white public
prejudice, while abolitionists relied on the regnant idealism of Christianity
and the American Revolution. Garrison was unafraid of the red herring of
intermarriage despite the impracticability of shifting white public opinion on
this volatile issue; his attitude was appreciated by the free Black community.[27]

The institution of marriage often shapes American social politics. Polyg-
amy served as a foil for federal-versus-Mormon tensions in the latter nineteenth century, interracial marriage was not legally resolved across the nation
until *Loving v. Virginia* in 1967, and marriage equality for lesbians and gay men
has marked the twenty-first century.[28] In explaining how marriage operates
socially, Stephanie Coontz demonstrates (while acknowledging the humor
of it) that what unites all marriage structures is how "since the dawn of
civilization, getting in-laws has been one of marriage's most important functions."[29] The vernacular "Would you let your daughter marry one?" points to
the uneasiness with social equality that undergirds various marriage battles:
do you want *those* people as your in-laws?

The threat of amalgamation, social leveling, and interracial marriage hov-
ered over the Canterbury school. By facing that threat head-on with her quip
about Moses's black wife, Crandall indicated that this canard would not derail
her project. Her enemies were going to use this specter no matter what she
said, so why back into a corner of denial? That very conundrum hampered
Child, despite having authored a novel (*Hobomok*) on interracial marriage
between a white woman and a Native man. In August 1831 she wrote an editorial against Northern racial prejudice, yet made an "unfortunate concession to
popular prejudice" when she declaimed interracial marriage, describing such
marriages as "in bad taste" and "unnatural." Garrison specifically critiqued
her, saying that only relationships between different species were unnatural.[30] Child did not repeat this error.[31] Crandall apparently had no hurdles to
overcome regarding interracial marriage and would not let fears of it be the
wedge to upend the academy. Although Crandall's opponents bruited her
witticism about, it never became ruinous to her case.

When the ad for Crandall's school appeared in the Saturday March 2 edition of the *Liberator*, the impact of its list of fifteen new endorsers, none from
Canterbury proper and the majority of them African American, incensed her

former supporters. The white leaders called a town meeting for Saturday, March 9.

The town meeting has an honored place in New England local politics, and Canterbury's leaders undoubtedly thought that a unanimous town meeting would have a power tantamount to the New Haven vote, shutting down the very idea of Black education in their vicinity. The town meeting also countered the prestige of Tappan and thwarted some new regional allies—the Benson brothers, Arnold Buffum, and May—by labeling them as outsiders. The local/foreign dichotomy became a major strategic plank in the white Canterbury elites' fight against the academy. The parallel to "states' rights" arguments, floated by white Southerners from the 1820s to the present day to blunt the drive for civil rights, is patent.[32]

On March 9 the town meeting commenced in a jampacked Congregational Church alive with dramatic shouts, declarations, boisterous hostility, and copious insults.[33] Only white men of Canterbury could speak; Crandall, as a woman, was disallowed. The official "moderators" then forbade Crandall's delegated representatives, May and Buffum, from speaking at all. Every description of the meeting highlights its rowdy—even menacing—atmosphere. The directors of the meeting strove to produce unanimity, forcibly if necessary, until shouting and removal became the (dis)order of the day.

Andrew T. Judson, the local representative to the Connecticut Assembly, established himself as the leader of Crandall's opponents. For a lawyer, his behavior seems unguardedly rash. This can be explained by his confidence that public opinion was with him and by his ambition to ride this controversy to regional and national prominence. Under Judson's polarizing rhetoric, this town meeting achieved the sharpest etching of the differences between the American Colonization Society and Garrisonian immediatism yet. Judson, who never regretted his actions, handed to William Lloyd Garrison a stark expression of heartless rhetoric with which to pillory colonization.[34]

May reports that though the church could hold "a thousand persons, sitting and standing," he and Arnold Buffum had to squeeze through a side door, yet ended up near the moderator Ashael Bacon.[35] Henry Benson and George Benson Jr. arrived a few minutes later. The report from Judson and company indicates that these "foreigners" caused the disturbance:

> *Arnold Buffum*, the agent of the Anti-Slavery Society, from R.I. the Rev. Samuel J. May, the Unitarian Minister of Brooklyn, and a Vice-President of the same Society, with two boisterous young men, also from R.I. entered the town meeting, *and took conspicuous posts in it*. To render the array still more imposing, some two or three stout negroes came into the meeting house, and took their places also. Who they were, or from whence they came, we know not.[36]

By contrast, May and Henry Benson report that the meeting was already in high dudgeon, as can be seen in the resolutions offered and accepted, which, in their tone as well as intent, signal hysteria against Crandall's school:

> WHEREAS it hath been publicly announced that a school is to be opened in this town, on the 1st Monday of April next, using the language of the advertisement, "for young ladies and little misses of color," or in other words, for the people of color, the obvious tendency of which would be, to collect within the town of Canterbury, large numbers of persons from other States, whose character and habits might be various and unknown to us, thereby rendering insecure the persons, property, and reputations of our citizens.[37]

From the start, the town meeting implied that the presence of people of color would affect property values and public virtue in the town, and to underline that, they mocked the respect Crandall's ad had adopted in referring to her Black students as "young ladies and little misses." Of course, there had been no such fear concerning out-of-town white women. The town meeting instead cast aspersions on the character of unknown young Black women as a class. They proceeded to pass resolutions that would render the compromise that May and Buffum had brought moot:

> *Thereupon Resolved,*—That the localities of a school, for the people of color, at any place within the limits of this town, for the administration of persons from foreign jurisdictions, meets with our unqualified disapprobation, and it is to be understood, that the inhabitants of Canterbury protest against it, in the most earnest manner.
>
> *Resolved*—That a Committee be now appointed, to be composed of the Civil Authority and Selectmen, who shall make known to the person contemplating the establishment of said school, the sentiments and objections entertained by this meeting, in reference to said school—pointing out to her, the injurious effects, and incalculable evils, resulting from such an establishment within this town, and persuade her to abandon the project.[38]

"Incalculable evils" predicted from a high school for teenagers? The resolutions written by the "Civil Authority and Selectmen" played so perfectly into Garrison's critique of colonization that he reprinted their reports without edits or comments.

The discussion of the resolutions was decidedly uncharitable. Judson compared Canterbury's situation to New Haven's struggle against the Manual Labor College and added that failure to stop Crandall's school would result in Canterbury becoming the next New Orleans (which he represented as a city of great unhappiness).[39] He also rained rhetorical fire on Crandall's "powerful conspirators," naming Tappan directly.[40] Judson's "philippic," as May described it, eschewed any sense of calm: "He vented himself in a strain of reckless hostility to his neighbor [Crandall]. . . . He twanged every chord that could stir the coarser passions of the human heart, and with such sad success that his hearers seemed to be filled with the apprehension that a dire calamity was impending over them."[41] Henry Benson reported the remarks were "wholly unworthy of a civilized, much less of an enlightened, christian community. . . . Those who have been most active in attempting the suppression of this school, may be honored now, but future ages will consign them to ignominy and shame."[42]

Needless to say, Judson and associates reported this differently. Canterbury's white leadership played the "outside agitator" card for public relations leverage, maintaining that these meddlers "conducted (themselves) in an improper manner. Their *talking, laughing,* and *notetaking* became offensive, and . . . aroused a spirit of manly indignation."[43]

White Canterburians declared their opposition to equality. The resolutions honed in on *"the leveling principles* imbibed by Miss C."[44] Thus they followed the ACS line, claiming that social equality and social coexistence of Black and white would prove impossible in the United States. The women who visited Crandall after the admission of Harris were worried about the loss of caste distinctions within a middle-class "finishing" school, while the male leaders focused on matters like church seating by caste, property values, and a marked preference for maintaining white supremacy.

The meeting ended peremptorily so that the vote could be unanimous. First, though, a surprising voice intervened—Reverend George S. White (1784–1852). The husband of Mary White, the first person to object to Crandall's school, this Episcopal minister sensed that the meeting was spinning out of control. He attempted to insert reason and calm, saying that Canterbury would not founder if the school were there, for "Miss Crandall is a Christian, and the evening and the morning prayer will daily ascend to the Father of mercies in their behalf, and he will vouchsafe his blessing." White also objected to an old colonial law against vagrants that was being rehabilitated for use against Crandall's students.[45] He was shouted down by the moderator, his warnings dismissed.[46]

When May and Buffum attempted to present their compromise, in which Crandall was willing to move to a quieter and less-conspicuous part of the town, they were brusquely denied. May claimed that they "silently presented" Crandall's letters to the moderator Ashael Bacon, but when he passed them to Judson, that practiced lawyer

[i]nstantly broke forth with greater violence than before; accused us of insulting the town by coming there to interfere with its local concerns. Other gentlemen sprang to their feet in hot displeasure; poured out their tirades upon Miss Crandall and her accomplices, and, with fists doubled

in our faces, roughly admonished us that, if we opened our lips there, they would inflict upon us the utmost penalty of the law, if not a more immediate vengeance.[47]

Note the reversal: having railed against the imagined violence that the school would bring, the townspeople threaten immediate violence against a founder of the Windham County Peace Society! Crandall is denied even proxy speech, having been forced to choose out-of-town representatives, since any Canterburians who might have sided with her had been cowed by their neighbors. Once her representatives were impugned as foreigners, she was officially rendered mute in absentia.

May would prove himself, time and again, a man who could think his way calmly through a situation in which others might be intimidated. Exhibiting peace principles by letting "the waves of invective and abuse dash over us," May waited until the meeting was officially adjourned; then, knowing he was violating no law, called, "Men of Canterbury, I have a word for you! Hear me!" Enough people stayed that May was able to cede the floor to Buffum, until they were forced outside, where they continued to answer questions and refute falsehoods.[48]

The importance of the town meeting of March 9 is manifold. It clarified the dualistic contours of the battle in Canterbury, since the townspeople were willing to stoke their vitriol before meeting a single out-of-town student: their anger against the school, like that of the white male citizens of New Haven, was based on an abstract but absolute disdain for social equality between Blacks and whites. They wanted a Canterbury—and, by extension, United States—that was monoracial or if it had to be multiracial, with an inviolable caste system in place. They silenced dissent in literal ways: shouting down or declaring out-of-order anyone who dared disagree.

Crandall's supporters, by contrast, were armed with real experience of African Americans as friends, neighbors, associates, and allies. Consider the "two or three stout negroes" present at the meeting. We can safely assume they opposed the meeting's resolutions! Their identity is unknown, but given Arnold Buffum's presence in Norwich, Connecticut, earlier in the week, they were quite likely from that town's Black community. That opens the possibility of those being such men as Frederick Olney, Charles Harris (fiancé of Maria Davis), or even David Ruggles. The prospect that Jehiel Beman from Middletown or one of his sons or associates might have made the journey cannot be dismissed, either. Whoever they were, these Black men stood as witnesses, their very "imposing" presence discomfiting the white leaders, even though the Black visitors did not speak. These free Black men, who made no threats of violence, had the violent tempers of the white attendees projected onto them.

White people committed to deconstructing racism can deploy their white privilege strategically. The interracial coalitions formed among the abolitionists seem to have understood (implicitly or explicitly) that, to gain the platforms necessary white abolitionists would *use* their positions and abilities instead of simply renouncing them. The experience that free Blacks had had of their protests and writings being ignored meant that they knew their critiques would go unheeded, but when white men started to impugn the motives of the American Colonization Society, that garnered an audience. Garrison was a master at this in the 1830s, using his position as an editor to amplify Black voices (most effectively in *Thoughts on African Colonization*) and to make privileged white men squirm. Later he neglected these strategies, most gratingly when he undervalued the talents of Frederick Douglass.[49] But at this budding stage of understanding what interracial social equality could mean, this division of duties between Black men and white men was a strategic necessity that came to the fore in the Canterbury struggle.

While Garrison is more famous and Tappan wealthier, May shines as the most consistent among Crandall's white allies. Despite his Unitarianism and her evangelical Baptist faith being theologically distant, they found common ground in Quaker-esque passive resistance and peace principles. May's Unitarianism, like Quakerism, theologically argued for the universal presence of the divine in all people. Dymond's ideas—willingness to suffer for the principles of Christianity, understanding what side of history one wants to be accounted on, and the intellectual potential of women—suffuse May's actions throughout the Crandall episode. He handled the morphing situation at the town meeting as well as could be—not defying the power of the town's officials but not allowing himself to be silenced.

Andrew Judson made a strategic blunder the next week by calling on May at his Brooklyn home on Monday, March 11. Judson and May had met prior to the Crandall scandal and "almost" formed a personal friendship. May surmised Judson suffered some pangs of guilt for his bullying at the town meeting. Indeed, Judson initiated this private meeting by saying "he had not become unfriendly" to May "and regretted that he had used some expressions and applied certain epithets" against him during the meeting.[50] But Judson's apology flipped into reiterating his opposition to Crandall. May responded by repeating her offer to move to a less-conspicuous location. Judson interrupted May's explanation:

> We are not merely opposed to the establishment of that school in Canterbury; we mean there shall not be such a school set up anywhere in our State. The colored people never can rise from their menial condition in our country; they ought not to be permitted to rise here. They are an inferior race of beings, and never can or ought to be recognized as the equals of

the whites. Africa is the place for them. I am in favor of the Colonization scheme. Let the niggers and their descendants be sent back to their
fatherland; and there improve themselves as much as they may, and civilize
and Christianize the natives, if they can. I am a Colonizationist. . . . The
condition of the colored population of our country can never be essentially
improved on this continent.[51]

May's report could be exaggerated, but the tone and content are congruent
with Judson's other recorded statements.

The problem in this discourse/debate between May and Judson is that
female and Black agency are absent. With the all-male town meeting and
this mano-a-mano debate, the narrative focus begins its drift away from the
people most intimately involved, the very people who launched the academy.
Their agency is eroded both structurally—Crandall and other women not
being able to attend the meeting—and by the arrogant dismissal of Judson
and his allies. May doesn't agree with that, but the ground of struggle between
white men was familiar enough for him to engage it. From another perspective, though, this is the ability that white male allies brought: they were able
to fight the rhetorical battle among white men and by doing so provided the
cover and distraction that enabled the school to operate.[52]

This meeting ended with Judson an implacable enemy to May. Judson's
mood of "high displeasure" never did improve.[53] On March 14, the committee
delivered the town meeting's resolutions to Crandall. By now she knew better than to be alone; she was flanked by her younger sister, Almira, and their
parents, Pardon and Esther.[54] This would be the last remonstrance by the white
male leadership of the town. Their own report says they arrived in a "formal
and becoming manner," urging Crandall to heed to the unanimous wishes of the
town, even offering to buy back her house if she gave up the school for Black
women: "This she declined. Nothing could overcome her determination to go
on."[55] Here we see the reemergence of female agency, followed by Crandall's
extending her network of female allies by spending the next few days with the
Benson family in Brooklyn, at their home dubbed "Friendship's Vale."[56]

It was here that she received the next salvo in the rhetorical battle: the
Liberator's coverage of the March 9 meeting, as reported by Henry Benson
and further dramatized by William Lloyd Garrison. Under the banner of
"HEATHENISM OUTDONE!" Garrison explained that he had "put the names
of the principal disturbers in black letter,—black as the infamy which will
attach to them as long as there exists any recollection of the wrongs of the
colored race. . . . This scandalous excitement is one of the genuine flowers
of the colonization garden."[57] The inflammatory effect of Garrison's coverage raised tensions, including for Crandall herself (and the Bensons, whose
favorite youngest son was the author of the highlighted letter). She wrote to

Garrison, entreating him to use "all mildness possible" rather than to enflame the wrath of her opponents, claiming that May and others agreed with her. However, her optimism that mildness might win "many friends in the town and vicinity" was mistaken; Garrison knew that. The battle had been joined, and neither side showed any tendency to surrender or compromise.

But this battle is not the most significant event around Crandall's second academy in March 1833. The truly new element was an earlier bombshell: the ad for Crandall's second academy was unprecedented in its racial balance, in its revelation of the depth and interracial cooperation within the abolitionist networks.

The New Academy's Fifteen Endorsers

In the narrative of Crandall's second academy, the dramatic town meeting of March 9 has eclipsed the seismic shift represented by the advertisement for her school, published one week earlier in the March 2 edition of the *Liberator*. With no holdovers from the first board of visitors,[58] this list showcases the full prestige and range of the abolitionist movement at that moment in time. Fifteen men signed on, eight Black and seven white. Aside from the roster of *Liberator* agents, no other early abolition enterprise is this racially balanced. Indeed, there was a trend toward having only token Black representation, that being thought more "expedient."[59] In New Haven, the whites had taken the lead (Jocelyn, Garrison, and Arthur Tappan), despite earlier organizing among free Blacks. While the New Haven Manual Labor College had maintained a "discreet balance" of Black and white, there was nothing "discreet" here—Blacks outnumber whites.[60]

The story of how these fifteen names came together has not been preserved. Crandall had met the majority of them by this time (remarkable, considering she had not even met Garrison until January 29). It is not safe to assume that Crandall put the entire list together nor that she was uninvolved with its assembly.

Whoever put it together (most likely Garrison and/or Tappan), it glows as a visible beacon of the growing immediate abolition network. With its laudatory racial balance, the list of Crandall's endorsers served two purposes. The first was functional: the ad was intended to recruit students. The *Liberator*'s subscription base was still largely African American, and so the presence of many well-known Black leaders on the list would have the salutary effect of reassuring Black parents.[61] The second was political. This advertisement appeared as tempers flared in Canterbury, guaranteeing its visibility. Crandall's school helped the *Liberator* reach national consciousness on its own terms, rather than reactively, as happened after Nat Turner and New Haven. The abolitionists took the initiative here, and so this ad serves as a worthy precursor to the founding of the American Anti-Slavery Society in December 1833 (whose documents were nowhere near as racially balanced).[62] This advertisement would accompany the whirlwind of press coverage of the Canterbury Academy, and so it provided evidence of Black achievement, visibility, and vision. Black and white names were arranged by geography rather than race (see table 1).

Tappan's name at the top was strategic, generating attention by his celebrity and wealth. The Black leaders—Peter Williams Jr., Theodore Raymond, Theodore Wright, James Hayborn, Samuel Cornish, James Forten, Joseph Cassey, and Jehiel Beman—constitute a living continuity with the beginnings of free Black institutions. Cornish was coeditor of the first Black newspaper, *Freedom's Journal,* whose call for the immediate abolition of slavery preceded Garrison's *Liberator* by four years. Forten and Cassey had mustered Black volunteers to defend Philadelphia during the War of 1812, a point that figured in (unsuccessful) attempts to establish Black citizenship.[63] These Black endorsers constituted a significant percentage of the visible Black male leaders in the Northeast.

Forten's presence on the list serves as the African American equivalent of Tappan's name among the white endorsers: his longstanding leadership in the Black community and relative financial affluence imparted instant legitimacy to middle-class Black readers. Forten, "the most highly respected black in Philadelphia,"[64] came from a freeborn lineage at least three generations long, acquiring his fortune primarily as a sailmaker. He helped convert Tappan from colonization into immediate abolition.[65] Forten had vacillated on whether to support or condemn the ACS (see chapter 1) until he sensed the unanimity of the free Black masses and staunchly opposed colonization.[66] The talents of his wife and daughters bolstered his consistent support for Black women's educational aspirations. A leader in Absalom Jones's African Episcopal Church in Philadelphia, Forten embodied respectability, a living reproof to colonizationist doctrines of Black inferiority.

Joseph Cassey (1789–1848), likewise, had the financial means to support many ventures in the Black community. A perfumer, hairdresser, real estate speculator, and moneylender, he was designated a "gentleman" in Philadelphia city directories—a rare title for a man of color. Like Forten, he had witnessed the benefit of women's education in his own household: his wife, Amy Williams (daughter of Reverend Peter Williams Jr.), was a significant activist.[67] Cassey was recruited by Forten to be a *Liberator* agent.[68] He and Forten provided much of the capital necessary to keep the *Liberator* going in its fiscally dicey early years.[69] At least three of Crandall's Black students were Philadelphians, likely personally recruited by Cassey and Forten.

Jehiel Beman (1789–1858) was minister to the African Methodist Episcopal Zion Church in Middletown, Connecticut.[70] This made him the closest

Table 1. Advertisement for Prudence Crandall's second academy

Text of the Advertisement	Commentary
Prudence Crandall Principal of the Canterbury, (Conn.) Female Boarding School	Crandall openly acknowledges her agency and role.
returns her most sincere thanks to those who have patronized her School. And would give information that on the first Monday of April next, her School will be opened for the reception of young Ladies and little Misses of color.	The language of "young Ladies and little Misses of color" implicitly—and to her opponents, quite explicitly—acknowledges equal social status of Black and white women.
The branches taught are as follows:—Reading, Writing, Arithmetic, English Grammar, Geography, History, Natural and Moral Philosophy, Chemistry, Astronomy, Drawing and Painting, Music on the Piano, together with the French language.	The latter half of this list of subjects indicates the level of the Canterbury Academy to be equivalent to a contemporary advanced-placement high school curriculum.
☞ The terms, including *board, washing*, and tuition, are $25 per quarter, one half paid in advance.	The cost put the academy out of reach for many free Blacks in the Northeast. The importance of the educational mission of the school, though, included not compelling the students to do manual labor while in attendance.
☞ Books and Stationary [*sic*] will be furnished on the most reasonable terms.	This is standard language for school advertisements of the time.
For information respecting the School, reference may be made to the following gentlemen, viz:	What follows is the list of fifteen endorsers, arranged by place, not by race. The commentary gives their race and occupation.
Arthur Tappan, Esq. N. York City	wealthy white businessman
Rev. Peter Williams N. York City	Black Episcopal priest
Rev. Theodore Raymond N. York City	aka J. T., or John T. Raymond, Black Baptist clergyman
Rev. Theodore Wright N. York City	Black Presbyterian clergyman
Rev. Samuel C. Cornish N. York City	Black Presbyterian clergyman and prominent editor of Black newspapers
Rev. George Bourne N. York City	white Presbyterian radical, leader in anti-Catholic movement
Rev. Mr. Hayborn N. York City	Black Baptist minister
Mr. James Forten Philadelphia	wealthy Black businessman
Mr. Joseph Cassey Philadelphia	wealthy Black businessman
Rev. S. J. May Brooklyn, CT	white Unitarian minister

Table 1. Continued

Text of the Advertisement	Commentary
Rev. Mr. Beman Middletown, CT	Black AMEZ minister
Rev. S. S. Jocelyn New-Haven, CT	white minister of a Black Congregational church
Wm. Lloyd Garrison Boston, Mass.	white editor of the *Liberator*
Arnold Buffum Boston, Mass.	white Quaker activist
George Benson Providence, R.I.	white businessman and activist (George Benson Jr.)
Canterbury, (Ct.) Feb 25, 1833.	This date was the Monday prior to the March 2 edition of the *Liberator*.

Source: Liberator, 3, no. 9, March 2, 1833, 35, and annotated.

African American endorser geographically. An early supporter of the *Liberator*, he was the paper's agent in Middletown and earlier for *Freedom's Journal*.[71] He organized a Home Temperance Society and the Connecticut State Temperance Society of Colored People.[72] Education reigned high on Beman's agenda for the free Black community.[73] In 1840, when the abolitionist split happened, Beman endorsed the more conservative evangelical organization, engaging in bitter feuding with former Garrisonian allies.[74]

Among the New York Black ministerial endorsers, Reverend John T. Raymond was just beginning what would be a prominent career as a Baptist minister. Originally from the Norfolk, Virginia, area, he was unable to return after the Nat Turner revolt because of laws against free Blacks.[75] He graced many renowned pulpits over his long career.[76] He became the first minister of the Zion Baptist Church, a New York City Black congregation hived off from Abyssinian Baptist in 1832.[77] From this position he participated in numerous abolitionist activities, working with Williams and Wright when they saw Nathaniel Paul off on his journey to Liverpool, England.[78] Raymond was active in the Black convention movement, hosting the New York State Convention after relocating to Albany in 1840.[79] He suffered a traumatic loss of eyesight in the late 1840s but persisted as an activist and minister. His presence on the list of Crandall's endorsers was one of his first public notices; given their shared Baptist faith, it is likely that he met with her in New York City. The contemporary Black chronicler William Cooper Nell notes, "Education, Anti-Slavery and Temperance always received . . . deserved attention" in the preaching of John T. Raymond, and "lecturers on the various reforms were cordially invited to address his church."[80] Known for working readily with white abolitionist allies and for his vocal support of the temperance cause, Raymond was involved in early Liberty Party efforts to run antislavery candidates.[81]

Reverend James Hayborn (ca. 1800–1835) is the endorser about whom the least is known. He was born enslaved, as noted by the Oneida Baptist Association in 1824:

> James Haborn [sic], a man of color, and a slave, belonging in Carlisle, Tompkins county, being present, the liberality of the public was solicited by J. Peck,[82] and others in his behalf. He appears to have been brought into the liberty of the gospel and received a call to preach Christ to dying sinners; but is holden in bondage by his master. A contribution was taken up of seventeen dollars and thirty five cents to aid in purchasing his liberty.[83]

Slavery wasn't abolished in New York State until 1827; like the famed Sojourner Truth, Hayborn's humanity was sacrificed to the legalistic machinery of gradualism.

Once free from captivity, Hayborn became the minister of the Abyssinian Baptist Church in 1832.[84] Judging from the scant record, Hayborn's three years at Abyssinian coincided with a marked increase in antislavery and racial-uplift programs as well as an increase in membership. The official history of Abyssinian Baptist notes that "under the leadership of Rev. James Hayborn, church membership had swelled to over three hundred, many of them women."[85] This evident desire on the part of women to participate in the church might have motivated (or affirmed) Hayborn's interest in women's education.[86] Hayborn, like all of Crandall's New York endorsers, worked with the Phoenix Society, a group dedicated to uplift that explicitly encouraged alliances between free Blacks and white allies.[87] Hayborn hosted the New York Auxiliary meeting of the Convention of Free People of Colour at Abyssinian Baptist in December 1832. This meeting honored the Irish Emancipator, Daniel O'Connell, and castigated the ACS.[88]

The remaining Black ministers among the endorsers are renowned in Black history: Peter Williams Jr. (1787–1840), Samuel Cornish (1795–1858), and Theodore Wright (1797–1847). The three shared the advantages of a base in New York City with affiliations to predominantly white denominations. These factors brought them some measure of respectability and attracted more affluent Blacks to their congregations.

Williams was the son of pioneering Black minister Peter Williams Sr., who is credited with cofounding the African Methodist Episcopal Zion Church (AMEZ) in 1805.[89] The younger Williams, though, was attracted to the Episcopal denomination, more formal and decorous than the fledgling AMEZ. His Black parish, St. Philip's Episcopal Church, was founded in 1809, its name commemorating the only apostle known to have baptized a Black African.[90] As early as 1808, Williams had achieved fame with his published sermon, *Oration on the Abolition of the Slave Trade*; so learned was this sermon that its authorship by a Black man was doubted, compelling Williams to get four attestations of his authorship.[91] Williams was not ordained until 1820, despite having worked with St. Philip's for more than a decade at that point. Among other institutional insults, he was not raised to the rank of a full priest until 1826.[92]

Williams Jr. functioned as a leader in the free Black community of New York City for over thirty years. In the oration that launched his career, he constructed a genealogy of abolitionist saints, from Woolman and Benezet to Wilberforce and Clarkson. Williams pushed for education and moral reforms in the free Black community. Though described as "mild and self-effacing,"[93] his speech "Slavery and Colonization," delivered on July 4, 1830, conveys his righteous anger and frustration:

> What hinders our improving here, where schools and colleges abound, where the gospel is preached at every corner, and where all the arts and sciences are verging fast to perfection? Nothing, nothing but prejudice. It requires no large expenditures, no hazardous enterprises to raise the people of colour in the United States to as highly improved a state as any class of the community. All that is necessary is that those who profess to be anxious for it should lay aside their prejudices and act towards them as they do by others.[94]

Williams's perceptive analysis of racial prejudice's role in shaping Black life in the North made him a natural ally for projects like Crandall's.

Williams supported myriad moral-reform movements, arguing that moral uplift aided one's Christian salvation.[95] He established a Dorcas Society for clothing poor children. He backed numerous high school ventures for Black youth in New York City, as well as initiating the New Haven Manual Labor College.[96] Endorsing Crandall's school was particularly appropriate, since he believed that prejudice against color was less fierce in rural areas than urban ones (this was to be proven erroneous).[97]

Williams, with Cornish, Wright, Forten, and Cassey, was an integral part of the network of leaders who, in the 1820s, undertook to create a national conversation among free Blacks. This included supporting *Freedom's Journal* and participating in the convention movement. His daughter Amy Matilda Williams Cassey married into the Philadelphia Black elite, connecting these communities and leaders.

Samuel Cornish (1795–1858) is a giant among antebellum African Americans. Born free in Delaware with a multiracial heritage, he moved to Pennsylvania in 1815. After studying for the Presbyterian ministry, he began preaching to free Blacks in New York City. In 1822 he established the First Colored Presbyterian (later renamed Shiloh Presbyterian Church), one of the most important Black churches in antebellum America.[98]

Arguably the best strategic thinker among Crandall's endorsers, Cornish understood the need for racially separate organizations but also looked forward to a day when they would not be necessary.[99] More important, he took action to counter white ignorance and malice by producing the earliest Black newspapers. Blacks had opposed colonization from the moment the scheme was promulgated, but the white press had neglected their resolutions.[100] When Cornish, together with John Russwurm, launched *Freedom's Journal* in March 1827, it provided both a political platform and a community newspaper for free Blacks. A national Black political network started forming with *Freedom's Journal*, the famed David Walker serving as an agent and author, as did Thomas and Nathaniel Paul.[101] *Freedom's Journal* failed when coeditor Russwurm defected into advocating Liberian colonization, costing the paper its credibility with Black readers.[102] Cornish briefly resuscitated the paper under the title the *Rights of All* in 1829, but that paper did not survive the year. Cornish's third newspaper venture—the *Colored American*—ran from 1837 to 1839 and contains valuable traces of Crandall's former students.[103]

While he was socially conservative in reinforcing clear lines of gender separation, Cornish persisted in demanding educational opportunities for Black women, declaring in 1834, "Every measure for the thorough and proper education of [black] females is a blow aimed directly at slavery."[104] Cornish supported numerous educational projects within the Black community and appealed to whites to assist in providing opportunities for schooling for Blacks.[105] He also had a perceptive understanding of what Crandall was accomplishing in Canterbury, noting that she was attacked because "she dared to teach" Black students "as if they were white—to treat them with the same delicacy and respect which an instructress is expected to extend to young ladies in good society."[106]

Cornish had a direct influence on Theodore Wright (1797–1847)—whose acumen concerning the persistence of racial prejudice within the abolitionist movement was noted earlier. Like Williams, Wright also had a famed activist father, R. P. G. Wright, an early advocate for Black higher education.[107] Preparing for the Presbyterian ministry, Theodore became the first Black graduate of Princeton Seminary in 1829. However, his way there was not smooth: he was subject to frequent harassment and exclusion. Wright chose not to fight back, maintaining instead, as he described it, "the comforting, but self-denying doctrine of nonresistance, so effective in curbing that vindictive spirit which naturally rises when suddenly assailed. Thankful am I that I was kept from lifting so much as a finger in self-defense."[108]

When *Freedom's Journal* started publishing, Wright exclaimed, "It came like a streak of lightning in the darkness; a clap of thunder."[109] Unfortunately, he was not alone in noticing the boldness of this new periodical. The principal of the seminary—Presbyterian theologian and controversialist Samuel Miller (1769–1850)—not only prohibited students (and faculty) from obtaining and reading the newspaper, he also attacked the entire enterprise as un-American, corrupting "the minds of Negro youth."[110]

These incidents in Wright's background point to a blend of idealism (the hope for higher education for Black youth) and realism (inevitable opposition) that marks this generation of Free Black leadership. Everyday prejudices against Black achievement continually dogged Wright's life: both he and his wife died from illness brought on by substandard segregated transportation.[111]

After graduating, Wright became the pastor of Cornish's Shiloh Presbyterian. This parish had a relatively affluent Black congregation, enabling Wright to feel secure in his finances and to speak out on the issues of the day. Known as a steadfast opponent of colonization, he built Shiloh into a large congregation abundantly involved in reform activities.[112] He was involved in the convention movement, built coalitions among Black leaders, and maintained personal relations and correspondence with white abolitionists.[113]

Taken as a group, Cornish, Wright, Williams, Raymond, Beman, Forten, and Cassey are an all-star cast of antebellum Black activists. Yet, previous writers on Crandall have glossed over their importance. The paucity of letters and other primary material addressing their role in the school accounts for this silence. But Crandall had to obtain students for her academy, and students were not going to be gained by the good wishes of white abolitionists alone. These Black men were the conduits through which students were gathered. There were also good strategic reasons for them *not* to take the visible lead in the Canterbury battle: trepidations concerning how the presence of out-of-town Black leaders would have affected the tenor of the debate in Canterbury and would have impeded their myriad existing responsibilities.

Crandall went to these Black leaders in New York City because their trust was more crucial even than the financial support of Tappan to the ultimate success of the school. Crandall's ability to deal with them directly rather than through a host of white male intermediaries likely signaled her seriousness and commitment to the cause as well as her ease in working across racial lines. These men would have been risking their reputations if they entrusted the young women of their community to a white person whom they did not know. In order to encourage students in a racist environment, Crandall had to establish in the entire Northeast what she had proven to Harris and Davis: her credentials as someone the free Black community could trust.[114] This entailed reciprocity in listening and learning and not imposing her own agenda. This nuanced dance reveals an intuitive intersectionality from Crandall and the Black male leaders who endorsed her school, as well as from the white abolitionist men assembling this ad.

The white endorsers also have compelling stories; the most prominent among them—Jocelyn, Tappan, Garrison, and May—having already been introduced. The other three, though, present an interesting cross-section of the growing white abolitionist ranks.

George Benson Jr. (1808–1879) followed in his father's footsteps, first as a merchant and then in pursuit of peace and abolition. George Benson Jr. had helped Crandall to meet Black parents in Providence. He would cut his political teeth assisting Crandall's school, attending town meetings, and writing missives on its progress to the *Liberator*. Later, George Benson Jr. joined the Quakers and founded the New England Non-Resistance Society in 1838. He was instrumental in the establishment of the Northampton Association, a utopic interracial communal experiment, which included Sojourner Truth and David Ruggles among its members.[115] Late in his life he moved to Kansas, becoming a state representative from Wakarusa.[116]

Arnold Buffum (1782–1859) exemplified the Quaker tradition, combining a manufacturing profession in haberdashery with spiritually grounded political work. Buffum was a tinkerer, devising improvements in the machinery for hat manufacture.[117] Long active in abolition, Buffum was an early convert to Garrisonian immediate abolition.[118] His daughter, Elizabeth Buffum Chace, wrote of how her father had spoken with formerly enslaved people during his youth and that "Never, in our large household, do I recall one word short of condemnation of the vile system" of slavery.[119]

In later years Arnold Buffum met stiff opposition to abolitionism among the Quakers of Indiana and was disowned by his meeting there because of objections to his abolitionist lecturing.[120] Buffum maintained the civil mode of debate that had characterized Quaker abolitionist pioneers like Anthony Benezet and John Woolman. In fact, in the midst of the Crandall crisis, Buffum was described in the abolitionist press as "a disciple and follower of Benezet, who teaches the *same* doctrine, but with more mildness and suavity."[121]

Another endorser influenced by Benezet was George Bourne (1780–1845), who is credited with initiating immediate abolition in America in the first two decades of the nineteenth century. He denounced slavery with enough force to lose his pulpit and be hounded from the South. His abolitionism, though, has been overshadowed by his unsavory leadership in organized anti-Catholicism.[122]

Bourne moved to the United States from England in the early nineteenth century. He worked as a minister and a newspaper editor, first in Baltimore, then in the Shenandoah Valley of Virginia. By 1810 he had developed a strong theological argument against slavery, relying on 1 Timothy 1 as well as the writings of John Wesley and Benezet. His strident tone and the offense he gave to his slaveholding neighbors led to his defrocking by the Presbyterians in 1818.[123]

Bourne published his argument in the landmark *The Book and Slavery Irreconcilable* (1816). Bourne raised a lone voice for immediate abolition with no recompense to slaveholders. With the rise of immediatism in the early 1830s, Bourne's foresight was acknowledged: he was welcomed into the growing movement. Significantly, he was left in charge of coediting the *Liberator* (with Oliver Johnson) at a transitional moment in Crandall's school: May 2, 1833, to September 29, 1833, while Garrison was in England.[124] Because of controversies dogging his name, Bourne asked for anonymity in his *Liberator* assignment, which means that some editorials supporting Crandall might well be Bourne's. Congruent with Crandall's work, his critique of slavery included an explicit critique of racism as a "depravity" of "pride."[125]

The controversies that clung to Bourne stemmed from his caustic critiques of Catholicism, exemplified in his editorship of the hysterically partisan periodical the *Protestant*. Although there are some extenuating circumstances in his family history for the fierceness of his anti-Catholicism (he was a direct descendent of John Rogers, the Bible translator and first Protestant martyr under Mary Tudor), Bourne seems to have imagined himself as a modern-day rhetorical heir to John Knox.[126] No innuendo against Catholicism was too outrageous for Bourne to publish, including fantasies of ritual rapes and murders.[127]

Bourne met his match when a young Philadelphia priest, Reverend John Hughes (1797–1864), hoaxed the editor of the *Protestant* with a fictional set of overwrought claims purporting to be the pope's master plan to sink the United States. Hughes went public with the scam, exposing Bourne's gullibility and diminishing his credibility. Hughes became the most famed Catholic bishop of the antebellum period. Bourne's temporary loss of face in this 1830 scandal led to his resignation from editing the *Protestant*.[128] This union of Protestant evangelical Christianity with antiimmigrant religious intolerance is a constituent part of nineteenth-century American history.[129] Although there is no evidence that Crandall shared Bourne's rabid detestation of Catholics, his extreme views provide a cautionary tale of how easily moral certitude can pass into vituperative fanaticism.

The remaining four white male endorsers—Garrison, Tappan, Jocelyn, and May—were closest to the conflict itself. Garrison and May focused on the politics and visibility of the incident, while Tappan bankrolled Crandall's legal defense. May was most involved in the daily battle, but Jocelyn gave Crandall the practical advice of a veteran of the same war. Together, these four men all contributed to the success of the academy and pioneered innovative ways to use their privilege to instigate change.

For instance, May had heard of Crandall as a successful local schoolteacher, but they had not met prior to the academy.[130] Just two days after the *Liberator* ad was published they were introduced, and May was instantly impressed, noting Crandall's "Quaker discipline . . . in every word she spoke, and in every expression of her countenance." She explained she could not attend the town meeting due to her gender. Since no Canterburian man would dare to support her, she requested that May act as her attorney and representative, which he agreed to do.[131] May's political perspicacity emerges: he appreciated a woman's political acumen and proved willing to undertake what his privilege made incumbent on him.

March 2 versus March 9

This roster of endorsers glints with honor that has only increased with time. The commitment it evinces for Black and female education and its unprecedented racial balance should have guaranteed it far-reaching fame. Yet, scholars focus more on the raucous town meeting of March 9.

This may be partly because Canterbury does not become a standard part of the biography of these men (excepting May). A few scholars have recognized the academy's centrality—William Mayer for Garrison, and Julie Winch for Forten—but most secondary literature ignores the signatories' involvement with Crandall's school. It is certainly possible that signing yet another endorsement was not a monumental event. But for the Black endorsers there were high stakes. They would be recruiting the daughters of their most esteemed friends to travel to a distant, hostile area of Connecticut. The young women of their communities who sought this education were at a vulnerable age, such that being subject to the ridicule and harassment of vigilantes could be especially hurtful, even sexually dangerous. The failure of the New Haven Manual Labor College forewarned Black leaders of potential dangers in Connecticut; it may also have alerted them to the naïveté of idealistic white leaders undisciplined by the constant stings of prejudice.

An additional Black activist, Nathaniel Paul, was not among the signatories to the school advertisement, but he was among the most consistent of Crandall's supporters. An early opponent of colonization, he had opened the doors of his First African Baptist church in Albany, New York, to Benjamin Lundy and helped launch *Freedom's Journal*.[132] From his position in England, where he lived for four years in the early 1830s, Paul assumed a prominent role in the transatlantic abolitionist network.[133] He spoke consistently about Crandall's school and the injustices she and her students suffered. Most notable, he dashed off a quick sarcastic letter, addressed to Judson but printed in the *Liberator*, promising to bruit about the "Christian . . . heroism" involved in "assail(ing) a helpless woman."[134] A Baptist minister with a keen interest in Black education, he married a white English woman.[135] His absence from the list of endorsers underlines the recruitment function of the Black names on that advertisement: this was one function Nathaniel Paul was not able to fulfill from Scotland.[136]

The advertisement published in the *Liberator* on March 2 constituted an advance in strategy over the failure in New Haven two years previous. The list of endorsers was fully integrated racially, geographically broad, with a good mix of professions and prestige. Their diversity provided strength to the school enterprise—Tappan the financier, May for local support, Garrison providing publicity nationwide, the Black ministers reassuring the students' parents. Compared to Jocelyn's unrealistic optimism in New Haven, this demonstrates an integrated strategy that combined the pragmatic and ideological. It would prove resilient until attacked on all fronts in the hot summer months of 1834.

The town protest meeting in Canterbury on March 9, by contrast, followed a well-worn racist script. A protest like this would have happened in almost any New England town if a similar school had been proposed. The town leaders of Canterbury followed the strategy that had proven itself in New Haven: strongarming overwhelming public disapproval to mimic the 700-4 vote of their neighbors to the southwest. There is a saying in military history that "generals always fight the last war, especially if they won it." By that analogy, Andrew Judson was Canterbury's status quo general, and his attempt to prevent Crandall's school from even existing—the result New Haven achieved—failed miserably. For all of the rhetorical sound and dramatic fury, the March 9 meeting failed of its goal: the school went forward.

Why does the meeting get the attention? Aside from its inherent drama, the town meeting laid bare the depth of Northern racism, proving free Black leaders and Garrison correct in their excoriating critiques of the ACS. Judson's reprehensible clarity in his unguarded attacks on African Americans helped amplify the case—a result both sides sought but which rebounded negatively (both short- and long-term) on colonizationism.

The town meeting is not insignificant but needs to be understood in context. Garrison's advice to George Benson prior to the meeting provides a strategic clue. Garrison mentions the importance of persistence in Canterbury, given the New Haven debacle:

> Miss C. must be sustained at all hazards. If we suffer the school to be put down in Canterbury, other places will partake of panic and also prevent its introduction in their vicinity. We may as well, first as last, meet this proscriptive spirit and conquer it.... The New Haven excitement has furnished a bad precedent, a second must not be given or I know not what we can do to raise up the colored population in a manner which their intellectual and moral necessities demand.[137]

Garrison, the pacifist field general, says, "Meet the proscriptive spirit and conquer it," specifically to further the "intellectual and moral necessities" of the free Black community. Muting colonizationist rhetoric was a step, not the end goal. The intellectual work of the school was the goal (despite Garrison's patronizing tone).

The March 9 meeting was a predictable show of power by a threatened white status quo. Ultimately there was nothing unusual about it. By contrast, the fifteen male signatories who endorsed Crandall's school were operating in a novel coalition with each other and the trio of women in Canterbury who had launched the enterprise. The publication of their endorsement opened a door to a future America.

CHAPTER 4

Martyrs in the Classroom
The Whip and the Prison

> I am asking you to hold fast to that faith
> written into our founding documents; that
> idea whispered by slaves and abolitionists.
> . . . A creed at the core of every American
> whose story is not yet written: Yes We Can.
> —Barack Obama

When the Canterbury Academy reopened in April 1833 for the reception of "Young Ladies and Little Misses of Color," the vision launched by Sarah Harris, Maria Davis and Prudence Crandall expanded to Black women, as students gradually arrived from all over the Northeast.

With the presence of actual Black women students, the Canterbury Academy became a decisively more realized venture than the New Haven Manual Labor College. Every day of life for the Canterbury Academy gave it more impact and history. The Canterbury school had become real, with pupils of flesh, blood, and mind.

While these students were eager to study, the white authorities in Canterbury did everything in their power to thwart them. They wanted to close the minds of free Blacks, mock their flesh, and even make their blood flow. For these first three months, the white Canterburians relied largely on coercive legal harassment, but always with the looming threat of physical violence. This chapter covers the first three months of the school's life, through Prudence Crandall's night in prison.

April 1833—The Students Arrive, the Law Is Invoked

Frustrated that the school was set to open, the white Canterburians sought to punish the students and the school physically and fiscally. The two-pronged strategy of vigilante violence and legal harassment went operational when the school and students "from abroad" became a reality.

Andrew Judson—the leader of Canterbury's white opposition—and his allies resuscitated existing vagrancy laws. Connecticut had always been a particularly rigid jurisdiction regarding inhabitants and their behavior. One contemporary noted, "In Connecticut the provisions to secure the safety of morals, are perhaps the most strict; and the operation of the laws also much fortified by the 'steady habits' of the people."[1]

A concern with the arrival of "outsiders" dated back to Puritan times and even England itself, steeped in stern moral judgment, xenophobic authoritarianism, and fiscal paranoia.[2] Enactment of these laws consistently made reference to not knowing these strangers or their habits, with disapproval being the automatic response. The material fear underlining these laws was that any stranger to the village would become a burden due to pauperism. In the case of Crandall's students, this carried the implication that free Blacks could never be materially successful and that their attendance at Crandall's school was doomed to failure.

As females, Crandall and the students could be imagined by their enemies as strangers to the making and administration of law and thus easily intimidated by it. Notwithstanding George S. White's perceptive objection to the vagrancy laws at the March 9 town meeting, their resuscitation went forward, unmasking a strongarmed status quo power.[3]

In his account of Crandall's school, Edward Abdy makes reference to a 1650 Colonial-era Connecticut law that forbid a "habitation to any younge man to sojourne" with a family, without the express consent of the village leaders. Abdy drily adds that "it was reserved for the nineteenth century, and the town of Canterbury, to exclude females."[4] This mention of the 1650 law has misled some to overlook the actual law by which Crandall's students were threatened with whipping, an oft-revised set of laws meant to prevent paupers from becoming a drain upon a town's treasury. The most recent revision of that law, far from being ancient in origin, dated from 1808, just twenty-five years prior to the Canterbury Academy. The relevant sections make clear the intent of the law, hostility against integrating newcomers:

> [T]he selectmen of any town . . . are hereby authorized . . . to warn any person not an inhabitant of this state to depart such town . . . and when any such person who shall be convicted of the breach of this act, in refusing to depart on warning as aforesaid, hath no estate to satisfy the fine, such person shall be whipped on the naked body not exceeding ten stripes.[5]

Authority is located squarely in a self-reinforcing status quo. The selectmen can decree whom they want and whom they do not want within their towns.

Opposition to free Blacks in towns like Canterbury, far from being a paper tiger, came with legal teeth.

The law focuses on the desirability of the sojourner while presuming likely indigence. From their deep reservoir of racist presumptions, the Canterbury leadership assumed that all free Blacks were undesirable and likely indigent—despite the fact that the students Crandall recruited were mostly middle class (being able to afford the tuition). Judson and his allies, though, expressed fears that the students would stay on in Canterbury or attract their families and other free Blacks and become a drain on the town.

The use of whipping as a punishment may very well have been specifically directed at free Blacks. The punishment of whipping is not part of the earlier 1650 codes, wherein whipping was applied to liars, not strangers.[6] The intimate connection between whipping and slavery remained in the consciousness of free Blacks; David Walker, upon attending a camp meeting revival in South Carolina, commented on a preacher who admonished the enslaved to obey their masters or fear the whip, revealing "surprise, to hear such preaching from a minister of my Master, whose very gospel is that of peace and not of blood and whips."[7] Walker's righteous disgust at any militant makeover of the Prince of Peace exemplifies a wider cultural movement against whipping in America. Richard Brodhead notes how the abolitionists' use of the lash as the symbol of slavery also led to questioning corporal punishment in education.[8] Crandall's proposed school would not use the lash; her Black students would be treated with the same genteel methods that Crandall's white, middle- and upper-class female students had received.

A more salacious angle cannot be discounted: whipping the naked bodies of Crandall's sexually mature female students may have been pornographically attractive to the Canterbury white male elite. Instances of women's bodies being exposed in slavery—whether in work, on the auction block, or in the administration of corporal punishment—are rife. The sadistic cruelty of Simon Northrup's master to the enslaved Patsey received cinematic portrayal in *Twelve Years a Slave* (2013), but incidents like this were tragically common and seared into the consciousness of Black women.[9]

Threatening Crandall's students with the whip was not only about invoking slavery and sexual dominance: it was also becoming an increasingly common tactic against Black learning and the spread of abolitionist ideas. In the immediate aftermath of the circulation of Walker's *Appeal*, the state of Georgia ordained that free Blacks who taught other Blacks to read were to be fined $500 and whipped; Savannah added a city ordinance prescribing thirty-nine lashes for the same offense.[10] In 1835 Amos Dresser (1812–1904), a white agent for the American Anti-Slavery Society, was whipped on his naked body for having copies of the *Liberator* with him in Nashville, Tennessee.[11]

In that same year, at Marion College near Hannibal, Missouri, white ruffians whipped an enslaved young girl trying to attend Sunday school.[12] The threat to Crandall's students was real.[13]

Ann Eliza Hammond, daughter of the Providence boardinghouse keeper Elizabeth Hammond, was the first out-of-state Black pupil at Crandall's school. Born August 18, 1816, she was sixteen in April 1833. Furthermore, her mother's work in maintaining a boardinghouse meant that issues of modesty and respectability were professionally important to the Hammond family, making Ann Eliza's role as the test case for this law all the more fraught.[14]

Samuel Joseph May thought that the town officials would lose nerve before legally ordering a student to be whipped as a vagrant. The language of the statute itself seemed ambivalent by excepting "apprentices" and "servants"—categories that could be stretched to include boarding students. Crandall herself was in favor of paying the $1.67 fine, but May felt that would not be wise, as it would establish an expensive precedent. Instead, May (via Arthur Tappan) made pledges to indemnify the town against further damages, obviating the pauperism argument.[15]

However, Judson and the selectmen refused to accept that bond, wasting no time taking the next step in this high-stakes standoff.[16] On April 13 the sheriff informed Crandall that they considered Ann Eliza Hammond a burden to Canterbury and on April 22 delivered a legal writ against her.[17] May was certain of Hammond's resolve:

> [I did] assure Miss Hammond that the persecutors would hardly dare proceed to such an extremity, and strengthen her to bear meekly the punishment, if they should in their madness inflict it; knowing that every blow they should strike her would resound throughout the land, if not over the whole civilized world, and call out an expression of indignation before which Mr. Judson and his associates would quail. But I found her ready for the emergency, animated by the spirit of a martyr.[18]

Crandall biographer Donald Williams chides May for his focus on the cause instead of expressing concern for the mental and physical health of a teenage girl.[19] However, such a critique underestimates the power of shared tropes of martyrdom. Christ himself, as the supreme figure in the Christian faith, models martyrdom. The lore and lure of early Christian history are crowded with martyrs. The Reformation rekindled the literal fires of ultimate self-sacrifice. As Maria Stewart put it in her initial 1831 pamphlet, striving for freedom necessarily brought the possibility of martyrdom, and that was not the fate to be most afraid of: "You can but die if you make the attempt (for liberty); and we shall certainly die if you do not."[20] Hammond's response of being willing to undergo physical punishment to further the cause of Black female education is not surprising.

Hammond's fearlessness won the day: the selectmen abandoned this line of attack and accepted a $10,000 bond when "it was seen that she was not frightened."[21] Crandall had likewise held firm; the balance of her doubts and her determination can be seen in two long letters she wrote to Simeon Smith Jocelyn in April. In the letter begun on April 17 and completed on April 20, Crandall opens with discouragement about how few students are in attendance. She writes about the writ against Hammond and says that she never expected such fierce opposition from professing Christians. Her language then adopts a decidedly evangelical tone, reminiscent of Stewart:

> I have put my hand to the plough and I will *never no never* look back—I trust God will help me keep this resolution for in Him only there is safety for *mine own arm never brought salvation.*
>
> I have had in the Providence of God to pass through many trying seasons but place them all together they are of small moment compared with the present scene of adversity—yet in the midst of this affliction I am as happy as at any moment of my life—I never saw the time when I was the least apprehensive that adversity would harm me.[22]

Crandall's bold attitude and sense of purpose through and within the struggle echo Garrison's experience in the Baltimore jail: "The court may shackle the body, but it cannot pinion the mind. . . . My soul flames as intensely, in prison, as out of it."[23] Dresser's supplications during his flogging led his tormenters to swear "G——d d——m him, stop his praying."[24] Black abolitionist William Cooper Nell expresses it pithily: "Imprisonment is a feature of martyrdom with which Abolitionists in the United States have become familiar. . . . But these persecutions are to be accepted as jewels in their crown, as seals of their devotion to the cause of millions now in the prison-house of bondage."[25] Such visible acts of resistance inspired Harriet Martineau to title her chronicles of the movement *The Martyr Age of the United States of America*.[26] In this moment in Canterbury, Hammond, Crandall, and May rendered passive-resistance performative.

But the teachers and students were not gathered together for martyrdom. The academy was about education and networking. Sometime between the resolution of the crisis around Hammond and the beginning days of May, Crandall took her students to Norwich, the nearest substantial town south along the Quinebaug River. One of her former students, Esther Baldwin, describes Crandall as going among the Black community with a bevy of Black women from New York City. The increasingly famous teacher "shook hands with the sexton," a remarkable interracial and cross-gender gesture that few white allies felt emboldened to take.[27] A few days later, she wrote in an editorial first published in the *Windham County Advertiser* that while she appreciated the support of the abolitionists, she had been "wholly self-moved in the plan" of opening her school for Blacks.[28] This was about agency: Crandall's, that of the Black community that wanted such schools open to their daughters, and those daughters who were now attending. The school trip to Norwich and this editorial together demonstrate the ongoing centrality of women's and Black community agency to the academy's existence.

The Black Law

Connecticut's so-called Black Law was specifically passed to thwart Crandall's school. While the Black Law created an air of continual uncertainty around the continuation of Crandall's second academy, it can best be interpreted as an overreach by Judson and his colonizationist allies; even one of the bill's coauthors, Philip Pearl, was embarrassed enough by its mean-spiritedness to guide its repeal a mere five years later, in 1838.

Judson, the moving spirit behind the Black Law, never felt such remorse. He wrote that during the 1833 assembly session, "I did not fail to carry every measure desired by me, and am grateful to this day for the kindness with which I was treated during the whole session."[29] Judson introduced, argued, and lobbied for the bill. His partisanship was noted as "unusual and made some talk."[30] The Windham County Colonization Society proclaimed Judson "the man they delighted to honor,"[31] since the Black Law's exclusionary impulse emblemized colonizationism's disdain for Black higher education.

The rapidity and apparent unanimity with which the Black Law passed the Connecticut legislature underscore white hostility toward free Blacks.[32] The law not only made a frontal attack on Black citizenship but also targeted Crandall directly; in fact, the law skirts dangerously close to being a bill of attainder against her and her family (for providing aid to an illegal school). Furthermore, the Black Law was indubitably ex post facto; the US Constitution expressly prohibits both attainders and ex post facto laws.[33] As with twenty-first century legal battles over marriage equality, the Black Law's impugning of citizenship rights for Blacks raised constitutional questions; while the legislators were acting as aggressors, their position was instantly transformed into a defensive one, wherein they had to prove a compelling state interest for maintaining their racial prejudice. This would be difficult but for the next century and more eminently possible because of the strength of white disdain for Black humanity.[34]

The legislative record of the bill indicates heightened panic in its sweepingly demeaning generalizations of free Black people. Much of this rhetoric harmonizes with colonizationist ideology, which by 1833 had become standard fare among white politicians. The Black Law, intended as a high mark of colonizationism, instead boomeranged into embarrassment.[35]

The debate—to the extent that there was one—assembled validation for the prejudices of the lawmakers, from a visit by a phrenologist (who argued against Black intelligence) to fears that the Maryland legislature was going to flood Connecticut by underwriting transportation of free Blacks from that state.[36] Judson had arranged for petitions from fifteen other towns in support of the proposed law, stating that the presence of free people of color was "an evil of great magnitude, a calamity."[37] But it is the report of Pearl's committee that lays bare the NIMBYism (not in my backyard) and racial prejudice. The free "colored people" are described as "an appalling source of crime and pauperism," who bring in their wake "immense evils within this State" and "would impose on our own people burthens which would admit of no future remedy and *can be avoided only by timely prevention*."[38] Crandall's opponents approved of Pearl's assessment enough to reprint the report in its totality as part of their *Statement of Facts* pamphlet.

Crandall's opponents did make some strategic adjustments. The Black Law is specifically an amendment to the earlier "Act for the admission and settlement of Inhabitants of Towns" that had been used to threaten Hammond with whipping. The last clause of the Black Law, in a kind of legal equivalent to an aside, enjoined whipping (and the negative publicity it had generated): "That so much of the seventh section of the act to which this is an addition, as may provide for the infliction of corporeal punishment, be, and the same is hereby repealed."[39] The cruel crudity of corporal punishment was abandoned.[40]

The logical leaps in the preamble reveal the Black Law's intended audience:

WHEREAS, attempts have been made to establish literary institutions in this State for the instruction of colored persons belonging to other states and countries, which would tend to the great increase of the colored population of the State, and thereby to the injury of the people.

This implies that Crandall's school was not running, calling it a mere attempt. The more damning evidence of the legislature's opinion comes in the assumption that the Black schools would lead to a marked increase in the free Black population, which would be injurious to "the people." In this instance of the unmarked case, the people meant are, of course, white people.

The first section of the Black Law targets "instruction or education of colored persons" as objectionable. Given that the original act excused servants (and, by extension, enslaved persons), this distinction made the stakes clear: Black higher education was proactively outlawed. The abolitionists were thus proven correct, as William Jay analyzed: "The law is intended to prevent the ingress of such blacks *only* as might come for the honorable and virtuous purpose of education, while not the slightest impediment is opposed to the introduction of cooks, waiters, scullions, shoeblacks, &c., in any number. The *best* are excluded, the *worst* freely admitted."[41]

The spiteful intent manifests in the mist net the law casts to ensnare everyone involved in Crandall's academy. While the students are still subject to being legally ejected from town, the monetary punishments fall on the teachers and supporters: "Each and every person who shall knowingly do any act forbidden as aforesaid (running such an Academy), or shall be aiding or assisting therein; shall, for the first offence, forfeit and pay to the treasurer of state, a fine of one hundred dollars, and for the second offence shall forfeit and pay a fine of two hundred dollars, and so double for every offence of which he or she shall be convicted. And all informing officers are required to make due presentment of all breaches of this act." Thus, merchants, supporters, and even family members were subject to the same escalating fines as Crandall herself was. The escalating fines were meant to intimidate Crandall and to obviate Tappan's deep pockets. The vindictive edge to the law was confirmed in June when Judson bullied her parents, Pardon and Esther Crandall, saying that the committee members were willing to make the law stronger if need be and that Prudence herself would be shown "no mercy" and would be treated like a horse thief or burglar.[42]

In another likely breach of constitutionality (here related to the Fifth Amendment), the Black Law's third section states that the students themselves "may be compelled to give testimony" against the school. While this is not whipping, it is the psychological equivalent, coercing the students to give evidence from their own lives that would aid in closing the very school they were attending and from which they benefitted.

A vicious, barbed spirit undergirds this law, which would germinate extensive bullying over the next fifteen months. Previous scholars have commented on some ambivalence in Senator Pearl's committee report, but there is no vacillation in the law itself.[43] As mentioned above, Judson paid a visit to Prudence's parents that even in the sometimes-sympathetic account of Ellen Larned comes across as cartoonish villainy.[44] In fact, the law itself treads the line between legal harassment and vigilante violence, uniting these two prongs by which Crandall's school was consistently attacked. In essence, it authorized vigilantism by indicating that the school's eradication was in the state's interest, the kind of plausible deniability inherent in announcing "will no one rid us of this meddlesome school."

The passage of the Black Law was the work of white males. In contradistinction to many moments in the story of the Canterbury Academy, the only players with any agency in this legal mechanism were white males, and even more specifically, white males with political power. They used their agency to reinforce their own status, most explicitly when they allowed that out-of-state Black scholars could be admitted with the "consent, in writing, . . .

of a majority of the civil authority, and also of the select men of the town in which such school, academy, or literary institution is situated." Consider, for instance, the three otherwise incidental, but socially influential Connecticut officials who signed the law into force: Samuel Ingham, Speaker of the Connecticut House of Representatives (1793–1881); Ebenezer Stoddard, lieutenant governor and president of the Senate (1785–1847), and Henry W. Edwards, governor (1779–1847).[45] All three of these men were able politicians, oft-elected to statewide office; they each served in the US Congress as well as in the state legislature.[46] By signing this law, they witness to how the Black Law's logic was accepted by the voting (all male and all white) public. Ingham, Stoddard, and Edwards are not the villains behind the Black Law, nor are they direct henchmen of Judson. Instead, they are simply markers of public opinion, average white male leaders of their time who were able to assess which way the wind was blowing. Their uncomplicated assent to the Black Law reveals the depth and breadth of white supremacy.

The Effects of the Black Law in Canterbury

When news of the Black Law's passage reached Canterbury on May 24, 1833, white citizens did rejoice and loudly: "On the receipt of the tidings . . . joy and exultation ran wild in Canterbury. The bells were rung and a cannon fired, until all the inhabitants for miles around were informed of the triumph."[47] This, too, can be read as a convergence of legal coercion and vigilante violence. The effect it had on the students—who by this time numbered over a dozen—can only be imagined, but if future events are any indication, they had collectively cultivated the spirit to face the tribulations of their school's pioneer status.

Judson took every opportunity to boast of his victory and predict the imminent closure of Crandall's school. His unwelcome intrusion with Crandall's parents and desire to prohibit family cooperation make his treachery patent.[48]

In the meantime, Crandall's white male supporters knew that the Black Law was suspect in the court of public opinion and constitutionally. They began working both angles immediately. Legally, they focused on the full faith and credit act of the Constitution: Article IV, Section 2. This was a fraught strategy, since Article IV, Section 2, Clause 3 included the requirement to return runaway slaves, and so it was commonplace to read Article IV against Black rights. But the abolitionists believed that free Blacks needed to be recognized as citizens and so looked for them to be included under Article IV, Section 2, Clause 1: "The Citizens of each State shall be entitled to all Privileges and Immunities of Citizens in the several States." If Blacks were citizens, Connecticut could not pass a law prohibiting their admission to a private academy.

Crandall's supporters chose to prove Black citizenship using the most vulnerable class of free Blacks: unmarried, young females. Crandall's lawyers would produce strong constitutional arguments in favor of Black citizenship, which would echo long after this case,[49] but using women as the test case raised questions that the legal system of 1833 wasn't prepared to answer. All women's citizenship rights were undetermined at this point in time.[50] The easiest routes to establishing citizenship—military service, voting, and property ownership—were closed to women of all races.

The immediate drama centered on Crandall's legal jeopardy. The abolitionists, including Crandall herself, decided to let the law take effect in order to expose its vile nature publicly. This meant that Crandall herself (not her students) would invite arrest and imprisonment.

Martyrdom, by its very nature, is demonstrative and performative. It involves the espousal of a cause volatile enough to provoke danger and then displaying the fortitude to withstand the punishment meted out by hostile authority. Those willing to undergo any form of martyrdom want their actions to be broadcast, their causes amplified by suffering. The early example of Socrates, who voluntarily chose to remain and accept his execution despite the ease with which he could have self-exiled, provides a clue: his actions and the disgrace of the Athenians who condemned him still resonate today. The attention that Christian communities give to every detail of Christ's Passion was, for Crandall and her allies, a transcendent example of visible suffering with ultimately redemptive results.[51]

May, George Benson Jr., and Crandall agreed it would be best to allow the law to function, thus "leaving her persecutors to show to the world how base they were, and how atrocious was the [Black] law."[52] This sort of strategy occurs often in movements for social change—Rosa Parks and John Scopes, for instance, volunteered to question the legitimacy of laws despite the certitude of being convicted. Thus, Crandall's own agency played a significant part in this episode: "I found that her resolution was equal to the trial which seemed to be impending, that she was ready to brave and to bear meekly the worst treatment that her enemies would venture to subject her to."[53] Challenging the law meant that when she was arrested for violations of the Black Law, she would have to endure being jailed rather than bailed out. Benson and May counseled all of Crandall's local supporters to not give bonds for her release when she was arrested.[54]

Crandall's imprisonment happened on June 27, 1833. Ashael Bacon and Ebenezer Sanger arrested Prudence and her sister Almira, bringing them to justice of the peace Rufus Adams, who read the complaint brought against them from Nehemiah Ensworth, whose daughters had been in Crandall's first academy. When it became clear that Almira was underage (majority for women being twenty-one) she was released, while bail for Prudence was set at a rather low $150 (roughly $5,000 in today's dollars).[55] But to the surprise of her enemies, no one paid that amount. May, at least according to his own account, had made the strategy and the stakes clear:

> People generally will not so soon realize how bad, how wicked, how cruel a law it is, unless we suffer her persecutors to inflict upon her all the penalties it prescribes. She is willing to bear them for the sake of the cause she has so nobly espoused. . . . If you see fit to keep her from imprisonment in the cell of a murderer for having proffered the blessing of a good education to those who, in our country, need it most, you may do so; *we shall not*.[56]

The response of Crandall's persecutors in this case? They swore a blue streak at the prudish pacifist May!

But it was May who had his pulse on the moment; upon hearing the key lock Crandall's cell, he pronounced: "The deed is done, completely done. It cannot be recalled. It has passed into the history of our nation and our age." He and Benson knew that "Miss Crandall's persecutors had . . . committed a great blunder" with this imprisonment. The next day, bail was provided, and Crandall "quietly resumed the duties of her school."[57]

Jailing as Performance Art

The above sequence of events concerning her night in jail doesn't do justice to Crandall's own agency and subjectivity. Her behavior that day has been oddly underexamined despite the fact that it goes well beyond stoic acquiescence. The accounts in Philip S. Foner and Josephine F. Pacheco, Donald E. Williams, and Susan Strane all admit that they are relying almost exclusively on May's firsthand account. Yet, we do have words from Prudence and a letter from her hand, written from jail, to the editors at the *Liberator*, and evidence of a second letter sent to one of the Benson brothers in Providence.[58]

First, her younger sister, Almira, is also overlooked, but she and Prudence went through the ordeal of arrest and arraignment together. Almira was released due to her age, and Prudence adds, in her letter from prison, "My sister after being bound over, was acquitted by the court, they having neglected to appoint her a guardian she being a minor."[59] This means that in their haste, Prudence's opponents had not even thought through basic logistical details of the arrest. Prudence was likely pleased that the Canterbury "selectmen" had made another strategic error, and equally glad that her sister didn't have to undergo the full imprisonment.

Next, the procession that carried Prudence from Canterbury to Brooklyn—a distance of about five miles—was noticeably hostile. She was alone during this procession, no known allies accompanying her. Nevertheless, she remained stoic, melding Quaker quietism and Baptist penchant for understated drama.

When she arrived at the jail, she and May had a momentary aside, where he offered to pay the bond if she was too afraid. With a rapidity signaling either a martyr's eagerness or defensiveness at being doubted, she quickly replied, "O no . . . I am only afraid they will not put me into jail." Most accounts of the arrest and jailing of Crandall stop there, but this was not the end of her reply to May. The rest of her commentary reveals that she, too, was thinking strategically: "Their evident hesitation and embarrassment show plainly how much they deprecate the effect of this part of their folly; and therefore I am the more anxious that they should be exposed, if not caught in their own wicked devices."[60] Crandall wanted her enemies to feel the public embarrassment that they had walked into of their own accord.

At the Brooklyn jail, the cell in which she was placed became a matter of some controversy. The jail did not see frequent use. The most recent resident was the notorious Oliver Watkins, who had murdered his wife. He had been imprisoned in the Brooklyn jail prior to his August 1831 execution. In his account, May makes it abundantly clear that the cell where Prudence stayed was the same as Watkins; May wrote *Some Recollections* long after the event, when he would have had even less reason to prevaricate.[61] He is also not shy about revealing that not posting bail was a strategic decision.[62] Much was made about a respectable young (white) woman being made to sleep in such a place. The *Windham County Advertiser* went so far as to declare that with her time in jail, Crandall had "Stepped out of the hallowed precincts of female propriety and now stands on common ground, and must expect common treatment."[63]

In a classic case of distraction from the primary issue, Judson and Adams decided to see deceit in the claim about Watkins's cell. Adams and Judson declared that Prudence "never was confined in the cell of Watkins the murderer. . . . This is part of the same contrivance to 'get up more excitement!' She was lodged in the debtor's room."[64] The men most responsible for creating a brouhaha to destroy Prudence's school seem unaware of the irony in their complaint about manufacturing excitement.

Prudence did not spend her night in prison alone. She was joined by a friend and ally, Anna Benson (1801–43), fourth daughter of George Benson Sr. Sexual propriety necessitated that anyone sharing her cell was female, but Anna's determination "to stay with Prudence for the duration, 'be the term long or short'" suggests another manifestation of female solidarity in the cause.[65] Anna Benson was not unimportant in her own right; she had three siblings who were deeply involved in support of Prudence's school and immediate abolition—George Jr., Henry, and Helen Benson, William Lloyd Garrison's soon-to-be-betrothed. A few months after the jailing, Anna accompanied her brother Henry on a trip to see the venerable Moses Brown; she was among the daughters who helped to sew the Jonathan Dymond pamphlets that the Windham County Peace Society distributed.[66] Like Prudence, Anna made her own religious decisions, becoming a Quaker by convincement.[67] Garrison was particularly close to Anna among his siblings-in-law, writing her very candid and emotionally open letters both before and after his marriage to Helen, evincing great respect for Anna's mind.[68] Finally, Anna helped to bring Olive Gilbert into the abolitionist movement during Prudence's crisis; they remained lifelong friends and despite the fact that Gilbert is critiqued for a condescending approach to Sojourner Truth, her acting as Truth's amanuensis remains key to feminist history. Anna joining Prudence in prison was an act of friendship and also a political statement.

Further evidence of Crandall's own political perspicacity emerges in the first postscript to her letter from jail: "Will you please send your Liberator the term of six months to Lydia Congdon Jewett City Conn.—she having paid to me for your agent Mr. Wm. Harris the sum of one Dollar. Do not fail to send her one next week."[69] Reflect for a moment on this: Prudence Crandall, in prison, takes the time to ensure that a recent Black woman subscriber, with whom she dealt directly ("having paid to me") will receive her copy of the *Liberator*.[70] She also reveals that she remains in regular contact with Sarah Harris's father, William Harris, especially in his role as agent for the *Liberator*. To borrow a leftist idiom, Prudence Crandall was performing "movement work," growing the alliance she had helped actualize with her school. Even the connection with Anna Benson can be seen as an example of this coalition building. In this brief jailhouse epistle, Crandall interacts, by name, with a Black man (William Harris), white male allies (May and George Benson Sr., who bails her out the next day), a Black woman (Lydia Congdon), and shares her cell with a white woman (Anna Benson). Crandall envisioned and actualized a different kind of America in that moment.

This is the fully vibrant Prudence Crandall, very much in charge of her own life and decisions, a conscious part of a movement for change, aware that she has cocreated something larger than herself with her school. Her performance of her minor martyrdom carries its own integrity. In the words of Martineau, Crandall's "conduct was to the last degree meek and quiet; nothing need be said about its courage."[71] While her enemies found her maddeningly contrary, she carried off this public performance with panache.

Crandall's politics always included Black women and men, more consistently than many other white abolitionists. From Black women in her immediate vicinity to establishing communication with the leadership network of free Blacks (both men and women), Crandall had listened to those who would be affected by her plan: the free Black community. And, for the entire time that the school operated—April 1, 1833, through September 10, 1834—Crandall was in daily, highly visible contact with Blacks: not only her students and Maria Davis but their families, Black *Liberator* agents, and local

Black residents.[72] Almost no other white abolitionists were able to sustain such interracial interaction without falling into condescension or shrinking in fear of public disapproval.

The social shunning generated by interracial contact of any kind intimidated many white abolitionists. Henry Bowditch, a decade *after* Crandall's school, recounted how merely walking down a street with his dinner guest Frederick Douglass produced scalding stares, triggering a personal epiphany for Bowditch.[73] Crandall was single for most of the time that her school was open, surrounded by hostile whites hurling amalgamationist slurs, yet she managed to live in an interracial, mixed-gender, class-crossing reality for eighteen months. And through all of this she kept her focus on the actual task of education. Thirty-six years later she recounted that the Black students and the two white women in the house—Crandall and her sister Almira—had all worked together as "our own washer women and kissed each other with as much freedom as though we had been all as white as snowbanks, but never for the purpose of being seen by the villagers."[74] Indeed, Crandall was not running her school as a publicity stunt—she had even offered to move the school to a less-visible part of town during the early days of the struggle.[75] Living an interracial reality and fostering (and therefore proving) the strength and ability of women's minds were not stunts to Crandall but a joyous vocation.

Despite the much greater feminist fame of the Grimké sisters, the Seneca Falls Convention, and Sojourner Truth, consider how the ever-budding feminism of Prudence Crandall in the early 1830s carries possibilities that were not fully explored then or now. The women supporters around Crandall and the formation of a woman's antislavery auxiliary in Windham County speak to how her actions galvanized the community. A protofeminist newspaper at the time, the *New York Female Advocate*, glimpsed the feminist dimension, condemning Judson (in all caps) for locking "FEMALES INTO PRISON, FOR SEEKING FEMALE IMPROVEMENT AND ELEVATION."[76] But during that time in jail, Crandall seems to have embraced not just the educational ideas but also the militant spirit of Maria Stewart. Above all, these two women—one white, privileged enough to receive an excellent education, the other Black and denied access to education—brought their innate intelligence to bear on race and gender in America, seeing beyond slavery to the superstructures of racism and sexism. The ultimate shared theme between Crandall and Maria Stewart is the self-authorizing of women for each other, an awakening solidarity to achieve what the dominant groups—whites and men—attempted to curtail: *female self-development.*[77]

CHAPTER 5

Young Ladies
and Little Misses
The Black Students
and Their Contexts

Teacher and pupils . . . evidently felt that it
was given to them to maintain one of the
fundamental, inalienable rights of man.
—Samuel J. May

Black women were instrumental in conceiving and launching Prudence
Crandall's second academy. This school was intended to assist Black women
materially and intellectually. Yet, in many retellings the students have little
individuality, becoming sentimental icons, cyphers, or benighted children.
It is time to say their names and share their stories. The success or failure
of Canterbury should rest with the educational outcomes of these Black
students, not the small-souled contempt of the white men of Canterbury. Of
the thirty-one Black women students whose names we know, research has
so far traced activities and achievements in the historical record for eighteen
of them. This means that two-thirds of these women were visibly active in
antebellum African American communities. At least six became teachers,
and six engaged in abolitionist activities. When the narrative of Canterbury
is misrepresented as white saviorism against a backdrop of persecution, it is
Black females' lives, aspirations, and educations that disappear.

The school was intellectually, vocationally, and politically vibrant, doing
what every institution of higher learning should do: extending an invitation
to the commonwealth of human knowledge while serving as the gateway
to full adulthood. Both Black education and women's education were taken
seriously. The academy produced a cohort of educated middle-class Black
women who proved to be effective teachers, activists, and spousal partners to
Black male leaders. The alumnae of Crandall's school in their "respectability"

provided a living riposte to colonizationist disparagements of Black character and potential.

For the story of Canterbury to be understood intersectionally, the light must shine on the principal actors who exercised their agency to make this interracial experiment work. Knowing the students' backgrounds provides access to their networks. Every Black family who sent a daughter to Canterbury did so from their own motivations and financial ability, via a network of mutual support.[1] The lives, struggles, and trajectories of each student whose life can be traced from existing evidence will be covered in this chapter (though due to women and African Americans being doubly neglected, much is lost).

Who Were the Students?

Diligent research by scholars has produced a still-growing list of thirty-one Black students. They hailed from at least four states, ranging in age from nine to twenty-three; however, exact dates are missing for many. Table 2 lists these students, with known and conjectured vital statistics.

The first thing to note is the ages of the students. They were primarily teenagers, not children learning the alphabet. The distortion that depicted them as raw youths stemmed from both the school's allies and enemies, but it deflects from the truth of the school's daring challenge to the racist status quo. Connecticut afforded its Black residents enough education to fit them for menial labor through the district schools (equivalent to elementary schools). The state, however, did not desire the breakdown of the racial caste system that universal *higher* education would create. The bulk of Crandall's students were of high school age, averaging almost seventeen years old in 1833.[2] This means the students were building on earlier education rather than starting as blank slates.

The next thing to note is that the students were clustered geographically. They hailed from four distinct geographic regions: Connecticut, Providence, New York City, and Philadelphia. Crandall had but one known student from Boston—Julia Williams. The free Black communities in these four areas were distinct from each other. Eastern Connecticut was a relatively rural area with opportunities for economic growth, while Providence's community was urban and comparatively poor. Philadelphia had a large community with both sacred and secular Black leaders, while effective clerical organizers dominated New York City.[3]

The students from eastern Connecticut were from towns along the Quinebaug River. The Quinebaug and Shetucket Rivers meet in Norwich, a recognized center for African Americans in antebellum eastern Connecticut. The combination of waterpower, industrialization, and African American

Table 2. Names and basic information of known Canterbury Academy students

Name	Birth and Death Dates	Residence	Spouse	Children	Source	Amount of Information
Benson, Mary Jane	—	—	—	—	Olney trial*	none to small
Bolt, Henrietta	b. ca. 1817 d. Apr 1870	New York	Theodore Breshow Vidal	yes	trials*	strong
Brown, Elizabeth	b. ca. 1822 d. 1898	Providence	John N. Smith	yes	Maritcha Lyons, many additional sources	extensive
Bustill, Elizabeth Douglass	b. ca. 1815 d. ca. 1915?	Philadelphia	Charles Jones	yes	family genealogy	strong
Carter, M. E.	—	New York?	—	—	second trial*	none to small
Congdon, Jerusha	b. Oct 10,1816 d. Dec 23, 1883	Lisbon, CT	William West	—	subpoena record, additional sources	strong
DeGrasse, Theodosia (Theodocia)	b. Apr 16, 1816 d. Mar 12, 1854	New York	Peter Vogelsang	—	trials*	strong
F., E.	—	Hartford, CT	—	—	temperance poem (1836)	none to small
Fenner, Amy (Amey)	b. ca. 1808 d. Feb 25, 1900	Jewett City, CT	Ransom Parker	yes	Olney trial,* Crandall-Harris letters	strong
Freeman, Polly	—	—	—	—	subpoena record	none to small
Glasko, Eliza	b. 1811 d. 1874	Jewett City, CT	John Peterson	yes	subpoena record; Crandall-Harris letters	strong
Glasko, Miranda	b. Aug 20 1820 d. July 7, 1894	Jewett City, CT	Thomas Overbaugh	—	Rowland Greene, The Colored American (1837)	strong

Table 2. Continued

Name	Birth and Death Dates	Residence	Spouse	Children	Source	Amount of Information
Hammond, Ann Eliza	b. Aug 18, 1816 d. after 1874	Providence	goes by birth name in 1870s	—	trials*	strong
Hammond, Sarah Lloyd	b. Jun 15 1824 d. —	Providence	—	—	second trial*	limited or inferential
Harris, Mary	b. Sep 29, 1817 d. May 15, 1900	Canterbury, CT	Pelleman Williams	yes	multiple sources	extensive
Harris, Sarah Ann Major	b. Apr 16, 1812 d. Nov 16, 1878	Canterbury, CT	George Fayerweather	yes	extensive range of sources	extensive
Henly, Elizabeth	—	Philadelphia	—	—	second trial*	limited or inferential
Johnson, J. K.	—	Philadelphia	—	—	artifact	none to small
Lanson, Harriet	b. 1817 d. 1835	New Haven	unmarried	no	obituary	extensive
Marshall, Gloriana Catherine (G. C.)	b. 1818–1824 d. —	New York	—	—	second trial; Olney trial*	limited or inferential
Miles, Mary Elizabeth	b. Apr 12, 1819 d. Oct 20, 1881	Providence	Henry Bibb; Isaac Cary	no	obituary by Alexander Crummell	extensive
Peterson, Ann	—	New York	—	—	trials*	none to small
Robinson, Maria	—	Providence	—	—	Olney trial; second trial*	none to small
Tucker/Goary, Julia (aka Maria)	b. ca. 1814 d. 1897	Canterbury CT	Jared Finnemore; Henry Yantis	—	The Gospel in All Lands	limited or inferential
Tucker/Goary, Virginia	—	Canterbury, CT	Pompey Johnson	—	The Gospel in All Lands	limited or inferential

Table 2. Continued

Name	Birth and Death Dates	Residence	Spouse	Children	Source	Amount of Information
Weldon, Catharine Ann	—	New York	—	—	trials*	none to small
Weldon, Eliza	—	New York	—	—	second trial*	none to small
Wilder, Anne Elizabeth (Amila)	—	New York	—	—	trials*	none to small
Williams, Julia	b. July 1, 1811 d. Jan 7, 1870	Boston (b. South Carolina)	Henry Highland Garnet	yes	obituaries, possibly subpoena	extensive
Willis, (unknown)	—	Providence?	—	—	Olney trial*	none to small
Wilson, Emila	—	—	—	—	second trial*	small to none
(unknown), Julia A. J.	b. May 21, 1823 d. Nov 1901	Albany	George Foote	no	autobiography; student at Albany school	extensive

* Trials are first Black Law trial (August 1833), second Black Law trial (October 1833), and Frederick Olney trial (March 1834).
Note: Residence is where an individual was living when she came to attend the academy.

knowledge of seafaring trades provided concrete opportunities for Black advancement and self-development. This Black community was small enough that they had robust networks, knew their white neighbors, and were ready and eager to seize the educational opportunity that Canterbury afforded their daughters.

The fathers of these eastern Connecticut students ranged from a yeoman farmer like William Harris to a common laborer like Caeser Tucker.[4] Preeminent among them was the highly successful Isaac C. Glasko (1776–1861), who was multiracial, having both Native and African lineages. He operated as an outfitter of marine tools who "furnished whaling implements to all New England ports."[5] Glasko developed such a strong relationship with the Kinnes (among Crandall's few white allies) that the two families share a graveyard in Griswold.[6] While Glasko was wealthier and more socially visible to the white community than most men of color, he still suffered under racism: his attempt to register to vote was denied.[7] He was also a local agent for *Freedom's Journal*, ensuring that the community in Norwich was part of national free Black networking.[8]

Glasko succeeded amidst the industrialization of the Quinebaug River Valley. He arrived in Griswold during the first decade of the nineteenth century and established a forge along the river. He married Lucy Brayton (1776–1849); Eliza (1811–74) and Miranda (1820–1894) were their two youngest daughters among seven children.[9] Eliza was one of the older students in Crandall's academy at twenty-two, and that fact, coupled with her local prominence, may explain why she was pressed to testify at Crandall's first trial (see next chapter). Given the family's proximity to the academy, it is not surprising that Eliza Glasko was the only student, along with Sarah Harris, to attend the school the day it opened.

The Glasko family was living in Jewett City in the 1830s, a manufacturing town close to Canterbury along the Quinebaug.[10] The Black woman whom Crandall was concerned should receive a *Liberator* subscription, Lydia Congdon, had a Jewett City address. In addition to the Glasko daughters, Amy Fenner came from this area, but nothing is known yet about her parentage. She was the oldest student in the school, being only five years younger than Crandall herself.

Jerusha Congdon's family lived in a Quinebaug River orbit that included Plainfield, Norwich, and Preston. Her grandfather Absalom Congdon had been enslaved as a child in Rhode Island before being manumitted by Samuel Coit in Preston in the late eighteenth century.[11] Jerusha Congdon's heritage included Native American ancestry.[12] She was also a distant relative of Amos Beman.[13] Jerusha was the oldest surviving child of the eleven born to James Congdon and Lydia Pelham Congdon. There was a family heritage in blacksmithing from Absalom, but the men of the family worked as laborers.

Jerusha Congdon, therefore, likely represents a less-privileged stratum of Black students than the Harris and Glasko families.

The Tucker/Goary sisters are known to the school primarily through a (fundamentally accurate) biographical sketch:

> When Miss Prudence Crandall was arrested and persecuted for teaching colored girls at her school in Canterbury, Conn, in 1833, there were among the pupils two sisters, the daughters of Caesar Tucker, a laboring man of the town, who had been given some eight months' tuition by the brave little Quakeress. When the power of the State of Connecticut was invoked to crush the daring school-ma'am, and she was thrown into jail, the parents of these two girls became frightened at the tumult of indignation that burst forth, and fled to Massachusetts, finding a home in Springfield, in that State.[14]

This story has the ring of truth in two respects. One is that Crandall was eager to fill the school in the early weeks, when the small number of scholars in attendance was threatening the viability of the enterprise. This makes the idea of supporting two pupils with financial aid a sensible gamble. The second is that local Blacks might well have been intimidated by the rhetoric spewing from Judson and other whites. The jailing of Crandall could have provoked some Blacks to move. Like Jerusha Congdon, the Tucker/Goary girls exemplify the Black working class, lacking the prestige of the elite Black families in urban centers. Mixing across class lines was common within the Black community, where economic vicissitudes and proximity to past enslavement created a perpetually shifting cline. For the students, this likely resulted in their academy being less class-conscious than white academies.

The family of William Harris, by contrast, had no intention of obliging Judson by departing Canterbury. At least two of their daughters—Sarah and Mary—attended the academy. Two other sisters, Celinda (1814–99) and Olive (1822–1902), might have attended, given that they were old enough and became prominent educators.

Harriet Rosetta Lanson hailed from New Haven. Her grandfather Laban Lanson served as a soldier during the American Revolution, while her father, William Lanson (ca. 1782–1851), a prominent free Black entrepreneur, fell on hard times personally, largely due to various forms of economic and social racism.[15] Jocelyn, who was probably Lanson's minister, became Harriet's guardian. The true cypher, "E. F." from Hartford, is known only through a temperance poem she recited at the Colored Temperance Convention of 1836.[16]

In most matters concerning the school, Julia Williams is an exemplary outlier. She was born in Charleston, South Carolina, in 1811, which made her among the oldest students and the only one of Southern origin. Her status at birth—enslaved or free—is still unclear, but her mother, Nancy, got the young

Julia and her sister Anna to Boston.[17] At the age of eleven, Julia Williams "embraced a religious life, and was baptized by immersion" by Daniel Sharp (1783–1853), whose Charles Street Baptist Church became an antislavery center in Boston.[18] It is possible that Julia Williams personally knew famous abolitionists like William Lloyd Garrison, Maria Stewart, and David Walker (perhaps even Maria Davis) before attending Crandall's school.[19] Julia Williams's quick intellect would have assuredly feasted on writings like Walker's *Appeal* and Stewart's "Pure Principles."[20]

The Rhode Island students include Elizabeth Smith, Ann Eliza and her sister Sarah Hammond, Mariah Robinson, and Mary Elizabeth Miles.[21] Of these, we have extensive biographical information on the postschool success of Smith and Miles, the latter better known as Mary Miles Bibb, second wife of the famed self-liberated Henry Bibb. Mary Elizabeth Miles was born into a Quaker family in Rhode Island in 1820. Little is known of her youth. The revelation that Mary Elizabeth Miles had been among Crandall's pupils—made by Canadian scholar Afua Cooper—makes it quite clear that the high school for Black women in Connecticut had surpassed Sarah Harris's modest goal to "get a little more learning" to becoming a catalyst for Black women's education and multifaceted involvement in the abolitionist struggle.[22]

Elizabeth Brown Smith's biography is presented by a former student of hers, Maritcha R. Lyons, in Hallie Q. Brown's *Homespun Heroines and Other Women of Distinction* (1926),[23] and has recently been filled out by scholars Kate Blankenship and Elizabeth Stevens. Elizabeth Brown's father, Cupid Brown, was born enslaved, but when his father gained manumission, he bought his children out of slavery. Cupid worked in maritime capacities, rising to a ship's steward in the 1830s; he and his wife, Margaret Roomes Brown, thus held tenuous middle-class status.[24] Elizabeth Brown Smith's earliest education was through Quakers in Providence; she was "(s)tudiously inclined" and "inducted into some branches then properly deemed 'too deep' for ordinary females."[25]

Ann Eliza Hammond and Sarah L. Hammond were the daughters of Elizabeth Hammond, whom Crandall met following her political rendezvous with Garrison in early 1833. The support that the Hammond family, mother and daughters, gave to the Canterbury experiment is extraordinary: Eliza Ann Hammond was the first out-of-state pupil to arrive and thus faced the full brunt of white Canterbury's anger, including the threat of whipping. This mother—the only non-Connecticut parent whom we know met Crandall prior to the school opening—entrusted the teacher with both her daughters. Ann Eliza, born August 18, 1816, was in her late teens at the time of the school. Sarah was the youngest pupil at Crandall's academy; her birthdate of June 15, 1824, would make her nine years old for most of the duration of the school.[26] Their parents, Thomas Hammond and Elizabeth Hall, had married

September 4, 1808; at the time of his death Thomas Hammond was able to leave an inheritance for his wife and daughters.[27]

Because the city had a small Black community, the Providence students likely knew each other; Elizabeth Hammond taking Crandall to meet other Black parents corroborates this.[28] Miles and Brown Smith both received Quaker educations in Providence. It is possible that George Benson Jr., who had become a Quaker by convincement, or Moses Brown, facilitated the enrollment of these Black Quaker women from Providence.

The only record of a woman with the last name of Willis at Crandall's academy comes from the trial transcript involving the fabricated charges of arson against Frederick Olney (March 1834).[29] Nothing about her age can be established. Although it has not yet been possible to determine her identity with certainty, it seems most likely that she was a daughter of George C. Willis (ca. 1787–1858) and his first wife, Martha Prophet. George Willis took a leading role in Black politics in Providence. A member of the prestigious First Baptist Church (Roger Williams's church), he was a Rhode Island representative to the Free Black conventions, an officer of the local Black Masons, and an agent for *Freedom's Journal*.[30] He was involved in virtually every political issue from the 1820s through the 1840s, most prominently in the effort to secure the franchise for Black men.[31] He chaired the "respectable meeting" of Black residents of Providence in October 1831 that was included in Garrison's *Thoughts on African Colonization*. Note this clarity of analysis in the wake of the New Haven failure:

> [W]e firmly believe, from the recent measures adopted by the freemen of the city of New Haven, in regard to the establishment of a College for our education in that place, that the principal object of the friends of African colonization is to oppose our education and consequent elevation here, as it will deprive them of one of their principal arguments for our removal.[32]

Furthermore, the hunger for education so manifest in the striving of Maria Davis and Sarah Harris at the start of the academy can be sensed in this resolution's plea as well:

> We are in this country a degraded and ignorant people; but ... our ignorance and degradation are not to be attributed to the inferiority of our natural abilities, but to the oppressive treatment we have experienced from the whites in general, and to the prejudice excited against us by the members of the Colonization Society, their aiders and abettors.[33]

These statements suggest that Willis would be an African American parent eager to send a daughter to a school like Crandall's. The 1830 census reveals three young Black females in his household—one between the ages of ten and twenty, and two below the age of ten. Willis had two marriages—the first to Martha Prophet, who died in 1818, and the second to Phyllis Ander-son, solemnized in 1820. This means that the female between the age of ten to twenty in the Willis household in 1830 is likely Martha's daughter, and the other two younger girls the daughters of Phyllis. If the Miss Willis who attended the school was the daughter of Martha Prophet, she would be yet another student of mixed-racial heritage. The Prophet family was a matri-lineal Narragansett clan descended from the "regionally renowned" elder Chloe Prophet.[34]

Maria (or Mariah) Robinson was also present at the time of the arson fire in 1834 that resulted in the Olney trial, but the context there implies Maria Robinson was working at the house rather than studying.[35] However, Maria Robinson was also mentioned in the writ of arrest from June 1833, there definitively listed as a student.[36] No free Black family of Robinsons in Rhode Island has yet been uncovered through public records.

The journey for individual women from Philadelphia to Canterbury was an expensive risk; none of the Forten daughters undertook it, for instance.[37] Crandall's Philadelphia students actually had more choices for schooling than those from Connecticut or Rhode Island. The students from Philadel-phia—Elizabeth Henly, J. K. Johnson, and Elizabeth Douglass Bustill—distill among them the problems attendant on researching the lives of marginalized people. Bustill came from a revered well-to-do family of free Black Quakers who played an integral part in the Black elite of that city. Henly appears as a delegate to the Remunerated Labor Conference and the Women's Anti-Slav-ery Convention in Philadelphia in 1838, representing the Northern Liberties Anti-Slavery Society along with famed dentist and activist James McCrum-mell.[38] By contrast, neither J. K. Johnson nor K. M. Johnson (the signatory of a box given to Crandall by a student soon after the closing of the school) have yet turned up in the records. However, the free Black person with the great-est means to educate his daughters and with a track record of cooperation with whites was the renowned self-made musician and bandleader Francis Johnson (1792–1844).

Francis (Frank) Johnson was among the most prominent performers of the early republic. He made a solid living as a musician, both from teaching and working the resort circuit in the summers; late in his career he staged a triumphant European tour and received a silver trumpet as a gift from the young Queen Victoria. While he was not primarily known as a political figure, he did compose a "Recognition March on the Independence of Haiti" and set a Sarah Forten poem to music, "The Grave of the Slave."[39]

In the 1830 and 1840 censuses, Johnson is listed as living in the Cedar Ward of Philadelphia, and there are "free colored females" in an appropriate age range to have been students of Crandall's: in 1830 there is one young woman in the age range from 10–23 (birth years between 1807 to 1820) and one woman in the older age group of 24–35 (birth years 1795–1806). In 1840 this number swells to four women between the ages of 24–35 (birth years 1805–16) and 2 in the younger age range of 10–23 (birth years 1817–30). The situation suggests that Francis Johnson, as a wealthy man, supported members of his extended family: whether the young women known to us only as J. K. and K. M. Johnson were his daughters, nieces, or unrelated to him is not discernible.[40]

Elizabeth Douglass Bustill came from one of the most prestigious and well-off lineages in antebellum Black America. She was the oldest daughter of David Bustill (1787–1866) and Elizabeth Hicks Bustill (married 1803); her father pursued teaching at one point in his life.[41] She was born in 1819. Elizabeth's middle name, Douglass, shows her relation, through one of her grandmothers, to the Douglasses, another significant Philadelphia free Black family. Her grandfather Cyrus Bustill (1732–1806) was a Quaker and leader of the free Black community during the years of the American Revolution. Elizabeth's grandmother Cyrus Bustill's wife Elizabeth Morey was Native American, so Elizabeth Douglass Bustill had mixed racial heritage.[42] Her brother Charles Hicks Bustill (1816–90) was Paul Robeson's grandfather.

A cousin of Bustill, Sarah Mapps Douglass (1806–82), wrote an emotional piece in "Sympathy for Miss Crandall" in July 1833, under her pseudonym "Zillah," published in the *Emancipator*. This remarkable testimony from a Black woman whose family legacy had already provided her with educational benefits speaks volumes for Black community solidarity with the students. Zillah spends far more time calling out white Christian hypocrisy and rousing Black women to educational action (in a tone reminiscent of Maria Stewart) than she does expressing sympathy with Crandall. She encourages Black women "to go forward. Let not the fear of insult deter any one from embracing this glorious opportunity. . . . For the sake of an education we might be willing to bear not only scornful looks, but oppressive acts. . . . Be courageous; put your trust in the God of the oppressed; and go forward!"[43]

The students who hailed from New York City form a most intriguing group but have proven to be difficult to research conclusively. The New York City students easily divide into two groups. The better-known ones—Henrietta Bolt, Theodosia DeGrasse, G. C. Marshall, and Ann Peterson—shared tangible connections to Peter Williams Jr. and St. Philip's Episcopal Church. They and their families were part of the network of those free Blacks who had a reasonable chance at gaining middle-class status and respectability. Eliza Weldon surfaces only once but significantly in pursuit of education when she attended Oberlin College's preparatory division in 1837–38.[44] The remaining six students are just names at this point, and even the connection to New York City is by necessity a tentative one: Mary Jane Benson, M. E. Carter,

Polly Freeman, Catharine Ann Weldon, Ann Elizabeth (or Amilia) Wilder, and Emila Wilson.[45] In the absence of more evidence, nothing more will be said about these latter women, aside from their roles at the trials.

Carla Peterson's meticulous 2011 study, *Black Gotham*, elegantly reconstructs the networks of the Black elite in New York City and how they "cohered around a number of institutions: the African Society for Mutual Relief; the Mulberry Street Schools; churches like St. Philip's or Mother Zion; newspapers like *Freedom's Journal*, the *Colored America*, the *New York Globe*, *Freeman*, and *Age*; and the annual conventions of colored people."[46]

Theodosia DeGrasse was born in New York City to George DeGrasse (1774–1862) and Maria Van Surley DeGrasse (1791–1861). Her father was born in Calcutta, India, and her mother was multiracial. The DeGrasse legacy is not only multiracial: it is ringed with fame. George DeGrasse was the "natural" son of "Admiral Count de Grasse, the commander of the French fleet that had helped George Washington triumph over the British at Yorktown in 1781." When he returned to France after the Revolution, his father left him in the newborn country under the care of Aaron Burr. In an 1802 letter to his own daughter Theodosia, Burr refers to "my man George (late Azar Le Guen, now George d'Grasse)." The connection to Burr explains why DeGrasse bestowed on the daughter who attended the academy the melodious name of Theodosia (which means "gift of God").[47] His liminal racial identity enabled George DeGrasse to receive US citizenship in the first decade of the nineteenth century.[48]

Theodosia's mother's line was, if possible, an even broader tapestry of possibilities. The line can be traced to Jansen Van Haarlem, better known as Murat Reis, an infamous Dutch pirate of the late 1500s who married a Moroccan woman.[49] His son Abraham Jansen von Salee moved to New Amsterdam (aka New York City), "where the phrase 'alias the mulatto' or 'alias the Turk' was regularly appended to his name."[50] Another source suggests that Maria Van Surley had German parents.[51] One of Theodosia's siblings, Isaiah, was reputed to be able to pass as white, and an article in the *Liberator* states that the young man had "no African blood in his veins."[52] This contradicts what Peter Williams, their pastor, said about the DeGrasse children having "a mixture of Asiatic and European with African blood."[53] The question of the meaning, indeed even the reality, of race is demonstrated in the complicated lives of Crandall's students, some of whom were multiracial (Sarah and Mary Harris, Theodosia DeGrasse, Elizabeth Douglass Bustill, and possibly the Willis daughter).

The DeGrasse family was economically secure, part of the rising Black middle class. They were members of St. Philip's Episcopal Church, placing Theodosia and her family in the milieu of Peter Williams Jr.'s constant activism and educational ventures. Her father ran a provisioning business in the Five Points neighborhood and was also involved in real estate. His burial at Brooklyn's Cypress Heights garden cemetery in 1862 points to financial success.[54] Her mother cast a wide net in the benevolent projects of Black New York City as a manager of the Dorcas Society and the Ladies Literary Society.[55] Theodosia brought to Crandall's academy a connection to the Black elite of New York City and an optimistic faith in the power of education. She is mentioned in Canterbury legal documents from June 1833 to March 1834, so she attended for most of the life of the academy.

Henrietta Bolt's mother, Margaret (b. ca. 1795), was originally from Jamaica; her daughter was born in New York City. Little else is known yet about her parents or background, though Henrietta would achieve an enviable financial security after the school.

Gloriana Catherine Marshall was known by her initials, G. C. at the academy. Like DeGrasse and Bolt, her family moved in the orbit of St. Philip's Church, but they did so in straitened circumstances. She was the daughter of Joseph Marshall (d. 1828) and Elizabeth Hewlitt Marshall (1779–1861). Her father was a house painter who managed to save enough to purchase a house for his family. After he died, the enterprising Elizabeth opened a bakery in part of the dwelling. She had four children to raise, of whom Gloriana Catherine was likely the youngest. The other three were Mary Joseph (b. 1815), Rebecca, and Edward. All three of Gloriana Catherine's siblings had an impact on Black history. While not much is known of her own life, Gloriana's family upbringing and the achievements of her siblings indicate a household with upwardly mobile aspirations that persistently sought education. The Marshall family—led by Elizabeth as a single mother after 1828—rubbed elbows with the wealthier Black elite; her children achieved the stability for which their parents had been striving.

Ann Peterson of New York has a frustratingly common name. There is an Ann Peterson listed as a manager of the Female Temperance Society founded by Black women in December 1833 in New York City; this is likely Crandall's student, either on a Christmas vacation from school or no longer enrolled.[56] Her first few months at Crandall's school had been grueling: like Ann Eliza Hammond, Ann Peterson was threatened with whipping, then subpoenaed to testify in the August 1833 trial. She was the first student to appear on the witness stand. The *Colored American* reports a "mental feast" of the Ladies Literary Society of the City of New York in 1837, with participation from both a Miss DeGrasse and a Miss Peterson; this could be a miniature class reunion of former Crandall students, or it could refer to John Peterson's sister Rebecca Peterson and Maria DeGrasse, a niece of Theodosia's, who were both teachers in New York City by 1837.[57]

The Courage of the Parents
of Crandall's Students

These sketches of what is presently known about each of the Black students in Canterbury suggest new ways to understand the academy. Table 3 presents a rough division of the prestige and the financial circumstances of the students' families within the free Black community in 1833–34. The solidarity of the students clearly overcame class stratification.

The active network around St. Philip's Church and Peter Williams Jr. means that we know a great deal about students whose families attended that congregation. By contrast, the lack of social status attached to the Baptist churches resulted in less notice of their activities in the Black press and in the *Liberator.* Records at all Black churches were often collateral damage of violence aimed at these institutions. Adequate membership rosters from Abyssinian Baptist would likely reveal identities of currently unknown students, and deep networks through Hayborn and Raymond (but likely not as financially secure as those at St. Philips). In considering class status, it is also important to remember that some students may well have come from families that had no leisure to attend literary societies or any inclination to be on temperance committees.

It is obvious that Crandall was willing to reach out to students in all economic situations; that speaks to how quickly she intuited the social stratification of free Blacks. At the same time, the prestige of an academy was alluring to the parents of the Black elite who hoped to dispel the calumnies against their race through educational achievement. It is no accident, therefore, that a significant percentage of her students came from elite (or striving-to-be-elite) families.

The parents and guardians who entrusted their daughters to the care of a woman in rural Connecticut need to be honored, too, for their bravery. These parents were taking an enormous leap of faith. Earlier chapters in the current volume have documented how the Black community had vetted Crandall. But there is a vast difference between heeding an endorsement and entrusting one's own children to someone unknown and to a place known to be hostile. But these parents were eager for their "daughters not only to succeed in every aspect of life but to exceed . . . and go much further" than they could.[58]

The students and teachers at the Canterbury Academy rose above the bullies. Daily life at the school went on no matter how much the vigilante violence and legal maneuvering against them escalated. The regular working of the academy should not be ignored. It is an accomplishment. As Kabria Baumgartner relates, the students "never knew what awaited them. But they went forward anyway." This persistence is crucial.[59] That daily life included

Table 3. Estimated class status of students of table 2

Fiscally Secure	Middle Class	Working Class	Unknown
Bolt	Brown	Congdon	Benson
Bustill	Fenner	Lanson	Carter
DeGrasse	Hammond (2)	Tucker/Goary (2)	Freeman
Glasko (2)	Marshall	Williams	Henly
Harris (2)	Miles	Peterson	Robinson
[Johnson]	[Willis]		Weldon (2)
			Wilder
			Wilson
			E. F.

Note: Names in square brackets indicate where these students would fit if the conjectures in this chapter about their identities turn out to be correct.

(in addition to Prudence and Almira) another pair of white siblings, William and Mary Burleigh, who also taught at the school. Supplies were brought in by the Crandall family and by local Blacks like Frederick Olney. There were regular visitors and a vigorous intellectual life, filled with debates and political controversies. All of the students had grown up under systems of racism and sexism that had disciplined them; no matter their financial status, they were not smugly privileged. They knew how to take care of their own needs, whether laundry, food preparation, religious devotion, or study. Crandall wrote, years later, of their happiness in one another; even without the urgency pushed by persecution, their mutual intellectual dedication would probably have been sufficient to foster this sense of community.

The legal battles, the violence, the inflammatory articles in the *Liberator*, and the openly racist retorts from locals—all of these are important to the story of Crandall's school. But the significance of the academy ultimately depends on what it reveals about women, about interracial cooperation, and about the power of education, more than constitutional subtleties or the vulgarity of racist behavior. The only reason to examine the repulsive particularities of white Canterbury is to remember that they were attempting to crush an experiment in human potential because they feared its success, not its failure. Much to their dismay, the academy succeeded: these "Young Ladies and Little Misses of Color" lived impactful lives.

CHAPTER 6

Ripples and Reflections in the Abolitionist Networks
Conventions and Curriculum

> Knowledge and comprehension are the
> joy and justification of humanity.
> —Alexander von Humboldt

Networks among free Blacks in the North and among Abolitionists (across race and gender) made an enterprise as complex and controversial as the Canterbury Academy possible. Once we forefront the agency of the politically marginalized—white women, Black women, and Black men—the webs in their intricacy reveal shared purpose and solidarity. Weaving in and around the necessarily fragile skeins constructed by the marginalized are the agency and actions of those white men who were listening attentively to the intelligence and aspirations of those whose access to education and political rights had been thwarted.

This chapter considers two distinct approaches to this dense interweave. The first concerns the free Black male elite who discussed the Canterbury school at their conventions and negotiated alliances with white men. The second considers how, through reading abolitionist literature, the students had their actions and agency reflected to them through the press.

The Black Convention Movement

The convention movement is a milestone in free Black self-development and organization. Strategies of respectability and racial uplift marked the six conventions held between 1830 and 1835, avowing that *"Education, Temperance* and *Economy"* were the best means of uplift.[1] The conventions stressed Black citizenship and the "incontrovertible" promises of the Declaration of Independence and the Constitution, which guarantee "in letter and spirit to every freeman born in this country, all the rights and immunities of citizenship."[2]

While these meetings were concerned with slavery, abolition was not their primary focus: the plight of free Blacks—whether through poverty, lack of access to resources such as education, or the unceasing and "unhallowed persecutions" of colonizationists—defined their agenda and trajectory.[3] The six conferences in the 1830s consistently endorsed higher education:

> If we ever expect to see the influence of prejudice decrease, and ourselves respected, it must be by the blessings of an enlightened education. It must be by being in possession of that classical knowledge which promotes genius, and causes man to soar up to those high intellectual enjoyments and acquirements, which places him in a situation, to shed upon a country and a people, that scientific grandeur which is imperishable by time, and drowns in oblivious cup their moral degradation.[4]

Two months into the life of the second Canterbury Academy, the 1833 convention was held in Philadelphia. Arnold Buffum attended, soliciting "encouragement and support" for Crandall's school.[5] In addition to Buffum's communication, the convention read a note from Simeon Jocelyn, who wrote that despite persecution Crandall's school "was in a flourishing condition, and only required the encouragement and support of those for whom it was opened, to triumph over the opposition."[6] The convention representatives accepted Jocelyn's report, and their political acumen probed how Canterbury's white elite had unmasked the rationale of the American Colonization Society:

> The recent appeal of the selectmen of Canterbury, (Conn.) to that Society, but too clearly demonstrates to the eyes of an enlightened public, that they have recognized it as an instrument, by which they might more fully carry into operation their horrible design of preventing innocent and unprotected females from receiving the benefit of a liberal education, without which, the best and brightest prospects of any country or people, must be for ever blasted.[7]

The convention's support for women's education constitutes a welcome break from the ambient sexism of the time.[8]

David Ruggles (1810–49), a significant Black thinker, was born and raised in Norwich, before leaving for New York City at the age of seventeen. By 1833 he worked as a traveling agent for the abolitionist newspaper the *Emancipator*.[9] Ruggles likely knew every Black family in Norwich; when he was born there were only 164 Blacks in the city (12 still enslaved). His connections in eastern Connecticut and New York ensured that he had solid information about Crandall and the students.[10] Black civil rights were a paramount concern for Ruggles. His major literary work at this time—a pamphlet concerning racial prejudice and the "bugbear" of intermarriage—dealt with issues and personnel (Garrison and May) involved in the Canterbury crisis. He denounced racism while nostalgically extolling the less-prejudiced Connecticut of his youth:

> How old are children, I mean white children, before this *"natural repug-nance"* shows itself? Just old enough to receive the elements of an incul-cated repugnance from five to fifteen years of age. In *bygone* days in New England, the land of steady habits, where my happiest hours were spent with my play mates, in her schools—in her churches. . . . Then—then, her morals were rich—she taught us sweet virtue! Then Connecticut, indeed, was the queen of our land!—then *nature*, never, *never!* taught us such sinful "repugnance!" She was *strong* to the contrary.[11]

At the 1833 convention, Ruggles introduced a motion that, sadly, is lost in its entirety: "Mr. David Ruggles, according to leave, presented a preamble and resolution, relative to the High School recently established by Miss Prudence Crandall."

Rather than act, though, the committee grew irresolute, deflecting the question by declaring that the communications from Buffum and Jocelyn were sufficient: "The committee are of the opinion that the preceding is included in the two communications before mentioned, but think that the utmost in our power should be done to sustain it, and therefore cheerfully recommend to our brethren, who may have girl children they wish to be well educated, to send them to her school."[12] This cheerful recommendation, while certainly welcome, did not address the fullness of the Black community's engagement with Crandall's project.

Ruggles's full statement would be especially fascinating to see, because he was decidedly less sexist than most free Black men of that day. For instance, he endorsed Maria Stewart, selling her collected works at his New York bookstore.[13] As Graham Russell Gao Hodges notes, this was a two-way street: Stewart and Lydia Maria Child had been major intellectual influences on Ruggles. His support of Crandall is another sign of his nascent profeminist perspective.[14] The dismissal of his motion in support of Crandall could be due to partisan rivalry between Philadelphians and New Yorkers,[15] or increasing uneasiness with coalition efforts involving white abolitionists, or Ruggles's own sometimes acerbic style. The puzzling fact remains that the 1833 convention supported Crandall's school more forthrightly when the motion came from whites than from a Black man.

The June 1834 convention in New York City occurred a month before disastrous riots in July. A guarded optimism emerges in the minutes concerning moral reform and the expansion of antislavery societies through which "the friends of the coloured man are evidently increasing."[16] The perception of Crandall's school at this moment was one of dogged continuity despite constant harassment. The main battleground had shifted from town meetings, threatened arrests, and legal badgering of the students to mere quotidian vigilantism, which, while unpleasant, did not interfere with the purposeful studiousness of the school's attendees. Thus, the convention passed the following resolution:

> On motion of Mr. Hinton, seconded by Mr. Hughes, *Resolved*, that this Convention do most cordially approve of the disinterested and truly philanthropic course of Miss Prudence Crandall of Canterbury, Con., in her devotion to the education of female coloured youth; and we do most cheerfully commend her to the patronage and affection of the people of colour at large.[17]

The two men making this motion were notable Black educational leaders: Frederick A. Hinton of Philadelphia (though here representing Carlisle, Pennsylvania) and Benjamin F. Hughes from New York City. Hinton had been part of the New Haven Manual Labor College committee in 1831 and a strong supporter of coalition efforts between Blacks and whites.[18] His support of the Female Literary Association of Philadelphia instigated Garrison's heralding of their activities in the *Liberator* in 1831.[19] Hughes was a longtime free Black educator in New York City. He had taken over the African Free School principal position in 1831 when the white teacher Charles Andrews defected to colonizationism.[20] Hughes was a close ally of Samuel Cornish and Peter Williams Jr., so his support for Crandall here epitomizes the larger network of free Blacks concerned with educational opportunities; he was also in touch with Nathaniel Paul, Crandall's advocate among Britain's abolitionists.[21] Hughes was a pedagogical reformer who encouraged critical thinking.[22] He may well have recommended pupils to Crandall's school.[23] The support of Hughes and Hinton marks a relative normality in the existence of the academy: their motion seems matter-of-fact and faced none of the skepticism (or fear of being duplicative) that Ruggles had experienced the year before (during the school's initially beleaguered status).

The initiatives of Hinton, Hughes, and Ruggles (from the previous convention) have passed unremarked by Crandall scholars, yet this increased support of the Canterbury school by free Blacks is significant. These men were educators and activists themselves and, within the limitations of socially pervasive sexism, supportive of women's education. These free Black conventions demonstrated the priorities, values, political perspectives, and networks of antebellum Black leaders. Canterbury being a part of their agenda is another indication of the integrated support the school garnered.

Black Women's Intellectual Feasts

From the late 1820s through the 1830s, free Black women were involved in a characteristically American antebellum passion: forming organizations and associations for benevolence and reform. In the early years of the republic, benevolent organizations had remained the province of upper-class whites; invitations were necessary to join. But Jacksonian democratizing impulses spurred a new era of middle-class and grassroots organizing. Women were often in the forefront of this energy: "In 1831 the number of female mutual aid societies in the city of Philadelphia outnumbered male mutual aid societies 27 to 16."[24] The needs of the Black community were especially acute, given an alarming reduction in white assistance, and the aching human needs of a beleaguered urban Black population.

Feminist scholar Anne Boylan noted that Black women's organizing "blended benevolence, mutual aid, self-improvement, community service, and social reform in ways that defied easy categorization."[25] Take, for instance, New York City's African Dorcas Society, whose mission was to provide clothing to destitute children in the community. The Dorcas Society shared considerable membership overlap and ideological ground with the Ladies Literary Society. Almost no member of the Black community had an assured economic status; even a seemingly secure middle-class status could be destroyed through racist violence.[26] Most crucially, especially in relation to Canterbury, Black women's self-development (such as increased literacy) was not for individual self-aggrandizement: skills gained through education functioned as community resources.

African American women's agency is best spotlighted through the growth in literary societies. These groups enabled a de facto academic atmosphere in which members helped each other learn through practice, sharing, and critique. The literary societies demonstrate that Black women in Northern urban settings longed to expand their horizons, preparing the way for their eventual entry into educational institutions like Oberlin and Black colleges after the Civil War.[27]

The term "literary" did not hew to a narrow definition. Reading material often came directly from the Black and abolitionist press. A marked expansion of literary societies corresponded to the launch and life of *Freedom's Journal* and again in the early days of the *Liberator*. Garrison consistently praised the work of literary societies, both male and female, during the early 1830s. Philadelphia's (male) Colored Reading Society, founded in the 1820s, maintained subscriptions to the *Genius of Universal Emancipation* and *Freedom's Journal*.[28] There is evidence, too, that schools with Black students used the African American press as reading material; the New York Free School held a subscription to *Freedom's Journal*.[29]

The Philadelphia Female Literary Society, formed in 1831, followed a suggestion from Jocelyn that the Black women there hold "mental feasts." The accomplished women of the Forten, Bustill, and Douglass families, among others, created an elaborate formal structure, with a constitution, officers, and a structure for anonymous critique.[30] New York's Phoenix Society—another educational project spearheaded by Samuel Cornish—also featured "mental feasts" for sharing original work.[31] The success of such intellectual events was lauded in the 1833 convention report.[32] In February 1834, Elizabeth Wicks addressed the African Female Benevolent Society of Troy, and, in the midst of the national prominence of the Crandall school, she spoke of how

> the colored population are exerting themselves in every direction for the improvement and cultivation of their minds whenever they are allowed the privilege of so doing; and, my friends, I think I see an opening in behalf of our oppressed race. The dark and stormy cloud that has forever been hanging over us appears in some measure to be gradually breaking away.[33]

The Phoenix Society explicitly endorsed Crandall at their July 1833 meeting, which was attended by at least four of her endorsers—Williams, Wright, Cornish, and Bourne. This took place soon after her arrest; the Phoenix Society minutes express outrage, promising "all the aid and cooperation which they can procure" and faith that "she may carry into ample and successful execution, the arduous, and beneficial object in which she is engaged." The crosscurrents of Black community support—in this case, explicitly across gender lines as well—is obvious.[34]

"Mental feasts" consistently combined themes of elevation with abolition. One of the finest examples of this comes from September 1832, commemorating the Female Literary Society's first anniversary. The eloquence and confidence of the writer-speaker testifies to the larger goals of female education. She states that the continuity of the literary society itself aids abolition and the enslaved, for "our interests are one . . . we rise or fall together." She is equally keen to use literacy against racism: "with the powerful weapons of religion and education, we will do battle with the host of prejudice which surround us."[35]

The Literary Societies linked learning to political activity, too. The New York Female Literary Society, launched in 1834, held fairs and raised funds for the publication of the *Colored American* newspaper, showing the unity of causes and the absence of separation between individual education and community advancement.[36]

The parallels between Canterbury and these literary societies, replete with mental feasts and abolitionist politics, are immense. Similar to the literary societies, the students at Crandall's school were reading the *Liberator*—in effect, watching their own struggle rivet the nation. Black women's self-consciousness

concerning the advantages to themselves and their community in developing and displaying their mental capabilities means that the students' goals
at Crandall's academy simultaneously fulfilled individual, communal, and
political goals. These young women knew for what they were striving.

Content and Context:
Movement Writings at the Academy

The curriculum at Prudence Crandall's second academy was distinctive for
its time period, anticipating twenty-first-century inclusive pedagogies. The
Canterbury Academy incorporated writings from free Blacks as a matter of
record, since the students were reading the *Liberator* and the *Unionist*. It
also seems quite likely that Crandall included writings by women authors
(both Black and white), and in another bold move, substituted the English
Quaker pacifist Jonathan Dymond for William Paley's more conventional
moral philosophy.[37]

Materials from the abolitionist press were available at the Canterbury
Female Academy. The students came from homes that supported the *Liberator*. The Black press had as part of its raison d'être the creation of a Black
reading public.[38] What made the academy academically unique was its combination of the standard educational curriculum of white schools with the
ethos and reading materials of a Black female literary society. An added fris-
son comes from the students reading about themselves, their school, and the
ongoing struggles of their free Black communities. Given that the school's
very existence stemmed from Crandall's being provided copies of the *Liberator* by Maria Davis and that the practice of reading the abolitionist press was
already a feature in African American schools and literary societies, we can
safely assume that the students were reading the *Liberator* alongside Davis
and their teachers.[39]

The students' own writings were present in the *Liberator*. First, and most
intriguing, is an antislavery essay in the April 6, 1833, essay, most likely from
Sarah Harris. The essay early announces that God "made all men equal"
and that it is only human depravity and selfishness that permit of slavery
and oppression. The essay then takes an emotional and idiosyncratic turn
stylistically:

> Notwithstanding our highly privileged America—highly privileged did I
> say? yes, and I repeat it again—highly privileged and blessed America, (for
> it is indeed blessed above all the nations of the earth for its moral and reli-
> gious improvements,) I say, notwithstanding all the light that beams upon
> us, we have still to lament the fact, that our American people have been
> and multitudes yet are, coworkers in the awful, heaven-daring sin, that of
> enslaving and destroying millions of our African brethren.[40]

This elaborate sentence proffers a complex blend of patriotism and critique, anticipating her reader's likely response with an internal dialogue while decrying the full horrors of the slave trade and enslavement itself.

One letter and two student essays were published by the *Liberator* in the leadup to Crandall's first trial in August 1833.[41] While these published excerpts were intended to show great accomplishment and to win support for the cause, the distinctiveness of the students' own voices can still be heard. One student recounted the difficulties inherent in being a young free Black woman traveling, noting that her "ride from Hartford to Brooklyn was very unpleasant, being made up of blackguards," such that she had to walk the last five miles. This same student indulged in sarcastically opining that Canterbury is beautiful, "all that is wanting to complete the place is *civilized men*."[42] Other student comments might leave white readers squirming, stating that the majority of whites "are so prejudiced against us that they will not suffer us to come up and be sharers in any of their privileges."[43]

By the same logic, three other abolitionist publications were accessible to the students: Lydia Maria Child's *Appeal in Favor of That Class of Americans Called Africans*, John Rankin's *Letters on American Slavery*, and the pro-Crandall newspaper the *Unionist*, published in Brooklyn, Connecticut. The two pamphlets were both published in 1833; Rankin's letters to his slaveholding brother were midwifed into print by the Providence Anti-Slavery Society in which the Benson brothers and Moses Brown were active.[44]

Child's *Appeal* contains references to Crandall's school and addresses the power of prejudice in a forthright manner.[45] She writes how the presence of slavery rebounds against the free people of color, such that *"laws operate oppressively"* against those who are trying to improve themselves—a fact that every student in that school knew as their lived reality.[46] Child shared the unbridled optimism of antebellum America; even as she writes her jeremiad, she praises the benefits of education:

> Of all monopolies, a monopoly of *knowledge* is the worst. Let it be as active as the ocean—as free as the wind—as universal as sunbeams! . . . Let the sons and daughters of Africa *both* be educated, and then they will be fit for each other. . . . Shall we keep this class of people in everlasting degradation, for fear one of their descendants *may* marry our great-great-great-great-grandchild?[47]

Addressing everything from the need for white activists to eradicate prejudice, to the question of intermarriage, to the thirst for knowledge that had driven Crandall's students to flock to Canterbury, Child's *Appeal* also modeled female literary achievement.

Rankin was not (yet) as militant as Child, and conceded too much to assumptions of racial degradation. But his opening letter dealt with prejudice, arguing strenuously for environmental rather than innate reasons for the lack of achievement by African Americans. He recognized how prejudice "fetters the mind" of its victims and "prevents that expansion of soul which dignifies man."[48]

Child's and Rankin's pamphlets were insistently advertised in the *Unionist*, which sold them from its offices.[49] This newspaper, which functioned from August 1, 1833, until at least the end of the school in September 1834, was funded by Arthur Tappan and edited by Charles Burleigh in Brooklyn, Connecticut.[50] Burleigh's brother and coeditor William worked as a teacher at the academy, along with their sister Mary. Their father, Rinaldo Burleigh, was an educator who worked at two of eastern Connecticut's finest academies, Woodstock and Plainfield.[51] The *Unionist* was formed to be a pro-Crandall newspaper at the height of the crisis; its pages covered the four trials affecting Crandall and her school with meticulous attention to detail. Unfortunately, only five issues of this newspaper survive, supplemented by scattered reprints of individual articles in other contemporary newspapers.[52] But what can be gleaned from the extant copies and excerpts support its inclusion in the curriculum of Crandall's students, especially given the focus of the paper and its coeditor being a teacher at the school.

The inclusion of these movement works should not be misconstrued as vanity, as these works offered much intellectually and pedagogically. Abolitionist writings were assuredly thought-provoking examples of rhetoric; they are still fruitfully studied that way. These abolitionist works significantly broadened the curriculum beyond what existed in most academies by including male and female, Black and white, and working class as well as privileged voices.

The *Unionist*, the *Liberator,* and Child's *Appeal* all explicitly praised the English Quaker Jonathan Dymond's philosophy. His systematic *Essays on the Principles of Morality, and on the Private and Political Rights and Obligations of Mankind* (1829) insisted that Christians renounce war and violence entirely, elevating the role of martyrdom (whether symbolic or real).[53] Abolitionists applied Dymond's nonviolence to the struggle against slavery and prejudice.[54]

My claim that the students read Dymond is based on having access to his writings while they were practicing the discipline of nonviolence. In addition to the Windham Peace Society's 1832 publication of Dymond's *On the Applicability of the Pacific Principles of the New Testament to the Conduct of States and on the Limitations Which Those Principles Impose on the Rights of Self-Defence*, extracts from Dymond's larger *Essays* were first published in the *Unionist*, as frontpage articles, prior to the issuance of the book in the United States.[55]

White male abolitionist intellectuals used Dymond's philosophy to address perceived shortcomings in the moral philosophy of rationalist William Paley

(1743–1805). A heuristic comparison of Paley and Dymond would pit them as enlightenment versus romantic. Paley, a Lockean famous for his "watchmaker" God analogy, was determined to prove the existence of God teleologically, through human reason alone. Paley was also a political realist who did not look for the same level of morality from nations as from individuals. Dymond, by contrast, was committed to the example of Jesus, rejecting any expediency that would place mere human reasoning above Christ's own rejection of violence and acceptance of self-sacrifice, whether for individuals or nations.[56]

The rationales for political activism among white male Abolitionists were imbued with rejection of Paley, especially in southern New England. It began when William Channing read Dymond's work, conveying it to George Benson Sr. with the commendation that it was exemplary because of "his uncompromising morality." Benson then shared the work and these insights with the aged Moses Brown and with his local ally Samuel J. May, stating that Dymond "has expos'd Archdeacon Paley's System of Morality—which makes expediency rather than Christian principles the rule for states."[57]

May expressed the hope that Dymond's *Essays* "will every where supersede the use of Dr. Paley's Moral Philosophy, which, though it has many excellencies, has some capital defects."[58] That was in late 1833; Charles Burleigh, another Windham County Peace Society member, then undertook to start the publication process in the *Unionist*, while Garrison was teasing epigrammatic highlights from Dymond in the *Liberator*.[59]

Reading Dymond for their moral philosophy would have been quite significant for Crandall's students. In rejecting expediency as legitimate for governments, Dymond endorsed cleaving to ethical absolutes. He privileged individual agency. He outlined a theory and rationale for civil disobedience (which would explicitly influence Thoreau's more famed articulation) that the students were practicing in their daily life in Canterbury.[60] Dymond's writings enabled them to posit themselves living the spirit of the New Testament while developing critical thinking skills for themselves and the benefit of their communities.

Moral philosophy functioned as the capstone of the educational process in both academies and colleges. Therefore, the lead teacher traditionally taught it. This practice was imported by Emma Willard into the female academies. That Crandall did this would seem to stem from the testimony of the student who wrote that

> you are aware that ever since we have been under Miss Crandall's instructions, it has been her utmost care to persuade us not to indulge in angry feelings towards our enemies—with unceasing and untiring earnestness has she plead with us to forgive them—and now let us try to abide by her counsel, and feel at peace with all men.[61]

With the Windham County Peace Society publicizing and publishing Dymond, with the *Liberator* and *Unionist* following that cue, and given Crandall's combined Quaker heritage and Baptist-inspired abolition activism, she opened her students to fresh philosophic perspectives that would emerge in countless small moments in African American resistance to dehumanization, circuitously leading to King's use of analogous concepts in the twentieth-century civil rights movement.[62]

The hope to replace Paley with Dymond in schools was fated to fall short. Paley remained enshrined as a cultural norm throughout the antebellum period. From the nearby Plainfield Academy, to Emma Willard's Troy Female Seminary, and the first women's colleges of Mt. Holyoke and South Carolina Female Collegiate Institute, Paley reigned in the field of moral philosophy.[63] This makes the exception of Canterbury all the more interesting: the students were exposed to advanced progressive work in philosophy, rather than the merely conventional.

An Accomplished School:
Achievements and Ripple Effects

In late August 1833 during a drought, the well water for the school was fouled with cow manure.[64] Prudence's father carted water two miles to keep the school functioning. Constant static harassment became the norm: Whites heaped abuse on the students whenever they left the schoolhouse, and most white villagers shunned everyone associated with the school.[65]

However, as Strane pointed out, Crandall and her allies might well have felt some optimism in the late summer of 1833 "as the advantage seemed to be turning toward Prudence like a welcome tide."[66] The founding of the partisan but presciently named *Unionist* and the publication of Child's *Appeal* were visible ripples troubling the pool of white complacency. Two other less-visible incidents, though, point to even deeper stirrings. White male students at Amherst College sent Crandall a note of strong support, and the people of nearby Plainfield (across the Quinebaug from Canterbury) formed an antislavery society.

The spark and financing for the *Unionist* stemmed from a surprise visit by Tappan to Canterbury, where he consulted with May about what was needed to keep the school going and growing. Tappan visited the school himself, meeting with Crandall and her scholars. Given how many of the students were gathered through networks of known allies and friends of the Tappans, he probably had a rich understanding of who they were, but his precise recollections are not recorded.[67]

Once launched, the *Unionist* provided rhetorically strong defense of the academy. Burleigh proved an able editor who "wielded a powerful weapon" with his pen. May attested that the existence of the paper assisted "mightily."[68]

The appearance of the *Unionist* demonstrably emboldened some white people in Crandall's neighborhood. The *Unionist* announced the organization of the Plainfield Anti-Slavery Society in late August 1833.[69] With a membership of forty-three people (both men and women) and visible leadership from the Burleigh family patriarch, Rinaldo (a deacon at Plainfield's Congregational Church), this organization made it clear that there were local white stalwarts in Crandall's camp.[70] Their 1834 annual report rehearsed the entire history of slavery while boldly denouncing racism against free Blacks. Perhaps the influence of direct contact with the students led the Plainfield Society to declare that the

> ruthless persecution of Miss Crandall and her school, has given signal notoriety to the strength and virulence of the prevailing prejudice against our colored brethren, which is alternately the immediate consequence and ultimate support of that *system* of oppression, under which they suffer. Nothing perhaps has so effectually brought their conditions and their claims before the public, as the contest about the Canterbury School. Being in the immediate vicinity, this has been an object of particular interest to us; and we are happy that we are able to close our Report with stating the fact, that the attempt to crush the benevolent enterprise of Miss Crandall has failed.

This optimism—which would so soon prove incorrect (this first anniversary meeting was held around August 1834)—does not detract from the accuracy of the analysis offered in a motion by Charles Burleigh, passed unanimously, affirming human equality:

> we regard the sentiment often expressed by the opposers of abolition, that the intellectual and moral character and condition of the colored man can never be elevated in this country—that he belongs to a class *"necessarily degraded,"* by causes "which neither humanity, nor legislation nor Christianity can remove," as utterly false; as slanderous both to our colored and our white countrymen; as a libel upon the constitution and laws, and above all upon the Creator of the colored man, and upon the Christian religion.[71]

Nor was this work limited to the attendees at the meeting. The annual report mentions meetings and addresses given in eleven different eastern Connecticut towns as well as antislavery literature "freely distributed" in the county. Charles Burleigh spread the news of Plainfield and Canterbury out of state when he attended the Providence Anti-Slavery Society meeting (with George Bourne).[72]

Simultaneously, though with even less fanfare, seventy-seven Amherst College students (almost one-third of the entire student body) formed an antislavery society on July 19, 1833.[73] At their second meeting, they passed a resolution "That we view with unqualified disapprobation and utter abhorrence the barbarous treatment of Miss Crandall, and that she is justly entitled to the prayers and sympathies of the Christian community while suffering persecution for her laudable and Christian efforts to instruct the ignorant and oppressed."[74] By the beginning of 1834, the Amherst Anti-Slavery Society had denounced the American Colonization Society and aligned itself with the newborn American Anti-Slavery Society.

Among the members of the society were two nephews of Arthur and Lewis Tappan, but the most daring participant was Humphrey Morse, who sometime in the fall of 1833 visited Canterbury to see conditions there for himself. His tantalizing entry in the minutes indicates that he used his white-skin privilege (and local anonymity) to hear an unfiltered version of what the opposition was saying. His brief report mentions he "had visited Miss C. and conversed with her neighbors—he mentioned some anecdotes—illustrating the bitter prejudice and persecution which were common in that part of Conn."[75] Morse's life was destined to be quite short; he died in 1836, not even two years after graduating from Amherst. But being "among the first to espouse the Anti-Slavery cause" stands out in his Amherst College alumni entry.[76]

The Amherst College Anti-Slavery Society survived only a few years. In 1835 college President Heman Humphrey squelched it. The students' connection to the American Anti-Slavery Society was too controversial for a college that drew students from the South, so Humphrey disbanded it, claiming it "inexpedient to keep up any organization, under the name of Anti-Slavery, Colonization or the like, in our literary and theological institutions."[77] But the awareness demonstrated by those seventy-seven students remained.[78]

Despite the pushback from "gentlemen of standing" like Humphrey, a slow turning of the tide of white public opinion had begun. Crandall's imprisonment had amplified the cause. The recruitment of the Burleighs to the movement; the Amherst students; the publication of writings by women like Lydia Maria Child—all pointed to the swing of a heavy pendulum. An increasing number of antislavery societies traced their formation to the 1833–34 period corresponding to Crandall's school.[79] While Canterbury was clearly not the sole cause for this effect, it was among the most visible galvanizing forces at that moment.

At the annual meeting of the New England Anti-Slavery Society, held in Boston in May 1834, one can see all the strands coming together: whites and Blacks, men and women, and people across generations. Moses Brown sent his greetings and his organizational enthusiasm from Providence, while the Amherst Anti-Slavery Society students were present (including Humphrey Morse). Garrison, May, George Bourne, and George Benson Jr. were present from among Crandall's endorsers as well as Charles Burleigh. Prudence Crandall basked in absentia in her lifetime membership accorded her, her name sharing the page with everyone from Brown and William Wilberforce to free Black Bostonians like Susan Paul and John Remond.[80] Nathan Winslow

(1785–1861), a Quaker from Maine, brought a resolution of commendation for female antislavery societies, adding a rhetorical flourish that found "the general cooperation of American females, in the sacred cause of emancipation, essential to the overthrow of slavery in this republic."[81] Paul, daughter of minister Thomas Paul, came with her Black students, who performed a hymn.[82] As Lois Brown persuasively argues, having these students sing about racism, colonizationism, and slavery literally showed African American youth "as free people of color and as agents of change in antebellum America."[83]

At this high point of success, support for Crandall's school was plentiful, including many "new recruits in this glorious war."[84] The report from the Plainfield society, presumably written by either May or Charles Burleigh, is more specific—and revealing. It paints a bleak picture of eastern Connecticut at the dawn of 1833, where only "two or three colored persons in the vicinity took the Liberator, but scarcely any body, except colored people, thought the paper worth reading."[85] The report then describes how Crandall's school awakened many more:

> The violence of opposition which was at once roused . . . served to defeat its own object. . . . Several who were at first strongly opposed to Miss Crandall's scheme, and to the Abolitionists . . . are now our most zealous and active Abolitionists; and one at least of this class may be found in the delegation from our Society to this Convention. . . . Converts were made to the Abolition faith.[86]

Among those converts were Vincent Hinckley (ca. 1781–1864), a lawyer in Plainfield, and his son Albert (1811–64), who was part of the Amherst Anti-Slavery Society. Vincent Hinckley, a personal friend of William Lloyd Garrison, became the vice president of the Plainfield Anti-Slavery Society and later of the Windham County organization.[87] Albert Hinckley visited Crandall's school often and testified during the August 1833 trial.[88]

What Maria Davis, Sarah Harris, and Prudence Crandall had started was burgeoning. This can be taken as a sign that their enemies did not succeed. No matter when or how the school was closed, the "violence served to defeat its own object."

How did this pendulum swing affect the students? From their vantage, being simultaneously subject to the catcalls of the village boys while also reading the good news from the *Liberator* and the *Unionist*, they must have perceived that change was occurring, and knew they were playing a part in making it happen. They also would have known that Crandall took the development of their minds seriously. For instance, during the first trial, Eliza Parkis, a young Black woman hired to do washing and housework for Crandall, was called to testify. Parkis said that Crandall employed her because "she did not wish to keep her scholars out of school to do work."[89] This means that, contrasted with manual-labor pedagogy, Crandall was eager to give Black women students the chance to develop their minds without suffering under "a load of iron pots and kettles."[90]

However, she could not shield them from all distractions thrust upon the school. From August 1833 to August 1834, four separate legal trials would hammer the skiff of the school. The students proved themselves capable mariners through these storms.

CHAPTER 7

Students on Trial

Thrice Inside the Courtroom

> It was to be expected that our white negro haters would seek our degradation, it is their habit to do so.
> —Frederick Douglass

Legal proceedings are staged to be intimidating: courtrooms relentlessly brandish the coercive power of the state. The trappings of uniforms, titles, and protocols, coupled with gamesmanship between judge, lawyers, and juries, render the setting unique. In antebellum America, the rights of white women and of all free Blacks were explicitly restricted in the law and courtroom, where high-status white men held all official roles. The Black students of Canterbury performed multiple times in this alien theater and did so with grace, composure, and success.

When the trials came, Prudence Crandall's coteachers, friends, students, and supporters were endangered along with her. Fortunately, her legal team was superb, an all-star cast of white male juridical thinkers. So insightful was their logic in defense of African American citizenship that it resurfaced in two of the most important cases in American legal history: overruled by the Taney court in its infamous Dred Scott decision (1857) and then positively affirmed by future US Supreme Court justice Thurgood Marshall and the NAACP lawyers in *Brown v. Board* (1954).[1]

The First Trial: August 1833

Previous chapters analyze the incorporation of significant alliances across lines of difference—among Black and white women, among Black and white Abolitionist men, within Black communities and families. The trials highlight another significant strand of allies—white men with significant political and legal power using their privilege to defend African American women's citizenship.

Henry Strong, Calvin Goddard, and William W. Ellsworth were Crandall's legal team for the first trial. William Wolcott Ellsworth (1791–1868), a congressman and noted constitutional expert, was the son of Oliver Ellsworth, third chief justice of the United States.[2] William Ellsworth became Connecticut's governor in 1838 and a state Supreme Court of Errors justice from 1847 to 1861.[3] Ellsworth's marriage to Emily Webster brought him a father-in-law of repute, Noah Webster. William Ellsworth was indubitably a member of the ruling-class elite, yet he used his position to establish arguments for Black citizenship and education.[4] Unlike many white Abolitionists, Ellsworth hired a young Black man, Holdridge Primus, from a prominent free Black family in Hartford.[5]

Calvin Goddard (1768–1842) had been mayor of Norwich and a US congressman.[6] As a Congregationalist, Goddard would have known many free Blacks in Norwich, including the Harris and Olney families, perhaps adding impetus to Goddard's resolve in pursuing this case.[7] Henry Strong (1788–1852), an "exact . . . profound and comprehensive" lawyer, also had connections to Norwich. Early in life he had operated a school for women.[8]

The constitutional implications of the case for Black citizenship constructed by Ellsworth, Goddard, and Strong have been analyzed effectively by Donald Williams in *Prudence Crandall's Legacy*. Therefore, my focus will be the subjective and objective positions of Crandall's Black students.

The students were present at the first trial as witnesses, a situation of grave danger. Their legal status as women was already dubious, and the status of free Blacks was precisely what was under discussion. The officials in the courtroom—judge, prosecutors, and attorneys—were all white men. The invective that Andrew Judson showed during the trial proceedings toward Crandall in particular, Blacks in general, and the Black students especially, resulted from a license he had granted himself in drafting and securing passage of the Black Law.

While the (self-)select(ed)men had decided against whipping Eliza Hammond, they did not intend to leave the students legally unmolested. The students were the subject of the trial, *subject* to the decisions of the court. They had to sit through arguments denying the citizenship rights of all free Blacks—including those who, like their families, had achieved a measure of respectability. Simultaneously the students had to "represent" their race, their comportment a performative refutation of the racism surrounding them. Being watched by a bevy of white men likely evoked uneasy echoes of the plight of enslaved Black women on the auction block.

As Elizabeth McHenry eloquently states, "Black Americans did not wait for legislative rulings to confirm their American identities."[9] These young women conducted themselves with a confidence beyond their years. Their abilities and ease in the situation helped the lawyers make the case. At stake were both female and Black citizenship.

For the first trial, held in Brooklyn on August 22–23, 1833,[10] subpoenas had been issued against students from outside of Connecticut whose names were known: Theodosia DeGrasse, Ann Peterson, Ann/Amelia (both names are used in court documents) Elizabeth Wilder, Catharine Ann Weldon, and Ann Eliza Hammond. Wilder returned home because of her mother's illness; the prosecution was annoyed by what they thought an evasion.[11] Weldon appears to have been a last-minute substitution for the missing Wilder. Connecticut resident Eliza Glasko, while not technically "illegal" as a student, was forced to testify to bolster the prosecution case.

Peterson was the first Black student called. Before she could testify, though, Crandall intervened, saying witnesses were unnecessary, because she would admit to breaking the law. But the cruelty toward the students was the intent of the prosecution, so they ignored the defendant. Before Peterson could speak, another white ally tried to shield the students: the lead attorney for the defense, William Ellsworth. He pointed out how, if an out-of-town student were to testify, it would create a situation of self-incrimination, forbidden by the Constitution. Ellsworth aimed to protect the students as much as possible while raising the jury's doubts concerning the Black Law's constitutionality. Ellsworth likely anticipated the countermove by the prosecutors: the lead lawyer for the prosecution, Jonathan Welch, read the third section of the Black Law that compelled the students to be witnesses: "Any person, not an inhabitant of this state, who shall reside in any town therein, for the purpose of being instructed as aforesaid, shall be an admissible witness in all prosecutions under the first section of this act, and may be compelled to give testimony therein." Ellsworth now struck directly at the constitutionality issue, doubting "the competency of the Legislature to compel a witness to testify, or to answer a question that might implicate him. . . . It was contrary to fundamental principles" of the nation for "the testimony of the witness" to "subject her to the penalties imposed by Statute."[12]

This was no mere legal gamesmanship; Ellsworth sought to unmask the spiteful malice drafted into the law. Judson fell into this trap, seizing the reins of the prosecution to argue that the students would not be charged with any crime. Surmising this wasn't convincing, he fell back on the law's own recognizance: "At all events . . . in this instance . . . the Legislature had expressly enacted that the pupils should be witnesses." Ellsworth drily replied to this tautology: "the question (is) whether the Legislature possess the power to compel a witness to convict himself." Ellsworth thus demonstrated how the law had been *designed* to humiliate the students at Crandall's school. It would place them in legal jeopardy that would either intimidate them into not testifying, or into leaving the school, or if they were brave enough to testify, into incriminating themselves. Judson was revealed as a bully in the legislature, a bully in the courtroom, and a bully in his neighborhood. Even though Judson won the legal point—Judge Joseph Eaton decided that the students could testify—Ellsworth had won a moral victory by questioning the Black Law's constitutionality, which induced Judson to expose his rancor.[13]

What were the Black women students experiencing during this drama? Knowing one's every action is used to "judge" one's "people" is an anxiety-provoking burden of being in a marginalized group. The students assuredly knew that their behavior would send signals to the jury, press, and spectators. They sought to disprove, in their very persons, the overheated rhetoric concerning free Blacks as a source of "injury" to the people of Connecticut. The students, having sought a place of learning, came equipped with the discipline to excel on the courtroom's political stage. The lawyers for Crandall had explained their strategy, and the students responded with a fine performance. The reporter from Hartford's *Connecticut Courant* broadcast their success, remarking that the students "were inferior to no others, in their conduct, language and appearance."[14]

The *Liberator* had published an essay earlier from one of Crandall's pupils (who, following female modesty codes, remained anonymous). Presented as a communication to her sister students in Canterbury, she reminds them, "It is very necessary that we all have the principle of forgiveness instilled into our hearts." She indicates both religious and social reasons for preferring forgiveness to suspicion or envy. But when she begins her second paragraph, this student-author makes a cogent racial analysis:

> We as a body, my dear schoolmates, are subject to many trials and struggles, and we all know to what they are attributable—it is the prejudice the whites have against us that causes us to labor under so many disadvantages. They are so prejudiced against us that they will not suffer us to come up and be sharers in any of their privileges. Oh, prejudice! prejudice!—Heaven grant thy reign may be short. My friends, although the white people may be so enraged against us as to try to break down every benevolent effort that is made in our behalf, and put every obstacle they can in our way to prevent our rising to an equal standard with themselves. . . . Let us be careful that we do not return evil for evil, but recompense it with good.[15]

The student does not mitigate her analysis with reference to those whites who are helping. This is key, not because the student was disregarding what Crandall and her supporters had tried to accomplish (the rest of the letter demonstrates that) but because she was exempting her allies from the category of "the whites" at that moment. This is implicit in her phrase, "we as a body," to describe those being subject "to many trials"—including an all-too-literal one. It is also interesting that the student—like Maria Stewart—makes prejudice the greater factor than slavery (which is not even mentioned) in creating and sustaining the oppression of African Americans.

The student essayist reveals that Crandall had been teaching the students nonviolent resistance:

> You are aware that ever since we have been under Miss Crandall's instructions, it has been her utmost care to persuade us not to indulge in angry feelings towards our enemies—with unceasing and untiring earnestness has she plead with us to forgive them—and now let us try to abide by her counsel, and feel at peace with all men.[16]

One can almost feel the student trying to convince herself, and her sister students, that this "unceasing and untiring" forgiveness is the best policy, tacitly admitting some frustration. The content of this student essay is corroborated in Simeon Jocelyn's obituary sketch of Harriet Lanson who "never uttered, to my knowledge, one unkind word towards the people of Canterbury; and . . . states that she is sorry for one of the principal persecutors of the school."[17] This was no mere garden-variety piety: it was a religiously inspired strategic attitude honed under actual persecution, amid daily insults intended to rouse resentment. The students' pacifist principles were a demanding, shared discipline, inculcated from religion in general and the school's instructors in particular.

A letter that Sarah Harris wrote soon after the trial reveals more about the students' perspective. First, she indicates that she was one of ten students present, despite the fact that the Black Law would not have applied to her as a Connecticut resident. She "was much pleased with Mr. Ellsworth's plea. He defended Miss Crandall's case eloquently inasmuch as he caused the jury to disagree, and of course, it was not decided." There is a sly pragmatism here, as Harris hints that the impact of Ellsworth's defense is judged by its effect. She then adds her hope that this and future court proceedings "will awaken the minds of people, and will cause the subject to be investigated by many—yes the proceeding of the Canterburians have given an impetus to our cause, and I trust will be the means of arousing the nations to their duty with respect to the condition of our colored population, and be the means of allaying the prejudice of Americans."[18]

In the 1950s and 1960s, King's principles of nonviolence were crucial to the success of the civil rights movement. These principles of nonviolence and passive resistance had to be taught, members of the movement had to be trained, and it was not always easy for participants to adhere to them.[19] Apparently, Crandall was engaged in a similar sort of teaching, inspired by Dymond, the peace movement, and the first inchoate stirrings of nonresistance within the abolition movement. Coteacher William Burleigh was a member of the

Windham County Peace Society and had launched his literary and political career with a poem published in the American Peace Society's *Calumet* periodical in 1832.[20] Their Black students were likely inspired by a different set of sources, starting from their communities and churches. As Samuel Ringgold Ward commented, "What class of whites, except the Quakers, ever spoke of *their* oppressors or wrongdoers as mildly as we do" of the whites who practice an "ever-present, ever-crushing Negro-hate?"[21] Canterbury merits a place in the annals of nonviolence as well as Black rights and women's education. The fact remains, to the great credit of the students as individuals and as a group, that not once did a student say or do anything to draw the ire of the village onto them—other than merely being in Canterbury to learn.

Judge Eaton overruled Ellsworth's objections; the students were "not protected, but must be examined." As Peterson went to the witness box, Ellsworth rose again, announcing "the witness had been advised not to answer interrogatories in regard to her knowledge of this School," due to his conscientious belief that the witness "could not be compelled to testify." In any nonresistant strategy, the difficulty arises when one is challenged. Despite the noncooperation that Ellsworth predicted, the prosecution went ahead and questioned Peterson. The interrogation included many specific questions—five "principal" ones are recorded in the trial transcript. But Peterson refused to answer any of them, replying that "she could not (answer them) without criminating herself."[22]

Frustrated by Peterson, the prosecution decided to test the mettle of some other students. Weldon and Hammond were called. They performed exactly as Peterson had, refusing to answer the questions posed, giving the same reason. The increasingly irritated prosecution "reserved . . . the right of moving that these witnesses be committed for a contempt of Court." Judson had stage-managed the Black Law to bring about this courtroom showdown, but these young Black women defanged the bully.[23]

What followed was a string of nonstudent witnesses. Even after Crandall's preacher, Levi Kneeland, was briefly jailed for contempt of court, the testimony the witnesses delivered fell short of proving the facts of the case. The prosecution became desperate enough to try an end around to the wall of silence from the students. They had to bring a student who was a Connecticut resident to testify; this required a new subpoena and a ride to Canterbury and back for a sheriff to bring Eliza Glasko to court. Despite not being as fully counseled as the others, she, too, "declined answering the questions propounded to her." At the breaking point, the prosecution called for Glasko to be jailed for contempt of court; the paperwork was set in motion. Finally the prosecution called another witness—a surprise to all—Mary Benson, one of the daughters of George Benson Sr. She was not in a position to have any plausible reason for silence, as she could not self-incriminate. Thus, she became the one who, however unwillingly, gave the prosecution what they wanted: evidence of Crandall teaching and boarding students known to be from outside of Connecticut.

Happy with their case, the prosecution rested. The sheriff prepared to cart Glasko off to prison, when Ellsworth "interposed and stated to the court that rather than have the girl committed he should advise her to testify again repeating that the course of the defendant's counsel in relation to the testimony of these girls, was dictated by an imperious sense of professional duty."[24] Ellsworth took the fall for the students here, protesting that their silence was ordered by him. His chivalric rhetoric was likely believed by the white men in the court, due to racist and sexist presumptions. But what Ellsworth did here was real: Glasko's reputation would not be sullied with resistance to the justice system or prison; Ellsworth acknowledged his vast professional latitude by recognizing these dynamics.

Glasko first stated the facts: yes, she was a student, as were the other women who refused to speak earlier. She identified their out-of-state hometowns and the subjects Crandall taught. To highlight the absurdity of calling the education they were receiving a crime, she concluded with piety: "The school was usually opened and closed with prayer—the scriptures were read and explained, daily, in her school—some portions were committed to memory by the pupils, and considered a part of their education." The students who appeared in the court—Peterson, Weldon, Hammond, and Glasko—demonstrated their solidarity, fortitude, and intelligence in comprehending the situation. None of them broke, or wavered emotionally, despite the full force of this all-white, all-male courtroom ranged against them. Men of power, wealth and unquestioned "respectability" were made to look like the bullies they were against four dignified "young ladies of color." These students stood ready to go to prison if need be. They declined any easy use of sentimental femininity, embracing instead what they had seen their teacher model. The student essayist had described how religion "supported our teacher amidst her trials, and when confined in this county prison, she could bear that bitter cup of persecution with patience and resignation."[25] The implication—that the students were prepared to follow her—shows in their behavior at the trial.

The plea from piety that Glasko made had an additional resonance behind it: Crandall and her students had recently been barred from attending the Congregational Church near the school. Crandall had originally intended to have preachers come to the house, but when that became logistically difficult, she "considered that I had done entirely wrong in depriving my scholars of the privilege of attending religious worship in this village."[26] She said she had been given permission to bring the scholars, though they would be confined to the balcony, the section normally reserved for Black attendees at those Northern white churches that allowed their attendance. However, in this case, the balcony would have been insufficient, and so the back pews were also opened: "Dr. Harris . . . said we might occupy the seat in the gallery appropriated to colored persons. Mr. Hough then remarked that the seat would not be sufficient for the scholars—Deacon Bacon then replied, that we might take the next pews until we had enough to be seated."[27] This original liberality, stingy though it was, evaporated. The students were banned.[28]

The *Unionist* ensured that this exclusion would be publicized. The *Connecticut Courant,* whose trial reporter had been won over to the school's cause, published the story: "Miss Crandall's pupils cannot attend public worship on the Sabbath, in the only church within three miles of Miss C's residence. . . . And this in a land professedly christian, in a State which boasts of its benevolent efforts to diffuse the blessings of the gospel among the distant heathen."[29] The students knew that their very *presence* in a house of worship in Canterbury had generated vituperation—and yet they were able to face these very same men, assembled in the courthouse to humiliate them. Such resolution commands respect.

Once testimony was completed, everyone listened to the closing arguments from Judson, Ellsworth, Strong, and Welch. These white men knew each other, their social circles overlapping from birth to college to the practice of law and politics. But for Crandall's Black women students, from their doubly disadvantaged status, hearing the prosecution's arguments against Black citizenship was likely traumatic: in the land of their birth, they listened as their citizenship was disparaged by those who held the power to shape it. Imagining them in that situation, with their real-time subjective responses to it, all the while needing to maintain the discipline of passive resistance and knowing that their every move, gesture, eye roll, or yawn was being monitored (teenagers often being indifferent to disguising their reactions), this can only be described as valiant.

Judson went first with his summation. Recognizing the impact of Ellsworth's attack on the constitutionality of the Black Law, he rushed to the law's defense. He painted a disingenuous picture of benign local authority where schools were under "the care and supervision of the select men and civil authority of each town."[30] His intent, though, was unveiled when he said that "the sole intention . . . of the act was, that colored persons, from another jurisdiction, should not be intruded into any town in this state, without a written permission from the select men." The verb "intrude" means to appear where one is unwanted; here it implies that the students are objects in a larger scheme designed by other actors, for the verb is used passively. Judson does not say that "colored persons are intruding" themselves but that they are *being intruded.* Not only would Judson actively deny that the students and their families are citizens but he also now stripped them of the agency that they had so ably demonstrated.[31]

Judson pressed on into increasingly thorny territory. He claimed the Black law was not as bad as prejudicial laws in other states and then added that it can't be unconstitutional because Blacks are not citizens and therefore are unprotected by constitutional guarantees.

As the students, subject to the laws of the nation and the decisions of this court, listened to this denial of their birthright citizenship, Judson was seduced by his own rhetoric. Claiming that the "public safety of this State, the preservation of its true interests, required this law to be enforced," he made a slippery-slope argument: the Southern states might send all their emancipated slaves "to Connecticut instead of Liberia," "overwhelming" the Nutmeg State's character. Judson's language revealed that the "true interests" of the State of Connecticut excluded the interests of Black people. When Judson veered into paranoid talk about the recent British West Indies emancipation, even the pro–Black Law Judge Eaton had to intervene to stop him. Perhaps embarrassed that he had conflated the courtroom with a stump speech, Judson corralled his fearmongering. He reminded the jury that even one instance of an out-of-state student was sufficient to convict Crandall and then rested his case.

Ellsworth began by conceding the facts: "True it was, the defendant has kept this school—'twas no secret, and whether that constituted a crime or not was for the jury to determine."[32] He asked the jury to decide if Crandall's actions were protected by a "higher power." Ellsworth let this phrase resonate in the jury's ears by suggesting that the law violated the Constitution, "the highest power known in our land."[33] Ellsworth masterfully played on the congruence between the American Revolutionary heritage and the shared Christian religiosity of the community. The testimony of the students came into high relief near the end of his remarks, when Ellsworth rhetorically inquired of the jury and echoed Eliza Glasko's testimony, "Were they prepared to say that teaching the Word of God was a crime? That it was a crime to teach children the Bible?"[34]

Ellsworth addressed the legal arguments forthrightly. Noting that Judson had made citizenship dependent on complexion, Ellsworth insisted it could only consist of birth or naturalization. He said that to deny birthright citizenship or limit it only to those granted the franchise would "denationalize" all women (white or Black). This made the question of female citizenship and the double burden carried by Black women visible. Judson's argument, Ellsworth contended, would also make a mockery of any nonvoting resident who appealed to the courts for redress. Ellsworth presciently surmised that the definition of citizenship would vex the nation for some time to come, foreshadowing the potential for this case to have abiding significance.[35]

Ellsworth then raised the obvious problem lodged in any exclusionary law that singles out an identifiable group: if the principle is allowed to pass unchallenged, it can be turned against any group, including the majority. Ellsworth says, what would stop Connecticut from erecting walls against the entry of all citizens from New York State? Or barring Roman Catholics from schooling?[36]

Having established these constitutional points, he could not refrain from disputing Judson's picture of the selectmen as benign. Ellsworth countered that placing permission for a Black Academy in the hands of local civic authority "was a mere parade of liberality—the select men of Canterbury would sooner shed their blood than grant Miss Crandall permission to keep this school. The power to license . . . is the power to deny."[37]

One of the linchpin texts for Ellsworth was the iconic Declaration of Independence; its citation by Crandall's lawyer doubtless reverberated with the students. The Declaration of Independence was vitally important to free Blacks; David Walker demanded:

> See your Declaration Americans!!! Do you understand your own language? Hear your language, proclaimed to the world, July 4th, 1776—"We hold these truths to be self evident—that ALL MEN ARE CREATED EQUAL!!![38]

Likewise, white abolitionists highlighted the glaring contradiction between the Declaration's bold claims of human rights and equality and the maintenance of slavery in the United States. In his 1832 *Thoughts on African Colonization*, Garrison proclaimed, "As long as there remains among us a single copy of the Declaration of Independence, or of the New Testament, I will not despair of the social and political elevation of my sable countrymen."[39]

Just as tellingly, those opposed to Black equality expressed increasing disdain for the "infidel, atheistic, French Revolution, Red Republican principle(s)" in the Declaration of Independence, the "bitter root of all our evils."[40] Southern ideologues excoriated the idealism of the Declaration. John C. Calhoun lambasted Jefferson's "false view" that people were equally capable of self-government, and George Fitzhugh pronounced the Declaration "absurd" and "dangerous."[41] Castigation of the Declaration had long Southern roots. Slaveowners in Virginia had objected to both the Virginia Declaration of Rights and the national Declaration of Independence when they were proposed in 1776:

> As soon as George Mason read the words of the preamble he had drafted to the Constitution, a bitter dispute arose over the clause "all men are by nature equally free and independent." Most planters objected, terming the words a "forerunner of civil convulsion," holding out the danger that Negroes would use them to claim their freedom. But the defenders of the clause, also slaveowners, insisted that there was no reason for the fear since the words did not apply to Negroes, who were not "constituent members" of the new independent state and nation about to be formed.[42]

In his summation Ellsworth makes these dual perspectives on the Declaration explicit. Either it means what it means literally—equality for all people—or the disguised segregated intent should be revealed by inserting the phrase "'except black people' . . . between each clause." Ellsworth hoped Judson "was not so ashamed of his republicanism" to edit the Declaration;[43] Judson's reply would emerge at the second trial.

When Ellsworth concluded by saying that "my appeal is to THE PEOPLE, and to THE PEOPLE I leave my client," the genuine breadth of the change possible in America might have broken through like a ray of sun from a storm cloud. In Ellsworth's "civic universalism," "the people" included not only the white men of the jury but everyone—Black and white, female and male—in that courtroom.[44] The Black students must have felt their worlds coming together: the world of their parents and free Black communities; the world as seen on the pages of the *Liberator* that valued the opinions and ideas of Black and white, women and men; the world of Canterbury where they were a part of an interracial experiment and witnesses to the pitched battle between a cognitive minority of whites who supported Black humanity and the vast majority who bitterly opposed civil rights.[45] The students could hear echoes of David Walker in Ellsworth's defense of their teacher and their education.

Henry Strong, Crandall's other lawyer, started by drawing the attention more squarely upon Crandall herself than Ellsworth had "a culprit is here arraigned—a female— . . . charged with giving instruction, but there was no pretence that she has inculcated bad principles. Her crime consisted in this, that she had given light to those who were in mental darkness."[46] He then contrasted two distinctly different laws passed in 1833—the outlawing of slavery in the British Empire and the Black Law of Connecticut. Next, he turned the jury's attention to the students whose testimony and behavior they had witnessed: "[Strong] rejoiced that her pupils had been before the jury, and that they had had opportunities of seeing them. Were they not worthy of being instructed? Had not the defendant entirely deferred to public sentiment, in relation to keeping the races separate?" The deportment of the students had exploded the myth of intellectual inferiority axiomatically presumed by the prosecution. Strong's point concerning Crandall's decision to switch to an all-Black student body was most likely meant to reveal the prosecution's insincerity. Strong exposed that deep hypocrisy in pointing out that the Black Law "does not prevent colored persons from coming to this State . . . for any earthly purpose except education."

Strong restated the citizenship argument: by the adoption of the federal Constitution "we were made one people." Judson and the legislature were borrowing the nullification strategy of South Carolina by claiming that Connecticut could make a law that would defy the Constitution. Strong hit a rich vein here: segregationist logic throughout American history relies on state's rights arguments, wryly suggesting, "A portion of our countrymen might wish to raise the Palmetto Banner, but the eagle and the stripes were our badge."[47]

Strong builds the argument for Black citizenship upon past practice, Black military service, and common sense, such as the fact that free Blacks could sue in court as citizens, not aliens. With his famed eye for detail, he deciphered and deconstructed many of Judson's examples of why Blacks should not be considered citizens. Strong dramatically pointed to the Black students, asking how the state legislature could decree that Glasko could and Hammond could not choose Crandall's academy for their education? By asking this question, Strong was tangentially assessing the performance of these two witnesses as demonstrating equal poise and the manifest usefulness of educating these two young women, who were obviously benefitting from their upbringing (demonstrating the respectability of their families) and their education. Presumably, the idea that these women might become charges on the town or lead a mass immigration of criminals to Canterbury appeared ludicrous in light of their poised performances.

Ellsworth and Strong laid the groundwork for future cases dealing with Black citizenship. The presence in the courtroom of Black women, hearing these arguments and giving the jury, prosecutors, and judges a living example of the people whose fates were being decided, deserves acknowledgment. The case is often reported as being about Crandall, but she never testified for either the prosecution or the defense. She was a silent witness, while her students spoke and (so to say) acquitted themselves. While the Black Law had been written to intimidate the students by compelling their testimony, the strategy boomeranged.

The final attorney to make closing arguments was Jonathan Welch. Compared to the previous three, his summation contains little remarkable: he defended the constitutionality of the law and said that Crandall could appeal if convicted here. He warned against sympathy for the defendant on the basis of gender and, oddly enough, conceded the fact of female citizenship when he did so, saying that her being a woman "altered not her rights. She had the same and none other rights, than every citizen."[48] He was not nearly so generous, though, about Black citizenship, which he felt was nowhere established; he even read the definition of "citizen" from the dictionary of Noah Webster—likely to needle Ellsworth's family connection to the lexicographer—to prove that Blacks were not within it. He used the laws against interracial marriage to advance his argument against Black citizenship. He also suggested that the defense team had reverted to the unconstitutionality of the law as the reason to acquit only after the evidence of the case against Crandall had been established despite their "closing the mouths of witnesses." It took "the grating doors" of the prison to "open dumb mouths."

This reference to the heavy-handed techniques of the prosecution seems a blunder on Welch's part.[49]

Welch made no reference to the students, and when he spoke of Black people, he was patronizing, ultimately issuing a dismissive rejection of Black citizenship. The students sat through this, too, with the knowledge that Welch's statements and the charge of the judge would be the last speeches the jury would hear. At the end of this long and literally trying day, they could not flinch, or look distracted, or show their anger. Their discipline again had to convey their humanity, and apparently it did. The jury returned three times, finally admitting "that there was no probability that they should ever agree." The vote was 7-5 for conviction.[50]

Because the decision was not unanimous, the case was sent forward to the next term of the Windham County Court. The official announcement set that for December,[51] but Judson and his allies were so anxious to see the school closed that they worked the machinery of the legal world to advance the date to early October, much to the surprise of Crandall's defense team and allies. Even without that change of schedule, though, the looming threat of a court-ordered end to the school, coupled with the constant vigilante harassment, must have added to the urgency with which the students and teachers in Canterbury pursued their studies.

The Second Trial: Restricting the Students' Agency

Judson was livid about the hung jury in the August trial. He had no intention of waiting—and allowing Crandall's school to operate—until December. He moved quickly and stealthily, acquiring new evidence and having Crandall arrested on September 26, 1833.[52] The selectmen had learned not to present a public relations boon to the abolitionists: two of Crandall's enemies paid bond to prevent her accruing more martyr points in jail.[53]

As Donald Williams analyzes, Judson intended to besmirch Crandall's credibility and character in this round.[54] The treatment of Crandall—trying to make her less sympathetic to the next jury—was not related to the facts of the case at all.[55] This was gratuitous character assassination by Judson and allies, who made sure that it was published widely. He obtained a letter from Richard Fenner stating that Crandall had deceived him about the purpose of her trip to Boston in January 1833.[56] Far worse, though, was Judson's attempt to instigate betrayal between two Black women. He obtained a letter from a young Black woman, Mary Barber, casting aspersions on how the school started, denying Sarah Harris's agency and reducing the academy to a white abolitionist plot.

Transparent though it may be, Judson's strategy created some flimsy counterevidence to Crandall's and Harris's version of events from the previous fall. Barber's testimony befuddled some scholars who examined Crandall's life, in particular Edwin Small and Miriam Small, who appear to have accepted it at face value.[57] More recent scholars—Strane and Donald Williams—have seen through it, the result of an improved understanding of race and gender dynamics. But if we look at the letter from the viewpoint of how it affected the Black women at the school, more dimensions of their resilience emerge.

Barber indicated in her September 10 letter to the court that she and Harris had both been live-in servants in the family of Jedediah Shepherd when

> Sarah informed me that she had been up to the House of Prudence Crandall, and Prudence Crandall enquired of her what her education was, she said in reply that it was but poor. She said that Miss Crandall then invited her to come to her school, and become a scholar with her white scholars and she would instruct her so that in 9 months or a year she could teach school. She further added during the same conversation that she never should have thought of going if Miss Crandall had not proposed it to her and she had concluded to go. Having understood that Sarah was to have been married at the ensuing Thanksgiving, an allusion was made to that circumstance, where Sarah replied, that she had given up that engagement and meant now to qualify herself to teach school and go to New Haven and take one. She said she felt very grateful to Miss Crandall, for she should not have thought of such a thing, if it had not been for her invitation.[58]

There are abundant reasons to be skeptical of this testimony. It disputes a conversation between Harris and Crandall to which Barber was neither privy nor present. Second, far from upsetting Harris's wedding plans, her wedding was still scheduled for November. Third, and most damaging, were the questions of how and why this testimony was produced at this moment in time. Williams suggests that "Judson and the prosecution clumsily influenced Barber's statement or perhaps drafted it themselves."[59]

Barber's testimony against Harris and Crandall was intended to *disempower* Harris, in order to assign the school's origins to a white person. Barber's testimony struck at the Black impetus for the school and the Black-white cooperation that had so marked its course to this moment. It tried to accomplish this by setting one Black woman's word against another. The classic divide-and-conquer stratagem was here aided (and abetted) by the stereotypical refusal of white people to believe that Blacks could create anything important. Peter Williams Jr. and David Walker both had their authorship questioned when their literary productions were considered too refined to have been written by Black men.[60] In this tangled web of racist and sexist assumptions, we have a removal of agency from one Black woman by another, likely at the prodding of white men of power, in order to cast responsibility onto a white woman.

The second trial, also held in Brooklyn, took place over two days. The speed with which it was called meant that some of Crandall's strongest supporters were not present, including May and Ellsworth. Her defense team this time consisted of Strong and Goddard, while the prosecution featured the perpetually rabid Judson and the esteemed Chauncey Cleveland.[61] The biggest difference, though, was the judge.

Chief justice of the Connecticut State Supreme Court of Errors, David Daggett (1764–1851) was a legal superstar at this point in his storied career. A cofounder of Yale Law School, his résumé included service in Connecticut's General Assembly, the US Senate, and mayor of New Haven.[62]

His fawning memorialist wrote that in Daggett's early career as a Federalist he had "political control of the State."[63] Once the Federalist party faded, Daggett was involved in organizing a Connecticut auxiliary to the American Colonization Society in 1818.[64] One of New Haven's most prominent residents, he was a vociferous opponent of the proposed Black college.[65]

Daggett did not wear his prominence lightly; on the contrary, he intimidated those around him. This would become meaningful in both the second and third trials and beyond to the Dred Scott decision.[66]

Frustratingly, even the pro-Crandall forces were less enthusiastic about recording the proceedings of the second trial: we do not have an official list of witnesses.[67] On the first day of the trial, October 3, the evidence was presented, and the attorneys gave their summaries.

The lack of discussion concerning the evidentiary phase of the trial has been explained by previous Crandall scholars in a number of ways—lack of preparation time for the defense and the certitude of the evidence. But the lack of reporting effectively erases the students while it shines the brightest light on socially preeminent white men, principally Judge Daggett. Spotlighting Daggett can be justified; his villainy is second only to Judson's in this Canterbury tale. But Daggett's place in history was guaranteed, while the African American women were predestined to marginal anonymity. This is an instance of white men hijacking the narrative of a Black women's academy.

Judson's summation to the jury provides the names of nine students involved in the October trial: M. E. Carter, Ann Eliza Hammond, Sarah Hammond, Catharine Ann Weldon, Eliza Weldon, Emila Willson [sic], C. G. Marshal [sic], Mariah Robinson, and Elizabeth Henly. However, it is not clear if all of them had testified or were in the courtroom. Although not fully specified, their homes were noted as Philadelphia, New York City, and Providence, making them, in Judson's words, "foreign persons of color." He also made reference to some of them returning with Crandall after a quick trip to New York City—which he implies extended to Philadelphia—in May 1833.[68] Assuming the students named by Judson were present, this is what they heard from him, repulsing the argument of equality from the Declaration of Independence:

> The *Declaration of Independence* has been quoted to sustain the (defense) argument, but . . . (when) was that declaration made? . . . perhaps every signer of that declaration, was himself a *slaveholder*, and that declaration did not dissolve those bonds. . . . Hence you see, that there ever has been in this country, a marked difference between the black and the white men. There is still that difference, and it is impossible to do it away. Those who claim to be the *exclusive philanthropists* of the day, will tell you this is prejudice. I give it no such name. It is entitled to no such appellation. It is *national pride* and *national honour* which mark this distinction. . . . It was a nation of *white men*, who formed and have administered our government, and every American should indulge that *pride* and *honor*, which is falsely called prejudice, and teach it to his children. Nothing else will preserve the *American name*, or the *American Character*. Who of you would like to see the glory of this nation stripped away, and given to another race of men?

Judson referred to Crandall's school as a "scheme, cunningly devised, to destroy the rich inheritance" of white Americans and force a "universal amalgamation of the two races," with Blacks "placed on the footing of perfect equality with the Americans."[69]

Friday morning, October 4, Daggett gave his charge to the jury. It was reprinted in full in the *Unionist*, the *Connecticut Courant*, and the *Liberator*. He cited laws that treated free Blacks (and Native peoples) as not being entitled to rights. From this body of evidence, Daggett encapsulated the argument thus:

> To my mind, it would be a perversion of terms, and the well known rule of construction, to say that slaves, free blacks, or Indians, were citizens, within the meaning of that term, as used in the Constitution. God forbid that I should add to the degradation of this race of men, but I am bound by my duty to say, they are not citizens.[70]

The students sat through this nearly hourlong oration from the chief justice only to endure his disingenuous crocodile tears. The jury took little time to decide unanimously against Crandall.

Counterintuitively, the outcome from this otherwise dismal legal ruling was more productive than destructive. The defense lawyers immediately appealed to the Connecticut Supreme Court of Errors; this meant that the conviction of Crandall was in abeyance until the Supreme Court's next session, which was not scheduled until July 1834. This provided the academy with a span of nearly nine months, with no scheduled formal legal harassment and plenty of time for Crandall's lawyers to prepare.

This nine-month respite is especially important in the lives and education of the students. The courtroom appearances and the stress that accompanied such proceedings had to be disruptive. The calendar was now set, or so they thought (the persecutors would foment another trial in March; see below). Breathing room for school studies had been won. This required Crandall to go on with her activities as if nothing had happened, a feat of which she proved more than capable, bristling the nerves of her enemies once again. The choice of language in this outraged editorial affirms the nonviolent resistance that Crandall was pioneering: "The peaceable and undisturbed manner . . . in which the Instructress has of late been permitted to go on with her school, in violation of the law which the people of this state have deliberately enacted, could hardly have been expected of her."[71] While Judge Daggett may have intimidated many of his colleagues on the bench and on the faculty, the women in this episode were not impressed. The students, Crandall, her sister Almira, and the Burleigh siblings carried on with what they were there to do: "to maintain one of the fundamental, inalienable rights" of women.[72]

The dangerous legal direction that Judson's and Daggett's arguments blazed brought another important white lawyer to the cause of Abolition: William Jay. The son of John Jay, the first chief justice of the Supreme Court, William was an able legal historian and researcher whose role in the abolitionist movement would prove substantial. In his September 30, 1833, letter to Samuel J. May, he said he hoped it would reach Brooklyn in time to be introduced into the trial. As May says, Jay's arguments might have "shaken even Judge Daggett's confidence in his own opinion, respecting the citizenship of colored people."[73] Unfortunately, it did not arrive in time, but May did well to share it with posterity, noting how Daggett's opinion against Black citizenship would "do inconceivable mischief in our country, if it be not corrected."[74]

I argue that what May and Jay did is *precisely* the role that white male abolitionists were best positioned to undertake. They were gathering the forces that could spearhead change in public, legal, and political spheres. Meanwhile, Crandall and the students surfaced *when necessary* in the legal circus, otherwise pursuing the learning for which the school was designed.

Inside the School,
October 1833 to June 1834

It was not unusual for an academy to encompass a wide range of student ages. In Canterbury, the ages spanned from at least nine to twenty-three. There were likely opportunities for older students to help the younger pupils; this was a regular pedagogical practice at the time, considered preparatory for the teaching vocation.[75]

The student-authored essay that appeared in the *Liberator* in early August was likely written by an advanced pupil, but the same principles of nonresistance were inculcated in younger students. Many years later Crandall shared a poem she had written for the four youngest scholars to recite at a mental feast.

> Four little children here you see
> In modest dress appear.
> Come listen to our song so sweet
> And our complaints you'll hear.
>
> 'Tis here we came to learn to read
> And write and cipher too.
> But some in this enlightened land
> Declare 'twill never do.
>
> The morals of this favored town
> Will be corrupted soon.
> Therefore they strive with all their might
> To drive us from our home.
>
> Sometimes when we have walked the streets
> Saluted we have been
> By guns and drums and cow bells, too
> And horns of polished tin.
>
> With warnings, threats and words severe
> They visit us at times
> And gladly would they send us off
> To Africa's burning climes.
>
> Our teacher too they put in jail
> Fast held by bars and locks!
> Did ere such persecution reign
> Since Paul was in the stocks?
>
> But we forgive, forgive the men
> That persecute us so
> May God in mercy save their souls
> From everlasting woe![76]

This poem can come across as infantilizing the students. But as with the case of Susan Paul's juvenile choir performing at antislavery events in Boston, the fact that Black youth were presenting sharp analyses of racism defies prejudice. The students projected their own agency, their alienation from "Africa's burning clime," their claim of the United States as "our home."[77] This poem has the added advantage of telling us something of Crandall's self-image. She compares herself to Paul, while emphasizing forgiveness.

Yet, she simultaneously pokes sarcastic fun at the preposterous claims of her enemies—that the town was in danger from her students and that learning the basics of literacy would "never do."

There is a fine line between patronization and partnering whenever an oppressed group is allied with more socially powerful groups. Some moments in this poem are cringeworthy, and have had the effect of reinforcing the notion that most students were there to learn elementary basics like reading. While this was patently false for the vast majority, there were younger pupils who constituted a cohort of elementary age students (primarily younger sisters of older scholars).[78]

The tincture of sentimentality is not as important as the ongoing protection of the students' identities. The reason it is so difficult to state precisely what students were in attendance at any time is that Crandall, her coteachers, and her allies realized the need for anonymity. No rosters have been located from the school; publications of student writings were anonymous. While anonymity was standard practice for women, here it also protected the students from targeted street harassment.[79]

In this extended period from the end of the second trial in early October 1833 to the disintegration that started in July 1834, the real educational work of the school accelerated. The students knew that the existence of the school was precarious, suspended in legal limbo, with their enemies hurling invective, stones, and statutes. Far from deterring the students, this opposition made them more diligent, their dedication aided by the knowledge that "they are being watched by those who are not their friends."[80]

One especially festive occasion was the double wedding of two couples intimately connected to the launching of the school. On November 26, Maria Davis married Charles Harris, while Charles's sister Sarah Harris married George Fayerweather. While their weddings did not immediately end the association of either woman with the school, their marriages would eventually take them away: the Fayerweathers to Rhode Island and Charles and Maria to Norwich.

These marriages, while not actualizing the specter of interracial marriage that haunted the school's enemies, presents the students' age far more cogently than the sentimental poem. How were these young Black women perceived sexually by the white people of Canterbury and of the United States? Widespread interracial sexual contact was the norm under slavery, while Northern white men patronized Black prostitutes in metropolitan areas. These sexual contacts led to children across a rainbow of color designations, such as quadroon, octoroon, or the more general mulatto. No one could claim—though many depraved whites tried—that Blacks and whites were separate species, given their obvious reproductive compatibility.

This means that illicit white male sexual desire for Black women cannot be discounted from the Canterbury kerfuffle. The white men of the North, though, werc used to accessing Black women's bodies at some distance from their quaint villages. Likewise, Southern men made it abundantly clear that they could do what they wanted with those whom they had enslaved (which included sexual abuse of men and women). The sexual fears aroused by having Black women students in Canterbury were based on the implied social status the school conferred on them, as well as patriarchal uneasiness around women's self-development and initiative. The Black women students frightened the Canterbury gentry because they were not playing into the script of subservience, sexual availability, and licentiousness that white men held as stereotypes of Black women. Any women's—but especially Black women's—higher education challenged patriarchal sexual codes and social power.

Fire at the School,
the Trial of Frederick Olney

Frederick Olney (1810–69), a free Black man from Norwich, was a longtime friend of the Harris family. He served as Norwich agent for the *Liberator* starting in 1833.[81] He was active in the abolitionist ranks and thus often delivered supplies to the Canterbury Academy to thwart white boycotts. He attended the 1834 Free People of Colour Convention in New York City, where he was hailed as a hero for his assistance to the academy.[82] The likelihood that he was one of the Black men present at the infamous town meeting of March 2, 1833, is increased by a letter from Henry Benson that they had been associates "for a long while and [I] believe him to be a very fine man."[83] He married Sarah Harris's sister Olive in 1844; his wife conducted a school for thirty Black children in New London, Connecticut.[84]

When he arrived at the school on January 28, 1834, he had come to visit his friends Maria and Charles Harris and to see one of the students in particular. He had promised to write to that student's mother as soon as he saw her daughter.[85] At the school, he noticed a mechanical problem with a clock, spoke with Prudence about it, went to the kitchen to visit with Charles and Maria, and then went to repair the timepiece. At some point in the morning, student Amy Fenner noticed smoke in the room. Mariah Robinson, another student, tried to enter the room but couldn't because of the smoke. Olney and Charles Harris raised the alarm, went outside, and deduced the location of the fire. Working with some of Crandall's white neighbors, they extinguished the fire before irreparable damage occurred. Olney's quick thinking and calm response to the crisis had saved the school.

Immediately all minds turned to the possibility of arson. A (literally) incendiary notice had been published in the Windham County *Advertiser* in late

December, warning that "a determination has been formed to BREAK UP the negro school in Canterbury."[86] Garrison leapt to print with the headline "Suspicious Occurrence," while hoping that even the morally bankrupt whites of Canterbury couldn't have gone this far.[87] Although Crandall's supporters expected little pursuit of suspects from law enforcement, they may not have anticipated the "turpitude" to which the enemies of the school would sink: Olney was arrested and accused of setting the fire, implying Crandall's collusion in a publicity-seeking arson.[88]

This meant another trial in the midst of what was supposed to be a respite from legal harassment. Students would again be under courtroom stress, intensified by a well-founded distrust in the judicial system's fairness toward young Black men.

Because no constitutional issues were at stake in this trial and because, until recently, full documents from the trial were unavailable, much less has been written about the impact this legal proceeding had on the school. The arrest and charges against Olney were so transparent—constituting blatant harassment of a Black man—that the jury's decision was quick and decisive, suggesting that they wanted to quash what had become an embarrassment for the opponents of the school. However, looking at this with early twenty-first-century eyes, the trial of Olney may be the most telling of the four legal proceedings. Black and female citizenship have now been (somewhat) *legally* secured; the three trials conducted around Crandall's academy are part of the history of that accomplishment. But the unequal and prejudicial manner in which the law looks at young Black male defendants remains all too persistent. The trial of Frederick Olney demonstrates that the Black community was already far too familiar with legal steamrolling and understood that solidarity was the strongest response.

The trial was held in Brooklyn, Connecticut, over three days, March 6–8, 1834. As with the first trial back in August, the presiding judges were Eaton, Griffin, and Chase.[89] From the students' perspective, they saw Frederick Olney, a young Black man, a friend to them and the school—who treated them with amity and concern (as well as saving them from a fire)—being tried on false charges.[90] At least five students testified this time: Mary Harris, Mary Jane Benson, Amy Fenner, Henrietta Bolt, and Mariah Robinson. The students not only defended their own education but sought to rescue a Black man from the jaws of injustice. If the defense was right, and Olney was innocent, it meant the fire was an attack on the school far more dangerous than verbal harassment. If the prosecution was right, and Crandall and Olney were in cahoots to give the school visibility by arson, then the students would know they were being used and that the academy had been a fraud.

How did the students perform under this pressure? Brilliantly. In fact, the strongest testimony in Olney's favor came from the students (and Charles and Maria Davis Harris). The students were able to report on Olney's where-abouts, the timing of events, and his exact location in relation to the fire with precise, consistent detail.

In the first half of the extant trial documents, Maria Robinson informed the court of Olney's purpose at the school—to deliver a care package to one of the students from her mother in New York City, then to write to that mother and let her know immediately how her daughter was. The next student to deliver key testimony was Fenner. She was the person to draw Olney's atten-tion to the fire, which was visible only as smoke. He then put his ear to the floorboards and "heard it roar." This showed that the fire was set from the outside.[91] Bolt then corroborated Fenner's testimony.

When she wrote her biography of Crandall, Susan Strane lamented that "only the prosecution half of the trial is recorded."[92] This is no longer the case. Due to a filing error, unknown copies of the *Unionist* were recently located at the Library of Congress, including one that includes the last third of the trial. And it is here that we find affirmation of the female and Black cultural investment in the school. The defense called Crandall's coteacher Mary Burleigh, a household servant Betsey Fish, Charles and Maria Harris, and, most crucial, New York resident Elizabeth Marshall (1779–1861), mother to academy student Gloriana Catherine Marshall.

Marshall's testimony deserves to be studied as a whole, as it proves the thesis of this book: Crandall's academy was run with deep engagement and cooperation from the free Black community.

> *Elizabeth Marshall* resides in the city of New York; on the 23rd or 24th of January last Olney left New York and took a letter, and bundle &c. to her little daughter at Miss Crandall's school at Canterbury; witness had before sent a bundle to her daughter which had miscarried in October last; Olney said he would write to witness as soon as he got to Canterbury and tell her whether he had found it or not and also tell her about her daughter; the Saturday night of the week following Olney's departure from New York, when witness returned home from her work, her eldest daughter told her that she had got a letter from Olney, and read it to her. (witness not being able to read); [The witness here produced a half sheet of letter paper writ-ten over, which he said was the letter read to her by her daughter; it was dated Canterbury January 28th 1834 and purported to be a letter from Frederick Olney to Mrs. Marshall; the other half of the sheet, which was the one containing the direction and post mark witness said she had used to light her lamp one morning, soon after receiving the letter, having risen before it was light.][93]

First, note the care and speed with which Olney moves to fulfill Marshall's request. Second, Elizabeth Marshall had tried previously to send a care pack-age to Gloriana, but—and one can only suspect foul play on the part of the

Canterburian whites—it had "miscarried." So rather than rely on the post office, this time Mrs. Marshall gave the package to Olney, a trusted emissary. This boosted his credibility in the eyes of the jury as well as corroborating his alibi. Marshall then indicated that she received the requested letter from Olney the Saturday following the fire, that being February 1.

The person who read that letter to her mother was Gloriana Catherine's oldest sister, Mary Joseph Marshall. She had attended the African Free School and thus was able to read Olney's missive to her mother, who admitted that she was not literate.

Consider the charm of the care package sent to a distant student, soldier, or other young person. A tangible sign of parental affection, bridging the miles with homespun warmth, the care package exudes an emotional pull. The key role of Olney's genuine alibi had remained clouded until now. Through this humble offering (made visible by the lightning bolt of the fire), the Olney trial gives us a glimpse of the school's everyday networking within the Black community. There is no better example of the ownership and investment that the free Black community had in Crandall's school than Elizabeth Marshall's willingness to travel from New York City to Canterbury, where she faced an imposing jury of white males from a town known to be hostile to free Blacks. Her willingness to expose herself to ridicule for her lack of literacy only underlines her commitment to the school that is now providing an educational opportunity for her youngest daughter. Elizabeth Marshall left a testimony of maternal devotion and community solidarity in rescuing a Black man from being framed.

The prosecution did not cross-examine Marshall, though they did try to call a few quick witnesses. But my hunch is that Marshall's testimony sealed the case, emotionally and legally. The jury unanimously acquitted Olney in less than fifteen minutes. When the house was being restored as a museum in the 1990s, the jury's verdict was confirmed: the fire had been set outdoors.[94] This outcome shows that Tappan and May had correctly surmised that a local pro-Crandall press would make a difference. Henry Benson noted, after the August 1833 trial, "*The Unionist*, which had been established at Brooklyn solely to support and defend this school is doing much good, and it is astonishing how rapidly public opinion is changing in favor of the school."[95] Benson's assessment is corroborated by the fact that an all-white male jury unanimously acquitted a Black male. The prosecution's evidence was transparently flimsy, an insult to the process of justice. The remarkable thing is that this was recognized so clearly.

The Olney trial also revealed how closely the vigilantes and selectmen were working together. Many years later a white man disclosed that he was supposed to "be one of the number who should burn the house of Miss Crandall" but had refused.[96]

Just as important, the trial also shows a series of women, Black and white, defeating blatant racism. From Maria Robinson to Amy Fenner to Maria Davis Harris to Mary Burleigh to Elizabeth Marshall, a parade of female witnesses (joined by Charles Harris) made the case. White women, Black women, and Black men working together won the case for Olney. The enemies of the school had intended this trial as a ritual scapegoating of a Black man. But the difference between ritual and legal proceedings is that the latter can have unexpected results due to the open processes in place. The Black students (in both the first trial and the Olney trial) actively produced the unexpected result.[97] The trial records showcased the performance of the students: they were prepared, emotionally strong, and intellectually sharp. They didn't make mistakes and proved more than equal to the challenges. The intimidating forces ranged against them did not overawe them.

The fire, though, signaled white Canterbury's increasing ferocity. This intensification was not merely a local phenomenon: it would stretch to the entire Northeast in the hot summer of 1834.

Prudence Crandall, by Francis Alexander. This formal portrait was painted in April 1834 at the height of optimism about the academy's long-term future. Division of Rare and Manuscript Collections, Cornell University Library, Ithaca, New York.

Sarah Harris Fayerweather, the African American student who first asked to be admitted to Crandall's school. Photograph ca. 1860s to 1870s. Courtesy of the Prudence Crandall Museum, Canterbury, Connecticut.

Mary Anderson Harris Williams, sister of Sarah Harris, Canterbury alumna who taught the newly emancipated in New Orleans during and after the Civil War. Photograph ca. 1870s to 1880s. Courtesy of Chuck Piper, descendant of Mary Anderson Harris Williams, and Judy Piper.

Form of Bond from Permanent Inmate.

I, the undersigned, having been received as a beneficiary of the "HOME FOR AGED COLORED WOMEN," a Corporation created by act of the General Assembly of Rhode Island, and located in the city of Providence, do hereby severally signify my assent to, and promise compliance with, the rules and regulations of the said Corporation existing at the date hereof, and as the same may from time to time be amended and modified. And in consideration of the benefits assured to me as such a beneficiary, under the rules and regulations aforesaid, I do hereby severally and respectively assign, set over, and convey unto the said Corporation, its successors and assigns forever, all and singular, the goods, chattels, and effects which I respectively may have brought with me into the house of said Corporation, or of which I may in any manner become possessed whilst an inmate of said house. And whereas, in the ordering of Providence it may occur that I shall be enabled both to relieve said Corporation from expense and outlay on my behalf in the future, and to reimburse it for such expense and outlay in the past, I do hereby severally and respectively appoint the President of said Corporation, for the time being, and her successor in office, my Attorney and Trustee, with full power to demand, recover and receive, and in her name as such Trustee, to sell and dispose of all estate and property, real or personal, to which I respectively may now be, or may hereafter become entitled. The said Trustee being hereby empowered and directed to apply and appropriate the proceeds of any collections or sales, so far as needful, to the reimbursement fully of said Corporation for its expense and outlay on my behalf, respectively, and being bound to account for whatever balance may remain (if any) to me respectively, or to my respective legal representatives. And the right of the Board of Managers to remove me from the home at any time, for any cause which they may deem sufficient, is hereby expressly recognized and assented to.

Name _Elisabeth H. Smith_

Signed in presence of _Isabel Fowler Ingraine_

December 27th 1893.

Elizabeth Brown Smith, a Canterbury Female Academy alumna, who achieved great renown as a teacher in Providence, Rhode Island, where she attempted to integrate an exclusive women's club. This signed document shows, however, that segregation doggedly followed her, as she was admitted to a senior residence "for colored women." Collection of the Rhode Island Black Heritage Society, Providence, Rhode Island.

Prudence Crandall Museum, 2023. The prominent home that served as the Canterbury Female Academy still stands and is an important part of the Connecticut Freedom Trail. Courtesy of the Prudence Crandall Museum, Canterbury, Connecticut.

Canterbury. John Warner Barber, illustration in *Connecticut Historical Collections* (1835). Barber, an ardent abolitionist, was one of the heroic four who voted in favor of the African American college in New Haven in 1831. In this engraving, the man in the foreground couple is pointing to the Canterbury Female Academy, whose windows and roofs are seen along the lefthand border, nestled behind a protective row of sturdy trees.

William Lloyd Garrison, editor of the *Liberator*, by Robert Douglass Jr., a Philadelphia artist, brother to educator Sarah Mapps Douglass, and first cousin of Elizabeth Douglass Bustill, one of the Canterbury students. Lithograph courtesy of Historical Society of Pennsylvania Portrait Collection, V88, box 69, Collection of the Historical Society of Pennsylvania, Philadelphia.

Peter Williams Jr. was a leading Episcopal minister to many of the students from New York City and a key endorser of the Canterbury Female Academy. Sketch from Daniel Alexander Payne, *Recollections of Seventy Years* (Nashville, Tennessee: AME Sunday School Union, 1888).

Theodore S. Wright was another clergyman who endorsed Crandall's school. Born in Providence, he experienced discrimination and violence during his years of study for the Presbyterian ministry at Princeton. His 1837 speech concerning the need for white abolitionists to root out their own internalized racism is deserving of more study. Lithograph by G. S. W. Endicott, from a daguerreotype by Plumbe. Image courtesy of the Randolph Linsly Simpson African-American Collection, folder 1249, box 50, Beinecke Rare Book and Manuscript Library, Yale University, New Haven, Connecticut.

REV. THEO. S. WRIGHT.
Pastor of the First Colored Presbyterian Church, New York.

Reverend Samuel Cornish, another Crandall endorser, edited three important African American newspapers in New York City from 1827 to 1839. Francis Kearney, Reverend Samuel Cornish, 1825, steel engraving, 7½ × 5¾, Print Division, PR.052.1, New-York Historical Society.

Simeon Smith Jocelyn aided Prudence Crandall directly. He had been the leading force in attempting to found a college for Black men in New Haven in 1831. His ward Harriet Lanson attended the Canterbury Academy as a student. Collection of the Massachusetts Historical Society, Boston.

The *Unionist* newspaper was established in August 1833 to provide a counterweight to the biased white supremacist local press. The motto shown here from the December 19, 1833 issue—"The Tyrants Foe, The Peoples Friend"—was more than rhetorical. The *Unionist*, edited by Charles Burleigh, embraced an expanded notion of "the people" that included all people of color and all women, and the paper was engaged in the fight against the tyrannical Black Law. Library of Congress; viewable at Rycenga and Szydlowski, *The* Unionist *Unified*.

An exposed beam uncovered during recent renovations at the Prudence Crandall Museum shows marks of charring from the vigilante attempt to destroy the school by fire in January 1834. Courtesy of the Prudence Crandall Museum, Canterbury, Connecticut.

Glass from windows, likely from the vigilante attack on the school in September 1834 that led to its closure. Found in archeological studies in 1977 and 1981. Photo by author; access to materials courtesy of the Prudence Crandall Museum, Canterbury, Connecticut.

The *Unionist* covered the trial and acquittal of Frederick Olney, who was falsely accused of attempting to burn down the school. This header, from the issue of April 10, 1834, shows that Charles and William Burleigh were coeditors; William was also teaching at the academy. Issue held by the Library of Congress; viewable at Rycenga and Szydlowski, *The* Unionist *Unified.*

VOICE OF THE FUGITIVE.

SANDWICH, CANADA WEST.

WEDNESDAY, JUNE 18, 1851.

VOLUNTARY CONTRIBUTIONS TO THE VOICE.

We feel truly grateful to J. T. Fisher of Toronto, C. W., Wm. Still of Philadelphia, Pa., Theodore Holly of Burlington, Vt., Rev. A. G. Beman of NewHaven Ct., Wm. G. Allen, of McGrawville, N. Y., and other friends of our cause, for their valuable and highly interesting contributions to the columns of our little sheet, and hope that they will not be " weary in well doing."

Excerpt from *Voice of the Fugitive,* June 18, 1851, a Canadian newspaper coedited by the self-liberated Henry Bibb and his wife, Canterbury alumna Mary Elizabeth Miles Bibb. Google News Archive, https://news.google.com/newspapers?nid=GO5CT2y9xrEC&dat=18510618&printsec=frontpage&hl=en.

Henry Highland Garnet, a preeminent Black activist and thinker of the nineteenth century, married Canterbury alumna Julia Williams. They met at the Canaan academy in New Hampshire, an interracial and coeducational venture launched soon after Canterbury, that ended in the violent destruction of that school in 1835. Photograph by James U. Stead, ca. 1881. National Portrait Gallery, Smithsonian Institution, Washington, DC.

Mary Joseph Marshall Lyons was the elder sister to Canterbury student Gloria Catherine Marshall. She accompanied her mother Elizabeth Marshall to Frederick Olney's trial in Canterbury. She lived a long activist life, with her husband Albro Lyons. Courtesy of the Harry A. Williamson Collection, Photographs and Prints Division, Schomburg Center for Research in Black Culture, New York.

Maritcha Lyons, daughter of Albro and Mary Joseph Marshall Lyons, became an activist for education and a fine writer. She was a personal friend to at least two Canterbury alumnae, Sarah Harris Fayerweather and Elizabeth Brown Smith. Courtesy of the Harry A. Williamson Collection, Photographs and Prints Division, Schomburg Center for Research in Black Culture, New York.

Carte de visite of Corporal John W. Harper, 1864, at the time he was serving in the Massachusetts Fifty-Fourth during the Civil War. In 1886 he wrote a letter in admiration of Crandall's actions. Collection of the Massachusetts Historical Society, Boston.

Two adult daughters of Sarah Harris Fayerweather and their husbands. One of the daughters, Isabella Fayerweather Mitchell, sent this picture to Crandall in Kansas in 1885. The specific identity of the people portrayed is unknown, but the photo conveys their secure class status. Courtesy of the Prudence Crandall Museum, Canterbury, Connecticut.

Fannie Barrier Williams was a leading force in Chicago's Prudence Crandall Literary Club and wrote a perceptive memorial to Crandall. Like Elizabeth Smith, she worked to integrate the exclusive women's clubs of the late nineteenth century. Photographer unknown. Scan of a ca. 1880 photograph of Fannie Barrier Williams, Public Domain, https://commons.wikimedia.org/w/index.php?curid=69699342.

CHAPTER 8

Patriarchal Marriage
and White Violence
The Closing of the
Canterbury Academy

> The unpreparedness of the educated classes,
> the lack of practical links between them and the
> mass of the people, their laziness, and, let it be
> said, their cowardice at the decisive moment
> of the struggle will give rise to tragic mishaps.
> —Franz Fanon, *The Wretched of the Earth*

Why did the school close precipitously in September 1834? The answer seems obvious. A night of total terror by Canterbury's white vigilantes, in which nearly every window in the school was destroyed and the building rendered uninhabitable, done with the more-than-tacit approval of the town's civic leadership, made it clear that far from dissipating, threats were increasingly lethal.

However, the closing drama is neither as predictable nor as simple as it appears. Crandall and the students had already persisted through an unconstitutional law, legal and extralegal harassment, and a fire. Crandall had offers to move her operations elsewhere, most notable to Philadelphia. For the remainder of her life, she retained interest in Black education but never again regained the traction she had established with the Canterbury Academy. So why did the school close when it did? Was it external forces—the riots, the threat of future trials, and the resultant uncertainty? Or, was it solely because of the attack on the school that September night? Or was the closing connected to personal matters impinging on Crandall?

Evidence can be marshaled for various arguments: Crandall's marriage, psychological exhaustion from the struggle, loss of interest from male abolitionists are among those proffered. I argue that a marked deterioration in white/Black and male/female cooperation within the abolitionist movement writ large in the summer of 1834 contributed to the shuttering of the school. White abolitionists, panicked by the violently negative reaction that interracial cooperation and social familiarity generated, lost some of their courage, notably Arthur Tappan, Joseph Parrish, and the Connecticut Supreme Court of Errors. At the same time, Crandall's marriage constrained her agency, moving her out of the liminality of being unmarried and into the patriarchal constructs of white society. Intersectional analysis must note both racism and patriarchal authority at work, even when they are not directly in cahoots.

This chapter charts major events shaping the lives of northern free Blacks in the summer of 1834. In June the Free People of Color Convention established a highwater mark for optimism, but this was washed away when the free Black community in New York City was torn apart by anti-abolitionist riots on the Fourth of July; a similar riot happened in Philadelphia in August. These riots targeted individuals and institutions connected to students at Crandall's academy: Peter Williams Jr., Arthur Tappan, Lewis Tappan, and James Forten. After these mob actions, some white abolitionists avoided being seen publicly and socially with their Black allies. This led to a realistic doubt on the part of free Blacks whether they could rely on white supporters.

At the third Black Law trial, held before the Connecticut Supreme Court of Errors in late July 1834, a majority of the supreme court judges were in favor of exonerating Crandall. But in deference to Justice Daggett they dismissed the case on a technicality instead. This meant Crandall was free to go on conducting her school, but it also meant her enemies could renew legal proceedings, restarting the whole legal sequence. A future that had seemed bright in June had clouded over by September.

Calvin Philleo:
Characterological Itinerancy

During the spring of 1834, Crandall received recognition indicating widespread support for her work, including international acknowledgment from women abolitionists in Edinburgh and Glasgow, Scotland.[1] In a triumphant visit to Boston in April, Francis Alexander painted her portrait; the resulting work conveys a sense of her resolute character, Quaker modesty in dress, and evangelical self-definition. A prominent Black man, John Bowers (1773–1844), donated a considerable sum to help pay for the portrait, declaring Crandall "one of those great heroines whose names but seldom adorn the Modern History of America."[2] Accolades were so prodigious that Garrison warned that Crandall "must be careful lest she be 'exalted above measure' . . . a situation like hers calls for sleepless vigilance."[3] Even as Garrison praised Crandall, she was on the threshold of a major transformation in her personal life. She was engaged to Baptist minister Calvin Philleo.[4]

She and Philleo had met in 1833, when he "came to visit my school as a friend to colored people."[5] His first wife, Elizabeth Wheeler Philleo, had died in late 1831. He had three children, ranging in age from eleven to twenty-one. Since his youngest—his son Calvin Wheeler Philleo—attended a boarding school in Suffield, and Canterbury was near the stagecoach route, it was convenient for Philleo to make regular stops to court Prudence.[6] Their courtship lasted several months, and Crandall learned many unsavory things that had been said of Philleo's conduct. In the end, she chose to overlook these problems and marry him.

Philleo was born in Dover, New York, on the Fourth of July in 1787. The family genealogy indicates that his parents were of differing religious opinions, perhaps setting the quarrelsome partisan religious tone that would be replicated in Prudence and Calvin's interactions.[7]

Calvin eventually adopted his mother's Baptist faith and became a minister. Philleo married Elizabeth Wheeler and started his first pastorate in Amenia, New York, in 1810. He had nearly continuous—though often brief—pastorates at Baptist churches through 1834. Calvin and Elizabeth's family grew with the birth of their three children: Emeline Conner Philleo (1812–85), Elizabeth Barnes Philleo (1815–41), and Calvin Wheeler Philleo (1822–58).

In 1825 he obtained the pastorate of the Second Baptist Church in Suffield, Connecticut, perhaps his most successful assignment. He built a local reputation as "an effective evangelist;" his most significant convert, Dwight Ives, became a leader in New England Baptist circles.[8] But Philleo's wandering and haranguing at length from the pulpit were liabilities even his supporters noted. Words like "eccentric" and "impulsive" cling to Philleo, even at his most effective: "Peculiar in his manner, he would neither be led nor driven; and yet there was a tenderness and warmth about his expression that would touch the gentlest nature."[9] By the late 1820s he extended his evangelical concerns to Pawtucket, Rhode Island, when, in the midst of a revival, he became the pastor of its First Baptist Church. Here, according to his bitter opponent, Jacob Frieze, Philleo "succeeded in converting to this faith, some twenty or thirty persons, women and children."[10] A participant in the revivals, George Foster Jenks, was more charitable. He had been skeptical but concluded Philleo was "not a false prophet" when he started to perform multiple baptisms on an almost daily basis.[11] In Pawtucket, too, Philleo was remembered for his "strong opinions and eccentric mannerisms."[12] His daughter Emeline judged his pastorate in Pawtucket as "very successful" until his wife's death in December 1831; he "was never long settled, after this period."[13]

Patterns discernable throughout his active pastoral ministry show Philleo to be, on the negative side, impulsive and polemical and given to wandering. On the positive side, they show him to be successful in winning converts, blessed with a powerful voice and a richly image-laden preaching style.

Philleo's battle with Frieze is revealing. Frieze was Pawtucket's newly arrived Universalist minister.[14] Universalists believe that a benevolent God wished salvation for all His creations, thus rejecting Calvinism root and branch. By contrast, Calvin Philleo laced his revivalist sermons with threats of hellfire, gratuitously adding that all Universalist ministers would roast in eternal flames. Frieze attended a sermon that Philleo delivered and was repulsed by his stress on a punitive deity. Frieze accused Philleo of picturing God as "a low, vulgar, and contemptable figure . . . (who) outrages all the better feelings of piety."[15] Like any Universalist, Frieze preferred reason to excesses of emotion and so launched his most blistering attacks on Philleo's revivalist methods, accusing him of manufacturing revivalist sentiment "by noisy dec-lamation, barefaced assumptions, and baseless assertions; and with the voice of terror, to overcome reason, to blind the understanding, warp the judgment, excite the animal passions, and to sever the very heartstrings of weak minded men, inexperienced youth, and tender females."[16] Frieze bequeaths an unflat-tering picture of Philleo as an "infuriate zealot" who "impiously assumed . . . the divine prerogative" for himself.[17] The atmosphere of chaos and arrogance that Frieze describes shadowed Philleo's career and character.

Helen Benson and William Lloyd Garrison were corresponding inten-sively in the early months of 1834 as their relationship approached a formal engagement. It is through their letters that we have the clearest indication that Philleo was not well received by Crandall's acquaintances; Rowland Greene, Henry and Helen Benson, and Samuel J. May, for instance, had largely negative reactions to Philleo.[18]

While Crandall had her own decided religious opinions and preferences, she maintained a more ecumenical practice than many: she remained friends with the Unitarian May and took her students to a variety of churches. But like many women of her time, Prudence seems to have found revivalist preach-ers fascinating and alluring.[19] When she first heard her future husband, she thought that a "man who can make a prayer like that must be a good man."[20]

Helen Benson bluntly shared with Prudence the rumors she had been hearing about Philleo, specifically that he was "wife-shopping" and had been offensive to some women during his "search."[21] During her triumphant visit to Boston in early April, Garrison commented, "Prudence has wholly given up Mr. Phillio [sic]."[22] Helen comforted Crandall about this loss of her prospects upon the latter's return to Connecticut from Boston, and Prudence simply said, "I am resigned." But Philleo was due to visit her soon.[23] Garrison became worried, presciently writing that Crandall's marriage "will seal her earthly destiny, either for good or evil."[24]

Philleo came prepared to overcome any misgivings Crandall had and responded to the rumors circulating around him. On June 7 Crandall and Philleo together made the rounds of Brooklyn, "extremely anxious to have her friends think well of him." They went to visit Helen Benson, who found Philleo's manners to be somewhat coarse. She admitted it was difficult to look beyond the prejudices she had already formed against him from the rumors she had heard. After Philleo had left, Crandall told Helen everything that had passed between them and that she was "perfectly satisfied with his explanations." Rather than calming Helen, this alarmed her, as Philleo's "acknowledgement in part made me believe more than ever that he was guilty of the many charges that had been laid against him." Helen could not even congratulate her good friend. For Prudence's part, she told Helen that Philleo was "the choicest blessing" heaven could have sent her and relayed the news that Calvin "said the school should be sustained" in Canterbury.[25]

Garrison met with Philleo later in June in Boston, and his first impression was neutral: "He certainly appears to be a good man."[26] That note, though, crossed in the mails with Helen's far more damaging report concerning Calvin's character:

> Mr. Philio leaves Canterbury to day from what I can learn they have been very happy together. Prudence says Mr. Tappan advised Mr. P. to go on with the school and he seems very willing to sustain it. Should he have any thing to do with it, I hope they will go out of the village of Canterbury for I do believe there will be no end to contention as long as they remain there. Prudence told me that Mr. Philio did advertise for a wife, & at the same time he was engaged to a lady who afterwards refused him, because of the various reports about him. She also stated that he called at a milliner's shop to see a lady for the first time, and if she was agreeable he intended to offer himself the next time he saw her—called some where & ascertained she had a husband; so sent her a note saying he should not fulfil his engagement to call again. Prudence thought nothing about the stories and it is not strange when we consider that he offered himself to her, the first call he ever made her: He will not let you look him in the face but holds his head down a good deal, seldom [gives] you a chance to look at his eyes which strongly indicates guilt. Perhaps I do wrong.[27]

Before she married him, Crandall knew the kind of man Philleo was, from his avid wife hunting to, as the incident with the milliner demonstrates, his lack of attention to detail.

There is no reason to doubt the sincerity of Philleo's abolitionism; he joined various antislavery societies over the course of his life. He sought out Garrison and Tappan and made all the right promises concerning the continuation of the school. The problem with Calvin is not found in his political sentiments but in his unreliability and increasingly shiftless life. His ability to bluster and thunder was not matched by constitutional fortitude. But he had a pronounced predilection for holding tight to bastions of patriarchal authority: minister, exhorter, and husband.

Anti-Abolition Riots in
New York City and Philadelphia

Horror and terror befell the free Black communities of the North in the summer of 1834. In July, New York City was racked by ten days of anti-abolitionist rioting, destruction and looting, encouraged by the press. Southerners applauded Northerners for "fighting our battles," sanctimoniously commenting that riots and mobs were fine in such a cause.[28] Similar riots occurred in Philadelphia in August; Black churches being again a favorite target of the mob.[29] The respectability and security that free Black community leaders thought they had won lay in the tattered ruins of churches and neighborhoods.

Among Crandall's endorsers, ten were from these two cities (Jocelyn had relocated to New York). Of those ten male leaders, evidence shows that seven of them were directly impacted by the riots, most dramatically Williams, Forten, and Arthur Tappan. At least twelve students came from New York and Philadelphia.

The Chatham Street Chapel, located close to Broadway in lower Manhattan, had become a center for revivalist and reform activity in New York City. Lewis Tappan purchased this former theater in 1832 for use by famed evangelist Charles Grandison Finney. The evangelicals delighted in this transformation: "Satan overthrown as the doors of another theatre are closed and a new church rises in its place."[30] Finney launched the chapel with one of his classic revivals, lasting seventy days. But the chapel was by no means limited to explicitly religious services. The Tappans arranged for benevolent organizations to meet at the chapel. The first national Sunday School Convention happened in October 1832, the inaugural meeting of the New York Anti-Slavery Society in 1833, American Peace Society annual meetings, and in June 1834, the Fourth Annual Convention of the Free People of Color.[31]

Their efforts, though, elicited outraged opposition, including from James Watson Webb (1802–84), the combative editor of the prominent *New York Courier and Enquirer*. Webb, "a nationalist of the chauvinist, racist extreme," used his editorial authority to broadcast his own virulent racism. Webb denounced immediate abolition from the start, leading the attacks on the proposed New Haven labor college, while remaining staunchly supportive of the American Colonization Society.[32] As the summer of 1834 heated up, Webb regularly stoked the furnace of racial prejudice.

Moves toward integration were happening within the abolitionist movement, most notably the election of three New York ministers (and Crandall endorsers)—Williams, Cornish, and Wright—to the American Anti-Slavery Society's executive committee. At an abolitionist meeting on May 6, Arthur Tappan said that seating at an abolitionist meeting would be without reference to color.[33] At the end of the month, a Female Anti-Slavery Society was formed at Chatham Street Chapel; this raised eyebrows and ire, since it meant that white women would be in the company of Black men.[34]

The volatile trigger for the violence was social equality between the races. In early June, Tappan invited Cornish to sit in his pew at Reverend Samuel Cox's Laight Street Church. White parishioners and some of the church trustees took offense at this "gross impropriety." As rumors of Tappan's social breach were bruited about town, Cox addressed the situation in his next sermon. To dramatize the unchristian nature of racial prejudice, Cox raised the question of Jesus's racial appearance, asking, "How white the Asiatics were, or how white must the complexion of the Savior be, were he now on earth, in order for us to tolerate his person or endure his presence."[35]

Webb lusted after ammunition like this. His editorial bellowed that Cox and the abolitionists merited social castigation:

> When they vilify our religion by classing the redeemer of the world in the lowest grade of the human species, when they debase the noble race from which we spring, that race which called civilization into existence, and from which have proceeded all the great, the brave, and good, that have ever lived—and place it in the same scale as the most stupid, ferocious and cowardly of the divisions into which the Creator has divided mankind, then they place themselves beyond the pale of all law, for they violate every law divine and human.[36]

While dehumanization of Blacks was the keynote of the *Courier and Enquirer*, Webb's racism here rose to an ontological level, aligning white supremacy with the mind and body of God. Webb's venom was calculated to whip up anger and violent resentment among his white readers; all too predictably, it worked.

Given their moralistic temperament and desire for respectability, the Tappan brothers and their Black ministerial allies had long been uneasy with the raucous celebrations that marked the Fourth of July in the free Black community. They embraced an opportunity to do something more solemn and meaningful. A "respectable committee of colored gentlemen" suggested a "Service of Commemoration" at Chatham Street. It was Lewis Tappan who suggested an integrated event, complete with Black and white choirs, a special new hymn from John Greenleaf Whittier, and a reading of the American Anti-Slavery Association's Declaration of Sentiments. Despite Finney's concern that integration could have dangerous consequences, the Tappans forged ahead, with Williams and Wright volunteering their churches' choirs.[37]

When this plan was announced, white racists decided to disrupt the meeting. With summer heat in the low nineties, a white man named George W. Bull gave a signal to a mob to commence, but a police officer present convinced them to desist from physical confrontation. Yet, Bull and his gang continued to act as bullies, shouting down the featured speaker, white abolitionist attorney David Paul Brown of Philadelphia, who angrily abandoned the podium, deprecating the citizens of New York.[38]

On the following Monday, July 7, a scheduling error for use of the chapel precipitated rioting. A prestigious white choir, the New York Sacred Music Society, normally used the chapel on Monday and Thursday evenings for rehearsals. According to Lewis Tappan, the choral society had indicated that they were not going to need it that day, so Black abolitionists had decided to rent the chapel to resume the rudely interrupted celebration of the Fourth (with an oration by Benjamin Hughes).[39] However, one of the leaders of the chorus, Dr. Rockwell, had not been informed of the cancellation and, seeing the chapel lit up, came in to see if a rehearsal was underway. When he saw African Americans taking the place of his choristers, he reacted with anger, commanding the speaker of that moment to stop. When he didn't, Rockwell and a few other white choristers stormed the stage to remove the speaker. A physical scuffle broke out, and Tappan thought the whites got the worst of the fighting.[40]

The New York press, of course, pushed a different interpretation. Webb dubbed the incident a "sooty usurpation" and an "outrageous violation of every feeling cherished in our society."[41] The *New York Transcript* indicated that the whites got reinforcements and won the day. They sarcastically added, undoubtedly to the delight of their working-class readership who disdained the busybody moralism of the evangelicals, "Never, probably, before, was such a scene exhibited in the house of God; and never, we will venture to say, was there such an one in those unrighteous days when the Chapel was a Theatre." The *Transcript* also impugned the courage of the Tappans, asserting that Lewis hid out to escape the mob.[42]

With the press intentionally inflaming ambient racism by circulating rumors of intermarriage in the abolitionist ranks, full-scale mayhem commenced on Wednesday, July 9. In the absence of an abolition event to disrupt, a mob broke into Chatham Street Chapel and held a mock meeting of their own. They invaded the Bowery Theater, intimidating and humiliating an English stage manager, before attacking the home of Lewis Tappan. They forced open the doors, smashed windows, and threw the furniture out into the street, pausing in their destruction only when they came across a painting of George Washington, which they lovingly preserved from harm.[43] With police closing in, the mob built a bonfire from Tappan's furniture before escaping.

The next evening rioters focused on Cox and moved en masse to his church. Vandalizing its windows and exterior, they repaired to Cox's home, but he had taken the precaution of moving his furniture and family to safer locations. The next day, when Cox came to survey the damage, he was taunted by boys who threw "dirty missiles at him."[44]

On the third night of rioting, part of the mob attempted to storm Arthur Tappan's store but were deterred by police. Simeon Jocelyn was also present; he walked among the crowd incognito to gauge their sentiments.[45] Then violence turned against free Blacks. The rioters swarmed through the Five Points district, where most free Blacks lived in what was a fairly integrated slum. Evidence of the organized nature of the mob can be discerned from the fact that white residents were told to put a candle in their window if they wished the wave of devastation to bypass their dwelling. The violence honed in on Black-owned homes and businesses, as well as five brothels where women were stripped and raped.[46]

Two buildings that the rabble savaged were Williams's St. Philip's Episcopal Church and James Hayborn's Abyssinian African Baptist Church. For over two hours, the mob systematically destroyed St. Philip's, including Williams's home. The damage at Abyssinian, where the windows "were broken to atoms," received less press attention but came on top of property disputes with white authorities that hampered the stability of the congregation.[47] When whites attacked Black churches, they were striking at the "organizational strength" of free Blacks; rioters often expressed a desire to crush what they perceived as Black arrogance, embodied in the separate churches of the Black community.[48]

What can be discerned from this explosion of mob disrule? First, it was widely understood that "gentlemen of property and standing" participated in the mob. Second, the press's role in stoking anti-abolitionist sentiment was transparent.[49] Third, as would happen time and again in riots of the 1830s, while both white Abolitionists and free Blacks were targeted, the Black community suffered more wanton destruction than whites. Lewis Tappan referred to the loss of his house and furniture—which he was able to quickly replace—as "a small sacrifice upon the altar of freedom."[50] By contrast, many impoverished Blacks were thrown out of their homes with few options for finding new dwellings. The fates of the assaulted sex workers remain unrecorded.

The outcome for Peter Williams Jr. is illustrative of larger structural issues. Williams served under Episcopal bishop Benjamin T. Onderdonk (1791–1861). Onderdonk, who had been bishop of New York since 1830, proved a persistent obstacle to Black progress in the denomination.[51] Like most Protestant churches, the Episcopal Church in America supported the American Colonization Society and remained wary of the American Anti-Slavery Society. Williams's association with immediate abolition raised Onderdonk's disapprobation even before the riots.

On the Saturday following the destruction, even as Williams was assessing the damage to his church, his congregation, and his life's work, he received a letter from Bishop Onderdonk. Starting with an expression of "sincere sympathy" for what had happened, the bishop immediately suggested the "prudent course" of resigning his "connexion, in every department, with the Anti-Slavery Society." He insisted that Williams not only resign from the Anti-Slavery Society but also publish that fact to the world. "My advice," says Onderdonk, "therefore is, to give up at once." He dresses this command in the cloak of Christian humility: "Let it be seen that on whichsoever side right may be, St. Philip's Church will be found on the Christian side of meekness, order, and self-sacrifice to common good and the peace of the community." Inverting the very notion of "pastoral" care, Onderdonk relentlessly asserted the ecclesiastical chain of command to a minister of an oppressed people whose church had just been decimated.[52]

Williams's reply of July 15 notes that he had sworn submission and obedience to the bishop. But he delays his resignation to tell his life story, starting with his father's service in the Revolutionary War. He says that his father's revolutionary zeal filled his young mind with "an ardent love for the American government." Williams clung to "the belief, notwithstanding the peculiarly unhappy condition of my brethren in the United States, that by striving to become intelligent, useful and virtuous members of the community, the time would come when they would all have abundant reason to rejoice in the glorious Declaration of American Independence."[53]

Williams pointedly addressed denominational support for the American Colonization Society. He indicated he never obstructed anyone who truly wanted to emigrate to Liberia and that he had assisted in establishing an Episcopal presence there, but Williams does make it clear that he cannot agree with the ACS's policies:

> In regard to my opposition to the Colonization Society it has extended no farther than that Society has held out the idea, that a colored man, however he may strive to make himself intelligent, virtuous and useful, can never enjoy the privileges of a citizen of the United States, but must ever remain a degraded and oppressed being. I could not, and do not believe that the principles of the Declaration of Independence, and of the Gospel of Christ, have not sufficient power to raise him, at some future day, to that rank.[54]

This lengthy diversion from the forced apology establishes four propositions that were vitally important to Black participation in Canterbury: the struggle for Black citizenship, the hope that respectability would foster white recognition and equality, continuous efforts to further Black education, and rejection of the premises of colonization as discouraging to Black self-improvement.

Williams served as mentor to a substantial number of students attending Crandall's school, with at least four being members of St. Philip's Church: Theodosia DeGrasse, Henrietta Bolt, Gloriana Catherine Marshall, and Ann Peterson. With Williams being forced to publicly distance himself from abolitionist activity, amidst indiscriminate attacks on free Blacks, the New York students would have had ample reason to be apprehensive about the future.

Williams was the only abolitionist *forced* to backtrack by ecclesiastical hierarchy. *Voluntary* recoiling from social equality emanated from Arthur Tappan and the white New York abolitionist newspaper the *Emancipator* throughout the remainder of July. Most white abolitionists were eager to distance themselves from rumors of intermarriage. Henry Ludlow, whose church had been attacked, was particularly pusillanimous, apologizing for widening the rift between the ACS and immediatists, vociferously denying that he had ever encouraged "amalgamation" between Blacks and whites.[55] Elizur Wright objected, "Amalgamation is too small a crime to be worth a *disclaimer*."[56] But his was a lone, private voice.

Arthur Tappan, up to this point a bold creator of Black-white alliances, was terrified of being seen in public with "any of his African American associates" after sharing his pew with Samuel Cornish was blamed for the 1834 riots.[57] His explanation is quite telling:

> Though I advocated the sentiment that as Christians we were bound to treat the colored people without respect to color, yet I felt that great prudence was requisite to bring about the desired change in public feeling on the subject; and, therefore, though I would willingly, so far as my own feelings were concerned, have *publicly* associated with a well educated and refined colored person, male or female, I felt that their best good would be promoted by my refraining from doing so till the public mind and conscience were more enlightened on the subject.[58]

Tappan meant to shield his Black allies from the racist violence rampant in New York, but patronizing attitudes still permeate this statement. He seemed oblivious to how the politics of respectability had just proven themselves wanting in the sack of St. Philip's Church. As the years went by, it became apparent that there was a gap between rhetoric and reality in the white evangelical wing of the abolitionist movement. For instance, the Tappan brothers never hired African Americans at their firm in any position that would allow for advancement; Black allies (including Jehiel Beman) called them out on this.[59] After the New York riot the white abolitionists were "more concerned with vindicating themselves and making themselves appear sympathetic than with the plight of their fellow sufferers" from the free Black community.[60]

Arthur Tappan had a difficult time sustaining his equilibrium after these riots. Compare this to Prudence Crandall: single for most of the time that her school was open, surrounded by hostile whites hurling slurs and stones, yet she and the students lived together in an interracial, mixed-gender, class-crossing reality for eighteen months. Throughout all of this they focused on the actual task of education. What Prudence and Almira Crandall, with William and Mary Burleigh, achieved at the Canterbury Academy in terms of a lived antiracist practice by whites was unprecedented. Theodore Weld admitted he knew "of no female, except Miss Crandall, who has resolution and self-denial enough to engage" in teaching young women of color.[61]

As with Crandall's night in jail, though, the riots created a new wave of abolitionist converts. Garrison wrote to Helen Benson that these were "perilous times," but some good could come out of it as "this shameful riot will ultimately advance the cause."[62] William Jay (son of John Jay) and William's son, John Jay (grandson of the former chief justice) both had their antislavery sentiments confirmed by the riots, as did future vice president Schuyler Colfax (1823–85), who witnessed the riots as a twelve-year-old boy.[63]

Perhaps the most significant addition to the ranks of the abolitionists, though, was the young African American Samuel Ringgold Ward (1817–66). Formerly enslaved, he and his family had escaped from Maryland when he was a child. He had been introduced to abolitionist ideas by Simeon Jocelyn. Eager to join an abolitionist society, Ward attended the meetings that provoked the riots and experienced the violence directly. The result of this—in an all-too-familiar parallel to Frederick Olney—was that Ward was incarcerated:

> The public watchman arrested the parties beaten instead of those committing the assault, and it was my lot to be among the former number. For the crime of being publicly assaulted by several white persons, I was locked up in the watchhouse throughout the night. Shortly after my imprisonment, four others were brought into the same cell by the officers of peace and justice, for the same crime. . . . My oath of allegiance to the antislavery cause was taken in that cell on the 7th of July, 1834.[64]

Ward went on to a long career as an antislavery editor and activist.[65]

The New York City press, most notably Webb's incendiary *Courier and Enquirer* and William Leete Stone's *Commercial Advertiser*, shed a few crocodile tears over the violence while endorsing the righteousness of the rioters' cause.[66] Hostile editors punctured the reputation of the Tappans, whose moralism had led to the closing of theaters and amusement parks.[67] The Southern press presented the unvarnished truth; the Charleston, South Carolina, *Courier* opined that the

> recent anti-abolition riots . . . cannot but be highly gratifying to the people of the south, as a strong, and indeed, conclusive manifestation that the public

sentiment of the north, will of itself suffice to put down that fanatical spirit of false philanthropy and real incendiarism.[68]

The Northern racism revealed in Canterbury was confirmed by these New York riots.

These riots were a tremendous setback for the free Black community, whose respectability and security were in shards. The capitulation by many white allies to existing mores and the backtracking on social equality must have been disappointing. Indeed, one can see in the development of increasingly independent Black institutions, like David Ruggles's Vigilance Committee, and the reestablishment of an independent Black press by Samuel Cornish with the *Colored American*, the frustration and discouragement with white allies that Theodore Wright would enunciate so powerfully.[69]

Furthermore, this nightmare of rioting was not over—in fact, the events of July mark the beginning of a spate of multiday urban riots against abolitionists. The violence from New York spread to Newark, New Jersey, where, once again, the issue allegedly concerned "amalgamation." There were two similar incidents closer to Canterbury. On July 9:

> An abolition riot took place at Norwich, Connecticut. It appears that some person from Boston had, the evening previous, preached an abolition sermon in the rev. Mr. Dickerson's first Presbyterian church in that city, which passed off quietly. The next evening he made a second attempt when a mob, headed by a band, marched to the church, proceeded up the broad aisle, took the parson from the pulpit, and forced him to march before them, at the same time playing the rogues' march, till they actually drummed him out of the place, threatening if he ever returned again to "give him a coat of tar and feathers."[70]

Similarly, there was some sort of kerfuffle around Scottish abolitionist Charles Stuart's appearance in Plainfield on July 11. Competing reports between the abolitionist press and William Leete Stone's *Commercial Advertiser* make it impossible to determine the precise truth.[71] But Stone's language, in the immediate aftermath of the New York riots, doubles down on the rhetoric that launched those explosions. He condemns the "pertinacious continuance of Miss Crandall's school . . . chiefly fomented by itinerant abolitionists" and now even "a foreign incendiary has contributed to fan the flame."[72]

These riots could be interpreted as backlash against the success of the burgeoning abolitionist movement. Historians have outlined the sources of unrest in this period, when rapid urbanization, extensive immigration, and the vicissitudes of an oft-depressed economy created large un- and underemployed young populations. Economic rivalry, class and race resentment, and the rapid pace of change in a transforming nation all contributed to the percolation and explosion of rioting. But to the abolitionists in that moment, this atmosphere of continual threats and violence must have been terrifying, especially since racial insult was nearly always a part of the atmosphere. The psychological toll on the denizens of the Canterbury Academy can be imagined.[73] A vice grip of violence was tightening around them, especially since the bugbear of interracial marriage had always figured in the sexually charged hysterics of the school's opponents.

These factors are important in considering the anti-abolitionist riot in Philadelphia in August 1834. The conflict started in an integrated working-class amusement hall dubbed "Flying Horses" for its famed carousel. On Friday, August 8, a skirmish between white volunteer fire-brigade members and some Black patrons occurred. When the Blacks bested their white opponents that night, a response was guaranteed to follow. On Saturday evening, Forten's son "was attacked on the street 'by a gang of fifty or sixty young [white] men.'" The disturbers of the peace took Sunday off, but the same gang that harassed the young Forten agreed to meet on Monday and "attack the niggers." Once again, though, the Blacks had the better of that encounter. This led to extensive rioting from August 12 to 15. The Flying Horses carousel was destroyed; the mob then rampaged through Moyamensing, an impoverished integrated neighborhood. While there was less-concerted action among the rioters than had been the case in New York the previous month, the Passover-like candles in the windows once again spread as a symbol among whites for their protection.[74]

Among many serious injuries, one Black person died. People fled the area, trying to eke out living quarters in the woods on the New Jersey side of the river for weeks afterward. Two major institutions were destroyed—a Masonic lodge and the famed African Presbyterian Church founded by John Gloucester.[75]

The composition and intent of the white mob in this riot has been the subject of much scholarly study and debate. There were significant differences between this mob and that in New York. The Philadelphia white rioters were younger and likely in economic competition with both skilled and unskilled Black workers. The economically stable Black middle class had been widely pilloried, making them an easy target for class resentment from poor whites. Satirical cards by Edward Clay, "Life in Philadelphia," included images of Blacks dressed like dandies but speaking with thick dialects and error-filled diction. The white city historian of the time, John Fanning Watson, located Black arrogance in their "separate churches" and expressed amazement that Blacks termed each other "gentlemen and ladies."[76] As Emma Lapsansky summarizes, "'upper-class' blacks were an acceptable target for [white] frustration, whereas upper-class whites were not."[77]

The press was not a major factor in the Philadelphia riot, and "gentlemen of property and standing" were not as obviously involved. But discerning the differences between the two riots has taken much critical scholarship, such that the differences were likely unclear to contemporary observers, who discerned a concerted attack on the Northern free Black community in its two major population centers. White rage wrecked Black institutions, mocking the politics of respectability.[78]

These two riots revealed that anti-abolitionist sentiment had become enflamed. It was equally obvious that white religious and civil authorities were more sympathetic to the ideology of the rioters than to the abolitionists; as Ward indicated, the victims were more likely to be prosecuted than the perpetrators.[79] Black leaders like Williams were reminded of "their place" in the social hierarchy, while white abolitionists backtracked on social equality.

White Canterbury had shown incessant hostility to Crandall's school. The harassment had been constant but below the lethal level (with the notable exception of the fire). The national publicity generated by the jailing of Crandall had chastened her enemies in this regard: they feared elevating her or the students into potent martyrs. But with the riots of 1834, the equation changed: the general approbation of the press for the mobs' disdain of social equality gave ample cover to Crandall's enemies. Crandall's school was a highly visible target, and the students' safety decreased daily as the national racial environment deteriorated.

The most pointed vigilante attack against Crandall's school came in early July.[80] The only known fatal victim of the school was a luckless feline saddled with immutable markings: black and white fur. This cat's throat was cut by hooligans in the village, its body impaled on a fence in the school's front yard. The ominous meaning was obvious, even in pre-Corleone days. Aside from mourning this innocent victim, killed for the color of its fur, Crandall and the students felt the chill of its message.

The Final Trial

At stake in the third Black Law trial was how the question of citizenship refracted through race, gender, age, and marital status. Prior to the trial, May caught the all-encompassing nature of the potential decision: "If this case shall be ultimately decided in accordance with Judge Daggett's opinion, we see not why our whole colored population will not be effectually disenfranchised. If their right to education is to be held alienable whenever their white brethren may be so disposed, what sure protection will they have for any other right?"[81] By raising the question of education as a right, May understood that "enfranchisement" encompasses more than voting rights. The right to education is contained within the "life, liberty and the pursuit of happiness" promised in the founding documents. If the court overturned Daggett's decision, they would have done so because they had recognized the universalism of these doctrines. But instead of overturning it, or confirming it, they punted.

The third trial took place in Brooklyn, Connecticut, on July 26, 1834. Four judges made up the panel of the Supreme Court of Errors: Daggett, Clark Bissell, Thomas Williams, and Samuel Church.[82] The other three justices trying the case did not say a word—at the time. So intimidated were they by Daggett and his power in the state's judicial system that they did not publicly raise their disagreements with his opinion. Judge Thomas Williams (1777–1861), Judge Clark Bissell (1782–1857) and Judge Samuel Church (1785–1854) had long, storied careers in Connecticut politics. Bissell served as governor in the late 1840s and was a colleague of Daggett's on both the supreme court and the Yale faculty. Thomas Williams, the brother-in-law of Crandall's attorney William Ellsworth, succeeded Daggett as chief justice of the Connecticut Supreme Court of Errors later in 1834. Church, too, would serve a turn as chief justice from 1847 until his death in 1854. One assumes these were men with strong opinions and the ability to take a stand in the midst of controversies. At this third trial on the Black Law, Chief Justice Daggett insisted on being present, though he could have recused himself from judging his own opinion. As Donald Williams drolly states, "Daggett's presence had a chilling effect on the ability of the other justices to frankly discuss and debate Daggett's rulings."[83]

During the July arguments before the court, Ellsworth referred to the students as "human beings" with no distinction based on gender or race, to make it clear that women were citizens despite not having the franchise. Judson countered with typical overstatements, calling the abolitionists "a few madmen or enthusiasts." His final summary featured a grandiloquent paean to white supremacy:

> Are we now called upon to adopt such construction of the constitution, as shall surrender the country purchased by the blood of our fathers, up to another race of men? Then I would appeal to this Court—to every American citizen, and say that America is ours—it belongs to a race of white men, the descendants of those who first redeemed the wilderness. The American name and character have been handed down to this generation, and it is our duty to preserve that character, and perpetuate that name. Let not the determination of this case aid those who are plotting the destruction of our constitution.[84]

Judson made it abundantly clear that the justices would be ruling on the constitutionality of exclusive white control over matters of citizenship.

Chauncey Cleveland, for the prosecution, reiterated that the Constitution of the United States clearly made a distinction based on color and that there were no substantial differences between slaves and free blacks when it came to questions of citizenship. He also referred to Crandall as "Prudy Crandall" and threatened the doctrine of nullification that was then popular in South Carolina. Cleveland's performance could not have helped the prosecution.[85]

Calvin Goddard gave the final speech to the state supreme court justices, a masterful look at the history of Black citizenship in the country. He gave some support to colonization, but said that neither the abolitionist or colonizationist debates nor the issue of slavery were at stake in this decision. It was about living up to the Declaration of Independence:

> We come in behalf of *three hundred and twenty thousand* free, native inhabitants of this free country in which we live. . . . [W]e come to claim for them the privileges secured to us all. . . . [W]e come in behalf of those, and the children of those, who, on the 4th of July, 1776, united in the self-evident truths then proclaimed to the world . . . "That all men are created equal.." . . . we come to ask *to pursue* that happiness . . . (t)o learn to read—to read the word of God, and to pursue happiness temporal—happiness eternal!

Goddard marked the urgency of the decision at this "moment of great public excitement regarding our colored population."[86]

After these arguments were presented, the justices of the court decreed that Daggett's ruling would be reversed because the prosecution had not mentioned, back in October, that "the school was set up without the license of the civil authority and selectmen."[87] If the issues at hand did not constitute a constitutional crisis, this would actually be comical. It is abundantly clear that the selectmen of Canterbury did not want this school to exist and had done all within their power to prevent it. Donald Williams thinks that the Supreme Court was so eager to avoid ruling on Daggett's opinion that they "stretched" or even "invented, a technical defect."[88]

The error made by the Connecticut Supreme Court of Errors came from supreme cowardice. Their nondecision helped no one. The lawyers for both sides were frustrated in their hopes of taking this case to the US Supreme Court.[89] The prosecution was alarmed that the Canterbury school had an indefinite lease on life. New rounds of legal wrangling were anticipated. Furthermore, the issues at stake in Crandall's case—most notable, Black citizenship—fell into legal limbo. By refusing to adjudicate the issue of Black citizenship, these justices merely kicked it down the road to US Supreme Court Chief Justice Roger Taney, who unequivocally and disastrously affirmed Judge Daggett's opinion in the Dred Scott case (1857).

The third trial marks a moment when white men took center stage, treating Black women, white women, and Black men as afterthoughts in a game between elites. In the hands of the prosecution, entire groups were mocked and derided. The extent to which the third trial constituted a conversation among white male equals intent on excluding others is awe-inspiringly awful.

No witnesses were called; everything came down to speeches by lawyers and private huddling by the justices. Among themselves the judges went into a lengthy discussion on Black citizenship, and all but Daggett "either held or inclined to the opinion that they were citizens."[90] Judge Williams states this plainly (and unapologetically):

> *Now* I have no hesitation in saying that my own opinion did not coincide with Judge Daggett's. . . . According to my recollection in the consultation in Brooklyn, Peters, J., absent, all of us differed from the Chief Justice so far as we expressed an opinion, but we *gave no definite opinion*, and when at Hartford *concluded to dispose of the case on other grounds* . . . [A]dvise me. . . . whether there ought to be any delicacy in saying what were our *impressions* on the subject, though *no judicial opinions were given*. For myself I must say that I *did not then doubt, nor since have doubted*, that our *respected friend was wrong* in his charge to the jury.[91]

Judge Williams had the power to make the right decision, as did the other judges. *But they chose not to do that.* These judges allowed an unconstitutional law to stand out of deference to Daggett and trepidation about the consequences of defying him.[92] White men, whose fame, prosperity, and legacy were already assured, had it in their grasp to decide a case that would have secured rights to an entire class of people. On the eve of the American Revolution, in 1773, Anthony Benezet had written that the hands of justice were moving too slowly for African Americans, due to "the fear of displeasing the powerful ones of the earth . . . and a want of feeling for the miseries of our fellow men."[93] The Connecticut Supreme Court of Errors continued that dubious tradition in placing Daggett's reputation above the lives of free Blacks. They deliberately chose to grasp at legal straws to avoid a confrontation with a judge who would be retiring within the year! If Fanon's analysis was in need of an illustration, here it is.

Marriage:
Prudence Crandall Is No More!

The first time that William Lloyd Garrison saw Prudence Crandall following her marriage to Calvin Philleo on August 12, he described it thus to his fiancée: "It seems then, that Prudence Crandall is no more! . . . Mrs. Philleo, who has taken her place . . . resembles her in all things precisely."[94] While Garrison presumably used the language of legal death teasingly, it pointed to an all-too-real fact: married women had no independent existence in the eyes of the law.

The wedding ceremony itself became politicized. Crandall and Philleo had asked Otis Whiton of the Congregational Church to preside; he agreed, but the very morning of the ceremony, he withdrew. Edward S. Abdy reports that Whiton had been offered a substantial monetary contribution to the church on the condition that he not perform the wedding, a fact showing opposition to the marriage either as part of the continuous harassment of Crandall or because Canterbury's thugs did not want a man living in the house.[95] The wedding also carried an air of tragedy because Crandall's minister, Levi Kneeland, lay on his deathbed; the couple traveled to Brooklyn to solemnize their wedding under Reverend Tillotson instead.[96]

The newlyweds took their honeymoon in Boston and Philadelphia. While in Boston they visited Garrison and Philleo's elder daughter, Emeline. Perhaps these first few days of marriage were happy, but Prudence's friends still had their doubts. Garrison was puzzled on how to evaluate Philleo, even after Philleo delivered two strong sermons at the African Meeting House in Boston.[97] Garrison used the words "eccentric" and "covetous" to describe Philleo. The first was consistent with earlier assessments from many sources; the second—the idea that Philleo was greedy—would prove to be true over the years; Philleo's poor judgment in money matters would hound Prudence and his children.

The excursion to Philadelphia was partly to explore the idea of relocating there, sparked by a visit to the school from Lydia White (1788–1871), the white proprietor of a famed free-produce store.[98] Despite the recent unrest, the abolitionist network there was better integrated than most (in both racial and gender dimensions, due to Quaker influence). When the newlyweds arrived in Philadelphia, they visited numerous activists, including Esther Moore (1774–1854) and Lucretia Mott (1793–1880). These white women, comprehending antiracism as part of abolitionism, were outstanding supporters of Black-white partnerships. They were also both active in the early woman's rights movement. Moore attended the Free Black convention in 1835; Martin Delany recognized her as one of the rare whites who would "permit of any of their measures to be questioned by a colored person."[99]

The Philleos made a number of excursions around Philadelphia's Black community—extensive enough to procure the possibility of up to fifty scholars for a relocation of Crandall's school.[100] Mott felt sure Crandall would relocate to Philadelphia.

But a cautious white abolitionist scotched this tantalizing possibility. Joseph Parrish (1779–1840) was president of the venerable Pennsylvania Society for Promoting the Abolition of Slavery. While Parrish and the Motts were on friendly terms (he was their family physician), they disagreed with him over women's rights and social equality of the races. The most famous incident occurred during May 1838, when the second annual Antislavery Convention of American Women became the first and only meeting ever held in the doomed Pennsylvania Hall. This convention angered Philadelphia's white racists so much that they burned down what they dubbed a "temple of amalgamation."[101] Escaping the mob, white and Black women delegates protected one another. The women made interracial cooperation tangible when they continued their meeting even after the destruction of the hall and passed this resolution (albeit, not unanimously) from Sarah Grimké:

> Resolved, That prejudice against color is the very spirit of slavery, sinful in those who indulge it, and is the fire which is consuming the happiness and energies of the free people of color.
>
> That it is, therefore, the duty of abolitionists to identify themselves with these oppressed Americans, by sitting with them in places of worship, by appearing with them in our streets, by giving them our countenance in steamboats and stages, by visiting them at their homes and encouraging them to visit us, receiving them as we do our white fellow citizens.[102]

Parrish was the type of Quaker who feared violence so much that he would melt into quiescence rather than risk confronting evil. Mott noted that he was afraid of the publication of this resolution, even weeks after the destruction of Pennsylvania Hall. Mott writes how Parrish "has left no means untried to induce us to expunge from our minutes a resolution relating to social intercourse with our colored brethren . . . and when he failed in this effort, he called some of the respectable part of the colored people together" to try to convince them.[103]

Given this timidity in the face of a momentous crisis—the destruction of Pennsylvania Hall—it is not surprising that four years earlier, with the possibility of the notorious Prudence Crandall moving to Philadelphia, Parrish squashed consideration until after the fall elections. By then it was too late. Parrish was reacting to riots, as Tappan had, pulling back in fear from social equality. Black abolitionists were in a different situation; they intimately knew the power of racism to distort and destroy their communities—viscerally, practically, and materially. They understood the riots as a serious setback but didn't abandon their principled struggle. Williams, though pressured to submit to ecclesiastical authority, made his "apology" more defiant than a mere concession, and while Forten felt discouraged to the point of depression, he kept organizing.[104] But leading white male abolitionists in New York and Philadelphia were significantly cowed and judged the costs of their ethical commitments as too high.

Whether cowardice, timidity, self-interest, or prudence, the reaction of white men is in stark contrast to how women like Mott, Crandall, and her students handled the same challenge. Crandall herself, though, was now more thoroughly enmeshed with direct white male authority, in the person of Calvin Philleo, than she had been at any point in the history of her school. Previously, she was not under the direct supervision of her father or her brothers. On the contrary: as the lead teacher at the academy, she had authority over a white male teacher, William Burleigh. In considering why the Canterbury Academy closed so precipitously in September 1834, the convergence of white male authority through Crandall's marriage and abolitionist white male faintheartedness reinforced patriarchal authority. Much as marriage and the prickly Philleo are easy to blame or as tempting as it is to say that the violence of the villagers won this battle by echoing the mob techniques from New York City and Philadelphia, it is the combination of factors that ended the school and buried Crandall in a forty-year cloak of relative anonymity and silence.

There was one male authority to whom Crandall had previously deferred to willingly: her minister Levi Kneeland. But when Crandall and Philleo returned from their extended honeymoon, they heard the devastating news that Kneeland had died. Kneeland's death meant that the one person who could have mediated between Prudence and Philleo with equal respect from and for both partners in the marriage was gone.

In addition to Kneeland's death, William Burleigh now became the object of the Canterburian cabal's legal harassment. Burleigh was served an indictment under the still-living Black Law with a trial date set for December.[105] On Tuesday, August 26, English visitor Edward Abdy returned once again to visit the school, since he knew the saga of the Canterbury Academy would expose American racism. Burleigh shared with Abdy the various badges of persecution and adulation Crandall had received. Among the latter were a Bible and concordance from "the Ladies of Edinburgh." It must have pleased Crandall to read the dedication they wrote on their gift:

> A mark of respect with which they regard the Christian courage of her conduct towards their colored sisters in the United States; and from a conviction that such consistent love and strength, could only be derived from the DIVINE AUTHOR of the SACRED VOLUME.[106]

The women of Edinburgh also singled out two Biblical passages: John 21:15 and Psalm 40:1–2. The first is when Jesus instructs Peter that the way to show his love for God is to "feed my lambs." The Psalm verse concerned the topic of uplift:

> I waited patiently for the Lord; and he inclined unto me, and heard my cry.
> He brought me up also out of an horrible pit, out of the miry clay, and set my feet upon a rock, and established my goings.
> And he hath put a new song in my mouth.[107]

The gift was dated March 5, 1834, but the multivalence of the Bible must have made this dedication prismatic for Crandall. Back in March it would have been possible for her to read them in relation to the project itself, assisting the Black community. But rereading them at the end of August, the "horrible pit" might well have been the ongoing hell of Canterbury, and the reality of her "goings" might have seemed prophetic (if she was still considering Philadelphia). Given the clarity with which Crandall had used the Bible in October 1832, when first approached by Sarah Harris, the ambivalence of her choices now might have occurred to her, even as the ultimate crisis of September dawned.

William Ellery Channing and the
Impact of the Black Students

There is one final example of white male hesitancy connected to the events of Canterbury. With a letter of introduction from May, Abdy sought an interview with America's foremost Unitarian theologian, William Ellery Channing (1780–1842). A day after leaving Canterbury, Abdy and Channing held a long discussion on racial prejudice. Channing does not emerge triumphant in this dialogue; he evaded the subject, raised straw arguments, and showed that he was ignorant of the plight of free Blacks, especially compared to Abdy, who had studied race relations and spoken with free Blacks.

Channing, among America's preeminent intellectuals, had many friends among the Garrisonians, most notably George Benson Sr. and May. He had been involved in the peace movement for over twenty years and blessed the Windham County Peace Society's publication of Jonathan Dymond's work.[108] He was, in principle, opposed to slavery but uncomfortable using his public influence in the cause. Like many respectable white leaders, he was distressed by the polemical "severity of (abolitionist) denunciation, the harshness of (their) epithets," which Channing believed at odds with pacifism.[109] However, between the fall of 1834 and the end of 1835, when he published his work *Slavery*, he had some slight change of heart.[110] What caused this? Three factors are usually cited: conversations he had with May, his alarm at the anti-abolitionist riots in the summer of 1834, and his conversation with Abdy.[111] All three factors point to the persecution and achievement of Crandall's school playing a part in Channing's transformation. But as too often happens with women's history, this salient connection has gone unnoticed.

Abdy insisted to Channing that their conversation focus on prejudice against free Northern Blacks, rather than slavery.[112] Channing cast aspersions on free Blacks, saying they were unsympathetic to one another and showed but "indifferent character." These socially commonplace assertions of white supremacy were easily refuted: Abdy had seen differently, knowing the students at Crandall's school and many Black ministers. Furthermore, he had seen ample evidence of Black solidarity, even noting (centuries before scholarship would affirm this self-evident fact) that free Blacks routinely aided self-liberating people fleeing enslavement.[113] The conversation wended its awkward way as Channing sought refuge in a variety of common canards, but Abdy observed that all Channing's gambits rested on the notion of Black inferiority and that white prejudice against them was "invincible." Abdy stated categorically that he "could not admit either the premises or the conclusion" of any assertions of racism in perpetuity.[114]

May also had a heart-to-heart conversation with Channing; May had the advantage of being a fellow Unitarian, a protégé of Channing's, and a trusted friend. But despite his usual deference to his respected teacher, May lost his patience with Channing's equivocation. At their meeting, soon *after* the forcible closing of Crandall's school, May was in no mood to hear that the problem lay with the tone of the antislavery advocates and, instead, challenged Channing:

> We are not to blame, sir, that you, who, more perhaps than any other man, might have so raised the voice of remonstrance that it should have been heard throughout the length and breadth of the land,—we are not to blame, sir, that you have not so spoken.[115]

Channing remained silent after this chiding; for May the "minutes seemed very long" before Channing "in the kindliest tones of his voice . . . said 'Brother May, I acknowledge the justice of your reproof. I have been silent too long.'"[116]

These two conversations—Abdy in August and May in October 1834, both fresh from seeing the persecution of the young Black women whom they knew personally in Canterbury—impressed upon Channing the need to lend his voice, weight, and credibility to the struggle. In October 1834, Channing preached an antislavery sermon and in 1835 published his book on slavery. However, he hadn't *fully* heard his interlocutors on the intrinsic connection between racial prejudice and slavery; May found Channing's *Slavery* to be "one of the most inconsistent books I have ever read," and Abdy wondered how he could have been credited with provoking Channing's sermon on slavery, because they hadn't discussed slavery.[117] In *Slavery*, Channing wrote that the abolitionists had

> preached their doctrine to the colored people, and collected these into their societies. To this mixed and excitable multitude, minute, heart rending descriptions of slavery were given in the piercing tones of passion; and slaveholders were held up as monsters of cruelty and crime. Now to this procedure I must object as unwise, unfriendly to the spirit of Christianity, and as increasing, in a degree, the perils of the slaveholding States. Among the unenlightened, whom they so powerfully address, was there not reason to fear that some might feel themselves called to subvert this system of wrong, by whatever means?[118]

Free blacks are "excitable," "unenlightened," and given to subversion and rebellion; the abolitionists come across as irresponsible demagogues gathering a mob. This is a classic case of reversal. What Channing lacked is what Abdy, May, and, above all, Crandall had achieved: lived, complex daily interactions with free Blacks in America.

The End of the School: September 1834

The first days of September were calm. Calvin and Mrs. Philleo attended the wedding of William Lloyd Garrison and Helen Benson in Brooklyn on September 4.[119] Three days later, Maria Davis Harris gave birth to her first son, accorded the bellwether name of William Wilberforce Harris.[120] The following Tuesday, September 9, a lineage of descent through Crandall's students began when Sarah Harris Fayerweather delivered her firstborn, appropriately named Prudence Crandall Fayerweather.[121] It should have been a happy time. But the rabble of Canterbury's "gentlemen of property and standing" wasn't about to permit the pursuit of happiness.

The assault of September 9 was well planned, coordinated, and thorough. The assailants crept up soundlessly, attacking on a prearranged signal. The sudden noise, the sounds of destruction, being roused from sleep—all aimed at terrorizing the inhabitants. The house was "assaulted by a number of persons with heavy clubs and iron bars" with "ninety panes of glass dashed to pieces."[122] There was some ransacking on the first floor, primarily destroying furniture. William Burleigh and Albert Hinckley were staying at the house that night and with Calvin Philleo tried to detect the perpetrators, but the vandals had already blended into the dark night.[123] Once all was quiet, the men headed downstairs. All of the immediate neighbors remained silent, seemingly unconcerned with this noisy eruption. Philleo and Hinckley went across the street, but Judson made it clear that he would have nothing to do with Philleo or his complaint.[124]

In the meantime, Prudence and Almira had huddled with the students. Knowing of the attacks on their neighbors and families in Philadelphia and New York, the students were justifiably frightened. Two students who were asleep in a ground-floor room awoke to glass strewn across their bed. Abdy reported that "the woodwork was in such a state when I saw it, that it had yielded to the blow [from the attackers], and remained suspended over that part of the bed where the girl's neck must have lain."[125] One student was said to have coughed up blood, she was so terrified.[126] These mature women also knew, instinctively, how male mobs treated women they wanted to disgrace.

When dawn came, Prudence, Almira, Calvin, and William were shaken by the damage. What if any of the students had been grievously injured or killed? What if any of the students had been sexually assaulted? What would the rabble do next if this attack did not succeed in ridding Canterbury of the school?

Neither Crandall nor her students wanted to die as actual martyrs. They pursued education for practical and philosophical reasons, not as a publicity stunt. The women were there to be educated, to better assist their own community in gaining an education in the decades to follow. Now many were afraid to spend another night in the house.[127]

What happened between sunrise on Wednesday morning and the closure of the school later that day, who was involved in the decision, and the role that Crandall played are unclear. When Abdy returned later in September, Prudence and Calvin spoke with him together about that awful night attack and the next day's decision, so to postulate an open rift between husband and wife concerning the closure of the school is not warranted. In his account, May deletes the agents in his wording: "After due consideration, therefore, it was determined that the school should be abandoned." But the totality of the project's end—"abandonment" rather than a temporary suspension, relocation, or defiant continuity—raises questions. The perseverance of Crandall, her fellow teachers, and her students had been solid to this point.[128]

Before the attack, the school's reputation and its apparent continuity into the future were assured. Adby refers to several new students who were enroute when the closure occurred, including two from Cuba, two from Hartford, one from Worcester, and one from Boston who arrived within a few days after the attack.[129] This signals trust on the part of the Black community and a widening circle of contacts, as these new arrivals would have represented an increase in geographic range.

Since their marriage, the Philleos had been in the company of the students, except when in Philadelphia, where they visited three outstanding white women abolitionists—Lucretia Mott, Esther Moore, and Lydia White. These three women were among the few female attendees and speakers at the December 1833 founding conference of the American Anti-Slavery Society.[130] The possibility that Calvin was dismayed to find his wife in such strong female company and that he might have looked askance at any Philadelphia plan as a result cannot be ruled out. Furthermore, the local women in Windham County had formed the Brooklyn Female Anti-Slavery Society in late June; the group included the Bensons and Olive Gilbert.[131] Again, Philleo might have intuited that he was deeper in radical petticoats than he wanted to be, or worse, that he would always play a supportive rather than a lead role in this marriage. His later conduct makes it clear that he intended to exercise a husband's prerogatives of unquestioned authority. Nothing was ever again mentioned of the idea of Crandall relocating to Philadelphia, despite the warm welcome she received from both the white abolitionist women and the parents in the Black community. The Philadelphia Female Anti-Slavery Society did indeed open a school for Black children in November 1834, with the young Mary Grew as the first white teacher; she was soon succeeded by Sarah Mapps Douglass. The opportunity for Crandall had been genuine but not taken.[132]

The absence of any investigation to discover the perpetrators meant there was no protection in Canterbury, even in the name of common decency. Crandall herself was shaken; May said, "Never before had Miss Crandall seemed to quail," but she did on the morning of the tenth. Therefore, it is certainly possible that she made a precipitous decision to close the school, not having a ready fallback plan. Her passive decision left an opening that Calvin Philleo would becloud with his own confused agenda.

Once the final decision had been made, Prudence was unable to make the announcement herself. Whether from humiliation at letting the townspeople win, or not wanting to upset the students more if her own tears mixed with theirs, or a sense of having let her allies and students down, or simple exhaustion, we cannot know.

Prudence asked Reverend May to gather the students and make the announcement instead. His narrative merits careful attention:

> The pupils were called together, and I was requested to announce to them our decision. Never before had I felt so deeply sensible of the cruelty of the persecution which had been carried on for eighteen months, in that New England village against a family of defenceless females. Twenty harmless, well-behaved girls, whose only offence against the peace of the community was that they had come together there to obtain useful knowledge and moral culture, were to be told that they had better go away, because, forsooth, the house in which they dwelt would not be protected by the guardians of justice, the men of influence in the village where it was situated. The words almost blistered my lips. I felt ashamed of Canterbury, ashamed of Connecticut, ashamed of my country, ashamed of my color. Thus ended the generous, disinterested, philanthropic, Christian enterprise of Prudence Crandall.[133]

May understood the historic moment, having seen the school firsthand for these many months. But note that he does not say the school had failed. The students had acquired "useful knowledge and moral culture" under that roof, through their readings, and in watching the drama of their own education unfold.

May's expression of multiple levels of shame is an act of antiracist courage. He knew, better than most white participants, the degree of Black-white alliance that made the Canterbury Academy a reality, an example of one possible American future. Like the humiliation of Peter Williams by Bishop

Onderdonk under ecclesiastic discipline, the mob had won a battlefield victory with the school's closure. But unlike Parrish in Philadelphia or Tappan in New York, May did not pull back from the struggle or blunt his understanding of interracial work. He faced the Black women students directly and felt the shame of being a member (albeit, a defiant reforming member) of the dominant group—white Protestant males.

Since "Prudence Crandall is no more!" the newcomer Calvin Philleo was the one in whose name the school was closed. An ad placed in local newspapers, concerning the sale of the house, made it clear that Philleo was assuming the authority that the law granted husbands, using the first-person pronoun in declaring, "I have therefore thought it proper and do hereby advertise the house and appurtenances thereof for sale."[134]

The students left for home over the next few days; Calvin guarded the house along with Burleigh and a few friends. One of Crandall's white allies, William Kinne, agreed to rent the house until it could be sold. While Crandall hinted to Abdy that she might consider traveling to England, that was never to be.[135] Crandall would now be subject to the unsettled life of her husband, Calvin. It would be his erratic whims, rather than her resolute, even stubborn obstinacy, that would determine her fate.

It is with reluctance that one turns from the unjaded, dauntless Prudence Crandall. Certainly, she felt the sting of being defeated. Many years later, when the Connecticut state legislature settled a pension on her, to atone for their past torments, she wrote, with evident bitterness:

> To tell the amount of loss occasioned by the destruction of my prospects in life to earn a respectable competency that I might not only sustain myself in independence from the labor of others but be enabled to do some good to the world of mankind besides is a question difficult to solve.[136]

In the case of her desire to work with the Black community around her, Crandall's dream, when deferred, became a dream denied. But for those eighteen months of existence, the school was a vision encompassed, a changing of human circumstances, in which the educator put her privilege in the service of ending prejudice, followed the logic of ideas from free Black women and men, and delighted in being educated herself in the process and struggle.

CHAPTER 9

You Are Trying to Improve Your Mind in Every Way
Lives after the Academy

A peculiar circumstance in the life of this fine-souled woman [Crandall] was her immediate and continuous obscurity after her marriage.
—Fannie Barrier Williams

The post-Canterbury narrative is diasporic. While every teacher knows the twinge of sadness that accompanies the end of the school year, when a group that has been meeting regularly is unlikely to ever be together again as a unit, the Canterbury Academy's end was perversely cruel. The very purpose of its existence had led to its precipitous destruction. The students dispersed, having learned lessons from books but also from the history they had cocreated. Through the crucibles of trials and tribulations, the students had long been prepared; as one of the Connecticut students wrote in the summer of 1833, "if we are compelled to separate, let us, adorned with virtue and modesty, earnestly and diligently pursue every thing that will bring respect to ourselves, and honor to our friends who labor so much for our welfare."[1]

In an explicitly patriarchal society, a woman's fate is tied to marriage. Those students who remained unmarried or who found husbands who respected them gained latitude to expand and nurture their talents. Sarah Harris, Julia Williams, and Mary Elizabeth Miles were fortunate, forming true partnerships with their husbands in the abolition struggle. By contrast, Prudence Crandall and Elizabeth Douglass Bustill were not as fortunate; their marriages resulted in restricted agency and lost visibility.

The Canterbury Academy had been a woman-initiated, woman-centered, and interracial project, where women learned from and with each other. Marriage, even within the homosocial "separate spheres" of the nineteenth century, disrupted the very possibility for such a woman-centered project to continue. Not all husbands would "permit" their wives to act independently. Female agency and solidarity were always subject to impingement.

After her magnified importance from 1832 to 1834, Prudence Crandall Philleo sinks from view for the remainder of the decade, while transformative changes occurred in the abolitionist movement. Women such as the Grimké sisters and Abby Kelley Foster gained prominence as public speakers and thinkers. The dynamic voices of Black women that had been present in Canterbury and earlier with Maria Stewart and the Black press were marginalized, as "apparently either racism or class bias—or both—prevented" white women abolitionists "from identifying with [Maria] Stewart."[2]

Meanwhile, the same style of riotous opposition that had broken out against abolitionists in the summer of 1834 crescendoed in violence. In 1835 Garrison was nearly lynched by a Boston mob, while the South Carolina post-office crisis—an attempt to block abolitionist literature from reaching the South—led to curtailment of free speech. President Andrew Jackson openly wished for the deaths of abolitionists.[3] Crandall's younger brother, Reuben, would be caught in the jaws of this infuriated white majoritarianism. Reuben's unjust imprisonment and premature death climaxed a three-year span of tragedies for Prudence's family, but she "might have been on the moon for all the help she was able to send her family."[4]

Under coverture, husbands had clear legal control over all financial, business, and family matters. Husband and wife were merged by erasing the woman's independence, stripping her of any interests apart from those of her husband. The young Elizabeth Cady Stanton (1815–1902) found herself haunted—and taunted—by New York's marriage law:

> The tears and complaints of the women who came to my father for legal advice touched my heart and early drew my attention to the injustice and cruelty of the laws. . . . He would take down his books and show me the inexorable statutes. The students, observing my interest, would amuse themselves by reading to me all the worst laws they could find.[5]

This candidly patriarchal system didn't intend women to exercise independent agency.

Prudence Crandall's union with Calvin Philleo hitched her to his pattern of itinerancy and shiftless lack of perseverance. He placed her financial future in constant jeopardy and secreted her away from the movement when she could have benefitted the most from it and when her vast experience of interracial relations could have contributed much that was needed.

All who have examined the relationship between Philleo and Crandall agree that this was not a happy marriage over the long term. Prudence took to the role of stepmother with enthusiasm and attention but never expressed a desire to have a child of her own. She repeatedly sought to distance her-self from her husband—financially, physically, spiritually, and (one assumes) sexually. The couple spent years apart from each other, especially in the 1840s, when Prudence moved to her family's land in Illinois to escape from her husband. She even advocated for divorce rights, though not personally pursuing this option.[6] This reminiscence registers her resistance:

> My whole life has been one of opposition. I never could find any one near
> me to agree with me. Even my husband opposed me, more than anyone.
> He would not let me read the books that he himself read, but I did read
> them. I read all sides, and searched for the truth whether it was in science,
> religion, or humanity.[7]

The key here is her realization—a legacy of both evangelical individualism and romantic rationalism—that both the exploration and the choice are hers and that any and all authorities—church, state, wealth, god, or husband—can and should be interrogated. But despite whatever prescient analysis of her situation Crandall had, it is undeniable that her voice was subdued in the forty years of her marriage from 1834 until 1874.[8]

On reflection, it is jarring that marriage inhibited someone as strong as Crandall who for two years had forthrightly opposed the racism of her vil-lage, state, and nation. She had resisted male domination in religion, when her Baptist conversion required her to oppose her brothers. Her inability to overcome the roadblocks of marriage testifies to the resilience of patriarchal systems.

She did leave the Baptists for spiritualism, an implicit rejection of her husband's ministerial authority. While she doesn't leap from the paradigm of marriage, she does neutralize Calvin's worst patriarchal authoritarianism and reemerges stronger after his death. But the process took decades.

Crandall's Peregrinations: Boonville and Albany

Staying in the Canterbury area after the school closed proved untenable. Calvin occasionally supplied the pulpit at Packerville Baptist after Kneeland's death, but his cantankerous character was not winsome: he preached often but "to a thin House" where "some few seemed to be happy."[9] By May 1835 the Philleos departed Canterbury, headed for Boonville, New York.

In 1835 Boonville might have seemed promising. It was an imagined access point to the far northern regions of New York State as the proposed site for a feeder to the Erie Canal. The town was well positioned for the lumber industry, including a new carriage and wagon factory.[10]

One of Calvin's most successful brothers, medical doctor Bonaparte Philleo, lived nearby.[11] He took an especial interest in the health of Calvin's younger daughter, Elizabeth.[12] Bonaparte Philleo was an avid participant in temperance and antislavery activity. Like his sister-in-law Prudence, he is described as "a man of strong religious nature, but had no sympathy with bigotry and entertained broad and liberal religious views."[13] Calvin's older brother Darius lived in nearby Russia, New York; many of this branch of the family were Universalists.[14] These in-laws likely provided Prudence with more intellectual diversity than her husband preferred.[15]

Except for a few legal traces concerning property, the "Boonville period is pretty blank."[16] Calvin Philleo had previously preached at Boonville between 1824 and 1826, in the glow of spiritual fire from Finney's Utica revivals.[17] Upon his return in 1835, it is not clear that Philleo was invited back to the pulpit. In fact, from 1837 forward the Baptist congregation there complained that there "was little, if any, regular preaching service, and no advancement was made in spiritual life or in membership."[18] This suggests that Calvin Philleo was either overlooked for the regular pulpit or that by 1837 he and Prudence had left town.

After the formal end of slavery in New York State in 1827, Troy and Albany had become centers of Black education, industry, and political ferment.[19] Three independent sources indicate that the Philleos relocated to Albany at some point. First is a quixotic report from the "African Education Society" (an organization usually associated with the American Colonization Society). They suggest that 120 Black students could all be accommodated in "Mrs. Philleo's school." This notice, from late June 1835, suggests that the Philleos may have had Albany as their next destination. But this same report casts aspersions on "the Anti-Slavery Society's interfering with the plan of promoting education among the coloured people," chiding abolitionists "to avail themselves of opportunities to converse with the coloured people."[20] Why would Crandall associate with them, or they with her?

Second, Julia A. J. Foote (1823–1901), an African American who became a well-known holiness preacher and the first ordained female deacon in the AMEZ denomination, wrote of the school venture:

> Mr. and Mrs. Phileos [sic] and their daughter opened a school in Albany for colored children of both sexes. This was joyful news to me. I had saved a little money from my earnings, and my father promised to help me; so I started with hopes, expecting in a short time to be able to understand the Bible, and read and write well. Again was I doomed to disappointment: for some inexplicable reason, the family left the place in a few weeks after beginning the school. My poor heart sank within me. I could scarcely speak for constant weeping.[21]

There is much to recommend the veracity of this brief report. Foote's auto-biography was intended to establish her legitimacy, so outright fabrication is unlikely. Elizabeth Philleo had chosen teaching as her profession, but her perpetually fragile health meant she always accompanied Calvin and Pru-dence.[22] Calvin's modus operandi had become starting and then abandoning new ventures inexplicably.

The third corroboration comes from the pages of the *Liberator*. George Thompson, addressing a public meeting of the Glasgow, Scotland, Ladies' Emancipation Society, assured them that the commemorative plate they "had presented to Miss Crandall, in token of their high esteem of that lady's zeal and devotedness in the cause of the negro, had been received with joy and gratitude, and that, though now married to the Rev. Calvin Philleo, of Albany, New York, she was still actively engaged in instructing the colored population."[23]

This reference from 1837 corresponds to the return to Albany of Nathaniel Paul, among Crandall's most enthusiastic Black supporters. Residing in Eng-land during the Canterbury controversy, Paul's labor in making the plight of the school visible to British abolitionists burnished Crandall's school with international fame. When he returned to Albany in 1837, he delved into a flurry of organizing efforts, culminating in the interracial "Union Society of Albany, Troy, and vicinity."[24] Paul, the new organization's president, and its secretary, Andrew Harris of Troy, vigorously promoted education.[25] They were candid on the necessity of combatting racism and slavery simultaneously, yet never excluded white allies.[26] The idea that Prudence Crandall found this area attractive is enhanced by the presence of an ally like Nathaniel Paul.

Reuben Crandall's Imprisonment and Trial

Prudence's notoriety tragically led to traumatic consequences for her younger brother. Reuben's career path, including college education at Yale and medical training, lifted his class status above his parents and siblings. He disapproved of Prudence first when she converted to the Baptists and then again when her second academy was just opening. In late April 1833 Reuben happened to share a steamboat ride with Andrew Judson, who appealed to Reuben to talk sense into his sister. Reuben replied that he hoped to "break up the school" but admitted that he was unsure of success because Prudence was "a very obstinate girl." While that wasn't news to Judson, Reuben expressed confidence that he could lure Almira away from Prudence's influence. Judson believed that Reuben "used his whole influence to break up the school."[27] So in distinction to her more supportive siblings, Hezekiah and Almira, there was friction between Prudence and Reuben. He had chosen upward mobil-ity and social respectability, while she had embraced moral principle and lost social standing as a result. This makes Reuben's fate ironic: he suffered martyrdom for the abolition cause.[28]

The situation that placed Reuben in mortal danger was complex. He went to Washington, DC, as the private physician of a family from Peekskill, New York.[29] Upon arriving in the summer of 1835, Reuben brought a large trunk filled with abolitionist literature, with a slip of paper bearing the imperative: "Read and Circulate." At the moment these papers were discovered, the national capital was in an uproar over an enslaved teenager, Arthur Bowen, who had attempted to murder his "owner," an elderly white woman, Anna Maria Thornton, the widow of the architect of the US Capitol. With tensions riding high, neighbors informed on Reuben Crandall and his box of incendiary abolitionist literature. Reuben was arrested on August 10.

Previous scholarship presents Reuben as uninvolved in abolitionist work. Strane downplays Reuben's confession of his antislavery principles at the time of his arrest, while highlighting his disinterest in actually circulating the pamphlets. Donald Williams contends that "Reuben was never an ardent abolitionist" despite acquiring "a modest collection of abolitionist literature."[30] In contrast, Morley describes this most enigmatic of the Crandall siblings succinctly but persuasively: "Reuben was more cautious than his famous sister but he did not lack conviction."[31] He focuses on Reuben's friendship with two leading members of the American Anti-Slavery Society: Charles Denison and Robert G. Williams.[32]

Reuben's opinion of his sister's school changed sometime after his conversation with Judson; presumably his family "catechized" him. Between his radical abolitionist network, the resolution of the entire Crandall family in the face of the crisis around Prudence's school, and possibly meeting some of his sister's Black students, he made a commitment to abolition.

Two days after Reuben's arrest, Washington, DC, was rocked by "the Snow Riots." Accomplished and successful free Blacks were targeted, such as the restauranteur Beverly Snow, as well as those all-too-familiar targets: Black schools and churches.[33] As with the 1834 riots, the white mob considered Black success and respectability threatening.

Reuben Crandall's arrest in the midst of this unrest made his guilt a foregone conclusion to prosecuting district attorney Francis Scott Key (1779–1843). Best-known for "The Star-Spangled Banner," Key's legal career in the District of Columbia is significant. A founder and leader of the American Colonization Society, he resolutely opposed the presence of free Blacks in America. Roger Taney and Key were related by marriage; Key helped launch the future chief justice's career. Their shared conservative middle-state perspective was diffident toward slavery but hard-set against Black civil rights.

In *The Rights of All*, Reverend Samuel Cornish had decried Key's racism years prior. Key had pronounced that nothing could ever overcome the prejudice that existed between whites and Blacks. Cornish thundered back that Key had made the devil "stronger than the Deity" or, worse, had turned God into

> a bat, or a mole, who should he dare to name the rights of the oppressed, would be driven by the poisonous affluvia of his prejudice into Capt. Symes' hole? How dare such a man to speak of the triumphs of the Cross, or the progress of light.[34]

Free Blacks were leagues ahead of their white allies in plumbing colonizationists' racist depths.

With name recognition bequeathed from his infamous sister, Reuben Crandall appeared a gift dropped in Key's lap. Like a medieval tyrant, Key kept Reuben in a dank cell for months—permanently wrecking Crandall's health—and did not even charge him with anything until January 1836, announcing then that he sought the death penalty.[35]

Jefferson Morley's study demonstrates that Key mismanaged his case against Crandall. Key's penchant for ideological speeches left judge and jury unconvinced.[36] Histrionically overstating the dangers posed by Reuben Crandall and the allegedly libelous pamphlets, Key asserted that white property rights outweighed freedom of speech and Black civil rights, anticipating Taney's infamous Dred Scott decision. He harped on the dangers of racial equality and amalgamation, hoping those tropes would be self-evidently malicious. He failed: the jury acquitted Reuben in under three hours.[37]

Reuben Crandall's fate is pertinent to any study of Prudence Crandall. The quick decision of the jury in Reuben's case shows that his sister's school had damaged the ACS's presumed beneficence. Perhaps, Key felt the prestige of the ACS slipping away. As one legal scholar put it, the trial seemed "an attempt to vindicate the Colonization Society" to the extent that "it is at times difficult to determine whether Key is working for the government or the Colonization Society."[38]

But regardless of whether Reuben was a committed abolitionist or not, his tragedy differs from that of his sister in the most salient way possible: there are no Black names among his associates. However noble his sacrifice, it was abstract compared to the interracial reality created in Canterbury.

Almira Crandall

The personal impact of Reuben's case was devastating and altered the Crandall family forever. The physical distance between Prudence and her birth family meant that she missed her sister Almira's wedding to John Rand in July of that same year. But that was the only *happy* event she missed; a cascade of struggles and tragedies was soon to deluge the Crandalls.

Prudence Crandall's youngest sibling, Almira Crandall, had been a co-teacher at the academy. Prudence nurtured, mentored, and protected her younger sister during the two years of the academy, but Almira also took a leadership role when Prudence was away or ill. She was subject to legal harassment at the time of Crandall's arrest, when Nehemiah Ensworth sought to detain her.[39] She also shared in the terror of vigilante harassment; it was she who wrote of one of the more resounding thuds of cheap terror:

> The Canterburians have been very quiet for a few days until Sabbath evening last when at half part 9 oclock a *stone* about the size of my hand and about an inch and a half in thickness was thrown by some one through a north window of our parlour passing through the curtain and scattering glass in every direction. The family had all retired save myself. I had but a very few moments before passed through the room. At half past ten something else was thrown with great violence against the house. By whom either was done we know not and can only pity them for their weakness.[40]

Two of the closest white allies of the school—Samuel J. May and Albert Hinckley—took the time to recognize Almira's contributions in 1834: "Resolved, That Miss Prudence and Miss Almira Crandall merit the warmest approbation of all friends of the colored race, for their persevering and untiring exertions to educate colored females, under a most bitter and unchristian persecution."[41] The few letters we have from her hand demonstrate a lively temperament and commitment equal to her sister's. Almira entertainingly pilloried the hysterical ravings of the Canterburian white elite as "the age of Goths and Vandals."[42] In a letter from April 1833, she outlines the outrages contemplated against Ann Eliza Hammond. She affirms what Prudence, Maria Davis, and Sarah Harris had launched:

> How bitter must be the repentance of Christians who discover themselves to be the persecutors of Gods [sic] intellectual creatures because he saw fit not to give them as pale faces as themselves! May God forgive them for verily *"they know not what they do"*![43]

She understands the students as thinkers, "intellectual creatures," who have been wronged. Almira also went on to teach Black students in Rhode Island.[44]

She married teacher John Rand in 1835. William Lloyd Garrison was impressed with him, describing him as "a pleasant, genteel and handsome looking man" who was "doing very well as a school teacher." The young couple moved to New York City, but Almira's health went into steep and rapid decline within a year.[45] She died in August 1837 back home in Canterbury.[46]

Almira's early death deprived history of another woman who might have been a leader. Compare, for instance, Harriet Beecher receiving strong sisterly mentoring from her older sibling, educator Catharine Beecher. Almira and Prudence could have made a similar tandem but mortality stifled that potential.[47]

Tragic Travels

The spiral of death cascaded for the Crandall family in 1838. Reuben Crandall traveled to Jamaica, where he died in January 1838. Far from being forgotten, he was memorialized by the first meeting of the Connecticut State Anti-Slavery Society. The assembled abolitionists apparently had no doubts about Reuben's affiliation, counting him as a "valuable citizen" of Connecticut and "a firm friend" of "the perishing slave."[48] Calvin Philleo was present at that 1838 meeting (with a residence listed as New London, Connecticut).

Pardon Crandall decided to leave the area that had brought so much sadness to his family. He traveled to Illinois, joining a large outmigration of New Englanders to the northcentral sections of the Prairie state.[49] His decision would reshape the Crandall family, initiating a substantial presence in Troy Grove and Mendota. When he returned to Canterbury, he took ill and died in July 1838. At Pardon's funeral three days later, Hezekiah's wife, Clarissa Cornell Crandall, died of a heart seizure.[50]

Evidence suggests that Prudence and Calvin were back in Connecticut around the time of Pardon's funeral, as Calvin was preaching in the area in August 1838.[51] The three years that Prudence had been distant from her birth family—1835 to 1837—had been stifling for her and disastrous for them. Never again would she be distant from her blood relations, whether from her own guilt, or the protection they offered her from Calvin's tyranny, or simply because she loved being around her headstrong kin.

Women's Rights and Women's Voices in the Abolitionist Movement

Although the history of women's participation in the abolitionist movement of the mid-1830s is not the burden of this volume, it is noteworthy to consider the accomplishments in this period and thus to measure the "feminist mental feast" that Crandall missed.

In May 1837, the first Anti-Slavery Convention of American Women was held. Though interracial, it was not fully integrated; for instance, Black women were not among the named officers. Black women in attendance included Maria Stewart, Sarah Mapps Douglass, Grace Douglass, Susan Paul, and Crandall Academy alumna Julia Williams.[52]

The second Anti-Slavery Conference of American Women, held in 1838, witnessed the destruction of Pennsylvania Hall, yet the women continued their convention even after that horrifying vigilantism. When the mayor of Philadelphia beseeched Lucretia Mott to desist from any interracial familiarity, she declined, saying, "It was a principle with us, which we could not yield, to make no distinction on account of color."[53]

This discloses the real consequences of Calvin Philleo's patriarchal authoritarianism. Prudence Crandall was not able to be present at these conventions; we can't even be sure how or if she was aware of them. Her sister Almira was deceased. The white female energy from the academy had dispersed. Black female energy was not as conspicuously central to the movement as it had been when Sarah Harris and Maria Davis had converted Crandall.

Some white women gained access to the public sphere through what Julie Husband terms "antislavery sentimentalism." Women spoke by claiming that they were defending the domestic sphere and highlighting suffering: "The women leaders of the antislavery movement pioneered a brand of antislavery sentimentality that put human suffering, especially as signaled by weeping and other physical signs, at the center of their appeals."[54]

Crandall's project, by contrast, was not about inducing tears but educating young women to take their role in society as teachers and activists. Her school was not sentimental, nor ornamental, nor a charity. The serious intellectual and moral work undertaken by the students and teachers in Canterbury are dimensions of the struggle that could have helped foster creative forms of cooperation between Black and white women.

The Noyes Academy

The day after the Canterbury Academy closed, September 11, 1834, the Noyes Academy in Canaan, New Hampshire, announced its intention to accept men and women, Black and white, to their course of study. The endorsers were an all-white male group. At its height the school had twenty-eight white and fourteen Black students. Among the Black students were two who assumed prominent roles as antebellum abolitionists and ministers: Henry Highland Garnet and Alexander Crummell.[55] Most conspicuous for this study, though, was Canterbury alumna Julia Williams. It was here that she met Henry Highland Garnet, her future husband.

The Noyes Academy, like Crandall's school, received widespread support from abolitionists, as the school received ample coverage in the *Liberator*. At a patriotic gathering in Plymouth, New Hampshire, on the Fourth of July in 1835, four Black male students—including Garnet and Crummell—addressed the crowd. They did not hesitate to critique colonization. Garnet contrasted "his own feelings with those proper" to celebrating the Fourth, before declaring it "the duty of every patriot and Christian to adopt the principles of the abolitionists . . . that every man who walked the American soil might tread it unmolested and free." On that Sunday, the four young Black speakers attended church with Nathaniel P. Rogers:

> Their presence proved no interruption to the services. They amalgamated with the congregation. The pew doors of our yeomanry, too respectable to be sneered down by the dandyism of the land, were opened to them, and they had the satisfaction of associating with their brethren and countrymen and fellow sinners, on proper and Christian footing. This I call *practical Antislavery*.[56]

The speeches of Garnet and Crummell at the Fourth of July celebration coincided with a meeting in Canaan that claimed the mantle of patriotism. A gang of white Canaanites, boasting they acted in "the spirit of '75," resolved to abolish the Noyes Academy. These white vigilantes took the news that the Black students were addressing public meetings as a further assault on "patriotism." They maintained no pretense of civic patience or legal maneuvering, preferring to maneuver nearly one hundred oxen. On August 10 (the same day, ironically, as Reuben Crandall's arrest in Washington, DC), they removed the Noyes Academy building from its foundation by hitching the animals to ropes bound round the schoolhouse and dumped the school in a pond, where the building remained as a potent symbol until it burned at the end of the decade.[57]

Perhaps, Crandall felt vindicated in her decision to close her school, since the danger to life and limb became patent in Canaan. In distinction to Canterbury and perhaps due to the coeducational nature of the school, students were less committed to nonresistance. Henry Highland Garnet, who with his family had self-liberated from enslavement, reportedly defended the academy with a gun.[58]

From Boonville to Albany and back to Canterbury, from Canaan to Reuben's jail cell in Washington, DC, this time period demonstrates how the energy of someone like Prudence Crandall could be stymied. Calvin Philleo effectively extracted his wife from her political role, her vocation, and her family. He was only able to do that for a few years, when she was most vulnerable and when his children, especially Calvin Jr., were young and in need of protection from their father's dictatorial ways. The lesson here is sobering: if marriage could sap the energy of a woman as strong as Crandall, how many more women were thus stifled?

"To Live for Usefulness":
Canterbury Academy Alumnae

The Black women who attended the second academy in Canterbury became an accomplished group of activists, professionals, mothers, and community leaders. Their success is outstanding for any academy's alumna list, even without the added pressures of racial prejudice and patriarchal norms.

At least six students became teachers: Miranda Glasko, Elizabeth Smith, Mary Harris Williams, Mary Elizabeth Miles Bibb, Ann Eliza Hammond, and Julia Williams. Six went on to documented activism in the abolitionist movement: Julia Williams, Sarah Harris Fayerweather, Eliza Glasko Peterson, Elizabeth Henly, Elizabeth Smith, and Mary Elizabeth Miles Bibb; two worked with freedmen after the war: Mary Harris Williams and Mary Elizabeth Miles Bibb (plus Elizabeth Smith's son, Isaac). At least three engaged with George Downing in efforts to integrate Rhode Island schools: Elizabeth Smith, Miranda Glasko Overbaugh, and Eliza Glasko Peterson. Three went on for additional education: Julia Williams, Mary Elizabeth Miles, and Eliza Weldon. Ten of these women married prominent male educators, activists, and community leaders: Bolt Vidal, DeGrasse Vogelsang, Fenner Parker, Glasko Peterson, Glasko Overbaugh, Harris Fayerweather, Harris Williams, Miles Bibb/Cary, Brown Smith, and Williams Garnet; they helped organize political events and educational enterprises.

Crandall's students put their education to use. While fulfilling roles perceived as proper for women, they surpassed those preconceptions, too. Notions of female respectability in the Black community always included community engagement and activism against racism and prejudice.[59] As a group, they fulfilled the call by one of their sister-students to "earnestly and diligently pursue every thing that will bring respect to ourselves, and honor to our friends."[60]

Not all of the students went on to lives of fame, though. Gloriana Catherine Marshall apparently died young, as there are no records of her after the school.[61] However, her siblings and niece Maritcha Lyons helped nurture the historic memory of the Crandall school.

Despite her early death, Harriet Rosetta Lanson's aspirations convey the trajectory of the lives of the students. When her final illness was upon her, Lanson did not fear death but regretted leaving because she "had hoped to live for usefulness." She wanted to fulfill the promise that her education had afforded her. As Simeon Jocelyn wrote in her remembrance, Lanson had glimpsed "the field of hope and usefulness to which immortal beings should be appointed."[62]

The most surprising disappearance from the historical records concerns Elizabeth Douglass Bustill. For a member of such a distinguished lineage to simply disappear from the historical record raises questions. Family historian Anna Smith Bustill boasted, "All families have records, but seldom are they so well preserved as that of the Bustill Family."[63] It takes considerable digging outside of the family records to discover the outlines of Elizabeth's life. She married Charles Jones (1810–80) in 1844. They had at least six children; Cornelia, one of the daughters, apparently got herself into some trouble romantically. This led to Elizabeth Bustill Jones traveling to Mississippi around 1870 to live with Cornelia and her family.[64] The records seem to indicate that Elizabeth Bustill Jones returned to Philadelphia later in her life; there are competing records of her death, one in 1898, the other in 1915 (which would make her the longest-surviving student from the academy).[65]

This speculative reconstruction, if correct, raises as many questions as it addresses. How did Elizabeth Bustill use her education? Did she assist in teaching the freedmen in the South? Was Elizabeth's marriage to Charles Jones somehow disgraceful, that it received no mention in the family history? As one of the students with high social standing, her meandering personal history is enigmatic. Whatever the story, the Bustills remain proud of her attendance at Crandall's academy.[66]

The mystery of the Tucker-Goary sisters became entangled with the history of Liberia and Sierra Leone, under the auspices of the American Missionary Association, an organization with radical abolitionist credentials.[67] The primary source on them—*The Gospel in All Lands*—relates a most unusual lineage of the surviving son of Virginia Tucker Johnson and Pompey Johnson: George Washington Johnson, who had been raised and influenced in Liberia by his aunt Maria Tucker Finnemore, was a prominent Liberian politician. The same newspaper report says Maria returned to Massachusetts after her husband died in Liberia, leaving George Washington Johnson in the care of C.T.O. King, a leading Black representative of the American Colonization Society and mayor of Monrovia in the 1880s.[68] Under King's tutelage, George W. Johnson rose to prominence, but he claimed his mother was a native African. The story of George W. Johnson, whose political nickname of "Reversible Johnson" arose from his flexibility, is difficult to corroborate in its details. He became a leading figure in Egbaland, promoting Egba identity, language, and self-government while also endorsing national unity.[69] Maria Goary Finnemore eventually moved to California where she was remarried to Henry Yantis; they had two children, neither of whom survived to adulthood.[70]

Julia Foote may have studied briefly with Crandall in Albany. She went on to a storied but stormy career in the AMEZ church. She and Crandall endorser Jehiel Beman clashed over Foote's enthusiastic religious style; Beman essentially banned her from further participation in his church, using blatantly sexist arguments to do so. Foote's memoir is an important document in African American women's religious history.[71]

Clusters and Paragons of Alumna

New York City and Rhode Island became centers for Crandall alumnae. Both of the Glasko daughters married educators based in New York City. There they lived in the same neighborhood as Henrietta Bolt Vidal, the Marshall family, Theodosia DeGrasse Vogelsang, and Ann Peterson.

Sarah Harris Fayerweather and Amy Fenner Parker moved to Rhode Island after their marriages, where Elizabeth Brown Smith worked as a teacher and later principal at the Meeting Street Primary School in Providence.[72] Recently, scholars Elizabeth Stevens and Kate Blankenship have uncovered evidence linking Amy Fenner Parker and Elizabeth Smith. Amy Fenner married Ransom Parker around 1837; Ransom was a property owner and an activist in many causes for racial equality in Rhode Island, including voting rights and school desegregation.[73] He served as principal of the Meeting Street Primary School in 1838 and hired Elizabeth Brown as a teacher. She stayed in that position, with distinction, for nearly half a century.[74] While receiving accolades for her pedagogical skills, Elizabeth remained active in antislavery causes, serving as a manager for the Providence Ladies' Anti-Slavery Society fair.[75] She married John N. Smith in the late 1840s, and their only child, Isaac Smith, was born in 1853.

Elizabeth Brown Smith taught at a segregated school but seems to have weathered the storm of controversy within Providence's Black community concerning the question of segregation and desegregation. Indeed, her son, Isaac, attended the integrated public high school in Providence.[76] Elizabeth Brown Smith always "maintained a lively interest in all groups working for uplift" and successfully intertwined intellectual and activist work through education.[77] Maritcha Lyons notes that Smith assisted "the 'Grand Old Man' of our people"—Frederick Douglass—then quoted Smith's pride in being among the abolitionists, those "real patriots who essayed such heroic service in stirring northerners' consciences just 'before the crisis.'"[78]

Elizabeth Smith also attained renown as a pianist and a piano teacher.[79] She fit the canons of "respectability" and "loved learning not only for learning's sake but for the privilege it gave her to aid in developing the mental growth and mental strength of the immature."[80] Her renown in Providence led to her application to join the prestigious, but all-white Rhode Island Woman's Club. Smith was rejected.[81] Elizabeth Buffum Chace—a classmate of Crandall and daughter of Crandall endorser Arnold Buffum—resigned her membership in the woman's club over this racism, declaring Smith's rejection a betrayal by white women "who for years had been pleading the cause of disfranchised womanhood, and now, for the sake of drawing into their circle women of the conservative, prejudiced classes, were willing to reject and to crush a woman more than disfranchised, worse than ill-paid, more outraged than themselves."[82]

Ann Eliza Hammond surfaces twice in the historical record after Canterbury. In 1836 she is coteaching with Ransom Parker—who would marry Amy Fenner—at the Providence English School for Colored Youth, under the principal, Reverend John Lewis. This educational venture mentions the same motivation as the Canterbury Academy: "Young men or young ladies of color who have it in their minds to engage in schools as teachers, will find it to their advantage to devote a part of their time to the study of these branches, and *the way is now open*."[83] While the Canterbury Academy and the Canaan Academy may have been shuttered by violence, the ripple in the pool that the women in Canterbury had started continued to flow outwards.

Ann Eliza Hammond is also known in much-later records, traveling to Cuba. She is on passenger lists from August 1873 and August 1874; judging from the names adjacent to hers, she was traveling alone, the intent of her trips unknown.[84] Given that she made these voyages under her maiden name, she likely had not married. Further, she had enough disposable income in her late fifties to afford such trips.

The Connecticut contingent of students, which had been quite strong, spread out in the years following the school. Eliza Glasko married John Peterson and moved to New York City. Her sister Miranda Glasko stayed with their parents until 1867, when she married Thomas Overbaugh and followed Eliza to New York City.[85] Olive Harris, who may have been a student, married Frederick Olney and lived in New London.[86] Maria Davis Harris lived with Charles Harris in Norwich, where they ran a restaurant and raised eight children.[87] Jerusha Congdon apparently stayed in the Windham County area, where her connections to her birth family were so strong that she is not even buried under her married name or with her husband.[88]

Both the New York City and Rhode Island clusters provide illustrations of activism and the strength of networks built while at the academy. Peter Vogelsang Sr., George DeGrasse, and Thomas Downing were leaders from the generation of the students' parents; they worked together as part of the Black elite of New York City in the 1820s and 1830s. John Peterson, George Downing, and Peter Vogelsang Jr. were part of a younger generation, along with the famed Henry Highland Garnet who, despite his frequent moves, was most associated with New York City in the 1840s and 1850s. Everyone in this leadership had direct connections through blood or marriage to alumnae of Crandall's Academy. They participated in intense debates about politics in the Black community, replete with frequent polemics, bitterness, and denunciation: it is important to recognize that however stressful such differences can be, they demonstrate the breadth of opinion that a functioning community will always have.[89] Because of their education in Canterbury, intelligent women gave their counsel and support to these Black male leaders. These women had sought out and fought for education, endorsed further education for their communities, and participated in the political debates themselves.

Among the Crandall alumnae, for instance, Mary Elizabeth Miles Bibb was part of a pitched rhetorical battle with Mary Ann Shadd Cary over questions of emigration to Canada and Black self-development. The invective was quite fierce—at one point Shadd Cary accused Henry Bibb of denying resources to refugees to Canada while his chickens rested on donated clothes![90] The Bibbs and their newspaper "favored black settlements, separate institutions, and white philanthropy to support them." Those aligned against them, including "Samuel R. Ward, Mary Ann Shadd Cary, and the *Provincial Freeman* group . . . urged blacks to be self-sufficient and to assimilate into Canadian society."[91]

While the Canterbury Academy can be considered part of the genealogy of Black nonviolent resistance, both Julia Williams Garnet and Mary Elizabeth Miles Bibb married men who considered violence defensible in the cause of justice. Henry Highland Garnet and Henry Bibb's views were incongruent with Dymond's and Garrison's nonresistance. But this demonstrates the importance of the training their wives received, for it is not in the manufacture of carbon copies that the mission of education rests. It is in fostering the ability to think critically.

As a self-liberated escapee from enslavement, and a survivor of antieducation vigilantism at Canaan, Henry Highland Garnet grew impatient with the pragmatic limits to moral suasion.[92] His most famous speech, given to a Black convention in 1843 in Buffalo, New York, called for the enslaved to revolt. It generated much vitriol, failing by one vote to receive the endorsement of the convention.[93] Julia Williams Garnet assisted her husband in the writing of this famous speech. When Maria Weston Chapman, the white associate editor of the *Liberator* excoriated the talk, Garnet responded with a scathing letter:

> You say that I "have received bad counsel." You are not the only person who has told your humble servant that his humble productions have been produced by the "*counsel*" of some anglo-saxon. I have expected no more from ignorant slaveholders and their apologists, but I really looked for better things from Mrs. Maria W. Chapman, an antislavery poetess, and editor *pro tem*, of the Boston Liberator. I can think on the subject of human rights without "counsel," either from the man of the West, or the women of the East. My address was read to but two persons, previous to its presentation at Buffalo. One was a colored brother, who did not give me a single word

of counsel, and the other was my wife; and if she did counsel me, it is no matter, for "we twain are one flesh."[94]

While the content of Julia Williams Garnet's advice is not known, we can infer from her educational odyssey that she would have brought a subtle mind to her husband's thesis, capable of anticipating counterarguments.[95]

Julia Williams Garnett maintained important relations with prominent white abolitionists, including Nathaniel Rogers and Gerritt Smith.[96] Rogers played an ongoing role in the life of Julia Williams, taking her into his household after the destruction of the Noyes Academy until she could return to Boston, where she became a teacher.[97] In addition to sustaining these strong ties, Julia accompanied her husband when he was assigned a missionary role in Jamaica by the Presbyterians. Here she taught school and broke local caste custom by teaching Black girls to sew—a job previously reserved for "brown" interracial women.[98] Once the Garnets had returned to New York City, Julia took a lead role in fundraising for the family of John Brown, hosting a meeting and establishing the "New York Liberty Fund."[99] Garnet preached in December 1862 that future generations would honor John Brown and recognize Nat Turner and Denmark Vesey as Brown's forerunners.[100] However, the Draft Riots of 1863 took a terrible toll on all of New York's African American population. For the Garnets, the riots must have seemed an awful recapitulation of the hatred they'd been fighting all their lives.[101] One of the institutions destroyed at that time, the Negro Orphan Asylum, had been a focus of charitable work for Julia and Henry (and likely other Canterbury alumnae).

When Julia Williams died of pneumonia in 1870, she was eulogized by two historically significant Black men: her widower, Henry Highland Garnet, and Alexander Crummell. Her husband wrote privately of this "gentle, sweet-tempered, God-loving woman," who had been a "perfect wife" to him.[102] Crummell's encomium noted how she "thirsted for education," persisting until she had "qualified herself for a teacher." Her sharp mind, impatient with racism in any form, coexisted with a sweet character: "She exemplified in her life all the virtues of a noble Christian woman. Her devotion to the antislavery cause, and her sacrifices for the fleeing fugitives, may not be recorded by human pen but the recording angel has written them." "The recording angel" being unavailable, we must accept Crummell's contention that her deeds outstripped the ciphers of them. The key link across her life highlighted in this memorial is Crummell's naming her "as a representative woman."[103] In 1837, when Julia Williams was chosen as a delegate from Boston to the Women's Anti-Slavery Convention in New York City, white abolitionist Anne Warren Weston explained that Williams was selected "because the coloured people regard her as one of themselves."[104] This means that for over thirty-five years, Julia Williams (later, Garnet)—friend to Prudence Crandall,

Nathaniel Rogers, and Gerritt Smith—was recognized in the Black community for the integrity of her commitment.[105] Julia Williams Garnet lived an antiracist life, maintaining alliances across the racial divide, while eschewing any simplistic resolution of the problems of race in America.

A great deal is known about Mary Elizabeth Miles, thanks to excellent scholarship by Afua Cooper and Kabria Baumgartner. In 1838 she was admitted to the integrated Young Ladies' Domestic Seminary in Clinton, New York, founded by abolitionist Hiram Kellogg. After graduation, she joined Samuel J. May at the State Normal School in Lexington, Massachusetts, in the mid-1840s.[106] From there she obtained a teaching job at the Wilberforce School in Albany in 1845, becoming its principal the next year. Here she developed a friendship with Gerrit Smith.[107] She met Henry Bibb in 1847, marrying him in 1848. Miles Bibb and her husband shared the intellectual work of editing the newspaper, the *Voice of the Fugitive*.[108] The first notice of this newspaper came from Miles Bibb, who sent the prospectus to Gerrit Smith.[109] In articles she wrote, including on the subject of education, she consistently championed the agency of Afro-Canadians and the heroism of fugitives. Scholar Afua Cooper speculates there were open disagreements, at least of emphasis, between Miles Bibb and her famed husband.[110] Kabria Baumgartner discovered a remarkable 1846 letter from Miles to Gerrit Smith, in which Miles foreshadows an intersectional analysis, in revealing that she had to contend with "not only . . . prejudice against poverty, prejudice against color but prejudice against her sex."[111] Scholar Bernell E. Tripp contends that the October 22, 1851, editorial on antiliteracy laws in slaveowning states was written by Mary Elizabeth Miles Bibb:

> A body of men premeditate keeping us in perpetual ignorance, because they know that if education reached us . . . the truth would be elicited that we were human beings, and might compel the same acknowledgement from our masters. Let us hear no more of our natural inferiority, for the above sentences admit our equality with the white enslaver,—they establish the fact that slaves can be converted into thinking beings.[112]

After the death of Henry Bibb, Mary Elizabeth Miles married Isaac Cary and continued to astound with her range of activities, including work as a teacher and an artist.

The first student, Sarah Harris Fayerweather, and Prudence Crandall corresponded later in their lives. Commiserating over the death of their friend Samuel Joseph May in 1871, Crandall expressed guarded optimism over the state of race relations in the postwar South: "This is a glorious time to work for humanity to hold up the labor question, temperance, woman's suffrage, and to put down cast[e]. I am sad for the colored people in the South, but I feel in hopes the[y] have seen the worst part of their affliction."[113]

Fayerweather made the long journey from Rhode Island to Kansas to visit Crandall in 1877. It is remarkable that she undertook this strenuous voyage in what turned out to be her final year. Maritcha Lyons described the elderly Fayerweather: "She was tall, fine looking and had a voice of peculiar sweetness. Her favorite attitude was sitting erect with clasped hands, while her steady gaze seemed to pierce far below the surface of things. She made a beautiful picture with abundant gray hair framing an almost colorless ivory face whose smile redeemed it from severity."[114] Even after Sarah's death Prudence stayed in touch with her children, confirming that the relationship between teacher and student was one of genuine friendship. Mere positive contact between Blacks and whites was remarkable enough in the late nineteenth century; friendship was a far-rarer jewel.

Learned Lines of Descent

The students' multigenerational legacies radiate into many trajectories in American history. One extraordinary example comes from Theodosia DeGrasse's husband, Peter Vogelsang Jr. He volunteered for the first Black regiment in the Civil War, the famed Massachusetts Fifty-Fourth, and survived the war. While Theodosia had died of consumption before the war, this connection of an alumna to the incorporation of Blacks into the Union Army illuminates the diffuse connections between Canterbury and Black history writ large.

Sarah Harris married blacksmith George Fayerweather. They lived in New London before moving to his birthplace of Kingston, Rhode Island. Their home became an abolitionist center in western Rhode Island. Sarah Harris Fayerweather followed the same path as Prudence Crandall, remaining allied with abolitionists across the factional divide. She maintained close friendship with both Garrison and Frederick Douglass (her seventh child was named Charles Frederick Douglass Fayerweather (1845–1914)).[115] Some of her children also became educators—Sarah M. Fayerweather in Delaware and George Fayerweather teaming up with his aunt Mary Harris Williams and uncle Pelleman Williams as part of a dynamic team of Black educators in Louisiana. He maintained close ties with the Black middle class in New York City, as evidenced by his serving as a pallbearer for Albro Lyons's funeral in 1906.[116] Isabella M. Fayerweather Mitchell (b. 1839) and Mary E. Fayerweather (b. 1836) corresponded with Prudence Crandall after the death of their mother, Sarah Harris. Isabella's daughter, Mabel Mitchell Perry, became a well-known piano teacher in Kingston. Her son, George Lewis—Sarah Harris's great-grandson—became the first Black student at the University of Rhode Island, in the class of 1915. The Harris family has consistently sustained their participation in education and civil rights.

An equally impressive multigenerational influence can be traced in the lives of Mary Harris Williams's descendants. Sarah Harris's younger sister remained engaged in both abolition and education.[117] She married an important Black educator, Pelleman M. Williams, in 1845. He had attended Amherst College and Dartmouth College. In 1849 he took a leadership role at the Connecticut State Convention of Colored Men.[118] Sometime in 1863 or 1864, Pelleman and Mary Harris Williams and their three children—Arthur, Mary Belle, and Pellemina—moved to New Orleans under the auspices of the abolitionist-led American Missionary Association (and later the Freedman's Bureau) where they worked as teachers. This included involvement with Straight University and its preparatory division. Straight had Blacks on its board of trustees and among its faculty, which won support within the Black community. George H. Fayerweather, son of Sarah Harris, was among the five Black trustees, while Pelleman Williams was on the faculty.[119]

Mary and Pelleman's son, Arthur P. Williams (1846–1920), attained great prominence in New Orleans as the lead teacher at the Fisk School for Boys. His wife, the remarkable Sylvanie Francoz (1847–1921), headed the contiguous Fisk School for Girls. Arthur Williams instituted a challenging curriculum while also making the turn toward honoring Black culture in its own right. He did this primarily in the realm of music; the school produced oratorios and classical concerts, including a production of *H.M.S. Pinafore*, while also bringing in local Black musicians who knew Creole traditions. The result was a key role for Fisk in the history of jazz: Louis Armstrong attended Fisk, and it is likely Buddy Bolden had preceded him.[120]

In addition to those famed students, Fisk School for Boys had two other teachers who played an important role in jazz history, James (1876–1945) and Wendell MacNeal (1878–1971).[121] They were the two oldest children of Pellemina Maria Williams and her husband, James MacNeal, and thus the nephews of principal Arthur Williams. The two of them became charter members of the famed Robichaux Orchestra, James on cornet and Wendell on violin. The Robichaux Orchestra's musical achievements included a blending of classical and jazz instrumentation and Dee Dee Chandler's innovative bass-drum pedal that spawned the modern drum set.[122] The brothers had not forgotten their activist heritage: in 1902 they helped organize the Negro Musicians Union in New Orleans.[123] Both brothers participated in the Great Migration north, where Wendell and his growing family settled in Illinois. His youngest surviving child, Zulme (Nuffie) Sybil MacNeal (1916–2008), maintained the jazz lineage through her marriage to Cab Calloway (1907–94).

Nuffie's older sister, Delia Lucille MacNeal Piper (1909–2006), chose a different course in raising her youngest son, Chuck Piper, withholding knowledge of his racial identity from him. While he remembers his grandfather Wendell, before Chuck started school the family moved from Chicago to rural Wisconsin, where they were light-skinned enough to pass as white. It was not until Chuck Piper applied for a passport in 1985 and had to produce a birth certificate that he discovered his own racial heritage and the illustrious family history of "a long line of social activists and unsung heroes who did extraordinary things."[124] This great-great-grandson of Mary Harris and his wife, Judy (an avid genealogist), have enriched the story of the school's legacy.[125]

The Harris family is not alone in sustained achievement through multiple generations. Julia Williams's granddaughter, Annie H. Barboza (1872–1923), continued her grandmother's legacy by becoming a teacher at Philadelphia's Mount Vernon school.[126]

Amy Fenner and her husband Ransom Parker were great-grandparents to Aida Laing (1896–1979), who married Frederick Douglass Pollard (1894–1986), better known to history as Fritz Pollard. Fritz Pollard Sr. was one of the first Black players in the National Football League, the first Black head coach in the NFL, publisher of the *New York Independent*, and an entertainment impresario who worked with Duke Ellington (among others).[127] Pollard and Laing's son Fritz Pollard Jr. (1915–2003), excelled in track and field, participating on the US team in the infamous 1936 Olympic Games held in Hitler's Germany. While the achievements of Jesse Owens at those games are rightly celebrated, Amy Fenner's great-great grandson continued the family legacy of challenging racism by winning a bronze medal.[128] He eventually held a high position in the US State Department's Equal Opportunity branch.[129] Sadly, he did not live to see his father honored: Fritz Pollard Sr. was inducted into the Pro Football Hall of Fame in Canton, Ohio, in 2005. Fritz Pollard Jr.'s son, Fritz Pollard III, and another grandson, Steven Towns, were there offering an incisive analysis of racism in their speeches honoring their grandfather.[130]

While Gloriana Catherine Marshall's fate is as yet unknown, her sisters' children went on to great prominence in the Northeastern Black middle class, especially through the writings of Maritcha Lyons. She was a pioneer in recording and maintaining Black women's history. This line of strong, smart women continues today with scholar Carla Peterson, whose brilliant *Black Gotham* contributed mightily to the threads of this book. Peterson is a direct descendent of Elizabeth Marshall's line.

Consider the range of accomplishment in these descendants of Crandall's students, spanning social justice, education, music, sports, and scholarship. This proves it imperative to reassess Crandall's Academy for Young Ladies and Little Misses of Color. The arc of its impact exceeds the venom of its attackers many times over. By this measure and by virtue of the uniquely diverse curriculum available to Crandall's students, the Canterbury Academy stands as a resounding success and a momentous achievement in the history of antiracism and women's education.

CONCLUSION

Hearing All the Voices

Anyone having as large self-esteem as I
have likes to be appreciated.
—Prudence Crandall, 1880

Distantly related by marriage and sharing an interest in temperance, Prudence Crandall and John Staples Smith (1823–92) started corresponding in the 1880s.[1] Their contact accelerated in 1885; Smith visited Crandall in Elk Falls, Kansas, where she had moved with her brother Hezekiah (when they were both in their seventies). Smith conceived the idea of obtaining a pardon and pension from Connecticut for Crandall, to mitigate its imposition of the Black Law.[2]

Back in Connecticut, Smith organized an efficient campaign, generating considerable attention and gaining significant allies. George S. Burleigh (1821–1903), brother to Charles, William, and Mary Burleigh, helped Smith generate a petition with over a hundred signatures from Canterbury, lamenting the "dark blot" that rested upon the village "for the cruel outrages inflicted upon a former citizen of our Commonwealth, a noble Christian woman."[3] A number of descendants of Crandall's persecutors became involved: Samuel Coit, son of sheriff Roger Coit; state Supreme Court Justice Elisha Carpenter, who had studied with Crandall prosecutor Jonathan Welch; and Thomas G. Clarke, a distant relation of Andrew Judson.[4] Descendants of those who supported Crandall also got involved; Henry Taintor, related to Crandall's lawyer William Ellsworth, testified in her favor. As the idea of compensating Crandall gained momentum, the press amplified the case to overcome a temporary loss of nerve by the legislators, leading to the granting of a yearly pension of $400 in April 1886.[5]

A wonderful end to the story, yet there are still inequalities to be articulated. While it is true that the legal maneuvering against the school injured Crandall, those most injured were Black women students, real and potential. And while Connecticut was able to soothe its conscience with this pension (which did enable Crandall to end her life vindicated and without fear of want), the actual social injury caused by the closure of the school—lack of access to higher education for Black women—was not repaired. Furthermore, except for Crandall herself, who was in touch with Sarah Harris Fayerweather's children during the pension controversy, no evidence has yet surfaced of attempts to reassemble or honor students from the academy. The State of Connecticut apologized for damaging the life prospects of an enterprising young white woman but didn't express remorse for having blocked the expansion of Black education.

Mark Twain, who knew a good story when he encountered one, supported the pension battle. His support gave the campaign a major public relations boost. Twain, though, *was* concerned about the larger issue. At the same time that he was offering to help Crandall, he was providing financial assistance to Warner Thornton McGuinn (1859–1937), a Black Yale law student. Twain had met McGuinn and sensed his potential but also noted how fiscally difficult it was for McGuinn to pay tuition. Twain wrote that whites had demeaned Blacks—his words were "ground the manhood out of them"—but however patronizing that sounds to our twenty-first-century ears, Twain's sense of responsibility comes through: "the shame is ours, not theirs, and we should pay for it."[6] And so he did.

Warner McGuinn went on to be a lawyer and civic leader in Baltimore. He led the fight for antisegregation laws in the wake of World War I and gave early support to women's suffrage. He was a leader on the Baltimore City Council, serving from 1919 to 1923 and 1927 to 1931.[7] He also served as a mentor and role model to Thurgood Marshall, who had an office adjoining McGuinn's in Baltimore.[8]

But before this distinguished career in Baltimore, McGuinn first practiced law in Kansas City, Kansas, and edited a Black paper, the *American Citizen* from 1889 to 1891. The final letter we have from Crandall's hand dates from December 1889. She proudly reports that she always read newspapers "edited by colored men that I can learn what they are doing for themselves."[9] Perhaps, Crandall meant McGuinn's paper, especially since a Black-run newspaper was a relatively rarity in Kansas. McGuinn was aware of Crandall's significance. When she died on January 28, 1890, the *American Citizen* ran two prominent memorials. The first was a brief obituary on page 1, entitled "The Negroes Friend" [sic].[10] More crucially, McGuinn's lead editorial filled a full column.

> Prudence Crandall is justly entitled to a foremost rank among the women who have lived in this century. . . . She was a woman of great breadth of mind, and of a heart so big that in it was a niche and nook for all the children of earth. She was a woman of settled convictions and an indomitable will power to carry into execution the promptings of her great heart. Having once conceived a thing to be right and practicable, she accepted no compromises, no apologies.

After he recounts the battle for the pension, his encomium extols Crandall:

> Fifty years make a great gap either in the improvement or degradation of a race. At the time of the introduction of the bill referred to [the pension,] the writer of this article sat in the same class, in the law school of Yale college, with a descendant of Judge Dagget who "charged so strongly" against Mrs. Crandall, and his presence excited no comment. . . . The grand old woman is gone, and ere this she has appeared before that tribunal where many, many of the decisions of this world are reversed and, if honesty, purity, fidelity, faithfullness [sic] and love count for anything in the heavenly courts, she has received the "well done thou good and faithful servant."[11]

The way that McGuinn writes about her suggests that he had either met her or heard from many people who had. McGuinn's assessment is congruent with other middle-class Black leaders, like Fannie Barrier Williams, T. Thomas Fortune, George Downing, and John Harper. The fact that Twain reached out to assist both Crandall and McGuinn in the mid-1880s shows how the loop of people working together for change can be traced, as they listened to one another, learned each other's stories, and assumed their shared humanity.

Ripples in the Pool of Complacency: The School's Legacy

Prudence Crandall reached out to the one Black family living in her town of Elk Falls, Kansas. In 1886 she wrote to Sarah Harris Fayerweather's daughter Isabella of this: "There is here a family by the name of Smith enterprising indeed. They have three daughters—first rate scholars to learn—when they come to see me we have such grand times. They sing and read their compositions to me, speak pieces, and show me their handw(riting)."[12] Mrs. Smith and her daughters attended Crandall's funeral, where Reverend Charles L. McKesson recalled Crandall embracing the girls, calling "them her 'dear daughters'" and "walk[ing] between them as lovingly as ever did their own mother."[13] Crandall had continued sharing her knowledge and skills freely.

Much of what we know of Crandall in the early 1880s comes from the work of an able academic historian, James Hulme Canfield (1847–1909). While teaching at the University of Kansas in 1881, he learned that Crandall lived in the state. He sent students to interview her, and from these reports and correspondence we have a snapshot of a lively Prudence engaging with Blacks as fellow citizens. Canfield's daughter, Dorothy Canfield Fisher (1879–1958), became one of the most important education reformers of the mid-twentieth century. Perhaps, Dorothy recalled hearing of Prudence Crandall, "keen-eyed . . . full of energy, and zealous in all good works."[14]

The pension struggle launched a spate of newspaper articles and reminiscences of the school. Most of the white press adopted a patronizing and/or congratulatory narrative. But far more important, Crandall's legacy was embraced by middle-class African Americans—the very group of people her school had so notably aided. As early as 1849 an early Black chronicler, William Cooper Nell, recognized Crandall as a "gifted philanthropist."[15] Nell's eminent successor, George Washington Williams (1849–91), wrote extensively about Canterbury in his magisterial *History of the Negro Race in America from 1619 to 1880* (1882), and Edward A. Johnson (1860–1944), whose textbook *The School History of the Negro Race in America* (1894) was briefly authorized for use in North Carolina schools, retold the story of Canterbury, lamenting that the students "whose only offense was a manifestation for knowledge" were deprived of their full education through "outrageous insults" and "all kinds of unpleasant and annoying acts" by the white Canterburians.[16]

When the pension movement began, the African Methodist Episcopal Church's *Christian Recorder* newspaper was an early endorser.[17] In early 1886 noted New York City editor, agitator, and economist T. Thomas Fortune (1856–1928) used the occasion of renewed interest in Crandall to remind his Black readership of her history and to solicit funds to assist her should the Connecticut General Assembly fail to do so.[18] He received three interesting responses: contributions from Brooklyn's (NY) Black community; smaller contributions from Middletown, Connecticut, Black women (including a Miss Elizabeth Beman); and an impassioned letter from Buffalo soldier and Massachusetts Fifty-Fourth Regiment veteran John Harper.[19] This last contribution is a crown jewel among Black remembrances of Crandall's efforts. From his post at Fort Meade in Dakota Territory, Harper reflects that when Crandall stood by Sarah Harris, "there were very few of her mind among the white people." He calls on Blacks to do something for "our living heroine who alone, away back in the dark days, dared to try and elevate the race." He describes his own situation as "an old soldier, one who belonged to the Old 54th Massachusetts Infantry, and I have a wife and ten children, yet I would like to give a little towards helping this woman."[20] Crandall's actions had resonated with African Americans.

It is not clear if Crandall ever saw this stirring testimony from Harper. What we do have is a direct exchange between Fortune and Crandall:

> An Interesting Letter from the Heroine of Canterbury- A Touching Reference to the Noble Workers of the Past.
>
> New York, March 23, 1886
>
> Mrs. P. C. Philleo, Elk Falls, Kan.
> *Respected Madam*:—I put a notice in my paper a few weeks ago, and as a result some of your friends of my race (colored) have handed me $5 for

your benefit, and as a mark of their appreciation of the priceless sacrifices you made for them in other days. I would be pleased to send you my check for $5 if I am correctly informed of your present address and if you would be pleased to accept the small testimonial.

Very respectfully,
T. Thomas Fortune[21]

T. Thomas Fortune's embrace of Crandall's cause was significant. He was still a young man, having been born into enslavement in Florida almost a quarter century after Crandall's Academy had ceased to exist. He had connections, though, to alumnae of the school through his activities as a prominent Black editorialist in New York City. He also took the lead in organizing Black literary societies for a new postwar generation.[22] In 1886 Fortune was at his most influential and energetic; his newspaper, the *New York Freeman*, was independent of any external control.[23] His controversial alliance with Booker T. Washington had not yet begun. He would later use his pen to advocate antilynching campaigns, listening to and working with Frances Ellen Watkins Harper and Ida B. Wells.[24] At this crucial juncture he boosted Crandall's visibility because "she was brave and loyal to the race when it cost something to stand by principle."[25]

Crandall's reply was written with alacrity, given the date:

Elk Falls, Elk Co., Kan.
March 28, 1886

T. Thomas Fortune, Esq., New York.
My Dear Sir:—I sincerely thank you for your kind letter of the 23rd instant. Of course you are aware of what the people of the famous town of Canterbury, Conn. have so nobly done of late on my behalf, and if their legislature would pay me but a little of what I consider they justly and honorably owe me my wants will be abundantly supplied. I do not consider myself an object of charity. I do not wish any person to give me one cent. Dealing with designing individuals I have lost much of my paternal patrimony, but I have enough left to carry me honorably to the grave. I want you, if you please, to hold on to that $5 till I see what the aforesaid legislature will pay to me.

Dear colored friends in Chicago, Ill. have a literary society which they have named the Prudence Crandall Club. I could only wish I was more worthy of the honor bestowed. In the greatness of their hearts they sent me a check for $25 which I hold in reserve, and if Connecticut will do her duty I shall be more than happy to return the same again to them for the benefit of the club. It would be one of the bright spots in my life if I were only able to attend their meetings.

The only one of your valuable paper I have seen is the one that contained the picture and a short history of that noble man, George Thomas Downing of Rhode Island. I cut the picture from the paper and put it in glass under a frame devoted to the photographs of Benjamin Lundy, William Lloyd Garrison, Wendell Phillips, Frederick Douglass, Oliver Johnson, Garrison's son and daughter, Mrs. Villard, Mrs. Sarah Harris Fay[er]weather and many other worthy ones who have been devoted to the best interests of humanity.

Yours truly, Mrs. P. C. Philleo[26]

Each paragraph here contains something of interest. In the first she outlines what she is owed by Connecticut, but she implies that African Americans do not owe her anything. In the middle paragraph, she reveals the existence of a Black literary society in Chicago that bears her name and of her deep desire to attend one of their meetings. They, too, had reached out and made a donation to her—which she hoped to return. There is a clumsiness here in how she handles the donation from Fortune's reader compared to the larger one from the literary club. But whatever awkwardness this reveals dissipates in the sharing of her personal Hall of Fame—a collection of photographs she retained under glass. Frederick Douglass, Sarah Harris Fayerweather, and George Downing are the Black Americans she mentions here, alongside many strong white Garrisonian abolitionists.[27]

The Prudence Crandall Literary Club (PCLC) in Chicago is a notable testament from middle-class educated Blacks of the significance they accorded the aging, white teacher. The club was cofounded in 1885 by S. Laing Williams and fellow Black lawyer, Lloyd Garrison Wheeler (1848–1909).[28]

The PCLC was a "tightknit well-educated group" that became "the most exclusive" of Chicago's Black clubs. While the club included both men and women, the women's group, led by Fannie Barrier Williams and Mary Jones, was more Black-centered than the male section. For these upwardly mobile Black women leaders, the PCLC functioned as a location for "intellectual stimulation and the development of a collective female political voice."[29] Fannie Barrier Williams, in particular, was a strong intellectual activist who desegregated the social clubs of white Chicago. Crandall corresponded with the PCLC, and while that correspondence has not yet come to light, her letter to T. Thomas Fortune clearly shows deep pride in this naming honor. Her statement, "It would be one of the bright spots in my life if I were only able to attend their meetings," testifies to Crandall's continued interest in Black learning.[30] After Crandall's death, Barrier Williams delivered a perceptive biographical sketch of her that highlights her unique actions, the effects of her bad marriage, and how "to the last she enjoyed any interchange of thought on the topics of the day."[31]

In Kansas itself, a direct descendent of Crandall's experiment had taken hold. Andrew Atchison (1855–1933), a white teacher based in Dunlap, Kansas (about a hundred miles north of Elk Falls), opened an academy for Black students.[32] Dunlap was one of the towns that received a large number of Exodusters—Southern Blacks who fled the violence of the South as Reconstruction imploded in 1877 and 1878. Atchison headed an institution dubbed the Colored Academy, starting in 1882.[33] In 1887 he published a short-lived newsletter, *Sweet Chariot,* "Devoted to the Interests of Colored Boys and Girls." The masthead included the lyrics to the eponymous spiritual of the periodical's title, an acknowledgment of Black culture's richness.[34] In the first issue, Atchison began a brief biography of Crandall with this encomium:

> How pleasant and helpful it is to recall the names of men and women who have excelled in wisdom and charity. I am learning the history of many such, and when I feel sad and discouraged I turn to them for comfort. Their lives collect the light of God's grace and they already shine as stars upon those who know their history. One of these, whose name ought to be treasured by the colored people, lives in this state. Her name in youth was Prudence Crandall.[35]

Next he tells of how his students, as part of their final examination under teacher Maggie Watson, were told the story of Crandall's academy, and each asked to write her a letter. Atchison indicates that he had been in touch with Crandall, who had "long shown a deep interest in our work" and "a life long interest in Christian education and reform work, and bears a fine and tender affection for those who engage heartily in this cause."[36]

The letters printed from the students and Crandall's replies to them are touching in their sweetness, perception, and continuity with her own teaching experience. Vina Jackson, the first student, expressed gladness at Crandall's love of children, education, and the poor. Crandall's reply starts, "My dear younger Sister," and compliments Vina's letter-writing prowess. Leanna Hale (ca. 1873–1900), the second young author, pens a rather scattered letter that focuses on Kansas wildflowers while also touching on school and Bible study. Crandall responds to her as "my dear little child" who is "trying to improve (her) mind in every way"—a recognition that the restlessness of Leanna's intellect might have its advantages. To Henry L. Pegg (1873–1940), the only male student included, Crandall assures him, "The elements of greatness are apparent in your kind letter. Keep it till you get to be a man that you can see how fast you can improve and how much."[37] Pegg worked as a teamster in the paper industry and enjoyed a long, happy marriage.[38] Crandall added how much she had enjoyed all these letters: "Only think how soon you will become teachers."[39] Crandall was still concerned with the development of Black education and the vocations of potential Black teachers, fifty years after the Canterbury Academy was forced to close.

Together, the acknowledgments from T. Thomas Fortune, John Harper, Fannie Barrier Williams, and Atchison's students uncover a virtually invisible strand of embedded respect for Crandall's innovative example within the Black middle class, a movement stretching back to David Ruggles and Sarah Mapps Douglass.[40] In the case of Fortune, his connection to George Downing, mentioned by Crandall, creates another live link to the Canterbury school—Downing was married to Theodosia DeGrasse's sister Serena.[41] Downing's work in education in both New York City and Rhode Island made him a kindred spirit to Crandall herself.[42]

The fact that several African American intellectuals acknowledged her in her elder years was likely quite affirming. At the end of her life, Crandall knew—whether through her contact with figures like Fortune and the Chicago elite, or her neighbor Mrs. Smith, or her former student Sarah Harris Fayerweather—that she *had* created the educational legacy she and her Black allies back in Canterbury had initiated. It is, alas, unsurprising that the public paid more attention to her quirky idiosyncrasies and the name of Mark Twain than to Fortune or Barrier Williams—or the photos of other activists from the martyr age that Crandall cherished, who had brought the promise of America a few steps closer to reality.

Intersectional Intellectual Growth

Crandall's story dovetails with *Brown v. Board of Education*—her lawyers' arguments in favor of Black equality before the law, first articulated in 1833, were recapitulated by the NAACP lawyers in the 1950s. While such connections quicken the heart of the historian, they expose the infuriating intransigence of racism in America and the inability of an earlier generation of activists to move the nation as far as their own vision had stretched.

This means the Canterbury Academy is relevant still. Discrimination and racist hostility to Black intellect and trivialization of women's minds are still all too frequent. The struggle in which Crandall and her students participated remains our struggle today.

The students undertook their education to better help their communities. All of the students whose heritages are known were at least one generation removed from slavery, underlining how Crandall's school was more concerned with fighting racism than eradicating slavery (though those goals were intertwined). Crandall and her students resolutely challenged assumptions of inferiority and inequality. But they weren't doing that as theater. The goal was Black female self-development and communal engagement with future generations through teaching. Those eighteen months in Canterbury when the students and Crandall persisted in their mutual learning is not a romantic drama but a goad to take up once again the transformations the past did not complete. Prudence Crandall is Connecticut's state heroine because we haven't lived up to what she did, not because we have accomplished what she, Maria Davis, and Sarah Harris started.

No one connected with Crandall's school ever abandoned women's education—notably the students but also allies like Samuel Joseph May and Henry Highland Garnet. Canterbury had conceived of Crandall's first academy as a way to improve the marriageability of their daughters. The second academy revealed that the project of women's education was not about marriageability. Education was about the female mind and the ability of women to make their way in the world.

As noted above, Crandall's last letter, penned to the children of William Lloyd Garrison in December 1889 (just a month before her death), spotlights her conscious intersectionality in a racially diverse America: "I am deeply interested in the progress of the colored people in every moral and intellectual growth. I take some paper all the time edited by colored men that I can learn what they are doing for themselves."[43] She chooses not to trust white sources alone but to listen to people of color directly. She intuitively and experientially understood the importance of perspective and context and the kind of agency expressed in an independent press. This is extraordinary for an eighty-six-year-old white woman in Kansas in 1889.

Unlike many abolitionists, Crandall did not write a memoir, but she left visible traces: newspapers, letters, and poems. It is frustrating that the story of this "fine-souled woman" has too often been reduced to simplistic sentimentality. It is even more galling that it is too often told without mentioning any of the African American women by name.[44] I know that Julia Williams, Mary Elizabeth Miles, Gloriana Catherine Marshall, Ann Eliza Hammond, Eliza Glasko, Miranda Glasko, Henrietta Bolt, Sarah Harris, and Maria Davis would tell the story quite differently, adding perspectives we should tune our ears to hear and incorporate into the nascent future they created in Canterbury.

Postscript

Over her last few decades, Prudence Crandall was a proponent of Spiritualism. It matters little to a person as strong-willed as Crandall whether or not scholars believe in communication with the dead. She maintains her end of the bargain with regular, if sometimes inconvenient, missives. Here's the latest via Prudence.

After receiving the proof pages for this book, a major discovery was made: an overlooked 1886 letter from Prudence Crandall Philleo revealed a student hitherto unknown: Elizabeth Susan Webb (1818–1888) of Philadelphia. She was the older sister of noted novelist Frank Webb (1828–1894), and a descendant of Aaron Burr through an interracial liaison he had. She married Geoffrey Iredell.

Crandall describes Elizabeth Susan Webb as "a beautiful young girl when at my school and I know she must be an interesting woman. Some years ago she wrote me and sent me the doings of the Womans Sufferage [*sic*] Convention that met at that time in Washington." She adds that Mrs. Iredell would remember the late Samuel J. May, "a friend in our time of need." Elizabeth Susan Webb Iredell's daughter Sarah Iredell Fleetwood (1849–1908) continues the remarkable multi-generational legacy of the Canterbury Academy students. She was a graduate of Howard University, and a major force in the professionalization of nursing as a career for Black women.

Kabria Baumgartner and I worked together to unearth this gem. We plan to co-write an article on this confirmation of the significance of the Canterbury Black students and Prudence Crandall.

Notes

Preface

1. Kendi, *Stamped from the Beginning*. "Antiracism" is a contemporary term. Some of the terms in use for "racism" in the nineteenth century include "colorphobia" and "prejudice." For more, see McLaughlin, "Anti-Slavery Roots of Today's 'Phobia' Obsession."

2. Consider the youthful Frederick Douglass bartering scraps of bread for scraps of learning, or the "hedge schools" among Irish Catholics resisting coerced Anglicanism; Blight, *Frederic Douglass*, 42–43, Elliott, *Catholics of Ulster*, 179–81; Hunt, "Biographical Sketch," xviii.

3. [Anonymous Black woman student], "The Separation," *Liberator* (Boston, MA) 4, no. 47, November 22, 1834, 186.

4. Baumgartner, *In Pursuit of Knowledge*, 24.

Introduction. A Luminous Moment

1. Stacey Robertson wrote that Crandall "was quickly harassed into closing" her school; James Brewer Stewart refers to the "ill-fated cause of Prudence Crandall, whose attempts to open a school for 'colored girls' . . . were thwarted by opponents." Robertson, *Hearts Beating for Liberty*, 28; J. B. Stewart, "New Haven Negro College," 337.

2. This is the subtitle of Edmund Fuller's unsatisfactory study, *Prudence Crandall: An Incident of Racism in Nineteenth-Century Connecticut*.

3. Flexner, *Century of Struggle*, 39–40; Act Designating Prudence Crandall.

4. I adopt Sarah Hoagland's definition of agency as the ability to act and make conscious decisions about one's action within structural constraints. Hoagland, *Lesbian Ethics*, 1.

5. For example, the *Woodville (MI) Republican* reprinted the *Hartford (CT) Courant*'s trial coverage from October 5, 1833.

6. *New-England Review* (Hartford, CT), reprinted in the *Springfield (MA) Republican*, March 23, 1833, 2.

7. See excerpts from Delany in Litwack, *North of Slavery,* 227–28; Wright, "Progress of the Antislavery Cause," 86–92; J. B. Stewart, "Emergence of Racial Modernity," 215–17.

8. M. Stewart, *Productions,* 16.

9. M. Stewart, *Productions,* 16. My surmise that Crandall could have read Maria Stewart—and complete confidence that the Harris family had—predates my reading of Susan Strane's work—but she, too, reached a similar conclusion. See Strane, *Whole-Souled Woman,* 24–25.

10. Julia Tucker and Virginia Tucker are mentioned as students at Crandall's Academy in W. H. Morse, "United States of Africa," in *Gospel in All Lands,* June 1891, 252–54. Thanks to Joseph Yannielli for this and for further research suggesting that the last name could be Goary (or Locks). Yannielli, personal email correspondence with author, September 2015–July 2016. Samuel Joseph May mentions that one student "has her expenses paid" by a woman who had been enslaved "and purchased freedom out of her own exertions." "Miss Prudence Crandall," 190. This might be Hester Lane, a formerly enslaved woman who lived in New York City and was active in benevolent and antislavery contexts. M. S. Jones, *All Bound Up Together,* 54–57. Edward Abdy wrote of Lane purchasing other African Americans from enslavement. Abdy, *Journal of a Residence,* 2:31–34. On Harriet Lanson's household work as financial aid, see *Liberator* (Boston) 6, no. 14, April 2, 1836, 56.

11. Jeffner Allen problematizes the binary of violence/nonviolence in *Lesbian Philosophy,* 43–46.

12. Ralph Foster Weld contends that Crandall "was shrewdly exploited by the abolitionists for the furtherance of their cause." *Slavery in Connecticut,* 22; cf. Richards, *Gentlemen of Property and Standing,* 39. The conservative New York *Commercial Advertiser* dismissed Crandall as merely "the instrument" of Buffum and Garrison. Strane, *Whole-Souled Woman,* 84; May, *Memoir of Samuel J. May,* 152. For a contemporaneous refutation of this theory, see *Liberator* (Boston) 3, no. 37, September 14, 1833, 147.

13. Judson and Daggett, *Andrew T. Judson's Remarks,* 22.

14. *Springfield (MA) Republican,* August 3, 1833, 1; Crandall, *Trial of Reuben Crandall,* 35.

15. *Liberator* 3, no. 21, May 25, 1833, 82, reprinted from the *Windham County (Brooklyn, CT) Advertiser,* letter to the editor, May 7, 1833; Small, "Prudence Crandall"; D. O. White, "Crandall School."

16. Mary E. Miles to Gerritt Smith, September 18, 1846, cited in Baumgartner, *In Pursuit of Knowledge,* 54, 240n31.

17. M. Stewart, *Productions,* 52.

18. Morton, "Beloved Image," 127–28. Thanks to Lou Turner, who gave me the elegant phrase "the luminous moment."

19. "Semi-Centennial at Packerville," *Windham Transcript* (Danielsonville, CT), October 24, 1878, TS, Prudence Crandall Museum, Canterbury, Connecticut.

Chapter 1. Crandall and Canterbury

1. Cayton, "Connecticut Culture of Revivalism," 359.

2. Jonathan Dymond said concerning Quaker women: "The public have . . . seen intelligence, sound sense, considerateness, [and] discretion." *Essays on the Principles of Morality*, 200–201.

3. Through her father, Prudence claimed descent from Elder John Crandall (1609–76), cofounder of the American Seventh-Day Baptist denomination. see McLoughlin, *New England Dissent*, 1:19–20, 62–70.

4. M. Welch, *Prudence Crandall*, 3; Strane, *Whole-Souled Woman*, 4.

5. M. Welch, *Prudence Crandall*, 2; Strane, *Whole-Souled Woman*, 4; Rena Clisby, "Canterbury Pilgrims," TS, 1947, Prudence Crandall Collection, Charles E. Shain Library, Connecticut College, New London, Connecticut, 8–9; Bartlett, *From Slave to Citizen*, 19.

6. Rena Clisby, "Canterbury Pilgrims," TS, 1947, Prudence Crandall Collection, Charles E. Shain Library, Connecticut College, New London, Connecticut, 26; Welch, *Prudence Crandall*, 1.

7. Rena Clisby, "Canterbury Pilgrims," TS, 1947, Prudence Crandall Collection, Charles E. Shain Library, Connecticut College, New London, Connecticut, 9.

8. Burr, "Quakers in Connecticut," 20.

9. Prude, *Coming of Industrial Order*, 34–64; Clark, *History of Manufactures*, 1:404; cf. Rappleye, *Sons of Providence*, and Kelsey, *Centennial History*, 34.

10. Moses Brown, to my knowledge, did not comment on Crandall's school, her apostasy from the Quakers being the likely reason. George W. Benson to Samuel Joseph May, August 20, 1833, Ms.A.1.2, 3:62, Anti-Slavery Collection, Boston Public Library.

11. Wesley's antislavery views in *Thoughts on Slavery* grew from discussions with Benezet; see Christie and Dumond, *George Bourne*, 8; Jones, *Moses Brown*, 12–16.

12. George Benson Sr. wrote about Brown's "veritable Testimony in favour of the proficiency and commendable Conduct of ABenezett's [*sic*] Scholars. I never before knew that you had been an eye witness of that fact." George Benson [Sr.] to Moses Brown, April 29, 1831, Moses Brown Papers, Rhode Island Historical Society, Providence, Rhode Island (hereafter referred to as RIHS). See also Jordan, *White over Black*, 447.

13. The earlier biography of Benezet by Brookes, *Friend Anthony Benezet*, has been superseded by M. Jackson, *Let This Voice Be Heard*. See also *Anthony Benezet, from the Original Memoir*, edited by Wilson Armistead. For cautionary notes against the canonization of Benezet, see Hodges, *Root and Branch*, 125; Goodman, *Of One Blood*, 7–8; however, Goodman recognizes that Benezet was among the most enlightened whites of his day on race. See also Carey, *From Peace to Freedom*.

14. Hornick, "Anthony Benezet," 399.

15. Woodson, "Anthony Benezet," 47–48.

16. M. H. Bacon, *Mothers of Feminism*, 62; Frost, *Quaker Family in Colonial America*, 114–15. Benezet's female students form an illustrious alumna group.

17. Armistead, *Benezet*, 18.

18. James Forten is often listed as a Benezet student, but Julie Winch disputes that in *Gentleman of Color*, 24–25. See also Jackson, *Let This Voice Be Heard*, 264n133.

19. P. Williams, *Oration on the Abolition*, 22–23.

20. Chandler, *Poetical Works*, 98–99; Child, *Appeal*, 230–31; I. V. Brown, *Mary Grew*, 16–17; [A. Grimké], *Appeal*, 32.

21. Thompson, *Moses Brown*, 282.

22. Thompson, *Moses Brown*, 287.

23. Moses Brown may have taken a subscription to the *Unionist*. See Henry Benson to Samuel J. May, August 13, 1833, and George W. Benson Jr. to Samuel J. May, August 20, 1833, RIHS.

24. Mary Peace Hazard, 1826–1827, autograph book from New England Yearly Meeting Boarding School, RIHS; Bingham, *American Preceptor*, 8. While still enslaved, Frederick Douglass famously obtained Bingham's *Columbian Orator*, sparking his full awakening to ideas of freedom; see Blight, *Frederick Douglass*, 43–47.

25. R. O. Davis, "Prudence Crandall," 240n9.

26. Drake, *Quakers and Slavery*, 120; Bartlett, *From Slave to Citizen*, 18, 22–23. In defense of Moses Brown, on hearing that the African Union he had helped sponsor included music at the service—which the Quakers did not condone—he wrote, "I don't approve of Singing Meeting and Some Other parts yet if it Suits the Colored people I shall not Oppose them." Brown, handwritten addendum on Jackson's pamphlet, RIHS; H. Jackson, *Short History*, 32.

27. May, "Miss Prudence Crandall," 180–81; Strane, *Whole-Souled Woman*, 7.

28. Lerner, *Creation of Feminist Consciousness*, 42–43.

29. Sklar, *Catharine Beecher*, 26–37.

30. Beecher, *Essay on Slavery*, 30–32.

31. Beecher's 1829 appeal to Hartford's citizenry, quoted in Sklar, *Catharine Beecher*, 96.

32. Beecher, "Female Teachers," quoted in B. M. Cross, *The Educated Woman in America*, 71–72.

33. Editorial, *Connecticut Courant*, November 16, 1830, quoted in Sklar, *Catharine Beecher*, 94.

34. *Liberator* (Boston) 7, no. 33, August 11, 1837, 129.

35. Her younger sister, Almira, may have joined her, since their dismissal by their Quaker meeting was considered simultaneously. Women's Minutes, book 3, East Greenwich Monthly Meeting, RIHS, 117.

36. Rena Clisby, "Canterbury Pilgrims," TS, 1947, Prudence Crandall Collection, Charles E. Shain Library, Connecticut College, New London, Connecticut, 14. See also Strane, *Whole-Souled Woman*, 9–10; M. Welch, *Prudence Crandall*, 10.

37. Donna Dufresne, conversation in person with author, spring 2002.

38. W. P. Garrison, *Benson Family*, 31–38.

39. C. Clark, *Communitarian Moment*, 18; W. L. Garrison, *Helen Eliza Garrison*, 8–9.

40. Stattler, "Guide to the Moses Brown Papers," 2; Thompson, *Moses Brown*, 282; Curti, *American Peace Crusade*, 45; Galpin, *Pioneering for Peace*, 38–39.

41. Curti, *American Peace Crusade*, 33.

42. George Benson to Moses Brown, April 14, 1824, Mss313.1.244, Moses Brown Papers, RIHS.

43. Yacovone, *Samuel Joseph May*, 29.

44. C. W. Dymond, *Memoirs, Letters and Poems*, 19.

45. "Dymond's Essays," *Liberator*, 4, no. 10, March 8, 1834, 89; Sumner, *Charles Sumner*, 2:335; Tolstoy, *Tolstoy's Writings*, 129, 286; Lynd, *Nonviolence in America*, xxi–xxv, and *Intellectual Origins*, 111, 117–19; Campbell, "Response to Jonathan Dymond"; R. M. Jones, *Later Periods of Quakerism*, 2:716–18; Brock, *Freedom from Violence*, 260–61, 358n3; Duban, "Thoreau, Garrison, and Dymond."

46. Rycenga, "Sun in Its Glory"; Ziegler, *Advocates of Peace*, 43; Brock, *Pacifism in the United States*, 498; J. Dymond, *On the Applicability of the Pacific Principles*; George Benson Sr. to Moses Brown, May 17, 1832, Moses Brown Papers, RIHS.

47. J. Dymond, *Essays on the Principles of Morality*, 410. The pamphlet is essentially the book's final essay.

48. J. Dymond, *Inquiry into the Accordancy of War*, 134.

49. J. Dymond, *Inquiry into the Accordancy of War*, quoted in Brock, *Quaker Peace Testimony*, 261.

50. Yacovone, *Samuel Joseph May*, 28–30.

51. George Benson Sr. to Moses Brown, May 17, 1832, RIHS.

52. W. P. Garrison, *Benson Family*, 38.

53. Yacovone, *Samuel Joseph May*, 30.

54. See Grace Jantzen on how the Virgin Mary's passivity and humility "made her a suitable recipient of God's favor" and that "if such lowliness is gender-related, then by a paradoxical twist women are especially privileged, at an advantage as candidates for exaltation." Jantzen, *Power, Gender, and Christian Mysticism*, 170.

55. Fox, *American Colonization Society*, 46–51.

56. Duignan and Gann, *United States and Africa*, 84.

57. Egerton, *Charles Fenton Mercer*; Fox, *American Colonization Society*, 50–51; Ammon, *James Monroe*, 522–23.

58. Dunne, "Bushrod Washington." He explicitly told his enslaved people that his leadership in the ACS did not mean he would ever manumit them. "Bushrod Washington," 27. Bushrod Island in Monrovia is named after him.

59. Foner, *History of Black Americans*, 587.

60. Goodman, *Of One Blood*, 17, see 16–20 for ACS founding. For middle-states emphasis, see Adams, *Neglected Period of Anti-Slavery*, 106.

61. Jefferson, *Notes on the State of Virginia*, query 14, 211. Note that Jefferson maintained this opinion throughout his life, writing in his final year, 1826, that "to the mixture of colour here . . . I have a great aversion," a quote that our era, knowing the descendants of Jefferson and Sally Hemings, reads with bitter irony.

62. Ammon, *James Monroe*, 187–89.

63. Jordan, *White over Black*, 564.

64. Jordan, *White over Black*, 551.

65. W. L. Miller, *Arguing about Slavery*, 73.

66. Goodman, *Of One Blood*, 17. See also Staudenraus, *African Colonization Movement*, 94–116.

67. Staudenraus, *African Colonization Movement*, 51.

68. Masur, *1831*, 49.

69. Perry, *Radical Abolitionism*, 9.

70. Warner, *New Haven Negroes*, 42.

71. Staudenraus, *African Colonization Movement*, 28–29.

72. Winch, *Gentleman of Color*, 177, 206; Foner, *History of Black Americans*, 581; Drake, *Quakers and Slavery*, 126.

73. Staudenraus, *African Colonization Movement*, 251.

74. The urge to rid the nation of free Blacks did not end with the Civil War; the ACS continued to solicit money and ships to take Blacks to Liberia, to aid in "the solving of the destiny of the African race in America." *New York Herald*, April 19, 1878, quoted in McNeely, "Assignment Liberia," 68.

75. Yacovone, *Samuel Joseph May*, 37; Staudenraus, *African Colonization Movement*, 127; Larned, *History of Windham County*, 2:398. Connecticut's Congregationalists dedicated every July 4th to support for the ACS. Keller, *Second Great Awakening*, 182.

76. Goodman, *Of One Blood*, 40–42; Mayer, *All on Fire*, 71–94; Yee, *Black Women Abolitionists*, 26; Sinha, *Slave's Cause*, 199, 216; M. H. Bacon, "One Great Bundle of Humanity," 23.

77. Drake, *Quakers and Slavery in America*, 123–25, 125n33. See also Winch, *Gentleman of Color*, 177, 206; P. Williams, *Discourse*, 15–16.

78. Staudenraus, *African Colonization Movement*, 19; Goodman, *Of One Blood*, 24; Winch, *Gentleman of Color*, 183, 186, 189.

79. Winch, *Gentleman of Color*, 183.

80. Winch, *Gentleman of Color*, 176–206. See also Julie Winch, "Leaders of Philadelphia's Black Community," 178–93.

81. Winch, *Gentleman of Color*, 191.

82. Winch, *Gentleman of Color*, 191. Resolutions from this meeting in W. L. Garrison, *Thoughts on African Colonization*, 2nd sec., 9–13. William Loren Katz asserts that with *Thoughts on African Colonization*, Garrison brought a significant number of whites to the same position that the Black masses in Philadelphia had achieved instantly in 1817. W. L. Garrison, *Thoughts on African Colonization*, 1st sec., xi. See also Winch, "Leaders of Philadelphia's Black Community," 184–85.

83. Winch, *Gentleman of Color*, 192–93.

84. Winch, *Gentleman of Color*, 196–97. See also Reed, *Platform for Change*, 128–33; "Address to the Humane and Benevolent Inhabitant of Philadelphia," in Woodson, *Negro Orators and Their Orations*, 52–55.

85. Even Black leaders in Liberia, such as the Virginian Baptist missionary Lott Cary, had disagreements and hesitations concerning the American Colonization Society. See Poe, "Lott Cary."

86. Burrows and Wallace, *Gotham*, 549. On Russwurm, see John Brown

Russwurm Collection, George J. Mitchell Department of Special Collections and Archives, Bowdoin College, http://library.bowdoin.edu/arch/mss/jbrg.shtml. See also Sagarin, *John Brown Russwurm*.

87. Burrows and Wallace, *Gotham*, 549.

88. Gross, *"Freedom's Journal"*; Swift, "Black Presbyterian Attacks on Racism," 53–57, and *Black Prophets of Justice*, 32–35.

89. Aptheker, *Documentary History*, 1:89; *Freedom's Journal*, August 10, 1827. Many scholars now think that "Matilda" may have been a pseudonym of Maria Stewart, given the thematic and stylistic continuity with her writings. Waters, *Maria Stewart*, 179.

90. This is not to say that "Matilda" encountered no sexism within the free Black community. As Hodges points out, an editorial in *Freedom's Journal* opines, "Women are not formed for great cares themselves, but to soften ours." Hodges, *Root and Branch*, 249; McHenry, *Forgotten Readers*, 57.

91. There are three excellent editions of Walker's *Appeal*: Walker, *One Continual Cry*; Walker, *David Walker's Appeal in Four Articles*, ed. Wilentz; and Walker, *David Walker's Appeal to the Coloured Citizens*. Peter Hinks's indispensable social biography of Walker is among the finest recent scholarly books: *To Awaken My Afflicted Brethren*.

92. Walker, *David Walker's Appeal to the Coloured Citizens*, xxvi–xxvii, 78.

93. Walker, *David Walker's Appeal to the Coloured Citizens*, 69–70; McHenry, *Forgotten Readers*, 102. Walker supported the Black enslaved poet George M. Horton. See *Freedom's Journal*, 2, August 8–October 8, 1828, 17–28; Gross, *Freedom's Journal*, 258–59n47, 49.

94. McHenry, *Forgotten Readers*, 41. Hinks refers to this as the "critical seaborne wing of the *Appeal*'s distribution." *To Awaken My Afflicted Brethren*, 149, 118–19.

95. Walker, *David Walker's Appeal to the Coloured Citizens*, 34 (article 2 of the *Appeal*).

96. Walker, *David Walker's Appeal to the Coloured Citizens*, 119n49; Schultz, *Culture Factory*, 167.

97. M. L. King, Jr., *I Have a Dream*, 102.

98. Sen, "Democracy and Its Global Roots," discusses how Alexis de Tocqueville highlighted public reasoning as a feature of the United States in the 1830s.

99. Karcher, *First Woman in the Republic*, 175.

100. Simeon Smith Jocelyn was known as Smith to his friends and family. Heinz, "Nathaniel Jocelyn," 5, 16, 39–40.

101. Sweeney, *Nathaniel Taylor*; Priest, "Revival and Revivalism"; J. E. Johnson, "Charles G. Finney."

102. Goodman, *Of One Blood*, 45; Swift, *Black Prophets of Justice*, 181.

103. H. Davis, "Northern Colonizationists," 656, 665; Sehr, "Leonard Bacon and the Myth of the Good Slaveholder."

104. H. Davis, "Northern Colonizationists"; Moss, *Schooling Citizens*, 54; Heinz, "Nathaniel Jocelyn," 32. Samuel Ringgold Ward, a close friend, indicates

Jocelyn "entered the ministry, on purpose to serve the colored people." Ward, *Autobiography of a Fugitive Negro*, 45.

105. Moss, *Schooling Citizens*, 37. Moss presents an excellent analysis of the New Haven Manual Labor School's failure and the preceding AIS efforts.

106. Warner, *New Haven Negroes*, 46–47, original emphasis.

107. Warner, *New Haven Negroes*, 81–82, 93.

108. The numbering of the Conventions of the Free People of Colour is confusing, as there was a meeting in 1830 in Philadelphia, which is not included in the standard numbering; however, many historians refer to it as the "first" convention. The convention to which I am referring here in 1831 is the one labeled "First" in documents, including the minutes. To be clear, there are six consecutive years of conventions: September 20–24, 1830, Philadelphia (unnumbered); June 6–11, 1831, Philadelphia, first convention; June 4–10, 1832, Philadelphia, second convention; June 3–13, 1833, Philadelphia, third convention; June 2–12, 1834, New York, fourth convention; June 1–5, 1835, Philadelphia, fifth convention. Minutes for all of these are available at http://coloredconventions.org/. See also Reed, *Platform for Change*, 135–56.

109. Two other white men in attendance—Thomas Shipley and Charles Pierce—are less well-known. Convention of the People of Colour, *Minutes and Proceedings*, 5.

110. See Jacobs, "David Walker and William Lloyd Garrison," for more on Garrison's encounter with Walker's ideas. While Jacobs stresses the strategic reasons for Garrison's interest in Walker's writing, rather than the philosophic, he still raises valuable insights into this pivotal moment in Black-white relations. I agree fully with Aileen Kraditor's suggestion, "In his comments on Walker's *Appeal*, Garrison . . . gave evidence of a trait that his scholarly critics have denied he possessed: the ability to admire and to see the point of view of someone he disagreed with." *Means and Ends in American Abolitionism*, 281. Garrison's openness to discussing the *Appeal* likely "earned him much credibility, just as Lundy's bitter condemnation of the *Appeal* in April 1830 must have further sunk his journal's hopes" with Black readers. Hinks, *To Awaken*, 113.

111. Warner, *New Haven Negroes*, 12–13.

112. Convention of the People of Colour, *Minutes and Proceedings*, 6.

113. Walker, *David Walker's Appeal to the Coloured Citizens*, 70–71.

114. Wright, "Progress of the Antislavery Cause," 89.

115. Simeon S. Jocelyn to William Lloyd Garrison, May 28, 1831, Ms.A.1.2, vol. 1, Anti-Slavery Collection, Boston Public Library.

116. J. B. Stewart, "New Haven Negro College," 332.

117. William Jay wrote a contemporary account of the New Haven Manual Labor College in *Inquiry into the Character*, 26–30. Maryland used the Turner Revolt to authorize state funds ($200,000) for colonization in 1832 and further restrict the rights of free Blacks to encourage emigration to Maryland's new African colony. Freehling, *Road to Disunion*, 206; Sagarin, *Russwurm*, 102.

118. Moss, *Schooling Citizens*, 62, 223n85.

119. James Watson Webb, quoted in *Liberator*, 1, no. 49, December 3, 1831, 195; Crouthamel, *James Watson Webb*, 56–57.

120. O. Johnson, *W. L. Garrison and His Times*, 123.

121. Franklin, "Education for Colonization," 97–98; H. Davis, *Leonard Bacon*; Swift, *Black Prophets of Justice*, 181–84, 194–95. See also the recent work to keep the planned college alive in the historic memory of Yale and New Haven, led by Michael Morand, Charles Warner, and Tubyez Cropper, especially in their film "What Could Have Been" (2021), https://www.youtube.com/watch?v=gmXF3N62Olo.

122. William Lloyd Garrison to George Benson, March 8, 1833, in W. L. Garrison, *Letters . . . Volume 1*, 212.

123. Litwack, *North of Slavery*, 125–26.

124. J. B. Stewart, "New Haven Negro College," 337.

125. French, *Rebellious Slave*, 60.

126. Moss, *Schooling Citizens*, 62.

127. Richards, *Gentlemen of Property and Standing*, 37–38.

128. *Liberator*, 1, no. 50, December 10, 1831, 198.

129. French, *Rebellious Slave*, 51–55, reference to Marshall, 53.

130. Richards, *Gentlemen of Property and Standing*, 21. Southern officials had similarly beseeched Otis to suppress free Blacks in his city concerning Walker's *Appeal* and *Liberator* and its circulation in the South. Walker, *One Continual Cry*, 46; Eaton, "Dangerous Pamphlet," 329; Hinks, *To Awaken My Afflicted Brethren*, 118–19.

131. Mayer, *All on Fire*, 122.

132. Richardson, *Maria W. Stewart*. Waters's new *Maria Stewart* significantly enhances knowledge of Stewart's youth and Boston life.

133. Quarles, *Black Abolitionists*, 20, and Pride and Wilson, *History of the Black Press*, 26–27. The subscription figure dates from the middle of the existence of the Canterbury Academy, April 1834. Pride and Wilson note that as the subscriber list started tilting toward white readers, concern with racism waned.

134. For a fuller analysis of the content and timing of Stewart's published essay, see Rycenga, "Maria Stewart, Black Abolitionist, and the Idea of Freedom."

135. Goodman, *Of One Blood*, 41–42.

136. Garrison confided to Grice that "it was too early to have published such a book." Bruce, *Origins of African American Literature*, 185. See also Young, *Antebellum Black Activists*, 8.

137. Ministers opposed to women's speaking "echoed the principal defenses of Negro slavery," claiming that empowered women would endanger society. "Ironically, antifeminist abolitionists, who interpreted the Bible allegorically when the issue was slavery, became fundamentalists when the issue was women's rights." Kraditor, *Means and Ends*, 43, 44.

138. *Liberator* 1, no. 36, September 3, 1831, 143.

Chapter 2. The Women and the Issues Are Joined

1. Robert Forbes hypothesized that Crandall's academy, if it had been permitted to function without harassment, would be remembered in the legacy of women's academies, including those of Catharine Beecher, Sally Pierce, and Emma Willard. Prudence Crandall Symposium, Canterbury, Connecticut, 2015.

2. Leonard Bacon opined that whites were to Blacks as Brahmins were to Sudras. See Jay, "Condition of the Free People of Color," 374.

3. Pease and Pease, *They Who Would Be Free*, 6–7; Litwack, *North of Slavery*, 220–21.

4. Richards, *Gentlemen of Property and Standing*, 3, 35.

5. *Windham County Advertiser* (Brooklyn, CT), November 9, 1831, 14; M. Welch, *Prudence Crandall*, 17–18.

6. The chemistry teacher, Andrew Cutler (1799–1876), the eldest son of a large Plainfield family, described himself as a scholar who "for seventeen years, been an excessive lame man, with nothing to do but to read, digest and teach a few scholars." Cutler, *English Grammar and Parser*.

7. Academies were not shaped by sectarian denominational concerns as colleges were. Sizer, *Age of the Academies*, 19–20; Rycenga, "Greater Awakening."

8. De Tocqueville, *Democracy in America*, 334.

9. M. Welch, *Prudence Crandall*, 19–20; Strane, *Whole-Souled Woman*, 12–13.

10. Strane, *Whole-Souled Woman*, 71; Amy Baldwin to Mary Clark, n.d., Baldwin Collection, Connecticut Museum of Culture and History, Hartford.

11. The Fayerweather Family Papers, 1836–1962, University of Rhode Island Special Collections and University Archives, Kingston.

12. Culpepper, "Philosophia."

13. Culpepper, "Philosophia," 7.

14. In the seven previous biographies of Crandall, Maria Davis being the conduit by which the *Liberator* reaches Prudence is mentioned without more elaboration. In almost every case, the only other reference to Davis comes with her marriage to Charles Harris. The exception is David White, who clarifies that Davis is never formally named as a student. M. Welch, *Prudence Crandall*, 18, 22; Fuller, *Prudence Crandall*, 14; Foner and Pacheco, *Three Who Dared*, 8–9; McCain, *To All on Equal Terms*, 13; D. E. Williams, *Prudence Crandall's Legacy*, 25–26; Strane, *Whole-Souled Woman*, 23–25, 233n13; David O. White, "Prudence Crandall," 1971, MS, Prudence Crandall Museum, Connecticut Historical Commission, Hartford, 22; Yacovone mentions Davis parenthetically, *Samuel Joseph May*, 202n6. Not surprising, Eleanor Flexner and Angela Davis in their feminist appraisals both zero in on the role of Davis. See A. Davis, *Women, Race, and Class*, 34–36, and Flexner, *Century of Struggle*, 38–40. In her brief article "A Canterbury Tale," Glee F. Krueger connected these female nodal points.

15. There has been confusion over Maria Davis's name in Crandall scholarship. Her gravestone, labeled "Ann Maria," definitively clarifies the spelling. The name was likely pronounced as "Mariah," as was common among Protestant New Englanders at the time. Maria Davis Harris's grave is a shared stone with her husband, Charles Harris, and two of their children, in Yantic Cemetery, Norwich, Connecticut. I have been unable to trace Maria Davis's Boston roots, but Boston city directories have one Black man with the name William Davis, who in 1825 is listed as a "labourer" living on George Street and in 1829–30 as a "waiter" residing on May Street.

16. Prudence Crandall Philleo to Ellen D. Larned, May 15, 1869, Connecticut State Library, Hartford.

17. *Liberator*, 1, no. 36, September 3, 1831, 36.

18. I had a wonderful conversation in 1999 with acclaimed Connecticut story-teller Gertrude Blanks, who confirmed my intuition of Maria Davis's centrality to the Canterbury story. Blanks had researched the academy and developed a one-woman presentation based on Maria. Grandy, "Blanks Turns Her Talents to Crandall Story."

19. The scholarly literature on antebellum Black Boston is exceptionally rich. See Horton and Horton, *Black Bostonians*; Jacobs, *Courage and Conscience*; Levesque, *Black Boston*. Samuel Snowden (ca. 1765–1850) served as the Black Methodist minister in Boston from 1818 to 1850, a remarkably long tenure. Thomas Paul (1783–1831), brother to Nathaniel Paul, was a Baptist. They were all strong supporters of Garrison and the *Liberator*. Mayer, *All on Fire*, 109.

20. Mayer, *All on Fire*, 109; attested to by John T. Hilton, *Liberator*, 19, no. 30, July 27, 1849.

21. Zelmire, "Unnatural Distinction," *Liberator*, 2, no. 30, July 28, 1832, 118.

22. *Boston Daily Evening Transcript*, September 28, 1830, quoted in Hinks, *To Awaken*, 151, original emphasis.

23. Swift, *Black Prophets of Justice*, 175; Hinks, *To Awaken*, 154; Mayer, *All on Fire*, 138; *Frederick Douglass' Paper* (Rochester, New York), 7, no. 43, October 13, 1854, 3, Amos Beman Scrapbook II, Beinecke Rare Book Library, Yale University.

24. Stewart's brief writing career in the pages of the *Liberator* includes the following:

- The pamphlet *Religion and the Pure Principles of Morality* is twice adver-tised, *Liberator*, 1, no. 41, October 8, 1831, 163, and *Liberator*, 1, no. 44, October 29, 1831, 175.
- Stewart's *Meditations*, a pamphlet, is advertised in the *Liberator*, 2, no. 13, March 31, 1832, 52.
- Address to the Afric-American [*sic*] Female Intelligence Society, *Liberator*, 2, no. 17, April 28, 1832, 66–67.
- Published in the "Lines" (poem), *Liberator* 2, no. 20, May 19, 1832, 80.
- A letter from M. W. S., "Cause for Encouragement," *Liberator*, 2, no. 28, July 14, 1832, 110.
- "Lecture Given at Franklin Hall," *Liberator*, 2, no. 46, November 17, 1832, 183.
- "Address at African Masonic Hall" in two consecutive issues, *Liberator*, 3, no. 17, April 27, 1833, 68, and 3, no. 18, May 4, 1833, 72.
- Stewart's farewell speech was apparently not printed in the *Liberator*; Garrison notes its reception by a "deeply interesting" audience. *Liberator*, 3, no. 39, September 28, 1833, 155.

25. Stewart begins her Franklin Hall (September 1832) lecture by declaring, "Tell us no more of southern slavery; for with very few exceptions . . . I consider our condition but little better than that. . . . Methinks there are no chains so gall-ing as those that bind the soul, and exclude it from the vast field of useful and scientific knowledge." Richardson, *Maria W. Stewart*, 45; Stewart, *Productions*, 51–52; *Liberator*, 2, no. 46, November 17, 1832, 183.

26. *Liberator*, 2, no. 28, July 14, 1832, 110. See Richardson, *Maria W. Stewart*, 43–44, for an annotated edition of this letter.

27. Stewart, *Productions*, 16.

28. *Liberator*, 2, no. 28, July 14, 1832, 110, original emphasis. Note how Angelina Grimké transmutes this logic into a declaration of female agency that is also explicitly antislavery: "The denial of our duty to act, is a bold denial of our right to act." *Appeal to the Women*, 14.

29. *Liberator*, 3, no. 21, May 25, 1833, 82–83, from Prudence Crandall letter to the editor, *Windham County Advertiser* (Brooklyn, CT), May 7, 1833.

30. Hinks, *To Awaken*, 93.

31. *Liberator*, 3, no. 21, May 25, 1833, 82–83, from Prudence Crandall letter to the editor, *Windham County Advertiser* (Brooklyn, CT), May 7, 1833, added emphasis.

32. Prudence Crandall Philleo to Ellen D. Larned, May 15, 1869, Connecticut State Library, Hartford, Connecticut; J. C. Hebbard, "Connecticut's Canterbury Tale from Real Life," 1886, MS, Kansas Historical Society, Topeka, Kansas, 2, added emphasis.

33. Rena Clisby, "Canterbury Pilgrims," TS, 1947, 29, Prudence Crandall Collection, Charles E. Shain Library, Connecticut College, New London, Connecticut.

34. Dvorak and Harris, "Washington Prepares to Pay Rosa Parks."

35. Parks, *Rosa Parks*.

36. Williams and Greenhaw, *Thunder of Angels*, 48. Claudette Colvin's actions were equally heroic to Parks's, but Colvin was shunted aside due to her age and status as an unwed mother.

37. Kaitlyn Greenidge, "'Sisterhood' Felt Meaningless."

38. Sarah Harris's ethnic background was multiracial. Turner, "Sarah Harris Fayerweather," 218.

39. Tucker, "Sarah Harris," 156.

40. Tucker, "Sarah Harris," 156–57.

41. *Liberator*, May 25, 1833, 82–83, letter Crandall sent May 7, 1833, to *Windham County Advertiser*. Noteworthy is how even the hostile actors—most likely Judson himself—who published their *Statement of Facts* affirm that the request came from Sarah Harris and was repeated before Crandall acceded, following Crandall's own statement, *Statement of Facts*, 5–6. In this description, Crandall refers to Sarah Harris as a "colored girl," despite the fact that Sarah was twenty years old at the time.

42. Stewart, *Productions*, 52. Another person influenced by the clarion jeremiads of Maria Stewart, Boston Black abolitionist Susan Paul, reinforced this sentiment a few years later, when she published the biography of one her students, hoping "this little book do something towards breaking down that unholy prejudice which exists against color." Paul, *Memoir of James Jackson*, 67.

43. Larned, *History of Windham County*, 2:403. Larned misreads Davis's name as "Marcia," corrected here for reading clarity.

44. Larned, *History of Windham County*, 2:403.

45. *Liberator*, May 25, 1833, 82–83. Amos Dresser uses this same passage from

Ecclesiastes when girding his loins to face whipping for carrying copies of the *Liberator*; see Dresser, *Narrative*, 16–17. Abby Kelley Foster, Crandall's erstwhile classmate at NEYMBS, used the Bible talismanically prior to her first public speech, being led to 1 Corinthians 1:26–27, on God choosing things the world finds foolish to prove his might. Speicher, *Religious World of Antislavery Women*, 38.

46. As Karen Jo Torjesen points out, Crandall's choice of Ecclesiastes is interesting because that book rejects the prizes of the world as vanity. If Crandall understood Ecclesiastes thus, she might well have been able to connect it to her renunciation of the side that held power and the giving up of the worldly accomplishments they could dangle before her, such as her successful first academy. Conversation, Spring 2001, Claremont, California. Crandall's siding with the tears here recalls one of Rosa Luxemburg's humanist letters from prison, where she states, "I am at home wherever in the world there are clouds, birds and human tears." Bronner, *Letters of Rosa Luxemburg*, 179–80.

47. *Liberator*, May 25, 1833, 82–83, letter Crandall sent May 7, 1833, to *Windham County Advertiser*. Original emphasis. Crandall ends the letter with another twist, vouching for Samuel J. May. In a society in which the testimony of women was frequently disregarded or dismissed, her attesting for a minister marks a clever reversal. Her last line, in fact, indicates the ultimate source of what May wrote: "[I] give this, my public declaration, in favor of the correctness of all the statements he has made, respecting myself and my school, many of which he made upon my authority. Respectfully yours, Prudence Crandall."

48. Samuel J. May mentions that William Harris "encouraged" Sarah and "gladly offered to defray the expense" of tuition, but the chronology is unclear. *Some Recollections of Our Antislavery*, 40.

49. Indirect male influence, such as Sarah Harris needing parental fiscal permission or Crandall drawing inspiration from male authors, is not being denied here. This is an argument about effective agency, not separatism.

50. Oliver Johnson mentions that some of Crandall's white students had known Harris from the district school, but Carl R. Woodward in his article on Sarah Harris points out that the family's move to Canterbury in early 1832 likely precluded Sarah being at the same district school with most of the white students. Although this is accurate, some of the students may have attended common schools south of Canterbury or attended schools with some of Sarah's siblings. Woodward, "Profile in Dedication"; O. Johnson, *W. L. Garrison*, 125.

51. Pardon Crandall to Andrew Judson, in W. L. Garrison, *Fruits of Colonization*, 5–6; Strane, *Whole-Souled Woman*, 27; D. E. Williams, *Prudence Crandall's Legacy*, 30.

52. Larned, *History of Windham County*, 2:403–4, 491; Strane, *Whole-Souled Woman*, 27–28; D. E. Williams, *Prudence Crandall's Legacy*, 30; M. Welch, *Prudence Crandall,* 24; Foner and Pacheco, *Three Who Dared*, 9; Fuller, *Prudence Crandall*, 14–15.

53. May, *Some Recollections*, 41–42. Clisby's recollections are of interest for including Maria Davis among the students: "Sarah Harris applied for admission

to the school and was accepted. The patrons were stirred to action by this, and a committee was appointed to visit her and demand that she take the colored girls out or they would remove their children. After duly considering the matter, Aunt staunchly replied: 'Take them out, then, I shall not deny these girls, Marcia [sic], and Sarah Harris, their right to learn.'" Clisby, "Canterbury Pilgrims," TS, 1947, Prudence Crandall Collection, Charles E. Shain Library, Connecticut College, New London, Connecticut, 29. Julie Roy Jeffrey's analysis of May's *Some Personal Recollections of Our Anti-Slavery Conflict* in *Abolitionists Remember* is excellent (27–59). She highlights May's agenda as "the vital importance of establishing an antislavery understanding of the past" and not allowing triumphant Northerners to forget about their complicity in slavery.

54. For an interesting parallel from Kentucky, see Myers, *Vice President's Black Wife*, 9, 115.

55. Kelly, *In the New England Fashion*, 74–76.

56. Clisby, "Canterbury Pilgrims," TS, 1947, Prudence Crandall Collection, Charles E. Shain Library, Connecticut College, New London, Connecticut, 34. The phrase "stiff-necked" might be traceable to Calvin Philleo.

57. Hornick, "Anthony Benezet," 399. Winch notes how Benezet was "(a)nxious to undermine notions of black intellectual inferiority." *Gentleman of Color*, 24.

58. Hornick, "Anthony Benezet," 403.

59. Goodman, *Of One Blood,* xix, 1–3.

60. May, "Miss Prudence Crandall," 182, added emphasis.

61. Theodore Dwight Weld (1803–95) was born a mere two months after Crandall, in Hampton, Connecticut, about ten miles from Canterbury.

62. Goodman, *Of One Blood,* xiv.

63. For more on how women contributed to this development, see Rycenga, "Greater Awakening."

64. Mayer, *All on Fire*, 214. See Jeffrey, *Abolitionists Remember*, 33–34, for a similarly effusive language of conversion from Samuel J. May. Interestingly, Judson adopts the language of conversion to deprecate Crandall in his cowritten letter with Rufus Adams, saying that in January 1833, "Miss C. was proselyted to the *immediate Abolition* faith," whose principles had "taken full possession of her mind." *Unionist* (Brooklyn, CT), August 8, 1833, 2.

65. D. B. Davis, "Emergence of Immediatism," 229. The willingness of Jesus to defy the literalism of his Pharisaic opponents (for instance, in the Good Samaritan parable, Luke 10:25–37) is one example of the spirit-versus-letter dynamic; Paul uses this dynamic in his argument against the need for circumcision, Romans 2:29.

66. Hinks, *To Awaken*, 233. This entire section owes much to Hinks's exegesis of Walker's *Appeal*.

67. M. Stewart, *Productions*, 59. This would have been available to Crandall through Maria Davis, falling into that period of 1832 prior to September, as it was published in the *Liberator*, April 28, 1832, 66–67.

68. Crandall to William Lloyd Garrison, January 18, 1833, MS A.1.2, 3:3, Anti-Slavery Collection, Boston Public Library.

69. Wright, "Progress of the Antislavery Cause," 90–91, emphasis added. See

also Beriah Green's speech in the *American Anti-Slavery Reporter* (New York City), 1, no. 6, June 1834, 88–90.

70. Goodman, *Of One Blood*, 234.

71. Litwack cautions that the antislavery movement was marked by "factionalism, extreme partisanship, narrow class attitudes, prejudice, and even hypocrisy, but it shared these weaknesses with nearly every organized social movement and political party in antebellum America." *North of Slavery*, 230.

72. *Liberator*, 3, no. 37, September 14, 1833, 147.

73. M. Stewart, *Productions*, 16.

74. M. Stewart, *Productions*, 3, 52.

75. Crandall to William Lloyd Garrison, January 18, 1833, MS A.1.2, 3:3, Anti-Slavery Collection, Boston Public Library.

76. D. E. Williams develops a similar idea about Crandall's political acumen on this point. *Prudence Crandall's Legacy*, 31.

77. M. Stewart, *Productions*, 4.

78. Mayer states categorically that she did not receive a reply from Garrison before going to Boston. *All on Fire*, 146.

79. This was the Marlboro Hotel. Strane, *Whole-Souled Woman*, 29. It was also the site for a workingman's convention called by the Universalist Jacob Freize in 1832. Grieve, *Illustrated History*, 98.

80. Mayer, *All on Fire*, 146.

81. Fuller, *Prudence Crandall*, 18–21; McCain, *To All on Equal Terms*, 26; D. E. Williams, *Prudence Crandall's Legacy*, 31, 44–46; Strane, *Whole-Souled Woman*, 28–31; Foner and Pacheco, *Three Who Dared*, 10–11; M. Welch, *Prudence Crandall*, 25–26. Mayer's account of this meeting seems to best understand the gender tensions and Crandall's boldness in conceiving of both the school and this meeting. *All on Fire*, 146.

82. Strane, *Whole-Souled Woman*, 28–29; Fuller, *Prudence Crandall*, 20–21.

83. Fuller, *Prudence Crandall*, 20–21.

84. D. E. Williams, *Prudence Crandall's Legacy*, 44–46, and Strane, *Whole-Souled Woman*, 28–31, present imagined reconstructions.

85. William Lloyd Garrison to George Benson, March 8, 1833, in W. L. Garrison, *Letters of William Lloyd Garrison, Volume I*, 212.

Chapter 3. Activating the Abolitionist Networks

1. Strane, *Whole-Souled Woman*, 31–33, describing the poverty in Providence's Black community, mentions that Crandall had likely not seen this side of Providence in her school days.

2. Crandall to William Lloyd Garrison, February 12, 1833, in Garrison and Garrison, *William Lloyd Garrison*, 316–17.

3. Crandall to William Lloyd Garrison, February 12, 1833, in Garrison and Garrison, *William Lloyd Garrison*, 316–17.

4. Crandall to William Lloyd Garrison, February 12, 1833, in Garrison and Garrison, *William Lloyd Garrison*, 316–17.

5. Crandall to William Lloyd Garrison, February 12, 1833, in Garrison and Garrison, *William Lloyd Garrison*, 316–17; W. P. Garrison, "Connecticut in the Middle Ages."

6. Conrad, *Perish the Thought*, 76. After meeting with a Haitian government official in 1824, Fanny Wright was forbidden from the grounds of Mount Vernon during Lafayette's triumphal tour. Morris, *Fanny Wright*, 81–82.

7. For instance, later that year, in November 1833, Williams, Cornish, and Wright evaluated a Mr. Rose who came with an emigration scheme, and they decided against trusting him. See Peter Williams, Theodore Wright, and Samuel Cornish to Gerrit Smith, May 3, 1835, box 40, Gerrit Smith Papers, Syracuse University, Syracuse, New York. William Miller's absence from the list of endorsers seems strange; in 1808 he cofounded the New York African Society for Mutual Relief, one of the first extensive cooperative networks among free Blacks in the North. Shirley Yee, "The New York African Society for Mutual Relief (1808–1860)," http://www.blackpast.org/. Miller was known for his capricious temperament; see the account of his disruptive role in the African Methodist Episcopal Zion Church (AMEZ). Hood, *One Hundred Years*, 70–71.

8. Child, *Anti-Slavery Catechism*, 29; A. Grimké, *Appeal to the Women*, 32.

9. Prudence Crandall to Simeon S. Jocelyn, February 26, 1833. Prudence Crandall Collection, Charles E. Shain Library, Connecticut College, New London, Connecticut.

10. Tappan, *Life of Arthur Tappan*, 133.

11. Tappan, *Life of Arthur Tappan*, 152.

12. Prudence Crandall to Simeon S. Jocelyn, February 26, 1833. Prudence Crandall Collection, Charles E. Shain Library, Connecticut College, New London, Connecticut.

13. *Liberator*, 6, no. 14, April 2, 1836, 56.

14. For Jocelyn's unbowed optimism, see the offhand remark by Henry Benson that Jocelyn "writes as if he saw not an obstacle in the way for the speedy emancipation of the slaves." Henry Benson to William Lloyd Garrison, February 8, 1833, in and Garrison, *William Lloyd Garrison*, 317n4.

15. Prudence Crandall to Simeon S. Jocelyn, February 26, 1833. Prudence Crandall Collection, Charles E. Shain Library, Connecticut College, New London, Connecticut.

16. Larned, *History of Windham County*, 2:404.

17. Abdy, *Journal of a Residence*, 1:200–203.

18. *Unionist* (Brooklyn, CT), 1, no. 2, August 8, 1833, 3.

19. The classic account is Richards, *Gentlemen of Property and Standing*, 5. The phrase in Richards's title can be traced to the *New-England Palladium & Commercial Gazette* (Boston) issue of August 14, 1835, which defended the mobs harrassing abolitionists Boston as *"gentlemen of property and standing"* who aimed to curb the threat of abolitionism. *Boston Mob*, 17; Mayer, *All on Fire*, 206–7, original emphasis.

20. *Statement of Facts*, 7.

21. George Benson Jr. to William Lloyd Garrison, March 5, 1833, in the *Liberator*, 3, no. 10, March 9, 1833, 39.

22. Strane, *Whole-Souled Woman*, 35; George Benson Jr. to William Lloyd Garrison, March 5, 1833, in the *Liberator*, 3, no. 10, March 9, 1833, 39.

23. *Statement of Facts*, 7.

24. Crandall's biblical support comes from Numbers 12, where Aaron and Miriam are displeased with Moses's having married an Ethiopian and are then cursed by God for doubting Moses's calling as a prophet.

25. Strane, *Whole-Souled Woman*, 36; D. E. Williams, *Prudence Crandall's Legacy*, 53.

26. See Litwack, *North of Slavery*, 105–6; Yee, *Black Women Abolitionists*, 130; Mayer, *All on Fire*, 115; Jeffrey, *Great Silent Army*, 92; Jacobs, "David Walker and William Lloyd Garrison," 13. Yee notes that Julia Williams, one of Crandall's Black students, was among those who signed a petition denouncing laws against intermarriage.

27. Jacobs, "David Walker and William Lloyd Garrison," 13.

28. For an insightful study of a later section of the tortured history of inter-racial marriage, see R. M. Griffith, *Moral Combat*, 83–120.

29. Coontz, *Marriage*, 33.

30. Karcher, *First Woman of the Republic*, 178–79. The original editorial of Child is in the *(Boston) Massachusetts Journal and Tribune*, August 6, 1831, 3, and is discussed in the *Liberator*, 1, no. 33, August 13, 1831, 129–30. For crediting Child with this unsigned editorial, see Karcher, *First Woman of the Republic*, 658n17.

31. In the *Appeal* Lydia Maria Child suggests that the freedom to marry is related to freedom of religion: "A man has at least as good a right to choose his wife, as he has to choose his religion. His taste may not suit his neighbors, but so long as his deportment is correct, they have no right to interfere with his concerns." Child, *Appeal*, 209. See Karcher, *First Woman of the Republic*, 189–90.

32. Connecticut flirted with state's rights during the Hartford Convention. The young Calhoun learned about disunion and nullification when studying law in Litchfield. M. L. Coit, *John C. Calhoun*, 36–40.

33. "Heathenism Outdone!" *Liberator*, 3, no. 11, March 16, 1833, 42; *Statement of Facts*, 7–8; W. L. Garrison, *Fruits of Colonization*, 3–6; May, *Some Recollections*, 43–46; Larned, *History of Windham County*, 404–5; Strane, *Whole-Souled Woman*, 41–45; M. Welch, *Prudence Crandall*, 30–32; Foner and Pacheco, *Three Who Dared*, 14–15; Fuller, *Prudence Crandall*, 24–29; D. E. Williams, *Prudence Crandall's Legacy*, 61–64.

34. Judson writes of 1833, "I did not fail to carry every measure desired by me, and am grateful to this day for the kindness with which I was treated during the whole session." Andrew Judson, "A Short Sketch of My Own Life," ca. 1847, MS, collection 247, Mystic Seaport Collections and Research Center, Mystic, Connecticut, 14.

35. May, *Some Recollections*, 44.

36. W. L. Garrison, *Fruits of Colonization*, 4, original emphases.

37. W. L. Garrison, *Fruits of Colonization*, 4.

38. W. L. Garrison, *Fruits of Colonization*, 4. See also Sillen, *Women against Slavery*, 13.

39. Strane, *Whole-Souled Woman*, 43. Note that John James Audubon

contemporaneously expressed distaste at the multihued diversity of New Orleans. Rhodes, *John James Audubon*, 176.

40. Henry Benson to William Lloyd Garrison, in *Liberator*, 3, no. 11, March 16, 1833, 42.

41. May, *Recollections*, 45.

42. Henry Benson to William Lloyd Garrison, in *Liberator*, 3, no. 11, March 16, 1833, 42. I am proud to do my part to cast "ignominy and shame" upon the white Canterburian leaders.

43. W. L. Garrison, *Fruits of Colonization*, 4, original emphasis.

44. W. L. Garrison, *Fruits of Colonization*, 5, emphasis added.

45. Henry Benson to William Lloyd Garrison, in *Liberator*, 3, no. 11, March 16, 1833, 42.

46. There is some confusion, in the primary sources, about the George S. White in question. Henry Benson identifies him as a "tanner." I follow D. E. Williams in feeling this was an error on Benson's part, because the rhetorical style, pious flourishes, and even the daring to speak in this hostile situation are all consistent with Reverend George S. White. See D. E. Williams, *Prudence Crandall's Legacy*, 63, 368–69n132, 133.

47. May, *Some Recollections*, 45.

48. May, *Some Recollections*, 46; Henry Benson to William Lloyd Garrison, in *Liberator*, 3, no. 11, March 16, 1833, 42.

49. For an excellent provocative analysis, see Kendi, *Stamped from the Beginning*, 182–86, 200–201; cf. Mayer, *All on Fire*, 371–74.

50. May, *Some Recollections*, 46.

51. May, *Some Recollections*, 47–48.

52. Whether May was aware of the cover he was providing is open for debate. While May's memoir stays focused on "northern moral complicity in slavery," Jeffrey also notes, "African-American individuals are not central to May's history." *Abolitionists Remember*, 27, 33, 49.

53. May, *Some Recollections*, 50.

54. Pardon Crandall to the Select Men of Canterbury, March 19, 1833, in Garrison, *Fruits of Colonization*, 5–6. Pardon Crandall in this letter also makes a telling comparison between Crandall's persecutors and the Puritan judges of colonial times, suggesting that Judson and company "are actuated by the same spirit that lited [*sic*] up the fires of Smithfield that banished Roger Williams the Quakers and Baptists from Boston and more particularly by the actors in the Salem witchcraft, when they tried to kill or lay the Devile Who, they imagined appeared to their inhabitants in form of a Black man."

55. *Statement of Facts*, 8.

56. Mayer, *All on Fire*, 178.

57. *Liberator*, 3, no. 11, March 16, 1833, 42.

58. Although Strane claims that Daniel Packer continued from the first to the second board, I have found no documentary evidence supporting that. Strane, *Whole-Souled Woman*, 38, 62.

59. Even back in the mid-1820s, the African Improvement Society's "board of

managers was to be formed of white and colored members, chosen in 'expedient' proportions." Warner, *New Haven Negroes*, 46–47n. Certainly, having any admixture of Black and white in leadership positions defied the racial segregation of the times, but the term "expedient" concedes much to white prejudice.

60. Leonard Bacon considered himself a "discreet man" in comparison to Garrison, for instance. J. B. Stewart, "New Haven Negro College," 335.

61. During the *Liberator's* initial year of 1831, there were about four hundred Black and fifty white subscribers. By 1833, the year of Crandall's Second Academy, the subscription list had about a thousand Black and five hundred white readers. Wesley, "Negroes of New York in the Emancipation Movement," 76.

62. The January 1832 founding of the New England Anti-Slavery Society had taken place at the African Meeting House, but the Black community retained its own Massachusetts General Colored Association rather than merging, which they did later. Mayer, *All on Fire*, 130; D. Walker, *David Walker's Appeal to the Coloured Citizens*, 129–30n99.

63. Ripley, *Black Abolitionist Papers*, 5:298n2.

64. Silcox, "Delay and Neglect," 457–58.

65. Wyatt-Brown, *Lewis Tappan*, 87.

66. W. L. Garrison, *Thoughts on African Colonization*; see also Winch, *Gentleman of Color*, 190–92, and *Leaders of Philadelphia's Black Community*, 172–92.

67. Willson, *Elite of Our People*, 10, 20, 162–63n110. Amy Matilda Cassey (1809–56) "became prominent among antislavery women as a founding member of the Gilbert Lyceum, an officer of the Philadelphia Anti-Slavery Society and Philadelphia Women's Association, and a participant in the city's annual antislavery fairs. Following Cassey's death in 1848, she married Charles L. Remond and continued her antislavery work in Salem, Massachusetts. In 1853, after being ejected from a Boston theater, she challenged the theater's racial discrimination in court and won a favourable decision." Ripley, *Black Abolitionist Papers*, 4:183n10.

68. James Forten to William Lloyd Garrison, December 31, 1830, in Ripley, *Black Abolitionist Papers*, 3:86.

69. Ripley, *Black Abolitionist Papers*, 3:85; Mayer, *All on Fire*, 110.

70. Housley, "Yours for the Oppressed," is the best source on the elder Beman; see also V. S. Welch, *And They Were Related*, 64–69. Jehiel's father chose the name "Beman" at his manumission, because he "wanted to *be a man*." Strother, *Underground Railroad in Connecticut*, 153–54.

71. *Liberator*, 1, no. 30, July 23, 1831, 117. Jehiel Beman was also the Middletown agent for the New Haven Manual Labor College. See Hewitt, "Sacking of St. Philip's Church," 16; Warner, *New Haven Negroes*, 204.

72. Quarles, *Black Abolitionists*, 94; Swift, *Black Prophets of Justice*, 175.

73. Jehiel Beman's son Amos Beman (1812–74) was involved in a repugnant episode at the newly opened Wesleyan University in Middletown in 1833. A white student and *Liberator* subscriber, Samuel Dole, agreed to tutor Amos Beman, conducting the sessions in Dole's dormitory room. Student harassment forced Dole and Beman off campus, but hostile students hounded them wherever they went, even writing a letter "deeming it derogatory to themselves as well as to the

university, to have you and other colord [*sic*] people recite here, do hereby warn you to desist from such a course, and if you fail to comply with this *peacable* [*sic*] request, we swear, by the ETERNAL GODS! That we will resort to forcible means to put a stop to it." Strother, *Underground Railroad in Connecticut*, 154–55.

74. Housley, "Life of Jehiel C. Beman," 22–24.

75. Dowling, "Sketches of New York Baptists," 299; Ripley, *Black Abolitionist Papers*, 2:266–67n2.

76. Among his sojourns were Zion Baptist in New York (1832–40), African Church in Albany (1840), First Independent Baptist Church in Boston (1840/41–43, 1845–47), Abyssinian Baptist Church in New York (1848–55), before returning to Zion Baptist for the remainder of his career (1855–61 or later). He was still preaching in 1861 and alive in 1870. "Sermon by Rev. J. T. Raymond; Zion Church," *New York Times*, December 1, 1861, print ed. The 1870 US Census record shows him living in Massachusetts but lists him as white. His death date is unclear. *1870 United States Federal Census, Population Schedule.*

77. Dowling, "Sketches of New York Baptists," 298–300.

78. *Liberator*, 2, no. 2, January 14, 1832, 5.

79. *Colored American* (New York), July 27, 1840. He also attended the first convention of the fledgling Liberty Party. See Horton and Horton, *In Hope of Liberty*, 242.

80. Nell, *Colored Patriots of the American Revolution*, 364. See also Finkenbine, "Boston's Black Churches," 186.

81. Horton, "Black New York and the Lincoln Presidency," 104.

82. John Mason Peck is a major figure in the antebellum decades of Illinois history and plays a cameo role in Calvin Philleo's restless history.

83. Oneida Baptist Association, *Minutes*, 4.

84. He followed the Abyssinian Baptist Church founders, brothers Nathaniel Paul and Benjamin Paul, in 1832.

85. J. A. Miller, "We've Come This Far," 24–33, 29. Hayborn inherited a temperance crusade, too, with forty pledges being recorded in the fall of 1831 from Abyssinian by agents of the New York City Temperance Society. Quarles, *Black Abolitionists*, 95.

86. McNeil, Robertson, Dixie, and McGruder, *Witness*, 19.

87. Convention of the People of Colour, *Minutes and Proceedings of the Third Annual Convention . . . 1833*, 39.

88. Henry Sipkins and Samuel Hardenburgh, "Meeting of the Free People of Color," *Abolitionist*, 1, no. 2, February 1833, 28; Quarles, *Black Abolitionists*, 132.

89. Peter Williams Sr. (1780–1823) worked with William Miller, Prudence Crandall's first contact in New York City, in the founding of the AMEZ. See E. D. Smith, *Climbing Jacob's Ladder*, 39–40.

90. Hewitt, "Sacking of St. Philip's Church," 20. The biblical reference is Acts 8:26–40.

91. P. Williams, *Oration on the Abolition*, 27–28; Townsend, *Faith in Their Own Color*, 29.

92. Townsend, *Faith in Their Own Color*, 38, 40, 41.

93. Townsend, *Faith in Their Own Color*, 29.

94. Woodson, *Negro Orators*, 80. Earlier in the speech, in an unfortunately prophetic moment, Peter Williams Jr. expresses the fear that the African Americans in Liberia could affect the Indigenous people of that area negatively, "infect(ing)" them as the European colonists did to Native Americans. The class divide and ethnic conflicts between American expatriate settlers in Liberia and native Africans have borne out this fear. Woodson, *Negro Orators*, 79–80.

95. Fordham, *Major Themes in Northern Black Religious Thought*, 41–42, mentions in particular Williams's 1817 sermon on the death of Paul Cuffee in relation to this theme.

96. *Colored American* (New York), January 26, 1839; E. D. Smith, *Climbing Jacob's Ladder*, 47; Swift, *Black Prophets of Justice,* 40–41, 61; Gross, "*Freedom's Journal* and *The Rights of All*," 275; Mabee, *Black Education in New York State*, 57–59.

97. Abdy, *Journal of a Residence*, 1:46–47.

98. The multiracial realities within the antebellum Black community were obvious to those within it but inimical to the binary racial categories of most white Americans, including many abolitionists. J. B. Stewart, "New Haven Negro College," 330–31, 334.

99. Bryant, "Race and Religion," 246–47.

100. Burrows and Wallace, *Gotham*, 549. This is one of the reasons why a work like Garrison's *Thoughts on African Colonization* was so significant as a sign of genuine solidarity.

101. Penn, *Afro-American Press and Its Editors*, 30; Walker, *David Walker's Appeal to the Coloured Citizens*, 69–70; Burrows and Wallace, *Gotham*, 549.

102. Burrows and Wallace, *Gotham*, 550; Winch, *Leaders of Philadelphia's Black Community,* 206, 228n102; Swift, *Black Prophets of Justice*, 41; Pride and Wilson, *History of the Black Press*, 17. Russwurm went to Liberia, where he established a newspaper and became involved in the politics of the expatriate Black community. Pride and Wilson, *History of the Black Press*, 19. Graham Russell Hodges feels that Russwurm's defection to colonization was spurred by his anger at white American racism. Hodges, *Root and Branch*, 199.

103. Pride and Wilson, *History of the Black Press*, 29–38; Wilson, *Whither the Black Press*, 25–51.

104. American Anti-Slavery Society, *First Annual Report*, 47–48. Yee argues that this part of the report was authored by Cornish. Yee, *Black Women Abolitionists*, 49. For Cornish's attacks on Fanny Wright, see Yee, *Black Women Abolitionists*, 115n11 and 13, 178–79, with comments from both 1828 and 1839.

105. *Colored American* (New York), November 23, 1839.

106. American Anti-Slavery Society, *First Annual Report*, 48.

107. Sorin, *New York Abolitionists*, 82; Swift, *Black Prophets of Justice*, 48–49; R. P. G. Wright was born in Madagascar and attended the 1817 anticolonization meeting in Philadelphia.

108. Perry, *Radical Abolitionism*, 113.

109. Reddick, "Samuel E. Cornish," 38.

110. Sorin, *New York Abolitionists*, 82–83.

111. "Rev. Wright's fatal illness was brought on by the exhaustion of walking miles uptown to see prospective donors and then miles back downtown, 'under the full muzzle of the July or August sun'" rather than submitting to the humiliation of public-transport segregation. Burrows and Wallace, *Gotham*, 856; for Wright's wife's death, see G. E. Walker, *Afro-American in New York City*, 19; *Emancipator*, October 26, 1837.

112. *Liberator*, 3, no. 9, March 2, 1833, 35; Burrows and Wallace, *Gotham*, 550.

113. Swift, "Black Presbyterian Attacks on Racism."

114. Crandall's spirited defense of her admission of Sarah Harris would have assured her that reputation locally. This is why the speculation that Maria Davis was present, as a servant, during some of the delegations from the townspeople is likely, though nonverifiable. Someone, other than Crandall, was getting the word out to the local southeastern Connecticut Black community that she was trustworthy, and Maria Davis is the most likely candidate for that, along with the Harris family. But Davis would have had the advantage of witnessing a greater number of interactions between Crandall and Blacks and between Crandall and her emerging white opposition.

115. Alonso, *Growing Up Abolitionist*, 58–59, 110.

116. W. P. Garrison, *Benson Family*, 51–54.

117. Salitan and Perera, *Virtuous Lives*, 13.

118. *Liberator*, 3, no. 8, February 23, 1833, 29, has a short piece on Buffum, who served as the New England Anti-Slavery Society's first president.

119. Salitan and Perera, *Virtuous Lives*, 96.

120. Salitan and Perera, *Virtuous Lives*, 101; Stevens, *Elizabeth Buffum Chace*, 40; Edgerton, *History of the Separation*, 40–41.

121. *Liberator*, "Colonization Meeting," repr. from *Genius of Temperance, Philanthropist, and People's Advocate* (New York), *Liberator*, 3, no. 15, April 13, 1833, 58; Stevens, *Elizabeth Buffum Chace*, 9, 237n21. Buffum also remained an optimist, writing in 1836 that abolition, temperance, and peace "are destined to elevate the moral and spiritual standard . . . be of good courage—the cause is onward." *Liberator*, 6, no. 42, October 15, 1836, 166.

122. Christie and Dumond, *George Bourne*; Theodore Bourne, "George Bourne"; Rodriguez, "Bible against American Slavery," 105–40; Blair, "Reverend George Bourne."

123. *Liberator*, 2, no. 34, August 25, 1832, 133–34. The New York Presbytery that restored his ministerial credentials issued Bourne a warning that "the want of prudence may be as great an obstacle to ministerial success as is the want of piety." Quoted in Blair, "Reverend George Bourne," 5.

124. Christie and Dumond, *George Bourne*, 96–97; Raffo, *Biography of Oliver Johnson*, 35. Interestingly, Oliver Johnson was newly married to Mary Ann White (1808–72), who was an early white activist for antislavery and women's causes; it seems likely that the attention given to the Crandall case in the *Liberator* was thus enhanced. Raffo, *Biography of Oliver Johnson*, 31–32.

125. G. Bourne, *Picture of Slavery*, 27, 176.

126. For more on John Rogers, see Daniell, *Bible in English*, 190–97.

127. Billington, *Protestant Crusade*, 116n139. The defense of Bourne's anti-Catholic crusade by his son is telling. See T. Bourne, "George Bourne," 79–81. While it is impossible to confirm the authorship of the notorious *Awful Disclosures of Maria Monk*, there were persistent rumors that Bourne had ghostwritten it, and he assuredly endorsed its weaponization against Catholicism.

128. Billington, *Protestant Crusade*, 55.

129. David Walker, in his *Appeal,* refers to Catholicism as "that scourge of nations" and regrets its presence in Haiti. *David Walker's Appeal to the Coloured Citizens*, 23.

130. May, *Right of Colored People*, 4; Clisby, "Canterbury Pilgrims," TS, 1947, Prudence Crandall Collection, Charles E. Shain Library, Connecticut College, New London, Connecticut, 11.

131. May, *Some Recollections*, 42–43. It is unclear whether May came with Benson Sr. or Jr.

132. Dillon, *Benjamin Lundy*, 137; Swift, *Black Prophets of Justice,* 27; Gross, "*Freedom's Journal* and *The Rights of All*," 266–68.

133. Quarles, *Black Abolitionists*, 130–31.

134. *Liberator*, 3, no. 47, November 23, 1833, 185; Strane, *Whole-Souled Woman*, 105; Nathaniel Paul to William Lloyd Garrison, August 31, 1833, MS A.1.2, 3:66, Anti-Slavery Collection, Boston Public Library. Sinha refers to Paul's joint appearances with Garrison as "the first triumph of interracial immediatism." Sinha, *Slave's Cause*, 221–22.

135. Mabee, *Black Education in New York State*, 51.

136. In later iterations of the advertisement, the names of Garrison and Buffum were dropped, and two other white men, Amos Phelps (1805–47) and Samuel E. Sewall (1799–1888), were substituted. See *Unionist* (Brooklyn, CT), 1, no. 2, August 8, 1833, 4.

137. William Lloyd Garrison to George Benson, March 8, 1833, in Merrill, *Letters of William Lloyd Garrison*, 1:212.

Chapter 4. Martyrs in the Classroom

1. Goodrich, *System of Universal Geography*, 112.

2. John Winthrop wrote in 1629, "All townes complaine of the burthen of theire poore." "Reasons for the Plantation in New-England," 71.

3. Vagrancy laws were later transmuted into the infamous antiimmigrant exclusion acts; see, for instance, the Immigration Act of 1917, which specifically forbids (in a long list of people excluded) "vagrants." February 5, 1917, H.R. 10384; Public No. 301, ch. 29, sec. 3. See Arnold-Lourie, "Inharmonious Elements" and "Racial Homogeneity."

4. Abdy, *Journal of a Residence*, 1:208.

5. State of Connecticut, *Public Statute Laws*, 674.

6. State of Connecticut, *Code of 1650*, 64–65.

7. D. Walker, *One Continual Cry*, 104.

8. Brodhead, *Cultures of Letters*, 13–16.

9. Bibb, *Narrative of the Life*, 112–13. See also D. G. White, *Ar'n't I a Woman*, 27–32. Bryant, *Victims and Heroes*, 15–23.

10. Grant, *Way It Was in the South*, 62.

11. Dresser, *Narrative of the Arrest*; Wood, "Nashville Now and Then: You Watch Your Mouth," *Nashville (TN) Post* August 5, 2007; O. Johnson, *W. L. Garrison and His Times*, 218; Nye, *Fettered Freedom*, 183.

12. A Subscriber, "Colonization in Missouri," *Emancipator and Journal of Public Morals* (New York City) 3, no. 5, February 3, 1835; Merkel, "Abolition Aspects," 245.

13. *Liberator*, 3, no. 20, May 18, 1833, 78.

14. Yee, *Black Women Abolitionists*, 53–54; Gamber, *Boardinghouse*.

15. May, *Some Recollections*, 51; Strane, *Whole-Souled Woman*, 68–69; D. E. Williams, *Prudence Crandall's Legacy*, 78–79; M. Welch, *Prudence Crandall*, 44–47; Foner and Pacheco, *Three Who Dared*, 41; Fuller, *Prudence Crandall*, 34–35.

16. Strane, *Whole-Souled Woman*, 69.

17. Hammond's first names are reversed in some primary sources, so she appears as both Ann Eliza Hammond and Eliza Ann Hammond. Prudence Crandall herself was unable to clarify this question when Wendell Garrison asked her. See Prudence Crandall Philleo to Wendell Phillips Garrison, May 5, 1881, in Alma Lutz Collection, Radcliffe Institute for Advanced Study, Schlesinger Library, Harvard University, where she admits, "I do not know whether Eliza or Ann came first in the name of Miss Hammond. It was her mothers [*sic*] own house where I was entertained (not a hired house) at the time you mention."

18. May, *Some Recollections*, 51.

19. Williams also claims that Crandall herself paid the fine for Ann Eliza Hammond, which he references from Pardon Crandall's May 1, 1833, letter to the Connecticut Assembly, in M. Welch, *Prudence Crandall*, 50–51. He maintains that Crandall cared more about the psychological health of Ann Eliza Hammond than May did. D. E. Williams, *Prudence Crandall's Legacy*, 81.

20. M. Stewart, *Productions*, 17. See also Bartlett, *Wendell Phillips*, 55–56.

21. O. Johnson, *W. L. Garrison*, 126. While the selectmen chose to abandon whipping as a strategy, the threat was not forgotten by Connecticut's African Americans. At the Connecticut State Convention of Colored Men in 1849, some progress in terms of education was noted: "No teacher need now fear *arrest, fine, and imprisonment,* for his labor of love in teaching a colored child. No colored young lady need tremble at a town's threatening of 'ten stripes on the naked back' for presuming to enter Connecticut in the pursuit of knowledge." *Proceedings of the Connecticut State Convention of Colored Men,* 17, original emphasis. In attendance at this conference was Pelleman Williams, spouse of Crandall alumna Mary Harris; they were wed in 1845.

22. Prudence Crandall to Simeon S. Jocelyn, April 17–20, 1833, in "Abolition Letters Collected," 83.

23. Mayer, *All on Fire*, 92, quoting William Lloyd Garrison to the *Newburyport (MA) Herald*, June 1, 1830.

24. Bibb, *Narrative of the Arrest*, 23.

25. *Boston Mob*, 73.

26. Martineau, *Martyr Age*.

27. Esther Baldwin to Amy Baldwin, May 4, 1833, Baldwin Collection, Connecticut Museum of Culture and History Research Center, Hartford, Connecticut; Strane, *Whole-Souled Woman*, 71. The Black sexton was likely Joseph Quy, who joined the church in 1826 and was the youngest son of Black Revolutionary War veteran Lebbeus Quy. Coit, *Historical Sketch*, 28. Thanks to Dale Plummer, June 23, 2017, email communication with author.

28. *Liberator*, 3, no. 21, May 25, 1833, 82, repr. of *Windham County Advertiser*, May 7, 1833.

29. Andrew Judson, "A Short Sketch of My Own Life," ca. 1847, MS, collection 247, Mystic Seaport Collections and Research Center, Mystic, Connecticut, 14.

30. "Canterbury," letter to the editor, (Hartford) *Connecticut Courant*, June 24, 1833, 2–3. Donald Yacovone deems this letter writer serious, but I sense irony and sarcasm. *Samuel Joseph May*, 49.

31. Jay, *Inquiry into the Character*, 37–38.

32. Fuller (*Prudence Crandall*, 38) and Foner and Pacheco (*Three Who Dared*, 22–23) state categorically that contemporary accounts indicate no "nay" votes on the Black Law.

33. Attainders and their abuse were among the chief complaints of the American colonists against their British overlords. The US Constitution specifically prohibits attainders and ex post facto laws in article 1, section 3, sentence 3.

34. The Connecticut and California decisions in favor of same-sex marriage equality hinged on the absence of any rationally compelling state interest for excluding same-sex marriage, despite the fact that there are copious compelling state interests in favor of marriage more generally (ease of property transfer on death, support of couples for each other during illness, stronger bonds between families, etc.). See Nussbaum, "Right to Marry." The notion of any compelling state interest in *denying* Black citizenship *and* in *denying* access to education to Blacks would eventually be disproven, but it would take the Civil War, the post–Civil War amendments, and the civil rights movement to even begin to make this real.

35. William Jay (1789–1858), son of Chief Justice John Jay, wrote an analysis of the Black Law and its colonizationist tendencies in *Inquiry into the Character*, 30–47.

36. (Hartford) *Connecticut Courant*, June 24, 1833, 2–3; Strane, *Whole-Souled Woman*, 74–75, 239n5. Despite Hegel's reputation for racism, he obliterated the pseudoscientific phrenology arguments for Black inferiority, recognizing that humanity lay in the combination of mind and spirit. He opined that the best way to disprove phrenological arguments was to punch out the person supporting phrenology: when "a man is told, 'You are so and so, because your skull-bone is so constituted,' this means nothing else than that we regard a bone as the man's reality. To retort upon such a statement ... would, properly speaking, have to go the length of breaking the skull of the person who makes a statement like that,

in order to demonstrate to him in a manner as palpable as his own wisdom that a bone is nothing of an inherent nature at all for a man, still less his true reality." *Phenomenology of Mind*, 365.

37. D. E. Williams, *Prudence Crandall's Legacy*, 83. These petitions are found in "Records of the Connecticut General Assembly," boxes 17–18, 1833, Connecticut State Library, Hartford. D. E. Williams lists the towns and the number of signatures. *Prudence Crandall's Legacy*, 374n19.

38. *Statement of Facts*, 8–10, contains the entire committee report, signed by Philip Pearl; added emphasis.

39. The text of the Black Law is printed in its entirety in *Statement of Facts*, 10–11.

40. In his excellent analysis of the legal aspects of Crandall's school, William Jay sighed, "Thus were the backs of Miss Crandall's pupils saved from the threatened laceration." *Inquiry*, 35.

41. Jay, *Inquiry*, 36.

42. Larned, *History of Windham County*, 2:408.

43. Strane, *Whole-Souled Woman*, 75; D. E. Williams, *Prudence Crandall's Legacy*, 83–84; Fuller, *Prudence Crandall*, 35–37.

44. Larned, *History of Windham County*, 2:407–9.

45. Ebenezer Stoddard had worked with Judson and Moses Warren on the surveying of the Connecticut-Massachusetts border in the mid-1820s.

46. Sketches of all three can be found in US Congress, *Biographical Directory of the United States Congress*, http://bioguide.congress.gov/scripts/biodisplay .pl?index=G000248.

47. May, *Some Recollections*, 52.

48. Larned, *History of Windham County*, 2:408; Strane, *Whole-Souled Woman*, 78–79.

49. Establishing Black citizenship with legal clarity had been on the agenda of the Black abolitionists and William Lloyd Garrison for years. An early issue of the *Liberator* expresses the opinion that citizenship should be easy to prove in court. *Liberator*, 1, no. 3, January 15, 1831, 10.

50. See Isenberg, *Sex and Citizenship in Antebellum America*. Her pithy summation: "Freeborn women had the appearance of citizenship but lacked the basic rights to be citizens." xii.

51. It is likely Crandall had read prison writings by Quaker women. Scheffler, "Prison Writings of Early Quaker Women."

52. May, *Some Recollections*, 53. Again it is unclear if the George Benson here is the younger or older man.

53. May, *Some Recollections*, 54.

54. May, *Some Recollections*, 54.

55. "Connecticut Barbarism," *Boston Advocate*, repr. *New Bedford (MA) Courier and Weekly Lyceum*, 7, no. 6, July 10, 1833, 2.

56. May, *Some Recollections*, 56, original emphasis.

57. May, *Some Recollections*, 56–57.

58. "Connecticut Barbarism," *Boston Advocate*, repr. *New Bedford (MA) Courier and Weekly Lyceum*, 7, no. 6, July 10, 1833, 2.

59. Prudence Crandall to "Mr. Editor" (of the *Liberator*), June 28, 1833, Boston Public Library, Anti-Slavery Collection, MS A.1.2, 3:45. Additional corroboration surfaced in the "Connecticut Barbarism" article. The prosecution, unaware of Almira's age, had three successive court-appointed guardians refuse to remand her to prison.

60. May, *Some Recollections*, 55.

61. May, *Some Recollections*, 54.

62. May, *Some Recollections*, 54; Yacovone, *Samuel Joseph May*, 49–50. In the more contemporaneous piece he wrote for Lydia Maria Child's *Oasis*, May states, "Her friends [chose] to let her opposers have their way for a season, that the odiousness of their new law might be made manifest." 186.

63. *Windham County Advertiser*, July 20, 1833, quoted in McCain, *To All on Equal Terms*, 34. The same newspaper carried the account of Watkins's execution two years previous. See "Execution of Oliver Watkins," *Windham County Advertiser*, 5, August 2, 1831, 52.

64. *Unionist* (Brooklyn, CT), August 8, 1833.

65. Henry Benson to William Lloyd Garrison, August 30, 1833, MS, VA.1.2, 3:64, Anti-Slavery Collection, Boston Public Library; Strane, *Whole-Souled Woman*, 82.

66. George Benson Sr. to Moses Brown, September 21, 1833, and George Benson Sr. to Moses Brown, May 17, 1832, Moses Brown Papers, Rhode Island Historical Society.

67. William Lloyd Garrison, *Helen Eliza Garrison*, 13.

68. William Lloyd Garrison to Anna Benson, May 20, 1834, in W. L. Garrison, *Letters of William Lloyd Garrison, Volume I*, 150.

69. Prudence Crandall to William Lloyd Garrison "Mr. Editor," June 28, 1833, MS A.1.2, 3:45, Anti-Slavery Collection, Boston Public Library.

70. This is almost certainly the Lydia Congdon listed in the 1850 census as a Black woman living in Preston City (contiguous with Jewett City). She is in the same household with two men named Daniel Congdon, but no relationships are described. She would have been born around 1802. *Seventh Census of the United States, 1850*. There is insufficient biographical information to establish the certitude of Lydia Congdon's relationship to Crandall's student Jerusha Congdon. Congdon was a very common white name in Rhode Island and eastern Connecticut. It seems likely that the smaller branch of Black Congdons was descended from people that a wealthy Congdon had enslaved. Jerusha Congdon's grandfather Absalom Congdon had been enslaved and given the name of Peter Perry. He was freed by Colonel Samuel Coit's will and given a life lease of land by Coit in 1791. The next year Absalom Congdon took out a public advertisement to renounce the name of Perry and return to his ancestral name of Absalom Congdon. (New Haven) *Connecticut Gazette*, 29, no. 1484, April 19, 1792, 4.

71. Martineau, *Martyr Age*, 15.

72. Frederick Olney, Charles Harris, and David Ruggles—all of whom play ongoing roles in African American life in southern New England—would be among Crandall's African American contacts.

73. John Jay Chapman, "William Lloyd Garrison," 13–14.

74. Prudence Crandall Philleo to Ellen G. Larned, March 7, 1870, Connecticut State Library, Hartford, Connecticut.

75. The offer to move the school to a less-conspicuous location was brought by May and Buffum to the infamous town meeting. May, *Some Recollections*, 47. In the April 20 codicil to Prudence's letter to Simeon S. Jocelyn, she says that May had heard of a positive offer from Reading, Massachusetts, to host her school. Prudence Crandall to Simeon S. Jocelyn, April 17–20, 1833, in "Abolition Letters Collected," 84.

76. Yacovone, *Samuel Joseph May*, 50, quoting from the *Emancipator*, quoting the *Female Advocate*, July 27, 1833. Another protofeminist, the young Henry Browne Blackwell, future husband of Lucy Stone, remembered that when he was eight, he and his siblings named a pair of horses Garrison and Prudence Crandall! *Old Anti-Slavery Days*, 142.

77. Sue Houchins, in her introduction to the four Black women writers (including Maria Stewart) in *Spiritual Narratives*, points out the discursive nature of Black autobiographical writing: these antebellum Black women writers "seized *authority*." Houchins, introduction, xxix.

Chapter 5. Young Ladies and Little Misses

1. May, "Miss Prudence Crandall," 190.

2. For the seventeen students with calculable ages, the average was 16.91. Eleven were teenagers, two were younger, and four were in their twenties.

3. There was a not-always-productive rivalry between New York City and Philadelphia for leadership of the free Black community nationwide, which created tension about where to hold the conventions.

4. W. H. Morse, "United States of Africa," *Gospel in All Lands* (New York), June 1891, 252.

5. Registration form application, February 27, 2001, Kinne Cemetery, Glasgo, Griswold Connecticut, 8, National Register of Historic Places, https://npgallery .nps.gov/NRHP/GetAsset/NRHP/01000351_text.

6. Registration form application, February 27, 2001, Kinne Cemetery, Glasgo, Griswold, Connecticut, National Register of Historic Places, 8, https://npgallery .nps.gov/NRHP/GetAsset/NRHP/01000351_text. Crandall's early teacher and ally Rowland Greene extolled the Glasgo family in an article in *Colored American* (New York), March 11, 1837.

7. Registration form application, February 27, 2001, Kinne Cemetery, Glasgo, Griswold, Connecticut, National Register of Historic Places, 9, https://npgallery .nps.gov/NRHP/GetAsset/NRHP/01000351_text. Leonard Bacon, erstwhile colonizationist and halfhearted abolitionist, is likely referring to Isaac Glasko: "Does the wealthy and respected colored man who manufactures axes in one of the eastern counties of Connecticut, find that axes cannot be sold at the market price, if the smith who makes them is black by nature as well as by trade?" Bacon, Review, 451.

8. *Freedom's Journal* (New York), August 3, 1827; Peter P. Hinks, "Connecting

Prudence Crandall: Black Education and Antislavery in Southeastern Connecticut before 1833," unpublished paper given June 2013, at the Prudence Crandall, Canterbury, Connecticut, 20.

9. Registration form application, February 27, 2001, Kinne Cemetery, Glasgo, Griswold, Connecticut, 8–9, National Register of Historic Places, https://npgallery.nps.gov/NRHP/GetAsset/NRHP/01000351_text.

10. Caulkins. *History of Norwich*, 448–49.

11. Brown and Rose, *Black Roots*, 84.

12. V. S. Welch, *And They Were Related*, 1. In the 1850 census, Jerusha, her husband, William West, and their children are listed as mulatto, but in the 1860 and 1880 censuses, the family is listed as Black. This typifies the slipperiness of racial categories in a hyperracialized America. US Census Bureau: *Seventh Census of the United States, 1850; 1860 United States Federal Census; Tenth Census of the United States, 1880.*

13. V. S. Welch, *And They Were Related*, 64f, 173f.

14. W. H. Morse, "United States of Africa," *Gospel in All Lands* (New York), June 1891, 252. Recently, researcher Susan Maciorowski found another published narrative of the Tucker family that confirms much of Morse's article; see "Fruit of Canterbury Plot: Descendants of Prudence Crandall's Students Working in Africa," *Norwich Bulletin*, May 11, 1909, 5.

15. Hinks, "William Lanson."

16. *Liberator*, 6, no. 31, July 30, 1836, 122. Kabria Baumgartner, who found this gem, thinks E. F. might be connected to Hartford's Morrison family; I wonder if she is the wife or sister of the convention's vice president, the activist Henry Foster. Mysteries remain!

17. Karttunen, "Nantucket Places and People"; Gould, *Diary of a Contraband*.

18. A. W. Smith, "Early Baptist Missionary Leaders," 336–38. Sharp has an impressive memorial at Mount Auburn Cemetery in Cambridge, Massachusetts; see King, *Mount Auburn Cemetery*, 38, illus. on 37; Alexander Crummell, "Died: Mrs. Julia Williams Garnet," *Christian Recorder* (Philadelphia), January 22, 1870.

19. Garrison traveled with Julia Williams in 1837 to the Woman's Anti-Slavery meeting in New York. William Lloyd Garrison to Helen Benson Garrison, New York, May 6, 1837, in W. L. Garrison, *Letters of William Lloyd Garrison*, 2:260–61.

20. Pasternak, *Rise Now and Fly to Arms*, 36. She may also have "organized fundraising bazaars for Samuel Ringgold Ward's *Impartial Citizen* in 1849," according to a footnote in Ripley, *Black Abolitionist Papers*, 1:499n1. There are hints that Williams or Garnet was related to Samuel Ringgold Ward, but I could not corroborate the connection.

21. The presence of Mary Elizabeth Miles (Bibb) at the Prudence Crandall school was unconfirmed until 2014. In her research on Miles, Afua Cooper reread the memorial oration delivered by Alexander Crummell that indicated Miles's attendance at the school. A mysterious name on the school list for years—Mary Elizabeth Wiles—thus became a resolved mystery, assuming a simple transposition error somewhere along the way from *M* to *W*! See Cooper, "*Voice of the Fugitive*," 135–53.

22. Cooper, "Legacy of the Prudence Crandall School;" Cooper, "*Voice of the Fugitive*"; Cooper, "Black Women and Work," 143–70; Cooper, "Ever True to the Cause"; Manheim, "Henry Bibb."

23. Peterson, *Black Gotham*. Both Maritcha Lyons and Hallie Q. Brown are part of the legacy of the Crandall school, having networks of connection to numerous alumnae of the academy. Lyons, in particular, was deeply imbricated by family and teachers in the entire New York City–to–Rhode Island educational exodus that happened after the Draft Riots of 1863 in New York City, when a sizeable number of well-educated Blacks moved to Rhode Island. It was here that Lyons studied under Smith and likely met Sarah Harris Fayerweather. Despite this, Lyons does make small factual errors in her account, for instance, making 1832 the year Crandall's school closed. H. Q. Brown, *Homespun Heroines*, 19. See also Mabee, *Black Education in New York State*, 116.

24. Blankenship, "Woman of Refinement and Education," 1–2.

25. H. Q. Brown, *Homespun Heroines*, 19.

26. Snow, *Alphabetical Index*, 28. Arrival dates at the school for the pupils is difficult to discern after the first few arrivals; departure dates are impossible to establish. This is not unusual for the time period—schools had not yet become the bureaucratic time-sinks of recordkeeping they are now.

27. Snow, *Alphabetical Index*, 200. Evidence for their comfortable status was corroborated in Crandall's May 5, 1881, letter to Wendell Phillips Garrison, indicating that it was Ann Eliza Hammond's "mothers [*sic*] own house where I was entertained (not a hired house)." Alma Lutz Collection, Radcliffe Institute for Advanced Study, Schlesinger Library, Harvard University, Cambridge.

28. Prudence Crandall to William Lloyd Garrison, February 12, 1833, MS A.1.2, 3:13, Anti-Slavery Collection, Boston Public Library. There is a Betsey Hammond among the African American members of the First Baptist Church in Providence, Rhode Island, likely Elizabeth Hammond. First Baptist Church, Providence, Rhode Island, *List of Members*, 46.

29. *Unionist* (Brooklyn, CT), 1, no. 36, April 10, 1834, 1.

30. First Baptist Church, Providence, Rhode Island, *List of Members*, 46; "A Correct History," *American* (Providence, RI), February 4, 1832; Rammelkamp, "Providence Negro Community," 30.

31. Cottrol, *Afro-Yankees*, 58, 69; H. Jackson, *Short History*, 4; Bartlett, *From Slave to Citizen*, 38; McLoughlin, *Rhode Island*, 132.

32. Garrison, *Thoughts on African Colonization*, sec. 2, 45.

33. Garrison, *Thoughts on African Colonization*, sec. 2, 44.

34. *Fifth Census of the United States, 1830*; Eldridge and Whipple, *Regenerations*, 35.

35. "*Maria Robinson* was at Miss Crandall's house at work on the 28th day of January," *Unionist* (Brooklyn, CT), 1, no. 36, April 10, 1834, 1.

36. Writ of Arrest, Nehemiah Ensworth, grand juror, to Rufus Adams, justice of the peace, June 27, Archives 920 C85W Main Vault, Connecticut Museum of Culture and History, Hartford, 183.

37. While three of Forten's four surviving daughters would have been of an

appropriate age to attend Crandall's school, the oldest, Harriet Davy Forten
(1810–75), was already married, and Mary Isabella Forten (1815–42) was con-
sumptive. Only Sarah Louisa Forten (1814–84) remains, and since her mother,
Charlotte Forten, was an accomplished teacher herself, there was no need for
her daughters to travel to Canterbury. Julie Winch, email with author, January
2023.

38. *Pennsylvania Freeman* (Philadelphia), March 15, 1838; and April 12, 1838.

39. Gardner, "Johnson, Francis," 287; Foner, *History of Black Americans*, 537.
He was attacked by a racist mob in Allegheny City, Pennsylvania, in 1843 follow-
ing a performance at the Temperance Ark, a local center for reform meetings.
Wilmoth, "Pittsburgh and the Blacks," 23–24.

40. Intriguingly, a J. H. Johnson also appears in the list of delegates to the
Remunerated Labor Conference, from the Junior Anti-Slavery Society, along with
Joseph Parrish Jr. If one of the Johnson females had been among the younger
students at Canterbury, being a representative from a youth group is not impos-
sible. *Pennsylvania Freeman* (Philadelphia), March 15, 1838. *Fifth Census of the
United States, 1830*, and *Sixth Census of the United States, 1840*.

41. A. B. Smith, "Bustill Family," 638–44, 641.

42. A. B. Smith, "Bustill Family," 638. Julie Winch notes that he was exhorting
free Blacks as early as 1787. *Leaders of Philadelphia's Black Community*, 147.

43. [Sarah Mapps Douglass] Zillah, "Sympathy for Miss Crandall," *Emancipator* (New York), July 20, 1833.

44. Oberlin College, *General Catalogue*, 1035.

45. In Carter G. Woodson's study of heads of families in 1830, there are four
Bensons, ten Carters, fourteen Freemans, and twenty-two Willson/Wilson names
in New York City. In ward 14—the same ward where Peter Williams Jr. lived—
were one Jacob Wilder and one Jacob Weldon; they each had seven people in
their household. The possibility that the Emila Wilson student might be a sister
or cousin to the noted Black educator William J. Wilson is a cherished hope of
this author. I have not yet been able to confirm either of these. The 1830 census
followed a protocol of naming only the head of household. Woodson, *Free Negro
Heads*. In May 1834, just weeks prior to violent anti-abolitionist riots in New York
City, there were numerous cases of Black men being kidnapped and sold into
slavery, including individuals named James Carter and William Carter. *American
Anti-Slavery Reporter*, 1, no. 6, June 1834, 92–94.

46. Peterson, *Black Gotham*, 29. It was through this book that the identity of
G. C. Marshall was ascertained, thus revealing that Peterson herself is a descendant of one of the school families.

47. Theodosia is often spelled with a *c* in place of the *s* in nineteenth-century
documents. Theodosia Burr (1783–1813) is famous now due to the musical *Hamilton*. Given her birth year of 1814, it is likely that she was named in memory of the
famed Theodosia Burr, who died in a shipwreck off the Carolina coast in early
1813 (but remained the topic of persistent rumors that she had been captured
or somehow survived).

48. Peterson, *Black Gotham*, 40.

49. For more on Murat Reis/Jansen Van Haarlem, see Tinniswood, *Pirates of Barbary*, and Ekin, *Stolen Village*.

50. Peterson, *Black Gotham*, 40–41.

51. Townsend, *Faith in Their Own Color*, 64.

52. Peterson, *Black Gotham*, 41; Townsend, *Faith in Their Own Color*, 65, 66–67.

53. Townsend, *Faith in Their Own Color*, 65.

54. Boylan, "Benevolence and Antislavery Activity," 127; Peterson, *Black Gotham*, 65; Walker, *History of Black Business*, 98.

55. Peterson, *Black Gotham*, 136–37; Boylan, "Benevolence and Antislavery Activity," 127. Maria Stewart was also a member of the Dorcas Society in New York City; this means that many of Crandall's students knew her personally later in their lives. Hodges, *David Ruggles*, 61.

56. *Emancipator* (New York), 34, December 21, 1833, 135.

57. *Colored American* (New York), "Of the Ladies Literary Society of the City of New York," September 23, 1837; Peterson, *Black Gotham*, 140.

58. Myers, *Vice-President's Black Wife*, 54–55.

59. Baumgartner, *In Pursuit of Knowledge*, 10.

Chapter 6. Ripples and Reflections in the Abolitionist Networks

1. Convention of the People of Colour, *Minutes and Proceedings of the First Annual Convention*, 5; original emphasis.

2. Convention of the People of Colour, *Minutes and Proceedings of the First Annual Convention*, 4–5.

3. Convention of the People of Colour, *Minutes and Proceedings of the Second Annual Convention*, 8.

4. Convention of the People of Colour, *Minutes and Proceedings of the Second Annual Convention*, 34.

5. Convention of the People of Colour, *Minutes and Proceedings of the Third Annual Convention*, 13.

6. Convention of the People of Colour, *Minutes and Proceedings of the Third Annual Convention*, 20–21.

7. Convention of the People of Colour, *Minutes and Proceedings of the Third Annual Convention*, 27.

8. Reed, *Platform for Change*, 150.

9. Hodges, *David Ruggles*, 93–94.

10. I agree with Hodges that Ruggles's proposal at the 1833 meeting suggests he had visited Norwich, where his family still lived. Hodges, *David Ruggles*, 11, 201.

11. Ruggles, *"Extinguisher" Extinguished!* 14.

12. Convention of the People of Colour, *Minutes and Proceedings of the Third Annual Convention*, 29, 30.

13. Hodges, *David Ruggles*, 60–61.

14. Hodges, *David Ruggles*, 79–84.

15. Reed, *Platform for Change*, 154–55.

16. Convention of the People of Colour, *Minutes of the Fourth Annual Convention*, 25.

17. Convention of the People of Colour, *Minutes of the Fourth Annual Convention*, 18.

18. McBride, "Black Protest against Racial Politics," 150–52, for background on Hinton.

19. McHenry, *Forgotten Readers*, 328n69.

20. Gross, *Freedom's Journal*, 273–74; Townsend, *Faith in Their Own* Color, 88. See also G. E. Walker, *Afro-American in New York City*, 99–100; *Freedom's Journal*, April 6, 1827.

21. *Liberator*, 4, no. 15, April 12, 1834, 59.

22. Hodges, *Root and Branch*, 218–19.

23. Hughes's school was under the auspices of St. Philip's Church, to which many of Crandall's New York City students can be traced. Foner, *History of Black Americans*, 572.

24. McHenry, *Forgotten Readers*, 57.

25. Boylan, "Benevolence and Antislavery Activity," 127.

26. For one example, consider Maria Stewart's loss of economic security through being cheated out of her late husband's war pension; Waters, *Maria W. Stewart*, 198–99. Boylan also mentions how in the New York City riots of July 1834 property-owning African Americans were particularly victimized by violence, Boylan, "Benevolence and Antislavery Activity," 123. This fragile grasp on middle-class status among free Blacks can be detected across the nineteenth century; the well-off Primus family of Hartford, Connecticut, for instance, still had one daughter, Henrietta, who worked as a domestic. F. J. Griffin, *Beloved Sisters and Loving Friends*, 12.

27. McHenry, *Forgotten Readers*, 68.

28. McHenry, *Forgotten Readers*, 51.

29. McHenry, *Forgotten Readers*, 93. See Peterson, *Black Gotham*, 76–78, for how Charles Andrews, a white teacher and defector to colonizationism, was replaced by Black teacher John Peterson, whose family is entwined with the Canterbury school.

30. Winch, "You Have Talents," 104–5. See also Mabee, *Black Freedom*, 150–51; Sterling, *We Are Your Sisters*, 110–13.

31. Mabee, *Black Education*, 58.

32. Convention of the People of Colour, *Minutes and Proceedings of the Third Annual Convention*, 33.

33. Wicks, *Address Delivered*, 115.

34. *Genius of Temperance, Philanthropist and People's Advocate* (New York), 4, July 10, 1833, 1.

35. *Liberator*, 2, no. 41, October 13, 1832, 162–63.

36. Porter, "Organized Educational Activities," 559, 568.

37. The full curriculum, including textbooks, is speculatively reconstructed in Rycenga, "Intellect and Abolition," 126–37. The list generated by Marvis Welch

is clearly faulty, *Prudence Crandall*, 17. Her sources are not credited, and she, too, was concerned about the list's integrity. Marvis Welch to Jessica Nashold, November 17, 1962, in possession of heirs of Jessica Nashold, Mendota, Illinois.

38. McHenry, *Forgotten Readers*, 86.

39. McHenry, *Forgotten Readers*, esp. 41, 51, and ch. 2, esp. 84–107.

40. *Liberator*, 3, no. 14, April 6, 1833, 55. In addition to Sarah Harris, this could have been written by Ann Elizabeth Hammond or Maria Davis.

41. In *Liberator*: 3, no. 25, June 22, 1833, 99; 3, no. 27, July 6, 1833, 106–7; 3, no. 31, August 3, 1833, 122. Other student writings appear in *Liberator*: 4, no. 2, January 11, 1834, 8; 4, no. 47, November 22, 1834, 186; and 6, no. 31, July 30, 1836, 122. All of these were published anonymously, likely due to gender conventions as well as protecting students and their families.

42. *Liberator*, 3, no. 25, June 22, 1833, 99, repr. from the *Anti-Masonic Intelligencer* (Hartford, CT).

43. *Liberator*, 3, no. 31, August 3, 1833, 122.

44. Rankin, *Letters on American Slavery*, v.

45. Child, *Appeal*, 212–13. Child's pamphlet was published August 5, 1833, prior to Crandall's first trial. Karcher, *First Woman of the Republic*, xxi.

46. Child, *Appeal*, 62, original emphasis.

47. Child, *Appeal*, 138, 140, original emphases.

48. Rankin, *Letters on American Slavery*, 12.

49. Both pamphlets are advertised in the *Unionist* (Brooklyn, CT), 1, no. 20, December 19, 1833, 3.

50. *Haverhill Gazette*, August 3, 1833; Strane, *Whole-Souled Woman*, 91–93; the *Liberator*'s report on the end of the school is taken from an article in the *Unionist*. See *Liberator*, 4, no. 38, September 20, 1834, 151.

51. J. C. Hebbard, "Contemporary Reformers: Prudence Crandall's Immediate Co-Workers," *Topeka (KS) Capitol*, April 13, 1886.

52. The five extant copies of the *Unionist* and all discovered reprints of *Unionist* material can be viewed at Rycenga and Szydlowski, "*Unionist* Unified," Digital Humanities Collection.

53. C. W. Dymond, *Memoirs, Letters, and Poems*, 19; Rycenga, "Sun in Its Glory," 241–59; Ziegler, *Advocates of Peace*, 43 (Ziegler gives a publication date of 1831, but all evidence points to 1832); Brock, *Pacifism in the United States*, 498; J. Dymond, *On the Applicability of the Pacific Principles*; George Benson Sr. to Moses Brown, May 17, 1832, Moses Brown Papers, Rhode Island Historical Society, Providence. Just as Dymond wrote that Christianity "wants men willing to *suffer* for her principles," Martin Luther King Jr. declared, "We shall match your capacity to inflict suffering by ours to endure it. We will wear you down by our capacity to suffer." Dymond, *Inquiry*, 148, and King, *Trumpet of Conscience*, 74. See also Garrison's reaction to the first letter he received from Angelina Grimké, William Lloyd Garrison to George W. Benson Jr., September 12, 1835, in Merrill, *Letters of William Lloyd Garrison*, 1:527.

54. Garrison was especially fond of Dymond. The *Liberator*, 4, no. 10, March 8, 1834, 39, refers to Dymond as "a prodigy among mankind—the Lord Bacon

of our times. His mind was like the sun in its glory, seldom showing the least obscuration."

55. Rycenga, "Sun in Its Glory"; Dymond, *On the Applicability of the Pacific Principles*; *Unionist*, 1, no. 32, March 13, 1834, 1, cols. 3–5, headlined "From Dymond's Essays on Political Rights and Obligations" and "Political Power is Rightly Exercised Only When It Subserves the Welfare of Community." This constitutes pages 237–40 from the complete *Essays on the Principles of Morality*. Given that the excerpt in the *Unionist* begins, "This proposition is consequent of the truth of the last," it is reasonable to speculate that this was an ongoing series. The previous section of the book is titled "Political Power is Rightly Possessed Only When It Is Possessed by Consent of the Community" (232–37).

56. The secondary literature on Paley is vast, while Dymond is little known outside of footnotes. Another Romantic, Coleridge, dismissed Paley in Aphorism 12 of *Aids to Reflection*.

57. George Benson Sr. to Moses Brown, May 17, 1832, Moses Brown Papers, Rhode Island Historical Society, Providence.

58. "Seventh Annual Report of the Windham County Peace Society," in *Calumet* (New York), 1, no. 17, January–February 1834, 514–18.

59. See *Liberator*, 2, no. 21, May 26, 1832, 81, and 2, no. 22, June 2, 1832, 85, for epigrams from Dymond; Garrison's children claimed that Dymond was one of their father's two favorite prose authors. Lynd, *Intellectual Origins of American Radicalism*, 111. The mainstream press, too, stressed the contrast between Dymond and Paley; see *American Traveler* (Boston), September 27, 1833.

60. Lynd, *Intellectual Origins of American Radicalism*, 111, 117–19.

61. *Liberator*, 3, no. 31, August 3, 1833, 122.

62. Ziegler, *Advocates of Peace*, 82. Consider, for instance, King's "Statement Delivered at the Prayer Pilgrimage Protesting the Electrocution of Jeremiah Reeves" (1958): "Our children, merely desiring equal education, are spat upon, cursed and kicked hither and yonder—but Father forgive them. Let us go away devoid of bitterness and with the conviction that unearned suffering is redemptive." *Papers of Martin Luther King, Jr., Volume IV*, 398. On King's philosophic background, see Steinkraus, "Martin Luther King's Personalism and Non-Violence."

63. Plainfield Academy, *Catalogue of the Trustees, Instructors, and Students*, 89, 72. New York writer and educator Caroline Kirkland edited an abridged edition of Dymond for use in schools, endorsed by Lydia Maria Child in *National Anti-Slavery Standard* (New York), August 4, 1842.

64. *Liberator*, 3, no. 39, September 28, 1833, 155; Strane, *Whole-Souled Woman*, 112.

65. David O. White, "Prudence Crandall," 1971, MS, Prudence Crandall Museum, Connecticut Historical Commission, Hartford, 32.

66. Strane, *Whole-Souled Woman*, 94.

67. Tappan, *Life of Arthur Tappan*, 156–58.

68. May, *Some Recollections*, 64.

69. "Anti-Slavery Society of Plainfield and Its Vicinity," *Abolitionist*, 1, no. 10, 1833, 159, from the *Unionist*, August 29, 1833.

70. New England Anti-Slavery Society, *Proceedings of the New England Anti-Slavery Convention*, 24.

71. Plainfield Anti-Slavery Society, *First Annual Report*, original emphasis.

72. Providence Anti-Slavery Society, *Reports and Proceedings*.

73. Records of the Amherst Auxiliary Anti-Slavery Society, July 19, 1833, Amherst College Special Collections, Amherst, Massachusetts, 1; Cochrane, "Anti-Slavery Movement in Hampshire County," 11.

74. "Anti-Slavery Society at Amherst College," *Abolitionist*, 1, no. 8, August 1833, 124–25; Records of the Amherst Auxiliary Anti-Slavery Society, July 24, 1833, Amherst College Special Collections, Amherst, Massachusetts, 2.

75. Records of the Amherst Auxiliary Anti-Slavery Society, December 4, 1833, Amherst College Special Collections, Amherst, Massachusetts. This meeting passed another resolution in support of Crandall.

76. An 1831 letter from Morse about religious matters is in the Amherst College Special Collections. Morse also gave a graduation oration contrasting Napoleon and prison-reformer John Howard.

77. Cochrane, "Anti-Slavery Movement in Hampshire County," 12. Heman Humphrey was being disingenuous here; he was allied with ACS leaders in the African Education Society, a group that held that Black education was solely for its "usefulness in Africa." African Education Society, *Report of the Proceedings*, 5. The two sons of Heman Humphrey, Edward and John, taught for a year at the Plainfield Academy and had William Henry Burleigh as a student. "Obituary, William H. Burleigh," *New-York Daily Tribune*, 30, no. 9345, March 20, 1871, 5.

78. Another leader of the Amherst College Anti-Slavery Society, Thomas Hervey (1812–47), contributed a poem to the *Unionist*, 1, no. 36, April 10, 1834, 4.

79. This includes the New Haven Anti-Slavery Society, formed by the Jocelyn brothers, among others, on June 4, 1833. See *Liberator*, 3, no. 35, August 31, 1833, 139. Oliver Johnson celebrates how "[t]wo young men, brothers, who were afterwards widely and honorably known in connection with the antislavery cause, were first brought to public notice during the Canterbury conflict . . . Charles C. and William H. Burleigh." *W. L. Garrison*, 127–28.

80. New England Anti-Slavery Society, *Second Annual Report*, 49.

81. New England Anti-Slavery Society, *Proceedings*, 6, 18; W. L. Garrison, *Letters of William Lloyd Garrison, Volume 2*, 516–17n11.

82. New England Anti-Slavery Society, *Proceedings*, 14, 50, 58.

83. L. Brown, "Out of the Mouths of Babes," 68.

84. New England Anti-Slavery Society, *Proceedings*, 22.

85. New England Anti-Slavery Society, *Proceedings*, 23.

86. New England Anti-Slavery Society, *Proceedings*, 24.

87. Plainfield Anti-Slavery Society, *First Annual Report*; W. L. Garrison, *Letters of William Lloyd Garrison, Volume 2*, 160, 161n5.

88. A conversation in September 1835 between Garrison and Albert Hinckley about student antislavery activism led Garrison to proclaim triumphantly "Colonization is dead—dead—dead." Garrison to Henry E. Benson, September 19, 1835, in W. L. Garrison, *Letters of William Lloyd Garrison, Volume 1*, 537. Ill

health prevented Hinckley from graduating. W. L. Garrison, *Letters of William Lloyd Garrison, Volume 2*, 160.

89. Judson, *Statement of Facts*.

90. Maria Stewart, "Religion and the Pure Principles of Morality," in Richardson, *Maria W. Stewart*, 38. After the summer of 1833 Crandall may have decided it was too dangerous to hire outside help, since she wrote to Ellen Larned, "For the most part we were our own washer women." Prudence Crandall Philleo to Ellen G. Larned, March 7, 1870, Connecticut State Library, Hartford.

Chapter 7. Students on Trial

1. See *Dred Scott v. Sanford*, para. 70, *Cornell Law School*, https://www.law.cornell.edu/supremecourt/text/60/393.

2. The town of Ellsworth, Maine, incorporated in 1800, was named after Oliver Ellsworth.

3. "Ellsworth, William Wolcott," *Biographical Directory of the United States Congress*, http://bioguide.congress.gov/scripts/biodisplay.pl?index=E000150.

4. D. E. Williams, *Prudence Crandall's Legacy*, 113–14. As a congressman, Ellsworth defended the treaty land claims of Native Americans. D. E. Williams, *Prudence Crandall's Legacy*, 113.

5. Beeching, "Reading the Numbers," 227. Holdridge Primus (1815–84) was father to Rebecca Primus, who taught freedmen in Maryland, and Nelson Primus, a well-known portrait artist based in Boston.

6. D. E. Williams, *Prudence Crandall's Legacy*, 114; "Goddard, Calvin," *Biographical Directory of the United States Congress*, http://bioguide.congress.gov/scripts/biodisplay.pl?index=G000248.

7. Tom Schuch located evidence that Goddard's brother Hezekiah assisted the Harris family directly in 1843. Tom Schuch, email correspondence with author, May 20, 2021.

8. Biographical information on Strong can be found in D. E. Williams, *Prudence Crandall's Legacy*, 114; Dwight, *History of the Descendants of Elder John Strong*, 1:751–52; Strong Family Collection, Beinecke Rare Book Library, Yale University, New Haven, Connecticut.

9. McHenry, *Forgotten Readers*, 29.

10. D. E. Williams, *Prudence Crandall's Legacy*, 113–29. I am indebted to Donald Williams's insightful account of the trial. Transcripts in the (Hartford) *Connecticut Courant*, September 2, 1833, 2, and September 9, 1833, 2, are reprints from the *Unionist*. The documents from the first half of the trial are also in the pamphlet *Statement of Facts*, 12–16. See also Weiner, *Black Trials*, 95–115.

11. The court documents indicate the four subpoenaed students: Theodosia DeGrasse, Ann Peterson, Ann Eliza Hammond, and Amelia/Ann Elizabeth Wilder. See *Statement of Facts*, 13; (Hartford) *Connecticut Courant*, September 2, 1833, 2. Strane conflates Wilder with Mary Elizabeth Wiles, but this is unlikely given the clarified identity of Mary Elizabeth Miles. Strane, *Whole-Souled Woman*, 95–96.

12. *Unionist*, August 29, 1833, repr. in *Connecticut Courant*, September 2, 1833, 2.

13. Judge Eaton should have recused himself, since as a legislator he had voted for the Black Law. See Abdy, *Journal*, 1:205; D. E. Williams, *Prudence Crandall's Legacy*, 116.

14. (Hartford) *Connecticut Courant*, August 26, 1833, 3.

15. *Liberator*, 3, no. 31, August 3, 1833, 122.

16. *Liberator*, 3, no. 31, August 3, 1833, 122.

17. *Liberator*, 6, no. 14, April 2, 1836, 56.

18. An Old Abolitionist, "Prudence Crandall's Boarding School," *Day* (New London, CT), October 15, 1892, 5. Thanks to Tom Schuch who discovered this long-lost gem.

19. Cooney and Michalowski, *Power of the People*.

20. William Henry Burleigh, "Original Ode," (New York) *Calumet*, 1, no. 10, November–December 1832, 316.

21. Ward, *Autobiography of a Fugitive Negro*, 28–29, original emphasis.

22. The word "criminating" was used synonymously with "incriminate" at this time; it is not a demeaning dialect. See the *Liberator*'s coverage of the trial of Frederick Olney, 4, no. 12, March 22, 1834, 47.

23. *Unionist*, August 29, 1833, repr. in (Hartford) *Connecticut Courant*, September 2, 1833, 2.

24. *Unionist*, August 29, 1833, repr. in (Hartford) *Connecticut Courant*, September 2, 1833, 2.

25. *Liberator*, 3, no. 31, August 3, 1833, 122.

26. Prudence Crandall to Solomon Payne, Andrew Harris, and Isaac Knight, in *Unionist*, August 29, 1833, repr. in (Hartford) *Connecticut Courant*, September 2, 1833, 2.

27. Prudence Crandall to Solomon Payne, Andrew Harris, and Isaac Knight, in *Unionist*, August 29, 1833, repr. in (Hartford) *Connecticut Courant*, September 2, 1833, 2.

28. The students were not long deprived of religious services. Packerville Baptist under Levi Kneeland welcomed the students, and at least one, Harriet Lanson, was "hopefully converted while at Canterbury school" under Kneeland's preaching. *Liberator*, 6, no. 14, April 2, 1836, 56; Rycenga, "Be Ashamed of Nothing but Sin."

29. *Unionist*, August 29, 1833, repr. in (Hartford) *Connecticut Courant*, September 2, 1833, 2. See also *Hartford (Baptist) Christian Secretary*, repr. in *American Repertory* (St. Albans, VT), September 5, 1833.

30. All quotes from Judson's summation are from the *Unionist*, August 29, 1833, repr. in (Hartford) *Connecticut Courant*, September 2, 1833, 2.

31. Even after the school closed, Judson insisted that Crandall's change from white to Black students had only been "at the instigation of Garrison and others." R. Crandall, *Trial of Reuben Crandall*, 35.

32. *Unionist*, August 29, 1833, repr. in (Hartford) *Connecticut Courant*, September 2, 1833, 2. Ellsworth's summation is divided between (Hartford) *Connecticut Courant*, September 2 and September 9, 1833.

33. *Unionist*, August 29, 1833, repr. in (Hartford) *Connecticut Courant*, September 2, 1833, 2.

34. *Unionist*, September 5, 1833, repr. in (Hartford) *Connecticut Courant*, September 9, 1833, 2.

35. Ellsworth's citizenship arguments span the *Unionist*, August 29, 1833, and September 5, 1833, repr. in (Hartford) *Connecticut Courant*, September 2, 1833, 2, and September 9, 1833, 2, respectively.

36. *Unionist*, September 5, 1833, repr. in the (Hartford) *Connecticut Courant*, September 9, 1833, 2. For an opposing perspective, see Maltz, "Fourteenth Amendment Concepts," 339–40. In "Whence Comes Section One," Barnett refutes Maltz.

37. *Unionist*, September 5, 1833, repr. in (Hartford) *Connecticut Courant*, September 9, 1833, 2.

38. *David Walker's Appeal to the Coloured Citizens*, 78.

39. W. L. Garrison, *Thoughts on African Colonization*, 146.

40. Quoted in Goen, "Broken Churches, Broken Nation," 31–32, 32n27; quote from Smyth, *Complete Works*, 7:543, 545.

41. Nye, *Fettered Freedom*, 96.

42. Foner, *History of Black Americans*, 320.

43. *Unionist*, August 29, 1833, repr. in (Hartford) *Connecticut Courant*, September 2, 1833, 2. The political world of Connecticut was a "small and familiar legal community." D. E. Williams, *Prudence Crandall's Legacy*, 116.

44. *Unionist*, September 5, 1833, repr. in (Hartford) *Connecticut Courant*, September 9, 1833, 2. "Civic universalism" is Weiner's phrase, which he traces from Ellsworth back to Granville Sharp. Weiner, *Black Trials*, 108.

45. Goodman, *Of One Blood*, 57, 56–61.

46. Henry Strong's summation is entirely within *Unionist*, September 5, 1833, repr. in (Hartford) *Connecticut Courant*, September 9, 1833, 2.

47. *Unionist*, September 5, 1833, repr. in (Hartford) *Connecticut Courant*, September 9, 1833, 2.

48. Jonathan Welch's summation is entirely within *Unionist*, September 5, 1833, repr. in (Hartford) *Connecticut Courant*, September 9, 1833, 2.

49. *Unionist*, September 5, 1833, repr. in (Hartford) *Connecticut Courant*, September 9, 1833, 2.

50. May, *Some Recollections*, 69.

51. *Unionist*, September 5, 1833, repr. in (Hartford) *Connecticut Courant*, September 9, 1833, 2.

52. *Unionist*, October 3, 1833, repr. in (Hartford) *Connecticut Courant*, October 7, 1833, 3.

53. M. Welch, *Prudence Crandall*, 84.

54. Williams's chapter on the second trial, "Judge Daggett's Decision," does an excellent job of covering the legal framework, social background, and impact of this trial in more detail than I do here. D. E. Williams, *Prudence Crandall's Legacy*, 131–47.

55. D. E. Williams, *Prudence Crandall's Legacy*, 134–36.

56. Strane, *Whole-Souled Woman*, 28–29; Fuller, *Prudence Crandall*, 20–21.

57. Small and Small, "Prudence Crandall," 509.

58. Mary Barber to the District Court, Canterbury, September 10, 1833, Prudence Crandall Museum, Canterbury, Connecticut.

59. D. E. Williams, *Prudence Crandall's Legacy*, 135. Williams also analyzes the falsehood about Harris's marriage. D. E. Williams, *Prudence Crandall's Legacy*, 135–36.

60. P. Williams, *Oration on the Abolition*, 27–28; Townsend, *Faith in Their Own Color*, 29; *Boston Daily Evening Transcript*, September 28, 1830, quoted in Hinks, *To Awaken*, 151. See also Russ, *How to Suppress Women's Writing*.

61. Cleveland's name is alternately spelled "Cleaveland."

62. Biographical information on Daggett can be found in Dutton, *Address at the Funeral*; "Daggett, David," *Political Graveyard*, http://politicalgraveyard.com/bio/daba-daigre.html; "Daggett, David," *Biographical Dictionary of the United States Congress*, https://bioguide.congress.gov/search/bio/D000002.

63. Dutton, *Address at the Funeral*, 11.

64. Hinks, "William Lanson," 19.

65. See Strane, *Whole-Souled Woman*, 109; Strother, *Underground Railroad*, 34; Antony Dugdale, J. J. Fueser, and J. Celso de Castro Alves, "Yale, Slavery and Abolition: The Town Meeting," *Amistad Committee*, http://www.yaleslavery.org/TownGown/tnmtg.html; O. Johnson, *W. L. Garrison*, 123.

66. Strane, *Whole-Souled Woman*, 109.

67. *Unionist*, October 10, 1833, repr. in (Hartford) *Connecticut Courant*, October 14, 1833, 2; D. E. Williams, *Prudence Crandall's Legacy*, 142.

68. Judson, *Andrew T. Judson's Remarks*, 6. "One girl has testified that the defendant went to New York and Philadelphia, and some of the girls by her named, returned with her."

69. Judson, *Andrew T. Judson's Remarks*, 21–22. In the early 1990s, the White Aryan Resistance had a widely distributed flyer that read, "White men *built this nation!! White men are* this nation!!!" Gilmore, *Abolition Geography*, 160, original emphasis.

70. *Unionist*, October 10, 1833, repr. in (Hartford) *Connecticut Courant*, October 14, 1833, 2; *Liberator* 3, no. 43, October 26, 1833, 170.

71. *Windham County (CT) Advertiser*, December 19, 1833, in M. Welch, *Prudence Crandall*, 87.

72. May, *Some Recollections*, 50.

73. "Are Free Colored Men Citizens," *Liberator*, 3, no. 43, October 26, 1833, 170, repr. from *Unionist*.

74. "Are Free Colored Men Citizens," *Liberator*, 3, no. 43, October 26, 1833, 170.

75. While it is unlikely that Crandall was using the Lancasterian monitorial system, due to the small size and advanced nature of the academy, its principles of intergenerational monitoring were likely known to the pupils, since many schools for African Americans utilized that system. See Kaestle, *Pillars of the Republic*, 41–43.

76. *Liberator*, 4, no. 2, January 11, 1834, 8; Prudence Crandall Philleo to Ellen Larned, May 15, 1869, Connecticut State Library, Hartford.

77. L. Brown, "Out of the Mouths of Babes."

78. For instance, Sarah Hammond would have been nine, and Miranda Glasko twelve in late 1833.

79. Anyone who has ever faced street harassment is aware that the attacker's power is increased if he calls his victim by name.

80. Miss Clarke, of Norfolk, Virginia, *American Missionary*, June 1864, 138, quoted in H. A. Williams, *Self-Taught*, 163.

81. Olney's name first surfaces in the January 19, 1833, issue; *Liberator*, 3, no. 3, January 19, 1833, 9. For the fire and Olney's trial, see Abdy, *Journal of a Residence*, 211; D. E. Williams, *Prudence Crandall's Legacy*, 160–63; Strane, *Whole-Souled Woman*, 117–20, 131; M. Welch, *Prudence Crandall*, 87–88; McCain, *To All on Equal Terms*, 38.

82. Convention of the People of Colour, *Minutes of the Fourth Annual Convention*, 18.

83. Henry Benson to Isaac Knapp, February 14, 1834, Ms.A.1.2, vol. 4, Anti-Slavery Collection, Boston Public Library.

84. Strane, *Whole-Souled Woman*, 233n10; Garnet, "Notes by a Traveler," 118. A journal by Olney has recently been transcribed in a Digital Humanities project, recounting ventures he had in seafaring trades, https://mcguirelibrary1998.omeka .net/exhibits/show/voyage-of-the-whaler-merrimac/introduction-and-history.

85. Strane, *Whole-Souled Woman*, 117, *Unionist*, April 10, 1834.

86. *Windham County (CT) Advertiser*, December 19, 1833, in M. Welch, *Prudence Crandall*, 87.

87. *Liberator*, 4, no. 6, February 8, 1834, 23.

88. This strategy had been foreshadowed in *A Statement of Facts*, when the white opponents claimed that street harassment of the students was either "boyish folly" or "chargeable upon some of the blacks belonging to the neighborhood." *Statement of Facts*, n5.

89. On Judge Eaton, see D. E. Williams, *Prudence Crandall's Legacy*, 115–16; Strane, *Whole-Souled Woman*, 96–97; Crosby, *Annual Obituary Notices*, 138.

90. *Unionist*, March 13, 1834.

91. *Unionist*, March 13, 1834.

92. Strane, *Whole-Souled Woman*, 243n2.

93. *Unionist*, April 10, 1834.

94. Kaz Kozlowski, longtime curator at the Prudence Crandall Museum, indicated that "the fire was set at the northeast corner of the building . . . at the front of the house," and "when the house was repainted in 2006, the contractors scraped the paint away from the clapboards on the north side." This revealed new lumber "pieced in" after the fire as a patch repair on the outside. Personal communication with author, 2003, reconfirmed 2023.

95. Henry Benson letter to William Lloyd Garrison, August 30, 1833, Ms.v.A.1.2, 3:64, Anti-Slavery Collection, Boston Public Library.

96. H. L. Read, "An Historical Romance: Prudence Crandall of Canterbury Green—The Instructor of Colored Children—Under Difficulties," *Hartford (CT) Courant*, December 21, 1880; D. E. Williams, *Prudence Crandall's Legacy*, 309.

97. George Benson Sr.'s family provided the students housing during the trial. William Lloyd Garrison to George Benson Sr., May 31, 1834, in W. L. Garrison, *Letters of William Lloyd Garrison*, 1:352. On the distinction between ritual and legal proceedings, I am indebted to Cynthia Estrada for sharing with me the following article: Lisa McGunigal, "The Criminal Trial of Anne Hutchinson: Ritual, Religion, and Law," *Mosaic: An Interdisciplinary Critical Journal* 49, no. 2 (2016): 149–66.

Chapter 8. Patriarchal Marriage and White Violence

1. "Captain Stuart will bring out with him a splendid present for Miss Crandall, obtained by me for her during my stay in *Edinburgh*. When I come I shall bring with me a piece of plate from *Glasgow* sent by the ladies there to Miss Crandall." George Thompson to William Lloyd Garrison, September 24, 1834, MS.A.1.2, vol. 4, Boston Public Library.

2. John Bowers to William Lloyd Garrison, Samuel E. Sewall, and Eleazer Mather Porter, May 14, 1834, Anti-Slavery Collection, Boston Public Library.

3. William Lloyd Garrison to Helen E. Benson, April 12, 1834, in Merrill, *Letters of William Lloyd Garrison*, 1:318.

4. For an overview of Calvin Philleo's career, see Rycenga, "Characterological Itineracy." There are numerous spellings of the name Philleo, including Phileo, Philo, and Fillow. Van Hoosear, *Fillow, Philo, and Philleo Genealogy*, 19.

5. Prudence Crandall to Emeline Connor Philleo Goodwin, after December 6, 1880, Kent Memorial Library, Suffield, Connecticut; cf. D. E. Williams, *Prudence Crandall's Legacy*, 150.

6. D. O. White, "Crandall School," 105–6. The school was likely the Suffield Academy, opened by the Baptists in August 1833. Evans, *History*, 36.

7. Van Hoosear, *Fillow, Philo, and Philleo Genealogy*, 48–49, 67–73 (Calvin's generation); Valerie LaRobardier, "Genealogies of the Early Settlers of Dover, Dutchess, NY and Collateral Families," http://www.doverdutchessgenealogy .com/f10.htm.

8. J. F. Smith, "Suffield and the Baptists," 11. Dwight Ives (1805–75) was a distant relative of the composer Charles Ives.

9. Stubbert, *Set Thee Up Way-Marks*, 23, 26.

10. Murphy, *Ten Hours' Labor*, 94.

11. George Foster Jenks, Journal, 1820s–1850s, August 5 and 12, 1829, Rhode Island Historical Society, Providence.

12. First Baptist Church, Pawtucket Rhode Island, *One Hundred and Fiftieth Anniversary*, 12.

13. Emeline C. Whipple to H. S. Sheldon, June 5, 1881, Kent Memorial Library, Suffield, Connecticut.

14. Hughes, "Jacob Frieze."

15. Frieze, *Letter to Rev. Mr. Philleo*, 3.

16. Frieze, *Letter to Rev. Mr. Philleo*, 2.

17. Frieze, *Letter to Rev. Mr. Philleo*, 23, 6.

18. For Rowland Greene, see Helen Benson to William Lloyd Garrison, June 2, 1834, Fanny Garrison Villard Papers, Houghton Library, Harvard University, Cambridge, Massachusetts, and Henry Benson to George Benson Jr., April 23, 1834, Anti-Slavery Collection, Boston Public Library. Years later George Benson Jr. confirmed that Philleo "is an unprincipled man." George Benson [Jr.] to Samuel Joseph May, June 13, 1839, Ms.A.1.2, 8:35, Anti-Slavery Collection, Boston Public Library.

19. Mintz, *Moralists and Modernizers*, 27.

20. Rena Clisby, "Canterbury Pilgrims." TS, 1947, Prudence Crandall Collection, Charles E. Shain Library, Connecticut College, New London, Connecticut, 32. This is hindsight. Crandall added that she had married him because "[s]omeone had to take care of him." Clisby adds that while Prudence "may not have loved Mr. Philleo," she "regarded him highly."

21. Helen Benson to William Lloyd Garrison, March 13, 1834, Fanny Garrison Villard Papers, Houghton Library, Harvard University, Cambridge, Massachusetts.

22. William Lloyd Garrison to Helen Benson, April 7, 1834, in W. L. Garrison, *Letters of William Lloyd Garrison*, 1:315–16.

23. Helen Benson to William Lloyd Garrison, April 9, 1834, and May 22, 1834, both in Fanny Garrison Villard Papers, Houghton Library, Harvard University, Cambridge, Massachusetts.

24. William Lloyd Garrison to Helen Benson, June 6, 1834, in W. L. Garrison, *Letters of William Lloyd Garrison*, 1:360.

25. Helen Benson to William Lloyd Garrison, June 9, 1834, and June 2, 1834, Fanny Garrison Villard Papers, Houghton Library, Harvard University, Cambridge, Massachusetts.

26. William Lloyd Garrison to Helen Benson, June 21, 1834, in W. L. Garrison, *Letters of William Lloyd Garrison*, 1:370.

27. Helen Benson to William Lloyd Garrison, June 18, 1834, Fanny Garrison Villard Papers, Houghton Library, Harvard University, Cambridge, Massachusetts.

28. *Greenville (SC) Mountaineer*, 6, no. 11, July 26, 1834, 3.

29. Runcie, "Hunting the Nigs."

30. Cole, "Free Church Movement," 290–91.

31. Cole, "Free Church Movement," 293; Galpin, *Pioneering for Peace*, 76; Convention of the People of Colour, *Minutes of the Fourth Annual Convention*, 3.

32. Crouthamel, *James Watson Webb*, 54, 55–57.

33. *New York Transcript*, 52, May 8, 1834, 2.

34. Swerdlow, "Abolition's Conservative Sisters," 34.

35. Tappan, *Life of Arthur Tappan*, 194, 195.

36. Weinbaum, *Mobs and Demagogues*, 23–24. For Cox's response, see Tappan, *Life of Arthur Tappan*, 195.

37. Hewitt, "Sacking of St. Philip's Church," 10–11.

38. *New York Transcript*, 102, July 7, 1834, 2; Tappan, *Life of Arthur Tappan*, 204.

39. *New York Transcript*, 104, July 9, 1834, 2. This is the same Benjamin Hughes who one month earlier endorsed Crandall's school at the Free Black Convention.

Reed, *Platform for Change*, 40, 197; Hinks and Kantrowitz, *All Men Free and Brethren*, 7, 52.

40. Tappan, *Life of Arthur Tappan*, 205–6.

41. Hewitt, "Sacking of St. Philip's Church," 13.

42. *New York Transcript*, 104, July 9, 1834, 2.

43. Headley, *Great Riots of New York*.

44. Headley, *Great Riots of New York*.

45. Tappan, *Life of Arthur Tappan*, 222.

46. Werner, *Reaping the Bloody Harvest*, 137.

47. *New York Evening Post*, July 12, 1834, 2; *New York Transcript*, 108, July 14, 1834, 2; Miller, "We've Come This Far," 29; McNeil, Robertson, Dixie, and McGruder, *Witness*, 19–20.

48. Emma Lapsansky, "Since They Got Those Separate Churches," 63. The African Methodist Episcopal Zion Church, located on Church at Leonard, sustained some damage in the riots, too, but its proximity to a newly opened opera house may have spared it more systematic violence, as the rioters "retired after dashing a few stones into the windows." *New York Evening Post*, July 12, 1834, 2. Cf. Museum of the City of New York's post on a visual artifact of these riots, "The Abolitionist Riots of 1834," https://blog.mcny.org/2012/04/03/the-abolitionist-riots-of-1834/.

49. *New York Evening Post*, July 12, 1834, 2.

50. Tappan, *Life of Arthur Tappan*, 209–10.

51. Onderdonk had his own problems, too, both theologically and controversially, when in the mid-1840s he was put on trial for what would now be called sexual harassment. The website *Anglican History* contains the documents on the all-white controversies in his life, with no mention of his treatment of Peter Williams Jr. or of Isaiah DeGrasse. Project Canterbury, http://anglicanhistory.org/usa/btonderdonk/.

52. Bishop Onderdonk to Reverend Peter Williams, July 12, 1834, in the *New York Spectator*, July 15, 1834, repr. in Sernett, *Afro-American Religious History*, 196–97. A Black congregant castigated Onderdonk's behavior as "pontifical" toward "an injured and persecuted congregation." *Liberator*, 4, no. 35, August 30, 1834, 139. A decade later, George Downing opposed Onderdonk on principle. Hewitt, "Mr. Downing," 243–46.

53. Reverend Peter Williams, open letter, July 15, 1834, in the *New York Spectator*, July 15, 1834, repr. in Sernett, *Afro-American Religious History*, 197–98.

54. Sernett, *Afro-American Religious History*, 199.

55. *Liberator*, 4, no. 31, August 9, 1834, 125.

56. Werner, *Reaping the Bloody Harvest*, 141. This paragraph is indebted to Werner's analysis. See also Goodman, *Of One Blood*, 126, for abolitionist opinion on amalgamation.

57. Burrows and Wallace, *Gotham*, 556.

58. Tappan, *Life of Arthur Tappan*, 201; Wyatt-Brown, *Lewis Tappan*, 176.

59. Wyatt-Brown, *Lewis Tappan*, 180.

60. Werner, *Reaping the Bloody Harvest*, 147

61. Dumond, *Antislavery*, 280.

62. William Lloyd Garrison to Helen Benson, July 15, 1834, in W. L. Garrison, *Letters of William Lloyd Garrison*, 1:376. See also *Liberator*, 4, no. 28, July 12, 1834, 111.

63. Tappan, *Life of Arthur Tappan*, 209–10, 420.

64. Ward, *Autobiography of a Fugitive Negro*, 47–48.

65. Burke, *Samuel Ringgold Ward*.

66. Wyatt-Brown, *Lewis Tappan*, 116–18; *Liberator*, 4, no. 28, July 12, 1834, 110; "The Riots in New-York, Gotten up by the 'Courier and Enquirer,' and the 'Commercial Advertiser,'" *Liberator*, 4, no. 30, July 26, 1834, 118. This last is a reprint from the Burleigh brothers in the *Unionist*.

67. *New York Transcript*, 106, July 11, 1834, 2.

68. Quoted in "Proslavery at the North," *American Anti-Slavery Reporter* (New York), 1, no. 8, August, 1834, 125–26, original emphasis; Werner, *Reaping the Bloody Harvest*, 143.

69. Wright, "Progress of the Antislavery Cause." For Ruggles's response to the riots and an interesting assessment of the effect of these riots, see Hodges, *David Ruggles*, 63–69.

70. *Niles Weekly Register* (Baltimore, Maryland), 46, July 19, 1834, 360, for both Newark and Norwich incidents. For more on Dickerson, see Hodges, *David Ruggles*, 67–69, and Dale Plummer, "United Congregational Church and Its Antecedents," TS, Archives, United Congregational Church in Norwich, Connecticut State Library, Hartford.

71. *Commercial Advertiser*, July 15, 1834, and August 7, 1834.

72. *Commercial Advertiser*, July 15, 1834.

73. Hirsch writes that these riots "made the parents very timid about trusting their children at long distances from their homes." "Free Negro in New York," 431.

74. Runcie, "Hunting the Nigs," 191; Lapsansky, "Since They Got Those Separate Churches," 63; 209; Runcie, "Hunting the Nigs," 191–92.

75. Brothers, *United States of North America*, 350; Lapsansky, "Since They Got Those Separate Churches," 64. For a sketch of First African Presbyterian's history, see Euell A. Nielsen, "First African Presbyterian Church, Philadelphia, Pennsylvania," *Black Past*, posted February 2015, http://www.blackpast.org/. Benjamin Hughes and Samuel Cornish also held pastoral tenures there.

76. Watson, *Annals of Philadelphia and Pennsylvania*, 261.

77. Lapsansky, "Since They Got Those Separate Churches," 71. She cites as confirmation an article in *Colored American* in 1838 that said, "Abolition is a mere pretext for these outbreakings. The same class of vagabonds who mob abolitionists, would as readily mob . . . the aristocracy could they do it with the same impunity." *Colored American* (New York City), June 2, 1838, 72.

78. See Stewart, "Emergence of Racial Modernity" for a broader approach to this historic moment.

79. Lapsansky, "Since They Got Those Separate Churches," 72.

80. William Lloyd Garrison to George W. Benson, July 10, 1834, in W. L. Garrison, *Letters of William Lloyd Garrison*, 1:374–75. Being in a rather giddy mood

with his engagement to Helen Benson, Garrison uses the death of the cat as the occasion for some groanworthy puns.

81. May, "Miss Prudence Crandall," 188–89.

82. Member of the Bar, *Report of the Arguments of Counsel*. It was also printed in the *Liberator*, 4, no. 39, September 27, 1834, 153–54, and 4, no. 41, October 11, 1834, 161–62. The third trial is covered in the earlier works on Crandall in Strane, *Whole-Souled Woman*, 146–48; Foner and Pacheco, *Three Who Dared*, 35–40; M. Welch, *Prudence Crandall*, 103–4; McCain, *To All on Equal Terms*, 38. Donald Williams's treatment is the most extensive and detailed, *Prudence Crandall's Legacy*, 191–203.

83. D. E. Williams, *Prudence Crandall's Legacy*, 193, 192.

84. Member of the Bar, *Report of the Arguments of Counsel*, 6, 10, 17, 22.

85. Member of the Bar, *Report of the Arguments of Counsel*, 23, 24. The doctrine of nullification was an effort, spearheaded by John Calhoun of South Carolina, to enable states to declare a federal law inapplicable in that state's jurisdiction.

86. Member of the Bar, *Report of the Arguments of Counsel*, 24.

87. Member of the Bar, *Report of the Arguments of Counsel*, 34.

88. D. E. Williams, *Prudence Crandall's Legacy*, 202.

89. "Miss Crandall," *New Bedford (MA) Courier and Weekly Lyceum*, 7, no. 6, July 10, 1833, 2.

90. John Hooker, letter to the editor, *Hartford (CT) Courant*, March 12, 1886, 2; also in Catterall, *Judicial Cases*, 4:415.

91. Catterall, *Judicial Cases*, 4:415–16, emphases added.

92. John Hooker, letter to the editor, *Hartford (CT) Courant*, March 12, 1886, 2; Catterall, *Judicial Cases*, 4:414, includes the following quote from the justices at the time: "On appeal counsel presented argument with respect to the principles on which the set was based, but the appellate court, after alluding to 'the excitement which always attends the agitation of questions connected with the interests of one class and the liberties of another, more particularly at the present time,' expressed a desire not 'to agitate the subject unnecessarily,' and decided the case on a technical defect in the information." John Hooker, Official Reporter of the Court, was the husband of Isabella Beecher Hooker, a key women's rights activist in Connecticut, suggesting another vector of Crandall's ongoing influence.

93. Quoted in Foner, *History of Black Americans*, 300. See also the tortured legal thinking that in 1828 kept Phoebe, a Black litigant, wrongfully enslaved in Illinois, as described in Heerman, *Alchemy of Slavery*, 106–7.

94. William Lloyd Garrison to Helen Benson, August 18, 1834, in W. L. Garrison, *Letters of William Lloyd Garrison*, 1:398–401.

95. Abdy, *Journal of a Residence*, 213.

96. Prudence Crandall Philleo to Ellen Larned, July 2, 1869, Charles J. Hoadley and George Hoadley Autograph Collection, Connecticut Museum of Culture and History, Hartford. In this letter, Crandall remembered the site of their wedding as Packerville, Connecticut, but Helen Benson, writing the day after the wedding, says it was in Brooklyn, Connecticut, with Reverend Tillotson. I follow previous Crandall scholars in preferring Benson's version. See *Liberator*, 4, no. 33, August

16, 1834, 131; Strane, *Whole-Souled Woman*, 148–49; McCain, *To All on Equal Terms*, 39; D. E. Williams, *Prudence Crandall's Legacy*, 205–7. Tillotson had been the minister to deliver the execution sermon for Oliver Watkins in 1831. *Windham County (CT) Advertiser*, 52, August 2, 1831; Strane, *Whole-Souled Woman*, 83. Tillotson became a major supporter of Black education; HBCU Huston-Tillotson University in Austin, Texas, bears his name.

97. William Lloyd Garrison to Helen Benson, August 18, 1834, in W. L. Garrison, *Letters of William Lloyd Garrison*, 1:398–401.

98. White's store was advertised in the *Liberator* and the *Unionist* when Crandall's school was operating. *Liberator*, 3, no. 16, April 20, 1833, 68; *Unionist*, 1, no. 20, December 19, 1833, 3. D. E. Williams states that Lydia White was a free Black, but this is incorrect. *Prudence Crandall's Legacy*, 209.

99. Delany, *Martin A. Delany*, 235. Delany misspells her first name as "Hester." He also mentions Gerrit Smith and William Lloyd Garrison as having similar "great and good hearts" tending to genuine equality between people.

100. Mott, *Selected Letters*, 29, in a letter dated September 13, 1834, from Mott to Phebe Post Willis.

101. Zaeske, *Signatures of Citizenship*, 123.

102. Anti-Slavery Convention of American Women, *Proceedings*, 8.

103. Sterling, *We Are Your Sisters*, 115–16; Tomek, *Pennsylvania Hall*, 156; Winch, *Gentleman of Color*, 304.

104. Winch, *Gentleman of Color*, 290, quoting Harriet Martineau from a letter to Charlotte Forten.

105. Abdy, *Journal of a Residence*, 208.

106. Abdy, *Journal of a Residence*, 209–10, original emphasis.

107. Psalm 40:1–3 (King James version).

108. George Benson Sr to Moses Brown, May 17, 1832, Moses Brown Papers, Rhode Island Historical Society, Providence. Samuel J. May was six when he first met his eminent mentor and worked with him in many contexts. May, *Memoir*, 19–21, 73–75.

109. May, *Some Recollections*, 172.

110. Channing, *Slavery*.

111. Kerber, "Abolitionists and Amalgamators," 37. For the causes of Channing's "conversion" to abolition, see also Martineau, *Martyr Age*, 22; Harwood, "Prejudice and Antislavery"; A. W. Brown, *Always Young for Liberty*, 224–31.

112. Abdy, *Journal of a Residence*, 217–18, 236.

113. Abdy, *Journal of a Residence*, 218–20. See Gara, *Liberty Line*.

114. Abdy, *Journal of a Residence*, 229–30; Mendelsohn, *Channing*, 243–45; Delbanco, *William Ellery Channing*, 128.

115. May, *Some Recollections*, 174.

116. May, *Some Recollections*, 174–75; cf. Yacovone, *Samuel Joseph May*, 70–72.

117. May, *Some Recollections*, 177–85; Abdy, *Journal of a Residence*, 236. See also Goodman, *Of One Blood*, 243–44; Mayer, *All on Fire*, 218–19.

118. Channing, *Slavery*, 155–56.

119. Mayer, *All on Fire*, 186; Strane, *Whole-Souled Woman*, 151.

120. Brown and Rose, *Black Roots*, 172.

121. Brown and Rose, *Black Roots*, 124. Prudence Crandall Fayerweather lived into adulthood; she is referred to in Prudence Crandall Philleo to Mary Fayerweather, March 23, 1879, Fayerweather Family Papers, Special Collections, University of Rhode Island, Kingston.

122. May, *Some Recollections*, 70–71.

123. The moon was one day shy of its waxing first quarter.

124. Abdy, *Journal of a Residence*, 304, for full conversation between Philleo and Judson.

125. Abdy, *Journal of a Residence*, 303–4.

126. "Prudence Crandall," *Kansas City (MO) Journal*, March 28, 1886, 12. Coverage of the attack can be found in Strane, *Whole-Souled Woman*, 151; Foner and Pacheco, *Three Who Dared*, 42–43; McCain, *To All on Equal Terms*, 39; M. Welch, *Prudence Crandall*, 107; D. E. Williams, *Prudence Crandall's Legacy*, 219–25; Abdy, *Journal of a Residence*, 303–8.

127. May, *Some Recollections*, 71.

128. Some have suggested that the "cruel attacks upon her school broke the teacher's spirit" (Mayer, *All on Fire*, 184) or that Garrison withdrew his support for the school after Crandall's engagement to Philleo. See Friedman, "Racism and Sexism in Ante-Bellum America."

129. Abdy, *Journal of a Residence*, 305.

130. May, *Some Recollections*, 92.

131. The Brooklyn Female Anti-Slavery Society was founded on June 29, 1834. At their first public meeting Garrison, May, and Charles Stuart were present as guests, and a letter from Lucretia Mott was read. Brooklyn's society was part of "the progress of female abolitionism in New England, which had bloomed into 65 female antislavery societies by 1836." Sinha, *Slave's Cause*, 275.

132. I. V. Brown, *Mary Grew*, 14–15.

133. May, *Some Recollections*, 71.

134. *Liberator*, 4, no. 38, September 20, 1834, 151.

135. Abdy, *Journal of a Residence*, 306.

136. Prudence Crandall Philleo to John S. Smith, January 30, 1886, Prudence Crandall Collection, Charles E. Shain Library, Connecticut College, New London, Connecticut.

Chapter 9. You Are Trying to Improve Your Mind in Every Way

1. *Liberator*, 3, no. 27, July 6, 1833, 106–7.

2. Yellin, *Women and Sisters*, 48.

3. Andrew Jackson to Amos Kendall, August 9, 1835, Library of Congress, https://www.loc.gov/resource/maj.11187_0036_0039/?st=gallery.

4. Strane, *Whole-Souled Woman*, 161.

5. Stanton, *Eighty Years and More*, 31–32.

6. Lydia Maria Child also supported women's rights in marriage but did not leave her own unfulfilling union. Karcher, *First Woman in the Republic*, 545.

7. Thayer, *Pedal and Path*, 213.

8. This includes not only the structural constraints of marriage but also elder care that Crandall provided to both her husband and her mother.

9. Packerville Baptist Records, entry, December 7, 1834, Records 1828–1928, Packerville Baptist Church, Connecticut State Library, Hartford.

10. Ryder, *181 Years*; Gordon, *Gazetteer of the State of New York*, 567–68; Durant, *History of Oneida County*, 419. Reference to the carriage factory comes from the files in the History and Genealogy Room, Erwin Library and Institute, Boonville, New York. For more on the Black River Canal, see the Boonville Black River Canal Museum, https://blackrivercanalmuseum.com.

11. Durant, *History of Oneida County*, 198–99.

12. Strane, *Whole-Souled Woman*, 172–73.

13. Van Hoosear, *Fillow, Philo, and Philleo Genealogy*, 73.

14. Karen E. Dau, "Herkimer County, NY Deaths from Universalist Sources, 1823–1878, part 3, Surnames O–Z," https://herkimer.nygenweb.net/vitals/herkuniversalistdeas3.html.

15. Darius Philleo was in regular contact with the family; Elizabeth Philleo to Calvin Wheeler Philleo, May 25, 1841, Calvin Wheeler Philleo Papers, Connecticut Museum of History and Culture, Hartford.

16. Calvin Wheeler Philleo to Joshua L. Spencer, September 10, 1850, Philleo-Norton Family Papers, Special Collections, Clements Library, University of Michigan, Ann Arbor; Marvis Welch to Jessica Nashold, December 29, 1962, in possession of descendants of Jessica Nashold, Mendota, Illinois.

17. W. R. Cross, *Burned-Over District*, 150.

18. Oneida Baptist Association, *Minutes of the Seventy-Second Anniversary*, 10.

19. Thornton, "Andrew Harris," 126–29.

20. *Daily Argus* (Albany, New York), August 5, 1835, 3. Calvin Philleo is also mentioned in a post office list in *Daily Argus*, February 2, 1836, 3.

21. Foote, *Brand Plucked from the Fire*, 39.

22. Elizabeth Philleo describes teaching she was doing in 1841 in Poland, New York. Elizabeth Philleo to Calvin Wheeler Philleo, May 25, 1841, Calvin Wheeler Philleo Papers, Connecticut Museum of History and Culture, Hartford.

23. *Liberator*, 7, no. 19, May 5, 1837, 74; *Liberator*, 4, no. 37, September 13, 1834, 146.

24. *Troy (New York) Daily Whig*, March 15, 1837, 2. The Black community in Albany had organized a meeting to denounce colonization in late 1833. *Liberator*, 3, no. 46, November 16, 1833, 182; *Colored American* (New York), April 1 and April 15, 1837.

25. Thornton, "Andrew Harris"; *Colored American* (New York), April 15, 1837, 1–2; Quarles, *Black Abolitionists*, 102–3.

26. Ripley, *Black Abolitionist Papers*, 1:42n11; Thornton, "Andrew Harris," 136–38; *Emancipator* (New York), May 16, 1839.

27. R. Crandall, *Trial of Reuben Crandall*, 34; Strane, *Whole-Souled Woman*, 163–64, 72; D. E. Williams, *Prudence Crandall's Legacy*, 229–30. Three different pamphlets were published on Reuben Crandall's trial. See Finkelman, *Slavery in the Courtroom*, 166–70.

28. Prudence did retain materials related to her younger brother. Prudence Crandall Philleo to Wendell Phillips Garrison, postcard, February 7, 1883, Prudence Crandall Folder, Radcliffe Institute for Advanced Study, Schlesinger Library, Harvard University, Cambridge, Massachusetts.

29. Morley, *Snow-Storm in August*. Morley's work relieves Prudence Crandall scholars from having to retell Reuben Crandall's entire story.

30. Strane, *Whole-Souled Woman*, 157–60; D. E. Williams, *Prudence Crandall's Legacy*, 228.

31. Morley, *Snow-Storm in August*, 109.

32. Morley, *Snow-Storm in August*, 109. Morley incorrectly identifies Williams as Robert C. when it is Robert G. Williams. See American Anti-Slavery Society, *Third Annual Report*, 31.

33. Morley, *Snow-Storm in August*, 153–55, 173.

34. *Rights of All* (New York), October 16, 1829. In 1818 American scientist Captain John Cleves Symmes postulated a hollow earth with openings at the poles.

35. Morley, *Snow-Storm in August*, 188; Strane, *Whole-Souled Woman*, 160; Goodell, *Slavery and Anti-Slavery*, 437.

36. Morley, *Snow-Storm in August*, 215.

37. Morley, *Snow-Storm in August*, 219–20. Reuben hastened to get out of Washington, DC, as soon as he was a free man. He was aided by Congressman William Jackson (1783–1855) of Massachusetts, another abolitionist. *Emancipator* (New York), March 8, 1838, 175. Jackson's election to Congress was noted with approbation by Charles Burleigh in *Unionist*, 1, no. 32, March 13, 1834, 3.

38. Finkelman, *Slavery in the Courtroom*, 170.

39. Quoted in Small and Small, "Prudence Crandall," 524; see also "Connecticut Barbarism," *Boston Advocate,* repr. in *New Bedford (MA) Courier and Weekly Lyceum*, 7, no. 6, July 10, 1833, 2.

40. Almira Crandall to George Benson, July 9, 1833, Ms.A.1.2, 3:51, Anti-Slavery Collection, Boston Public Library; *American Repertory* (St. Albans, VT), 12, August 1, 1833, 40.

41. New England Anti-Slavery Society, *Proceedings*, 18. See also May, "Miss Prudence Crandall," 190.

42. Almira Crandall to Henry Benson, April 30, 1833.

43. Almira Crandall to Henry Benson, April 30, 1833, original emphasis.

44. W. H. Burleigh, *Poems*, 139–41. This contains an elegiac poem written by William Burleigh about his coteacher Almira, followed by a biographical note on Almira.

45. W. L. Garrison *Letters*, 2:163.

46. C. M. Burleigh, "Journal," August 19, 1837, foreword.

47. John W. Rand moved to Indiana and later Kentucky after Almira's death, remarrying and raising a family while teaching.

48. Connecticut Anti-Slavery Society, *Charter Oak*, 6.

49. Magdol, *Antislavery Rank and File*, 16. On settlement patterns from New England to Illinois, see Kofoid, "Puritan Influences"; Meyer, *Making the Heartland Quilt*; Pooley, "Settlement of Illinois."

50. Rena Clisby, "Canterbury Pilgrims," TS, 1947, Prudence Crandall Collection, Charles E. Shain Library, Connecticut College, New London, Connecticut, 12; Strane, *Whole-Souled Woman*, 168.

51. Philleo is mentioned in the records of Packerville Baptist Church on February 5, 1838, August 19, 1838, September 2, 1838, and February 3, 1839. The earliest date would correspond to a letter that Crandall received from her father, Pardon, saying that Philleo had visited Canterbury in the aftermath of Reuben's death. The letter's implication, supported by Marvis Welch and D. E. Williams, is that Calvin had the temerity to ask Pardon for money. Packerville Baptist Church, records 1828–1928, Connecticut State Library, Hartford, Connecticut; M. Welch, *Prudence Crandall*, 125–27; D. E. Williams, *Prudence Crandall's Legacy*, 234.

52. Zaeske, *Signatures of Citizenship*, 84–88, for convention coverage.

53. Speicher, *Religious World of Antislavery Women*, 101.

54. Husband, *Antislavery Discourse*, 20, 16.

55. Thomas Paul Jr. was also a student at Noyes Academy, the son of Thomas Paul Sr. and nephew to Nathaniel Paul. For more on the Paul family, see Lois Brown's introduction to Paul, *Memoir of James Jackson*.

56. *Liberator*, 5, no. 30, July 25, 1835, 118; Wallace, *History of Canaan*, 294–95, original emphasis.

57. Wallace, *History of Canaan*, 255–96; N. B. Smith, "Historian's Notebook," 23–24.

58. Pasternak, *Rise Now*, 14–15; Schor, *Henry Highland Garnet*, 15; Hutchison, *Let Your Motto Be Resistance*, 4–7; Simmons, *Men of Mark*, 531.

59. Baumgartner, "Dear Jesus," 8–9.

60. *Liberator*, 3, no. 27, July 6, 1833, 106–7.

61. Given the continued association of the Marshall family with New York's Black middle class, the lack of records for G. C. Marshall is surprising to both this author and Carla Peterson. Carla Peterson, personal correspondence and conversations with author, 2015–17.

62. *Liberator*, 6, no. 14, April 2, 1836, 56.

63. A. B. Smith, "Bustill Family," 638.

64. *1870 United States Federal Census*. See also Compiled Military Service Records of Volunteer Union Soldiers Who Served with the United States Colored Troops: Infantry Organizations, 47th through 55th, National Archives, Washington, D.C., Ancestry.com.

65. My reconstruction of the life of Elizabeth Douglass Bustill Jones is largely indebted to Joyce Mosley and Clay Wilfour, who have also conducted family research on the Bustill line.

66. A. B. Smith, "Bustill Family," 641.

67. Yannielli, "Logic of the Antislavery Movement"; Joseph Yannielli, personal email communication with author, 2015 and 2016.

68. Morse, "United States of Africa," 252–54; Burrowes, *Power and Press Freedom*, 117.

69. Morse, "United States of Africa"; Echeruo, *Victorian Lagos*, 104.

70. "Henry Yantis," *Find a Grave*, https://www.findagrave.com/memorial/104814484/henry-yantis.

71. Foote, *Brand Plucked from the Fire*; Ripley, *Black Abolitionist Papers*, 3:456n13; Housley, "Yours for the Oppressed," 23–25.

72. H. Q. Brown, *Homespun Heroines*, 28.

73. Cottrol, *Afro-Yankees*, 99, 124–25; McLoughlin, *Rhode Island*, 132; Lemons and McKenna, "Re-enfranchisement of Rhode Island Negroes," 6, 8.

74. Blankenship, *Woman of Refinement*, 2–3.

75. *Liberator*, 14, no. 35, August 31, 1844, 139; Blankenship, *Woman of Refinement*, 3.

76. In the 1860 Census John N. Smith, Elizabeth H. Smith, and Isaac Smith live in Providence, Rhode Island, along with her mother, Margaret Brown. *1860 United States Federal Census*, Providence Ward 3, Providence, Rhode Island.

77. H. Q. Brown, *Homespun Heroines*, 19, 21.

78. H. Q. Brown, *Homespun Heroines*, 21.

79. H. Q. Brown, *Homespun Heroines*, 18–22.

80. H. Q. Brown, *Homespun Heroines*, 21.

81. Elizabeth Stevens, email correspondence with author, February 2023.

82. Stevens, *Elizabeth Buffum Chace and Lillie Chace Wyman*, 80; Blankenship, *Woman of Refinement*, 7.

83. *Liberator*, 6, no. 31, July 30, 1836, 123, added emphasis. Lewis also inaugurated the Providence Temperance Society and a night academy for Black adults; he was friends with Garrison and Amos Beman. See also Cottrol, *Afro-Yankees*, 62, and Sherer, "Negro Churches in Rhode Island," 20–21, 24.

84. Ann Eliza Hammond is on the steamship *City of Merida* from Havana, Cuba, to New York City, September 1873 and August 1874. National Archives, Washington, DC: *Passenger Lists of Vessels Arriving at New York, New York, 1820–1897*; Microfilm Serial or NAID:M237; RG Title: Records of the U.S. Customs Service; RG: 36. Ancestry.com: New York Passenger Lists, 1820–1957, rolls 381, 392.

85. New York City Department of Health, Division of Vital Statistics, *Marriage Registers, Extracts from Manhattan (1869–1880) and Brooklyn (1895–1897)*, https://www.ancestry.com/discoveryui-content/view/146791:7854.

86. Baumgartner reaches the same conclusion. *In Pursuit of Knowledge*, 233n45.

87. Brown and Rose, *Black Roots*, 172.

88. "Jerusha Congdon," *Find a Grave*, https://www.findagrave.com/memorial/84590572/jerusha-west.

89. Peterson, *Black Gotham*.

90. Mary Ann Shadd Cary to George Whipple, December 28, 1852, in Ripley, *Black Abolitionist Papers*, 2:245–55, 250; Washington, "I Am Going Straight to Canada," 176–77.

91. Ripley, *Black Abolitionist Papers*, 2:31.

92. Mabee, *Black Freedom*, 155–56.

93. The text of Garnet's speech with a brief introduction can be found at "(1843) Henry Highland Garnet: An Address to the Slaves of the United States," *Blackpast.org*, 2007, https://www.blackpast.org/. See also Forbes, "Every Man Fights for His Freedom," 156.

94. Woodson, *Mind of the Negro*, 194–95. Hutchinson notes that Garnet "often credited" Julia as "the source of many of the ideas he expressed in his speeches." *Let Your Motto Be Resistance*, 8.

95. See a similar insight by Sinha, *Slave's Cause*, 418.

96. Pasternak, *Rise Now*, 39, 57.

97. "Obituary of Mrs. Julia Williams Garnet," *Christian Recorder* (Philadelphia, Pennsylvania), January 22, 1870. See also "Honor to Whom Honor Is Due," *Liberator*, 10, no. 33, August 14, 1840, 131.

98. *Slave* (London), April 1854. I thank Richard Blackett for this reference.

99. Quarles, *Blacks on John Brown*, 19; Swift, *Black Prophets of Justice*, 313.

100. Schor, *Henry Highland Garnet*, 185–86.

101. Peterson, *Black Gotham*, 232–37; Schor, *Henry Highland Garnet*, 197–99; Pasternak, *Rise Now*, 113–14. The records of the New York Phoenix Society were destroyed in these same draft riots; I suspect that hints on the identities and families of some Crandall students were in those lost documents. Cromwell, *Early Negro Convention Movement*, 10.

102. Pasternak, *Rise Now*, 144.

103. *Christian Recorder* (Philadelphia), January 22, 1870.

104. Anne Warren Weston to Deborah Weston, April 18, 1837, Ms.A.9.2.9, vol. 28, Anti-Slavery Collection, Boston Public Library.

105. *Christian Recorder* (Philadelphia), January 22, 1870; Yee, *Black Women Abolitionists*, 103.

106. Martin Delany wrote that Miles attended a normal school in Albany, New York, but later historians have championed the Massachusetts school. See Delany, *Condition, Elevation, Emigration*, 132. See also Mabee, *Black Freedom*, 155, and Cooper, "Ever True to the Cause," 23.

107. M. I. Hughes, *Refusing Ignorance*, 50, 90.

108. Cooper, "*Voice of the Fugitive*," esp. 143–45.

109. Mary E. Bibb to [Gerrit Smith], November 8, 1850, in Ripley, *Black Abolitionist Papers*, 2:108–12; Cooper, "*Voice of the Fugitive*," 143.

110. Cooper, "*Voice of the Fugitive*," 143–45.

111. Baumgartner, *In Pursuit of Knowledge*, 54, 240n31.

112. Tripp, "Mary Miles Bibb," 18–19.

113. Prudence Crandall to Sarah Harris Fayerweather, July 26, 1871, Fayerweather Family Papers, Special Collections, Library, University of Rhode Island, Kingston.

114. H. Q. Brown, *Homespun Heroines*, 28. See also Strane, *Whole-Souled Woman*, 201–2; Clisby, "Canterbury Pilgrims," TS, 1947, Prudence Crandall Collection, Charles E. Shain Library, Connecticut College, New London, Connecticut, 34–35.

115. Helen Benson Garrison to Sarah Harris Fayerweather, June 5, 1863, Fayerweather Family Papers, Library Special Collections, University of Rhode Island Kingston; Woodward, "Profile in Dedication," 10; Turner, "Sarah Harris Fayerweather," 220.

116. Turner, "Sarah Harris Fayerweather," 220; "Genealogical Record," Henry Albro Williamson collection, reel 1, Schomburg Collection, New York Public Library, New York, 5.

117. "Remittances," *Liberator*, 7, no. 23, June 2, 1837, 91.

118. "African Americans @ Dartmouth College, 1775–1950: Pelleman M. Williams," *Black Alumni at Dartmouth Association*, http://badahistory.net/view .php?ID=133. In the 1850 Census Pelleman and Mary were in New Haven, Connecticut; in 1860 in Norwich, Connecticut. *Seventh Census of the United States, 1850; 1860 United States Federal Census.*

119. R. C. Morris, *Reading, 'Riting, and Reconstruction*, 111–12; Blassingame, *Black New Orleans*, 128–29. George H. Fayerweather was also involved in vocal music in New Orleans, according to Blassingame, *Black New Orleans*, 142.

120. Trotter, *Music and Some Highly Musical People*, 343; Kennedy, *Chord Changes on the Chalkboard*, 2–3; Blassingame, *Black New Orleans*, 141; Marquis, *In Search of Buddy Bolden*, 29.

121. Wendell was named for white abolitionist orator Wendell Phillips.

122. Piper and Piper, "Passport to History," 35–36. On Dee Dee Chandler, see Jaina, "Birth of the Drum Set."

123. Piper and Piper, "Passport to History," 36.

124. Piper and Piper, "Passport to History," 34.

125. Chuck Piper and Judy Piper attended the May 2015 Prudence Crandall Symposium in Canterbury. Chuck writes movingly of how he is "conflicted by the realization that what my parents did in leaving behind family and all that they knew in Chicago was in large part for my benefit. Their action provided me unfettered opportunities based only on ability. On the other hand, I now realize that this move resulted in lost opportunities to know and to interact with my aunts, uncles, and cousins." Piper and Piper, "Passport to History," 34–35.

126. *Greater Camden City Directory, 1910–1911*, 91.

127. Eschenbach, "Fritz's Fame."

128. Both Fritz Pollard and Fritz Pollard Jr. are well documented in the annals of sport. The best longform articles are Eschenbach, "Fritz's Fame"; Menzies, "Black History Month"; "Fritz Pollard, Class of 2005," *2021 Pro Football Hall of Fame*, Canton, Ohio, http://www.profootballhof.com/players/fritz-pollard/.

129. Menzies, "Black History Month"; "Fritz Pollard Jr.," *International Olympic Committee*, https://olympics.com/en/athletes/frederick-douglas-jr-pollard. Additional pictures of Fritz Pollard Sr. can be found at Brown University Library, http://library.brown.edu/cds/pollard/atbrown.html. Thanks to Louis Mazza.

130. "Fritz Pollard, Class of 2005," *2021 Pro Football Hall of Fame*, Canton, Ohio, http://www.profootballhof.com/players/fritz-pollard/.

Conclusion. Hearing All the Voices

1. Smith's wife was a niece to Hezekiah Crandall's first two wives.

2. Prudence Crandall Philleo to John S. Smith, January 30, 1886, Prudence Crandall Collection, Charles Shain Library, Connecticut College, New London, Connecticut.

3. *Kansas City (MO) Weekly Journal,* March 28, 1886, quoted in Strane, *Whole-Souled Woman,* 217.

4. D. E. Williams, *Prudence Crandall's Legacy,* 316; Prudence Crandall Philleo to Samuel Coit, February 9, 1886, in the *Hartford (CT) Courant,* February 17, 1886, 2.

5. Donald E. Williams Jr. provides an excellent retelling of the pension struggle. *Prudence Crandall's Legacy,* 317–23.

6. The definitive account is in Fishkin, *Lighting Out for the Territory,* 99–107; Schiff, "Old Yale"; Frederick N. Rasmussen, "A Little Help from Twain," *Baltimore Sun,* February 17, 2001; "Rare Letter Shows Twain Offering Aid for Black Law Student at Yale," *Providence (RI) Journal,* March 14, 1985.

7. "Warner McGuinn, Lawyer, Born," African-American Registry, undated, accessed March 31, 2024, http://www.aaregistry.org/historic_events/view/warner-mcguinn-lawyer-born.

8. Edwin McDowell, "From Twain, a Letter of Debt to Blacks," *New York Times,* March 14, 1985.

9. Prudence Crandall Philleo to the children of William Lloyd Garrison, December 6, 1889, MS, Am 1906, Houghton Library, Harvard University.

10. *American Citizen* (Kansas City, KS), 2, no. 49, January 31, 1890, 1.

11. *American Citizen* (Kansas City, KS), 2, no. 49, January 31, 1890, 2.

12. Prudence Crandall to Mrs. Isabella Mitchell, a daughter of Sarah Harris Fayerweather, March 14, 1886; David O. White, "Prudence Crandall Philleo: Letters from Kansas," 1972, TS, Prudence Crandall Museum, Canterbury, Connecticut, 39n20.

13. C. L. McKesson, "Prudence Crandall Philleo: Funeral Address," *Moline (IL) Republican,* 8, no. 41, February 7, 1890, 1; Strane, *Whole-Souled Woman,* 214–15, 227–28. A brief obituary published in the Baltimore German-language paper *Der Deutsche Correspondent* suggests Crandall's actions were hailed amongst the radical German Americans immigrants from 1848. January 31, 1890, 1.

14. James Hulme Canfield, "Prudence Crandall," *Topeka (KS) Daily Capital,* October 18, 1885. For more on James Hulme Canfield, see C. Thomas, "James Hulme Canfield."

15. W. C. N. [William Cooper Nell], "Boston, July 15," August 24, 1849, *North Star* (Rochester, NY).

16. George W. Williams, *History of the Negro Race,* 2:149–57; E. A. Johnson, *School History of the Negro People,* 32–34. George Washington Williams coined the term "crime against humanity" in his *History of the Negro Race.*

17. *Christian Recorder* (Philadelphia), February 4, 1884, repr. from *Philadelphia Evening Transcript.*

18. *New York Freeman*, January 30, 1886.

19. *New York Freeman*: February 27, 1886, for Harper; March 20, 1886, for Brooklyn; April 10, 1886, for Middletown.

20. *New York Freeman*, February 27, 1886. Harper finishes his letter with an encouragement for Blacks to move to the Dakota Territories: "This is going to be a great county. I would like to see more colored people come out here and take up claims. Those who have come are doing well."

21. *New York Freeman*, April 10, 1886.

22. Peterson, *Black Gotham*, 333–35, 346, 348.

23. Thornbrough, *T. Thomas Fortune*, 85.

24. Ratzlaff, "Ida B. Wells," 155.

25. *New York Freeman*, February 27, 1886.

26. *New York Freeman*, April 10, 1886.

27. The Prudence Crandall Museum holds the original photographs from her Kansas home.

28. Hendricks, *Fannie Barrier Williams*, 45–46, 53–54; W. H. Pruden, "Lloyd Garrison Wheeler." The PCLC held a meeting in 1885; see "Chicago," *Cleveland Gazette*, December 19, 1885.

29. Hendricks, *Fannie Barrier Williams*, 56–57.

30. *New York Freeman*, April 10, 1886.

31. Mrs. S. Laing Williams (Fannie Barrier Williams), "A Herald of Freedom," *Inter Ocean* (Chicago), August 3, 1891, 6.

32. Nelson, *To the Stars*; brochure for the Colored Academy, Andrew Atchison Principal, Dunlap, Morris County, item 21, vols. 5 and 6, Negro Clipping, 103–5, Kansas State Historical Society, Topeka.

33. *Topeka (KS) Weekly Tribune*, January 1882, vols. 5 and 6, Negro Clipping, Kansas State Historical Society, Topeka.

34. *Sweet Chariot* (Dunlap, KS), 1, no. 1, September 1, 1887, 1, Kansas State Historical Society, Topeka.

35. *Sweet Chariot* (Dunlap, KS), 1, no. 1, September 1, 1887, 3.

36. *Sweet Chariot* (Dunlap, KS), 1, no. 1, September 1, 1887, 3.

37. *Sweet Chariot* (Dunlap, KS), 1, no. 1, September 1, 1887, 3.

38. Joyceann Gray, email with author, May 2022.

39. *Sweet Chariot* (Dunlap, KS), 1, no. 1, September 1, 1887, 3.

40. Charlotte Forten Grimké also mentions the Canterbury Academy to prove that New England's racism was persistent; see "Colored People in New England."

41. Serena DeGrasse attended the Young Ladies Domestic Seminary in Clinton, New York, in the late 1830s, where she studied alongside Canterbury alumna Mary Elizabeth Miles. Baumgartner, *In Pursuit of Knowledge*, 47, 238n2.

42. Peterson, *Black Gotham*, 277–80.

43. Prudence Crandall Philleo to the children of William Lloyd Garrison, December 6, 1889, MS, Am 1906, Houghton Library, Harvard University.

44. The phrase "full-souled" comes from Mrs. S. Laing Williams (Fannie Barrier Williams), "A Herald of Freedom," *Inter Ocean* (Chicago), August 3, 1891, 6.

Bibliography

Abdy, Edward S. *Journal of a Residence and Tour in the United States of North America, from April, 1833, to October, 1834.* 3 vols. London: Murray, 1835.

"Abolition Letters Collected by Captain Arthur B. Spingarn." *Journal of Negro History* 18, no. 1 (1933): 78–84.

An Act Designating Prudence Crandall as the State Female Hero. Connecticut Senate Bill No. 362, Public Act No. 95-20. May 1995.

Adams, Alice Dana. *The Neglected Period of Anti-Slavery (1808–1831).* Boston: Ginn, 1908.

African Education Society. *Report of the Proceedings at the Formation of the African Education Society, Instituted at Washington, December 28, 1829, with an Address to the Public, by the Board of Managers.* Washington, DC: Dunn, 1830.

Allen, Jeffner. *Lesbian Philosophy: Explorations.* Palo Alto, CA: Institute of Lesbian Studies, 1986.

Alonso, Harriet Hyman. *Growing Up Abolitionist: The Story of the Garrison Children.* Amherst: University of Massachusetts Press, 2002.

American Anti-Slavery Society. *First Annual Report of the American Anti-Slavery Society; with the Speeches Delivered at the Anniversary Meeting, Held in Chatham-Street Chapel, in the City of New-York, on the Sixth of May, 1834, and by Adjournments on the Eighth, in the Rev. Dr. Lansing's Church; and the Minutes of the Society for Business.* New York: Dorr and Butterfield, 1834.

American Anti-Slavery Society. *Third Annual Report of the American Anti-Slavery Society with the Speeches Delivered at the Anniversary Meeting; Held in the City of New-York, on the 10th May, 1836, and the Minutes of the Meetings of the Society for Business.* New York: Dorr, 1836.

Ammon, Harry. *James Monroe: The Quest for National Identity.* New York: McGraw-Hill, 1971.

Anniversary Record of the Golden Wedding of Mr. and Mrs. Thomas Lathrop. Plainfield, Connecticut: C. F. Burgess, 1881.

Anti-Slavery Convention of American Women. *Proceedings of the Anti-Slavery*

Convention of American Women, Held in Philadelphia. May 15th, 16th, 17th, and 18th, 1838. Philadelphia: Merrihew and Gunn, 1838.

Aptheker, Herbert, ed. *A Documentary History of the Negro People in the United States*. Vol. 1. New York: Citadel, 1969.

Armistead, Wilson, ed. *Anthony Benezet, from the Original Memoir*. Philadelphia: Lippincott, 1859.

Arnold-Lourie, Christine. "'Inharmonious Elements' and 'Racial Homogeneity': New England Exceptionalism and Immigration Restriction." *Review of Faith & International Affairs* 19, no. 3 (2021): 33–45.

Bacon, Leonard. Review of Mrs. Child's *Appeal in Favor of That Class of Americans Called African*. *Quarterly Christian Spectator* 6 (September 1834): 445–56.

Bacon, Margaret Hope. *Mothers of Feminism: The Story of Quaker Women in America*. San Francisco: Harper and Row, 1986.

Bacon, Margaret Hope. "'One Great Bundle of Humanity': Frances Ellen Watkins Harper." *Pennsylvania Magazine of History and Biography* 113, no. 1 (1989): 21–43.

Barber, John Warner. *Connecticut Historical Collections, Containing a General Collection of Interesting Facts, Traditions, Biographical Sketches, Anecdotes, etc., Relating to the History and Antiquities of Every Town in Connecticut, with Geographical Descriptions*. New Haven, CT: Durrie and Peck, 1837.

Barnett, Randy. "Whence Comes Section One? The Abolitionist Origins of the Fourteenth Amendment." *Journal of Legal Analysis*, March 2011. http://paperity .org/p/34475332/whence-comes-section-one-the-abolitionist-origins-of-the -fourteenth-amendment.

Bartlett, Irving H. *From Slave to Citizen: The Story of the Negro in Rhode Island*. Providence, RI: Urban League of Greater Providence, 1954.

Bartlett, Irving H. *Wendell Phillips: Brahmin Radical*. Boston: Beacon, 1961.

Bartlett, Irving H. *In Pursuit of Knowledge: Black Women and Educational Activism in Antebellum America*. New York: New York University Press, 2019.

Baumgartner, Kabria. "'Dear Jesus, This Is Death': Julia Williams Garnet and African American Womanhood in Late Nineteenth Century America." Unpublished paper, 2003.

Baumgartner, Kabria. *In Pursuit of Knowledge: Black Women and Educational Activism in Antebellum America*. New York: New York University Press, 2019.

Beecher, Catharine E. *An Essay on Slavery and Abolitionism, with Reference to the Duties of American Females*. 2nd ed. Philadelphia: Perkins, 1837.

Beeching, Barbara J. "Reading the Numbers: Census Returns as Key to the Nineteenth Century Black Community in Hartford, Connecticut." *Connecticut History* 44, no. 2 (2005): 224–47.

Berry, Henry. *The Speech of Henry Berry, (of Jefferson), in the House of Delegates of Virginia, on the Abolition of Slavery*. Richmond, VA: n.p., 1832.

Bibb, Henry. *Narrative of the Life and Adventures of Henry Bibb, an American Slave, Written by Himself*. With an Introduction by Lucius C. Matlack. New York: Self-published, 1849.

Billington, Ray Allen. *The Protestant Crusade, 1800–1860: A Study of the Origins of American Nativism*. Chicago: Quadrangle, 1964. First published 1938 by Macmillan.

Bingham, Caleb. *The American Preceptor; Being a New Selection of Lessons, for Reading and Speaking*. 10th ed. New York ed. New York: Evert Duyckinck, 1817.

Blackwell, Henry Browne. *Old Anti-Slavery Days. Proceedings of the Commemorative Meeting, Held by the Danvers Historical Society, at the Town Hall, Danvers, April 26, 1893, with Introductions, Letters, and Sketches*. Danvers, MA: Danvers Mirror, 1893.

Blair, Charles William. "The Reverend George Bourne: Rockingham's Pioneer Abolitionist." *Harrisonburg-Rockingham Historical Society Newsletter* 32, no. 1 (2010): 1–5.

Blankenship, Kate. *A Woman of Refinement and Education: A Biography of Elizabeth H. Smith, Black Principal of the Meeting Street Primary School in Providence, Rhode Island*. Providence, RI: Providence Preservation Society, 2023.

Blassingame, John W. *Black New Orleans, 1860–1880*. Chicago: University of Chicago Press, 1973.

Blight, David W. *Frederic Douglass: Prophet of Freedom*. New York: Simon and Schuster, 2018.

The Boston Mob of "Gentlemen of Property and Standing": Proceedings of the Antislavery Meeting Held in Stacy Hall, Boston, on the Twentieth Anniversary of the Mob of October 21, 1835. Boston: R. F. Wallcut, 1855.

Bourne, George. *Picture of Slavery in the United States of America*. Middletown, CT: Hunt, 1834.

Bourne, Theodore. "George Bourne, the Pioneer of American Antislavery." *Methodist Quarterly Review*, 4th ser., 64, no. 34 (January 1882): 68–91.

Boylan, Anne M. "Benevolence and Antislavery Activity among African American Women in New York and Boston, 1820–1840." In *Women and Sisters: The Antislavery Feminists in American Culture*, edited by Jean Fagan Yellin, 119–37. New Haven, CT: Yale University Press, 1989.

Brock, Peter. *Freedom from Violence: Sectarian Nonresistance from the Middle Ages to the Great War*. Toronto: University of Toronto Press, 1991.

Brock, Peter. *Pacifism in the United States: From the Colonial Era to the First World War*. Princeton, NJ: Princeton University Press, 1968.

Brock, Peter, ed. *The Quaker Peace Testimony 1660 to 1914*. York, UK: Sessions Book Trust, 1990.

Brodhead, Richard H. *Cultures of Letters: Scenes of Reading and Writing in Nineteenth-Century America*. Chicago: University of Chicago Press, 1993.

Bronner, Stephen Eric, ed. *The Letters of Rosa Luxemburg*. New ed. Atlantic Highlands, NJ: Humanities, 1993.

Brookes, George S. *Friend Anthony Benezet*. Philadelphia: University of Pennsylvania Press, 1937.

Brothers, Thomas. *The United States of North America as They Are; Not as They Are Generally Described: Being a Cure for Radicalism*. London: Longman, 1840.

Brown, Arthur W. *Always Young for Liberty: A Biography of William Ellery Channing*. Syracuse, NY: Syracuse University Press, 1956.

Brown, Barbara W., and James M. Rose. *Black Roots in Southeastern Connecticut, 1650–1900*. Detroit: Gale Research, 1980.

Brown, Hallie Q. *Homespun Heroines and Other Women of Distinction*. 1926. Edited by Randall K. Burkett. New York: Oxford University Press, 1988.

Brown, Ira V. *Mary Grew: Abolitionist and Feminist (1813–1896)*. Selinsgrove, PA: Susquehanna University Press, 1991.

Brown, Lois. "Out of the Mouths of Babes: The Abolitionist Campaign of Susan Paul and the Juvenile Choir of Boston." *New England Quarterly* 75, no. 1 (2002): 52–79.

Bruce, Dickson D. *The Origins of African American Literature, 1680–1865*. Charlottesville: University of Virginia Press, 2001.

Bryant, Jerry H. *Victims and Heroes: Racial Violence in the African American Novel*. Amherst: University of Massachusetts Press, 1997.

Bryant, Joan. "Race and Religion in Nineteenth-Century America." In *Perspectives on American Religion and Culture*, edited by Peter W. Williams, 246–58. Malden, MA: Blackwell, 1999.

Burke, Ronald K. *Samuel Ringgold Ward: Christian Abolitionist*. New York: Garland, 1995.

Burleigh, Cyrus Moses. "Journal Commencing on the First Day of July, 1837 and Diaries." In *American Poetry, 1650–1900: Part II*. New Haven, CT: Research Publications, 1975.

Burleigh, William Henry. *Poems*. Philadelphia: J. Miller M'Kim, 1841.

Burr, Nelson R. "The Quakers in Connecticut: A Neglected Phase of History." *Bulletin of Friends Historical Association* 31, no. 1 (1942): 11–26.

Burrowes, Carl Patrick. *Power and Press Freedom in Liberia, 1830–1970*. Trenton, NJ: Africa World, 2004.

Burrows, Edwin G., and Mike Wallace. *Gotham: A History of New York City to 1898*. New York: Oxford University Press, 1999.

Campbell, Alexander. "Response to Jonathan Dymond, on Insolvency." *Millennial Harbinger*, 4th ser., 3 (October 1853): 586–88.

Carey, Bryccham. *From Peace to Freedom: Quaker Rhetoric and the Birth of American Antislavery, 1657–1761*. New Haven, CT: Yale University Press, 2012.

Catterall, Helen Tunnicliff, ed. *Judicial Cases Concerning American Slavery and the Negro*. Vol. 4: Cases from the Courts of New England, the Middle States, and the District of Columbia. 5 vols. 1936. New York: Octagon, 1968.

Caulkin, Frances M. *History of Norwich, Ct., from Its Possession by the Indians to the Year 1866*. Norwich, CT: Self-published, 1866.

Cayton, Mary Kupiec. "The Connecticut Culture of Revivalism." In *Perspectives on American Religion and Culture*, edited by Peter W. Williams, 353–65. Malden, MA: Blackwell, 1999.

Chandler, Elizabeth Margaret. *The Poetical Works of Elizabeth Margaret Chandler*. Philadelphia: Howell, 1836.

Channing, William Ellery. *Slavery*. Boston: Munroe, 1835.

Chapman, John Jay. "William Lloyd Garrison." In *The Selected Writings of John Jay Chapman*, edited by Jacques Barzun, 3–138. New York: Funk and Wagnalls, 1968.

Child, Lydia Maria. *Anti-Slavery Catechism*. 2nd ed. Newburyport, MA: Whipple, 1839.

Child, Lydia Maria. *An Appeal in Favor of That Class of Americans Called Africans*. Boston: Allen and Ticknor, 1833.

Christie, John W., and Dwight L. Dumond. *George Bourne and The Book and Slavery Irreconcilable*. Wilmington: Historical Society of Delaware, 1969.

Clark, Christopher. *The Communitarian Moment: The Radical Challenge of the Northampton Association*. Ithaca, NY: Cornell University Press, 1995.

Clark, Victor S. *History of Manufactures in the United States*. 3 vols. New York: McGraw-Hill, 1929.

Cochrane, James C. "The Anti-Slavery Movement in Hampshire County (1830–1860)." Master's thesis, Amherst College, 1948.

Coit, George D. *A Historical Sketch of the Second Congregational Sunday School of Norwich, Connecticut, Delivered Sunday Evening, December 16, 1894*. Norwich, CT: n.p., [1894?].

Coit, Margaret L. *John C. Calhoun: American Portrait*. 1950. Reprint. Columbia: University of South Carolina Press, 1991.

Cole, Charles C., Jr. "The Free Church Movement in New York City." *New York History* 34, no. 3 (1953): 284–97.

Connecticut Anti-Slavery Society. *Charter Oak*. Pamphlet. Hartford: Connecticut Anti-Slavery Society, 1838.

Connecticut State Convention of Colored Men. *Proceedings of the Connecticut State Convention of Colored Men, Held at New Haven on September 12th and 13th, 1849*. New Haven, CT: William H. Stanley, 1849.

Conrad, Susan P. *Perish the Thought: Intellectual Women in Romantic America, 1830–1860*. New York: Oxford University Press, 1976.

Convention of the People of Colour. *Minutes and Proceedings of the First Annual Convention of the People of Colour; Held by Adjournments in the City of Philadelphia, from the 6th to the 11th of June Inclusive, 1831*. Philadelphia: Self-published, 1831.

Convention of the People of Colour. *Minutes and Proceedings of the Second Annual Convention, for the Improvement of the Free People of Color in these United States, Held by Adjournments in the City of Philadelphia, from the 4th to the 10th of June Inclusive, 1832*. Philadelphia: Martin and Borden, 1832.

Convention of the People of Colour. *Minutes and Proceedings of the Third Annual Convention for the Improvement of the Free People of Colour in These United States, Held by Adjournments in the City of Philadelphia, from the 3rd to the 13th of June Inclusive, 1833*. New York: Self-published, 1833.

Convention of the People of Colour. *Minutes of the Fourth Annual Convention for the Improvement of the Free People of Colour in the United States, Held by Adjournments in the Asbury Church, New-York, from the 2nd to the 12th of June Inclusive, 1834*. New York: Self-published, 1834.

Cooney, Robert, and Helen Michalowski. *Power of the People: Active Nonviolence in the United States*. Philadelphia: New Society, 1987.

Coontz, Stephanie. *Marriage, a History: How Love Conquered Marriage*. New York: Penguin, 2006.

Cooper, Afua. "Black Women and Work in Nineteenth-Century Canada West: Black Woman Teacher Mary Bibb." In *'We're Rooted Here and They Can't Pull Us Up': Essays in African Canadian Women's History*, coordinated by Peggy Bristow, 143–70. Toronto: University of Toronto Press, 1994.

Cooper, Afua. "Ever True to the Cause of Freedom—Henry Bibb: Abolitionist and Black Freedom's Champion, 1814–1854." *Northern Terminus: The African Canadian History Journal* 3 (2005–6): 21–32.

Cooper, Afua. "The Legacy of the Prudence Crandall School in Canada: Mary Miles Bibb and Black Education." Talk presented at "No Small Courage": A Symposium on the Lives and Legacies of Prudence Crandall's African-American Students, Part Two, May 21, 2016, Canterbury Municipal Building, Canterbury, Connecticut.

Cooper, Afua. "The *Voice of the Fugitive*: A Transnational Abolitionist Organ." In *A Fluid Frontier: Slavery, Resistance, and the Underground Railroad in the Detroit River Borderland,* edited by Karolyn Smardz Frost and Veta Smith Tucke, 135–53. Detroit: Wayne State University Press, 2016.

Cottrol, Robert J. *The Afro-Yankees: Providence's Black Community in the Antebellum Era.* Westport, CT: Greenwood, 1982.

Crandall, Reuben. *The Trial of Reuben Crandall, M.D., Charged with Publishing Seditious Libels by Circulating the Publications of the American Anti-Slavery Society, before the Circuit Court for the District of Columbia, held at Washington, in April, 1836, Occupying the Court the Period of Ten Days.* New York: H. R. Piercey, 1836.

Cromwell, John W. *The Early Negro Convention Movement.* The American Negro Academy, Occasional Papers no. 9. Washington, DC: American Negro Academy, 1904.

Crosby, Nathan. *Annual Obituary Notices of Prominent Persons Who Have Died in the United States for 1857.* Boston: Phillips, Sampson, 1858.

Cross, Barbara M. *The Educated Woman in America: Selected Writings of Catharine Beecher, Margaret Fuller, and M. Carey Thomas.* New York: Teachers College Press, 1965.

Cross, Whitney R. *The Burned-Over District: The Social and Intellectual History of Enthusiastic Religion in Western New York, 1800–1850.* Ithaca, NY: Cornell University Press, 1950.

Crouthamel, James L. *James Watson Webb: A Biography.* Middletown, CT: Wesleyan University Press, 1969.

Crummell, Alexander. "Died: Mrs. Julia Williams Garnet." *Christian Recorder,* January 22, 1870.

Culpepper, Emily. "Philosophia: Feminist Methodology for Constructing a Female Train of Thought." *Journal of Feminist Studies in Religion* 3, no. 2 (1987): 7–16.

Curti, Merle. *American Peace Crusade 1815–1860.* 1929. New York: Octagon Books, 1973.

Cutler, Andrew. *English Grammar and Parser, Made Up of Proverbs, Interesting Anecdotes, Prose and Poetical Selections: Addressed to School Examining Committees; Teachers, and Scholars a Little Advanced in Understanding.* Plainfield, CT: Bennet and French, 1841.

"Daggett, David." *Biographical Dictionary of the United States Congress*. https:// bioguide.congress.gov/search/bio/D000002.

Daniell, David. *The Bible in English*. New Haven, CT: Yale University Press, 2003.

Davis, Angela. *Women, Race, and Class*. New York: Random, 1981.

Davis, David Brion. "The Emergence of Immediatism in British and American Anti-slavery Thought." *Mississippi Valley Historical Review* 48, no. 2 (1962): 209–30.

Davis, Hugh. *Leonard Bacon: New England Reformer and Antislavery Moderate*. Baton Rouge: Louisiana State University Press, 1998.

Davis, Hugh. "Northern Colonizationists and Free Blacks, 1823–1837: A Case Study of Leonard Bacon." *Journal of the Early Republic* 17, no. 4 (1997): 651–75.

Davis, Rodney O. "Prudence Crandall, Spiritualism, and Populist Era Reform in Kansas." *Kansas History* 3, no. 4 (1980): 239–54.

Delany, Martin. *The Condition, Elevation, Emigration, and Destiny of the Colored People of the United States, Politically Considered*. Philadelphia: Self-published, 1852.

Delany, Martin. *Martin A. Delany: A Documentary Reader*. Edited by Robert S. Levine. Chapel Hill: University of North Carolina Press, 2003.

Delbanco, Andrew. *William Ellery Channing: An Essay on the Liberal Spirit in America*. Cambridge, MA: Harvard University Press, 1981.

de Tocqueville, Alexis. *Democracy in America*. Vols. 1 and 2. Translated by Henry Reeve. Electronic Classics Series. Pennsylvania State University. pdf document.

Dillon, Merton. *Benjamin Lundy and the Struggle for Negro Freedom*. Urbana: University of Illinois Press, 1966.

Douglass, Sarah Mapps [Zillah]. "Sympathy for Miss Crandall." *Emancipator* (New York), July 20, 1833.

Dowling, John. "Sketches of New York Baptists—No. IV: Rev. Thos. Paul and the Colored Baptist Churches." *Baptist Memorial and Monthly Record*, September 1849.

Drake, Thomas E. *Quakers and Slavery in America*. Gloucester, MA: Peter Smith, 1965.

Dresser, Amos. *Narrative of the Arrest, Lynch Law Trial, and Scourging of Amos Dresser: at Nashville, Tennessee, August, 1835*. Oberlin, OH: Self-published, 1849.

Duban, James. "Thoreau, Garrison, and Dymond: Unbending Firmness of Mind." *American Literature* 57, no. 2 (1985): 309–17.

Duignan, Peter, and L. H. Gann. *The United States and Africa: A History*. Cambridge: Cambridge University Press, 1984.

Dumond, Dwight Lowell. *Antislavery: The Crusade for Freedom in America*. Ann Arbor: University of Michigan Press, 1961.

Dunne, Gerald. "Bushrod Washington and the Mount Vernon Slaves." *Supreme Court Historical Society 1980 Yearbook*, 25–29. Washington, DC: Supreme Court Historical Society, 1980.

Durant, Samuel W. *History of Oneida County, New York 1667–1878*. Philadelphia: Everts and Fariss, 1878.

Dutton, Samuel W. S. *Address at the Funeral of Hon. David Daggett, April 15, 1851*. New Haven, CT: Maltby, 1851.

Dwight, Benjamin Woodbridge. *The History of the Descendants of Elder John Strong, of Northampton, Mass.* 2 vols. Albany, NY: Joel Munsell, 1871.

Dymond, Christopher William. *Memoirs, Letters and Poems of Jonathan Dymond, with Bibliographical Supplements.* Bristol, UK: John Bright, 1907.

Dymond, Jonathan. *Essays on the Principles of Morality, and on the Private and Political Rights and Obligations of Mankind.* London: Adams, 1829. 1st American ed. New York: Harper, 1834.

Dymond, Jonathan. *An Inquiry into the Accordancy of War with the Principles of Christianity, and an Examination of the Philosophical Reasoning by Which It Is Defended: With Observations on Some of the Causes of War and on Some of Its Effects.* 3rd ed. Corrected and enlarged. Philadelphia: William Brown, 1834.

Dymond, Jonathan. *On the Applicability of the Pacific Principles of the New Testament to the Conduct of States: And on the Limitations Which Those Principles Impose on the Rights of Self-Defence.* 1st American ed. from the 2nd London ed. Brooklyn, CT: People's Press, A. F. Lee, 1832.

Eaton, Clement. "A Dangerous Pamphlet in the Old South." *Journal of Southern History* 2, no. 3 (1936): 323–34.

Echeruo, Michael J. C. *Victorian Lagos: Aspects of Nineteenth Century Lagos Life.* London: Macmillan, 1977.

Edgerton, Walter. *A History of the Separation in Indiana Yearly Meeting of Friends.* Cincinnati: Achilles Pugh, 1856.

Egerton, Douglas R. *Charles Fenton Mercer and the Trial of National Conservatism.* Jackson: University Press of Mississippi, 1989.

Ekin, Des. *The Stolen Village: Baltimore and the Barbary Pirates.* Dublin: O'Brien, 2006.

Eldridge, Elleanor, and Frances H. Whipple. *Regenerations: Memoirs of Elleanor Eldridge.* Edited by Jocelyn Moody. Morgantown: West Virginia University Press, 2014.

Elliott, Marianne. *The Catholics of Ulster.* New York: Basic Books, 2001.

Eschenbach, Stephen. "Fritz's Fame." *Brown Alumni Magazine*, March–April 2005.

Evans, Philip Saffrey. *History of Connecticut Baptist State Convention, 1823–1907.* Hartford, CT: Smith-Linsley, 1909.

Finkelman, Paul. *Slavery in the Courtroom: An Annotated Bibliography of American Cases.* Washington, DC: Library of Congress, 1985.

Finkenbine, Roy E. "Boston's Black Churches: Institutional Centers of the Antislavery Movement." In *Courage and Conscience: Black and White Abolitionists in Boston*, edited by Donald M. Jacobs, 169–89. Indianapolis: Indiana University Press, 1993.

First Baptist Church, Pawtucket, Rhode Island. *One Hundred and Fiftieth Anniversary 1805–1955.* Published by First Baptist Church, Pawtucket, Rhode Island, 1955.

First Baptist Church, Providence, Rhode Island. *A List of Members of the First Baptist Church in Providence: With Biographical Sketches of the Pastors.* Providence, RI: Brown, 1832.

Fishkin, Shelly Fisher. *Lighting Out for the Territory: Reflections on Mark Twain and American Culture*. New York: Oxford University Press, 1996.

Flexner, Eleanor. *Century of Struggle: The Woman's Rights Movement in the United States*. Cambridge, MA: Belknap, 1959.

Foner, Philip S. *History of Black Americans: From Africa to the Emergence of the Cotton Kingdom*. Westport, CT: Greenwood, 1975.

Foner, Philip S., and Josephine F. Pacheco. *Three Who Dared: Prudence Crandall, Margaret Douglass, Myrtilla Miner: Champions of Antebellum Black Education*. Westport, CT: Greenwood, 1984.

Foote, Julia A. J. *A Brand Plucked from the Fire: An Autobiographical Sketch*. Cleveland: Lauer and Yost, 1886. Facsimile in *Spiritual Narratives*, edited by Sue Houchins. New York: Oxford University Press, 1988.

Forbes, Ella. "Every Man Fights for His Freedom: The Rhetoric of African American Resistance in the Mid-Nineteenth Century." In *Understanding African-American Rhetoric: Classical Origins to Contemporary Innovations*, edited by Ronald L. Jackson II and Elaine B. Richardson, 155–70. New York: Routledge, 2003.

Fordham, Monroe. *Major Themes in Northern Black Religious Thought, 1800–1860*. Hicksville, NY: Exposition, 1975.

Fox, Early Lee. *The American Colonization Society 1817–1840*. Johns Hopkins University Studies in Historical and Political Science, ser. 37, no. 3. Baltimore: Johns Hopkins, 1919.

Franklin, Vincent P. "Education for Colonization: Attempts to Educate Free Blacks in the United States for Emigration to Africa, 1823–1833." *Journal of Negro Education* 43, no. 1 (1974): 91–103.

Freehling, William W. *The Road to Disunion: Volume 1: Secessionists at Bay, 1776–1854*. New York: Oxford University Press, 1991.

French, Scot. *The Rebellious Slave: Nat Turner in American Memory*. Boston: Houghton Mifflin, 2004.

Friedman, Lawrence J. "Racism and Sexism in Ante-Bellum America: The Prudence Crandall Episode Reconsidered." *Societas* 4, no. 3 (1974): 211–27.

Frieze, Jacob. *Letter to Rev. Mr. Philleo: Dedicated to the People of Pawtucket*. Pawtucket, RI: n.p., 1829.

Frieze, Jacob. *Two Discourses, Delivered in the Universalist Church, in Pawtucket, on Sunday, August 30, 1829. On the Subject of Religious Excitements*. Pawtucket, RI: Chronicle, 1829.

Frost, J. William. *The Quaker Family in Colonial America: A Portrait of the Society of Friends*. New York: St. Martin's, 1973.

Fuller, Edmund. *Prudence Crandall: An Incident of Racism in Nineteenth-Century Connecticut*. Middletown, CT: Wesleyan University Press, 1971.

Galpin, W. Freeman. *Pioneering for Peace: A Study of American Peace Efforts to 1846*. Syracuse, NY: Bardeen, 1933.

Gamber, Wendy. *The Boardinghouse in Nineteenth-Century America*. Baltimore: Johns Hopkins University Press, 2007.

Gara, Larry. *The Liberty Line: The Legend of the Underground Railroad*. 1961.

Lexington: University Press of Kentucky, 1996. Page references are to the 1996 edition.

Gardner, Eric. "Johnson, Francis." In *American National Biography: Supplement 2*, edited by Paul R. Betz and Mark C. Carnes, 286–87. New York: Oxford University Press, 2005.

Garnet, Henry Highland. "(1843) Henry Highland Garnet: 'An Address to the Slaves of the United States.'" *Blackpast.org*, January 24, 2007. https://www.blackpast.org/.

Garnet, Henry Highland. "Notes by a Traveler." *Emancipator* (New York) 10, no. 30, November 19, 1845, 118.

Garrison, Francis Jackson, and Wendell Phillips Garrison. *William Lloyd Garrison, 1805–1879: The Story of His Life Told by His Children*. Vol. 1, 1805–35. New York: Century, 1885.

Garrison, Wendell Phillips. *The Benson Family of Newport, Rhode Island, Together with an Appendix concerning the Benson Families in America of English Descent*. New York: Nation Press, 1872.

Garrison, Wendell Phillips. "Connecticut in the Middle Ages." *Century* 30, September 1885, 780–86.

Garrison, William Lloyd. *Fruits of Colonization*. Boston: Garrison and Knapp, 1833.

Garrison, William Lloyd. *Helen Eliza Garrison: A Memorial*. Cambridge, MA: Riverside, 1876.

Garrison, William Lloyd. *The Letters of William Lloyd Garrison, Volume I: I Will Be Heard! 1822–1835*. Edited by Walter M. Merrill. Cambridge, MA: Belknap, 1971.

Garrison, William Lloyd. *The Letters of William Lloyd Garrison, Volume II: A House Dividing against Itself*. Edited by Louis Ruchames. Cambridge, MA: Harvard University Press, 1971.

Garrison, William Lloyd. *Thoughts on African Colonization: or an Impartial Exhibition of the Doctrines, Principles, and Purposes of the American Colonization Society. Together with the Resolutions, Addresses and Remonstrances of the Free People of Color*. Boston: Garrison and Knapp, 1832. Reprint, New York: Arno Press, 1968.

Gilmore, Ruth Wilson. *Abolition Geography: Essays towards Liberation*. London: Verso, 2022.

Goen, C. C. "Broken Churches, Broken Nation: Regional Religion and North-South Alienation in Antebellum America." *Church History* 52, no. 1, 1983, 21–35.

Goodell, William. *Slavery and Anti-Slavery: A History of the Great Struggle in Both Hemispheres; with a View of the Slavery Question in the United States*. 1852. New York: Negro Universities Press, 1968.

Goodman, Paul. *Of One Blood: Abolitionism and the Origins of Racial Equality*. Berkeley: University of California Press, 1998.

Goodrich, Samuel Griswold. *A System of Universal Geography, Popular and Scientific: Comprising a Physical, Political, and Statistical Account of the World and Its Various Divisions; Embracing Numerous Sketches from Recent Travels, and Illustrated by Engravings of Manners, Costumes, Curiosities, Cities,*

Edifices, Remarkable Animals, Fruits, Trees, and Plants. Boston: Carter, Hendee, 1832.

Gordon, Thomas F. *Gazetteer of the State of New York*. Philadelphia: Collins, 1836.

Gould, William B., IV. *Diary of a Contraband: The Civil War Passage of a Black Soldier*. Stanford, CA: Stanford University Press, 2002.

Grant, Donald Lee. *The Way It Was in the South: The Black Experience in Georgia*. Athens: University of Georgia Press, 1993.

Greater Camden City Directory, 1910–1911, Containing the Names and Addresses of the Inhabitants, Together with a Business Directory of the City and an Appendix of Useful Information. Philadelphia: C. E. Howe, 1909.

Grieve, Robert. *An Illustrated History of Pawtucket, Central Falls and Vicinity. A Narrative of the Growth and Evolution of the Community*. Pawtucket, RI: Pawtucket Gazette and Chronicle, 1897.

Griffin, Farah Jasmine, ed. *Beloved Sisters and Loving Friends: Letters from Rebecca Primus of Royal Oak, Maryland, and Addie Brown of Hartford, Connecticut, 1854–1868*. New York: One World, 1999.

Griffith, R. Marie. *Moral Combat: How Sex Divided American Christians & Fractured American Politics*. New York: Basic Books, 2017.

[Grimké, Angelina]. *Appeal to the Women of the Nominally Free States, Issued by an Antislavery Convention of American Women*. 2nd ed. Boston: Knapp, 1838.

Grimké, Charlotte Forten. "Colored People in New England." Letter to the editor of the *Evangelist*. Manuscripts for the Grimke Book. Digital Howard. *Howard University*. https://dh.howard.edu/ajc_grimke_manuscripts/37.

Gross, Bella. "*Freedom's Journal* and *The Rights of All*." *Journal of Negro History* 17, no. 3 (1932): 241–86.

Harwood, Thomas F. "Prejudice and Antislavery: The Colloquy between William Ellery Channing and Edward Strutt Abdy, 1834." *American Quarterly* 18, no. 4 (1966): 697–700.

Headley, Joel Tyler. *The Great Riots of New York, 1712 to 1873, including a Full and Complete Account of the Four Days' Draft Riot of 1863*. New York: Treat, 1873.

Heerman, M. Scott. *The Alchemy of Slavery: Human Bondage and Emancipation in the Illinois Country, 1730–1865*. Philadelphia: University of Pennsylvania Press, 2018.

Hegel, G. W. F. *Phenomenology of Mind*. Translated by J. B. Baillie. New York: Harper, 1967.

Heinz, Bernard. "Nathaniel Jocelyn: Puritan, Painter, Inventor." *Journal of the New Haven Colony Historical Society* 29, no. 2 (1983): 2–44.

Hendricks, Wanda A. *Fannie Barrier Williams: Crossing the Borders of Region and Race*. Urbana: University of Illinois Press, 2014.

Hewitt, John H. "Mr. Downing and His Oyster House: The Life and Good Works of an African-American Entrepreneur." *New York History* 74, no. 3 (1993): 229–52.

Hewitt, John H. "The Sacking of St. Philip's Church, New York." *Historical Magazine of the Protestant Episcopal Church* 49, no. 1 (1980): 7–20.

Hinks, Peter P. *To Awaken My Afflicted Brethren: David Walker and the Problem of Antebellum Slave Resistance*. University Park: Pennsylvania State University Press, 1997.

Hinks, Peter P. "William Lanson." Unpublished paper, 2008. Word document.

Hinks, Peter P., and Stephen Kantrowitz, eds. *All Men Free and Brethren: Essays on the History of African American Freemasonry*. Ithaca, NY: Cornell University Press, 2013.

Hirsch, Leo H., Jr. "The Free Negro in New York." *Journal of Negro History* 16, no. 4 (1931): 415–53.

Hoagland, Sarah Lucia. *Lesbian Ethics: Toward New Value*. Palo Alto, CA: Institute of Lesbian Studies, 1988.

Hodges, Graham Russell Gao. *David Ruggles: A Radical Black Abolitionist and the Underground Railroad in New York City*. Chapel Hill: University of North Carolina Press, 2010.

Hodges, Graham Russell Gao. *Root and Branch: African Americans in New York and East New Jersey, 1613–1863*. Chapel Hill: University of North Carolina Press, 1999.

Hood, J. W. *One Hundred Years of the African Methodist Episcopal Zion Church; or, the Centennial of African Methodism*. New York City: A.M.E. Zion Book Concern, 1895.

Hornick, Nancy Slocum. "Anthony Benezet and the Africans' School: Toward a Theory of Full Equality." *Pennsylvania Magazine of History and Biography* 99, no. 4 (1975): 399–421.

Horton, James Oliver. "Black New York and the Lincoln Presidency." In *Lincoln and New York*, edited by Harold Holzer, 98–125. New York: New-York Historical Society, 2009.

Horton, James Oliver, and Lois E. Horton. *Black Bostonians: Family Life and Community Struggle in the Antebellum North*. New York: Holmes, 1979.

Horton, James Oliver, and Lois E. Horton. *In Hope of Liberty: Culture, Community, and Protest among Northern Free Blacks*. New York: Oxford University Press, 1998.

Houchins, Sue. Introduction to *Spiritual Narratives*, edited by Sue Houchins, xxix–xliv. New York: Oxford University Press, 1988.

Housley, Kathleen. "'Yours for the Oppressed': The Life of Jehiel C. Beman." *Journal of Negro History* 77, no. 1 (1992): 17–29.

Hughes, Marian I. *Refusing Ignorance: The Struggle to Educate Black Children in Albany, New York, 1816–1873*. Albany: Mount Ida, 1998.

Hunt, Mary E. "Biographical Sketch [of Mary Daly]." In *The Mary Daly Reader*, edited by Jennifer Rycenga and Linda Barufaldi, xv–xix. New York: New York University Press, 2017.

Husband, Julie. *Antislavery Discourse and Nineteenth-Century American Literature: Incendiary Pictures*. New York: Palgrave Macmillan, 2010.

Hutchinson, Earl Ofari. *"Let Your Motto Be Resistance": The Life and Thought of Henry Highland Garnet*. Boston: Beacon, 1972.

Isenberg, Nancy. *Sex and Citizenship in Antebellum America*. Chapel Hill: University of North Carolina Press, 1998.

Jackson, Henry [reputed]. *A Short History of the African Union Meeting and School-House, Erected in Providence (R.I.) in the Years 1819, '20, '21; with Rules for Its Future Government.* Providence, RI: Brown and Danforth, 1821.

Jackson, Maurice. *Let This Voice Be Heard: Anthony Benezet, Father of Atlantic Abolition.* Philadelphia: University of Pennsylvania Press, 2010.

Jacobs, Donald N., ed. *Courage and Conviction: Black and White Abolitionists in Boston.* Bloomington: Indiana University Press, 1993.

Jacobs, Donald N. "David Walker and William Lloyd Garrison: Racial Cooperation and the Shaping of Boston Abolition." In *Courage and Conviction: Black and White Abolitionists in Boston,* edited by Donald N. Jacobs, 1–20. Bloomington: Indiana University Press, 1993.

Jaina, Nick. "The Birth of the Drum Set." *Smithsonian Folkways Magazine* (Winter/Spring 2015).

Jantzen, Grace. *Power, Gender, and Christian Mysticism.* Cambridge: Cambridge University Press, 1995.

Jay, William. "Condition of the Free People of Color." In *The Free People of Color,* 371–95. Facsimile ed. of 1853 ed. New York: Arno, 1969.

Jay, William. *Inquiry into the Character and Tendency of the American Colonization, and American Anti-Slavery Societies.* [New York]: R. G. Williams, 1838. Reprint, New York: Negro Universities Press, 1969.

Jefferson, Thomas. *Notes on the State of Virginia: An Annotated Edition.* Edited by Robert Forbes. New Haven, CT: Yale University Press, 2022.

Jeffrey, Julie Roy. *Abolitionists Remember: Antislavery Autobiographies and the Unfinished Work of Emancipation.* Chapel Hill: University of North Carolina Press, 2008.

Johnson, Edward A. *A School History of the Negro People in America.* Raleigh, NC: Edwards and Broughton, 1894.

Johnson, James E. "Charles G. Finney and a Theology of Revivalism." *Church History* 38, no. 3, September 1969, 338–58.

Johnson, Oliver. *W. L. Garrison and His Times.* Boston: Houghton, 1881. Reprint, Miami: Mnemosyne, 1969.

Jones, Augustine. *Moses Brown: His Life and Services.* Providence, RI: Rhode Island Printing, 1892.

Jones, Martha S. *All Bound Up Together: The Woman Question in African American Public Culture, 1830–1900.* Chapel Hill: University of North Carolina Press, 2007.

Jones, Rufus M. *The Later Periods of Quakerism.* 2 vols. London: Macmillan, 1921.

Jordan, Winthrop D. *White over Black: American Attitudes toward the Negro.* Chapel Hill: University of North Carolina Press, 1968.

Judson, Andrew Thompson, and David Daggett. *Andrew T. Judson's Remarks, to the Jury, on the Trial of the Case, State v. P. Crandall: Superior Court, Oct. Term, 1833: Windham County, Ct.* Hartford, CT: John Russell, printer, [1833].

Kaestle, Carl F. *Pillars of the Republic: Common Schools and American Society 1780–1860.* New York: Hill and Wang, 1983.

Karcher, Carolyn L. *The First Woman in the Republic: A Cultural Biography of Lydia Maria Child.* Durham, NC: Duke University Press, 1994.

Karttunen, Frances. "Nantucket Places and People: Much More Than a Barber on Main." *Yesterday's Island, Today's Nantucket* 38, no. 18, August 28–September 3, 2008.

Keller, Charles Roy. *The Second Great Awakening in Connecticut.* 1942. Hamden, CT: Archon, 1968. Page references are to the 1968 edition.

Kelly, Catherine E. *In the New England Fashion: Reshaping Women's Lives in the Nineteenth Century.* Ithaca, NY: Cornell University Press, 1999.

Kelsey, Rayner Wickersham. *Centennial History of Moses Brown School 1819–1919.* Providence, RI: Moses Brown School, 1919.

Kendi, Ibram X. *Stamped from the Beginning: The Definitive History of Racist Ideas in America.* New York: Nation Books, 2016.

Kennedy, Al. *Chord Changes on the Chalkboard: How Public School Teachers Shaped Jazz and the Music of New Orleans.* Studies in Jazz 41. Lanham, MD: Scarecrow, 2005.

Kerber, Linda K. "Abolitionists and Amalgamators: The New York City Race Riots of 1834." *New York History* 48, no. 1 (1967): 28–39.

King, Martin Luther, Jr. *I Have a Dream: Writings and Speeches That Changed the World.* Edited by James M. Washington. San Francisco: Harper, 1992.

King, Martin Luther, Jr. *The Papers of Martin Luther King, Jr., Volume IV: Symbol of the Movement, January 1957–December 1958.* Edited by Clayborne Carson, Susan Carson, Adrienne Clay, Virginia Shadron, and Kieran Taylor. Berkeley: University of California Press, 2000.

King, Martin Luther, Jr. *The Trumpet of Conscience.* New York: Harper and Row, 1967.

King, Moses. *Mount Auburn Cemetery, including also a Brief History and Description of Cambridge, Harvard University, and the Union Railway Company.* 19th ed. Cambridge, MA: Moses King, 1883.

Kofoid, Carrie Prudence. *Puritan Influences in the Formative Years of Illinois History.* Springfield: Illinois State Journal, 1906.

Kraditor, Aileen. *Means and Ends in American Abolitionism: Garrison and His Critics on Strategy and Tactics, 1834–1850.* New York: Vintage, 1969.

Krueger, Glee F. "A Canterbury Tale: Sarah Ann Major Harris and Prudence Crandall." Textiles in Early New England: Design, Production, and Consumption. *Dublin Seminar for New England Folklife Annual Proceedings* 22 (1997): 233–35.

Lapsansky, Emma. "'Since They Got Those Separate Churches': Afro-Americans and Racism in Jacksonian Philadelphia." *American Quarterly* 32, no. 1 (1980): 54–78.

Larned, Ellen D. *History of Windham County, Connecticut: A Bicentennial Edition.* 1874. 2 vols. Chester, CT: Pequot, 1975.

Lemons, J. Stanley, and Michael A. McKenna. "Re-enfranchisement of Rhode Island Negroes." *Rhode Island History* 30, no. 1 (1971): 3–14.

Lerner, Gerda. *The Creation of Feminist Consciousness: From the Middle Ages to Eighteen-Seventy.* New York: Oxford University Press, 1993.

Levesque, George A. *Black Boston: African American Life and Culture in Urban America, 1750–1860*. New York: Garland, 1994.

Litwack, Leon. *North of Slavery: The Negro in the Free States, 1790–1860*. Chicago: University of Chicago Press, 1961.

Lynd, Staughton. *Intellectual Origins of American Radicalism*. Indianapolis: Bobbs-Merrill, 1966.

Lynd, Staughton, ed. *Nonviolence in America: A Documentary History*. Indianapolis: Bobbs-Merrill, 1966.

Mabee, Carleton. *Black Education in New York State: From Colonial to Modern Times*. Syracuse, NY: Syracuse University Press, 1979.

Mabee, Carleton. *Black Freedom: The Nonviolent Abolitionists from 1830 through the Civil War*. New York: Macmillan, 1970.

Magdol, Edward. *The Antislavery Rank and File: A Social Profile of the Abolitionist Constituency*. New York: Greenwood, 1986.

Maltz, Earl M. "Fourteenth Amendment Concepts in the Antebellum Era," *American Journal of Legal History* 32, no. 4 (1988): 305–46.

Mancini, Jason R. "Glasgo: Isaac Glasko Forges a Life." *Connecticut Explored*, Summer 2016. https://www.ctexplored.org/glasgo-isaac-glasko-forges-a-life/.

Marquis, Donald M. *In Search of Buddy Bolden: First Man of Jazz*. Rev. ed. Baton Rouge: Louisiana State University Press, 2005.

Martineau, Harriet. *The Martyr Age of the United States of America*. Boston: Weeks, Jordan, 1839.

Masur, Louis P. *1831: Year of Eclipse*. New York: Hill and Wang, 2001.

May, Samuel J. *Memoir of Samuel J. May*. Edited by George Barrell Emerson, Samuel May, and Thomas J. Mumford. Boston: Roberts Brothers, 1873.

May, Samuel J. "Miss Prudence Crandall." In *The Oasis*, edited by Lydia Maria Child, 180–91. Boston: Benjamin C. Bacon, 1834.

May, Samuel J. *The Right of Colored People To Education, Vindicated. Letters to Andrew T. Judson, Esq., and Others in Canterbury, Remonstrating with Them on Their Unjust and Unjustifiable Procedure Relative to Miss Crandall and Her School for Colored Females*. Brooklyn, CT: Advertiser Press, 1833.

May, Samuel J. *Some Recollections of Our Antislavery Conflict*. 1869. Miami: Mnemosyne, 1969.

Mayer, Henry. *All on Fire: William Lloyd Garrison and the Abolition of Slavery*. New York: St. Martin's Press, 1998.

McBride, David. "Black Protest Against Racial Politics: Gardner, Hinton and Their Memorial of 1838." *Pennsylvania History* 46, no. 2 (1979): 149–62.

McCain, Diana Ross. *To All on Equal Terms: The Life and Legacy of Prudence Crandall*. Hartford: Connecticut Commission on Arts, Tourism, Culture, History, and Film, 2004.

McHenry, Elizabeth. *Forgotten Readers: Recovering the Lost History of African American Literary Societies*. Durham, NC: Duke University Press, 2002.

McLaughlin, Don James. "The Anti-Slavery Roots of Today's 'Phobia' Obsession." *New Republic*, January 29, 2016.

McLoughlin, William G. *New England Dissent 1630–1833: The Baptists and the Separation of Church and State.* 2 vols. Cambridge, MA: Harvard University Press, 1971.

McLoughlin, William G. *Rhode Island: A History.* New York: Norton, 1986.

McNeely, Patricia G. "Assignment Liberia: 'The boldest adventure in the history of Southern journalism.'" In *Seeking a Voice: Images of Race and Gender in the 19th Century Press*, edited by David B. Sachsman, S. Kittrell Rushing, and Roy Morris Jr., 67–76. West Lafayette, IN: Purdue University Press, 2009.

McNeil, Genna Rae, Houston Bryan Robertson, Quinton Hosford Dixie, and Kevin McGruder. *Witness: Two Hundred Years of African-American Faith and Practice at the Abyssinian Baptist Church of Harlem, New York.* Grand Rapids, MI: Eerdmans, 2014.

A Member of the Bar. *Report of the Arguments of Counsel, in the Case of Prudence Crandall, Plff. in Error, vs. State of Connecticut, before the Supreme Court of Errors, at Their Session at Brooklyn, July Term, 1834.* Boston: Garrison and Knapp, 1834.

Mendelsohn, Jack. *Channing: The Reluctant Radical.* Boston: Little, Brown, 1971.

Menzies, Amanda. "Black History Month: Jesse, 'Fritz' and Der Führer." *University of North Dakota News*, February 2016. http://und.edu/news/2016/02/fritz-pollard.cfm.

Merkel, Benjamin G. "The Abolition Aspects of Missouri's Antislavery Controversy." *Missouri Historical Review* 44 (1950): 232–54.

Meyer, Douglas K. *Making the Heartland Quilt: A Geographical History of Settlement and Migration in Early Nineteenth-Century Illinois.* Carbondale: Southern Illinois University Press, 2000.

Miller, James A. "We've Come This Far: A History of the Abyssinian Baptist Church." In *We've Come This Far: The Abyssinian Baptist Church: A Photographic Record*, edited by Bob Gore, 24–33. New York: Stewart, Tabori, and Chang, 2001.

Miller, William Lee. *Arguing about Slavery: John Quincy Adams and the Great Battle in the United States Congress.* New York: Vintage, 1995.

Mintz, Steven. *Moralists and Modernizers: America's Pre–Civil War Reformers.* Baltimore: Johns Hopkins University Press, 1995.

Morley, Jefferson. *Snow-Storm in August: The Struggle for American Freedom and Washington's Race Riot of 1835.* New York: Anchor, 2012.

Morris, Celia. *Fanny Wright: Rebel in America.* Urbana: University of Illinois Press, 1984.

Morris, Robert C. *Reading, 'Riting, and Reconstruction: The Education of Freedmen in the South 1861–1870.* Chicago: University of Chicago Press, 1981.

Morton, Nelle. "Beloved Image." In *The Journey Is Home*, 122–46. Boston: Beacon, 1985.

Moss, Hilary J. *Schooling Citizens: The Struggle for African American Education in Antebellum America.* Chicago: University of Chicago Press, 2009.

Mott, Lucretia Coffin. *Selected Letters of Lucretia Coffin Mott.* Edited by Beverly

Wilson Palmer, with Holly Byers Ochoa and Carol Faulkner. Urbana: University of Illinois Press, 2002.

Murphy, Teresa Anne. *Ten Hours' Labor: Religion, Reform, and Gender in Early New England*. Ithaca, NY: Cornell University Press, 1992.

Myers, Amrita Chakrabarti. *The Vice President's Black Wife: The Untold Life of Julia Chinn*. Chapel Hill: University of North Carolina Press, 2023.

Nell, William Cooper. *The Colored Patriots of the American Revolution, with Sketches of Several Distinguished Colored Persons: To Which Is Added a Brief Survey of the Condition and Prospects of Colored Americans*. With an introduction by Harriet Beecher Stowe. Boston: Robert F. Wallcut, 1855.

Nelson, Donald Frederick. *To the Stars over Rough Roads: The Life of Andrew Atchison, Teacher and Missionary*. Cambridge, MA: TidePool, 2008.

New England Anti-Slavery Society. *Proceedings of the New England Antislavery Convention, Held in Boston on the 27th, 28th, and 29th of May, 1834*. Boston: Garrison and Knapp, 1834.

New England Anti-Slavery Society. *Second Annual Report of the Board of Managers of the New-England Antislavery Society, Presented January 15, 1834. With an Appendix*. Boston: Garrison and Knapp, 1834.

New York City. Department of Health, Division of Vital Statistics. *Marriage Registers, Extracts from Manhattan (1869–1880) and Brooklyn (1895–1897)*. Ancestry.com. https://www.ancestry.com/discoveryui-content/view/146791:7854.

Nussbaum, Martha. "A Right to Marry? Same-Sex Marriage and Constitutional Law." *Dissent Magazine*, summer 2009.

Nye, Russel B. *Fettered Freedom: Civil Liberties and the Slavery Controversy 1830–1860*. Lansing: Michigan State University Press, 1963.

Oberlin College. *General Catalogue of Oberlin College, 1833–1908, including an Account of the Principal Events in the History of the College, with Illustrations of the College Buildings*. Oberlin, OH: Oberlin College, 1909.

Oneida Baptist Association. *Minutes of the Oneida Baptist Association. Held at Fenner, on the 25th and 26th of August, 1824, Together with Their Circular and Corresponding Letter*. New York: Oneida Baptist Association, 1824.

Oneida Baptist Association. *Minutes of the Seventy-Second Anniversary of the Oneida Baptist Association Held with the Boonville Baptist Church, Boonville, N.Y., Tuesday and Wednesday, Oct. 4–5, 1892*. Waterville, NY: Times Book, 1892.

Parks, Rosa. *Rosa Parks: My Story*. Edited by James Haskins. New York: Dial, 1992.

Pasternak, Martin B. *Rise Now and Fly to Arms: The Life of Henry Highland Garnet*. New York: Garland, 1995.

Paul, Susan. *Memoir of James Jackson, The Attentive and Obedient Scholar, Who Died in Boston, October 31, 1833, Aged Six Years and Eleven Months*. Edited by Lois Brown. Cambridge, MA: Harvard University Press, 2000.

Pease, Jane H., and William H. *They Who Would Be Free: Blacks' Search for Freedom, 1830–1861*. New York: Atheneum, 1974.

Penn, I. Garland. *The Afro-American Press and Its Editors*. 1891. New York: Arno, 1969.

Perry, Lewis. *Radical Abolitionism: Anarchy and the Government of God in Anti-slavery Thought*. Ithaca, NY: Cornell University Press, 1973.

Peterson, Carla L. *Black Gotham: A Family History of African Americans in Nineteenth-Century New York City*. New Haven, CT: Yale University Press, 2011.

Philleo, Prudence Crandall. "Letters of Prudence Crandall Philleo to George Harris Richardson," *Negro History Bulletin* v. 13, no. 1 (Oct 1, 1949), p. 15.

Piper, Chuck, and Judy Piper. "A Passport to History." *Jazz Archivist* 23 (2010): 30–36.

Plainfield Academy. *A Catalogue of the Trustees, Instructors, and Students of Plainfield Academy, Plainfield, Ct. for the Year, Ending August, 1832*. Brooklyn, CT: Advertiser Press, 1832.

Plainfield Anti-Slavery Society. *First Annual Report of the Plainfield Anti-Slavery Society*. Plainfield, CT: Plainfield Anti-Slavery Society, 1834.

Poe, William A. "Lott Cary: Man of Purchased Freedom." *Church History* 39, no. 1 (1970): 49–61.

Pooley, William Vipond. "The Settlement of Illinois from 1830 to 1850." History ser. *Bulletin of the University of Wisconsin* 1, no. 4 (1908): 287–595.

Porter, Dorothy. "The Organized Educational Activities of Negro Literary Societies, 1828–1846." *Journal of Negro Education* 5 (1936): 555–76.

Pride, Armistead S., and Clint C. Wilson II. *A History of the Black Press*. Washington, DC: Howard University Press, 1997.

Priest, Gerald L. "Revival and Revivalism: A Historical and Doctrinal Evaluation." *Detroit Baptist Seminary Journal* 1 (Fall 1996): 223–52.

Providence Anti-Slavery Society. *The Reports and Proceedings of the First Annual Meeting of the Providence Anti-Slavery Society. With a Brief Exposition of the Principles and Purposes of the Abolitionists*. Providence, RI: H. H. Brown, 1833.

Prude, Jonathan. *The Coming of Industrial Order: Town and Factory Life in Rural Massachusetts 1810–1860*. New York: Cambridge University Press, 1983.

Pruden, William H., III. "Lloyd Garrison Wheeler (1848–1909)." In *The Encyclopedia of Arkansas History and Culture*, June 16, 2023. http://www.encyclopedia ofarkansas.net/encyclopedia/entry-detail.aspx?entryID=8050.

Quarles, Benjamin. *Black Abolitionists*. 1969. New York: Da Capo, 1991.

Quarles, Benjamin. *Blacks on John Brown*. Urbana: University of Illinois Press, 1972.

Raffo, Steven M. *A Biography of Oliver Johnson, Abolitionist and Reformer, 1809–1889*. Lewiston, NY: Mellen, 2002.

Rammelkamp, Julian. "The Providence Negro Community, 1820–1842." *Rhode Island History* 7, no. 1 (1948): 20–33.

Rankin, John. *Letters on American Slavery. Addressed to Mr. Thomas Rankin, Merchant at Middlebrook, Augusta Co., Va*. Boston: Garrison and Knapp, 1833.

Rappleye, Charles. *Sons of Providence: The Brown Brothers, the Slave Trade, and the American Revolution*. New York: Simon and Schuster, 2006.

Ratzlaff, Aleen J. "Ida B. Wells, Crusader against Lynching." In *Seeking a Voice: Images of Race and Gender in the 19th Century Press*, edited by David B.

Sachsman, S. Kittrell Rushing, and Roy Morris Jr., 151–60. West Lafayette, IN: Purdue University Press, 2009.

Reddick, L. D. "Samuel E. Cornish." *Negro History Bulletin* 5, no. 2 (1941): 38.

Reed, Harry. *Platform for Change: The Foundations of the Northern Free Black Community, 1775–1865*. East Lansing: Michigan State University Press, 1994.

Rhodes, Richard. *John James Audubon: The Making of an American*. New York: Vintage, 2004.

Richards, Leonard L. *"Gentlemen of Property and Standing": Anti-Abolition Mobs in Jacksonian America*. New York: Oxford University Press, 1970.

Richardson, Marilyn. *Maria W. Stewart, America's First Black Woman Political Writer*. Bloomington: Indiana University Press, 1987.

Ripley, Peter C., ed. *The Black Abolitionist Papers*. 5 vols. Chapel Hill: University of North Carolina Press, 1985–92.

Robertson, Stacey M. *Hearts Beating for Liberty: Women Abolitionists in the Old Northwest*. Chapel Hill: University of North Carolina Press, 2010.

Rodriguez, Richard. "The Bible against American Slavery: Anglophone Transatlantic Evangelical Abolitionists' Use of Biblical Arguments, 1776–1865." PhD diss., Florida International University, 2017. https://digitalcommons.fiu.edu/etd/3511.

Ruggles, David. *The "Extinguisher" Extinguished! or David M. Reese, M.D. "Used Up."* New York: Ruggles, 1834.

Runcie, John. "'Hunting the Nigs' in Philadelphia: The Race Riots of 1834." *Pennsylvania History* 39, no. 2 (1972): 187–218.

Russ, Joanna. *How to Suppress Women's Writing*. Austin: University of Texas Press, 1983.

Rycenga, Jennifer. "'Be Ashamed of Nothing but Sin': Prudence Crandall, Levi Kneeland, and Connecticut Baptists." *American Baptist Quarterly* 34, no. 3–4 (2015): 324–42.

Rycenga, Jennifer. "Characterological Itineracy: The Career of Calvin Philleo." *American Baptist Quarterly* 39, no. 3 (2020): 247–68.

Rycenga, Jennifer. "A Greater Awakening: Women's Intellect as a Factor in Early Abolitionist Movements, 1824–1834." *Journal of Feminist Studies in Religion* 21, no. 2 (2005): 31–59.

Rycenga, Jennifer. "Intellect and Abolition: Reconstructing the Curriculum at Prudence Crandall's Academy for Young Ladies and Little Misses of Color." In *Schooldays in New England, 1650–1900. The Dublin Seminar for New England Folklife Annual Proceedings 2015*, edited by Peter Benes, 126–37. Deerfield, MA: Dublin Seminar for New England Folklife, 2018.

Rycenga, Jennifer. "Maria Stewart, Black Abolitionist, and the Idea of Freedom." In *Frontline Feminisms: Women, War and Resistance*, edited by Marguerite Waller and Jennifer Rycenga, 297–324. New York: Garland, 2000.

Rycenga, Jennifer. "The Sun in Its Glory: The Diffusion of Jonathan Dymond's Works in the United States, 1831–1836." *Quaker Studies* 26, no. 2 (2021): 241–59.

Rycenga, Jennifer, and Nick Szydlowski. *The* Unionist *Unified: Connecticut's First*

Immediate Abolitionist Newspaper. Digital Humanities Collection. *San Jose State University*, 2023. https://sjsu-library.github.io/unionist/.

Ryder, Ron. *181 Years in Boonville, N.Y.: Facts, Dates and Trivia—1795 to 1976*. Boonville, NY: Boonville Graphics and Country Books, 1976.

Sagarin, Mary. *John Brown Russwurm: The Story of Freedom's Journal, Freedom's Journey*. New York: Lothrop, 1970.

Salitan, Lucille, and Eve Lewis Perera, eds. *Virtuous Lives: Four Quaker Sisters Remember Family Life, Abolitionism, and Women's Suffrage*. New York: Continuum, 1994.

Scheffler, Judith. "Prison Writings of Early Quaker Women: 'We Were Stronger Afterward Than Before.'" *Quaker History* 73, no. 2 (1984): 25–37.

Schiff, Judith Ann. "Old Yale: Pioneers." *Yale Alumni Magazine*, January–February 2006, 80–81.

Schor, Joel. *Henry Highland Garnet: A Voice of Black Radicalism in the Nineteenth Century*. Westport, CT: Greenwood, 1977.

Schultz, Stanley K. *The Culture Factory: Boston Public Schools, 1789–1860*. New York: Oxford University Press, 1973.

Sehr, Timothy J. "Leonard Bacon and the Myth of the Good Slaveholder." *New England Quarterly* 49, no. 2 (1976): 194–213.

Sen, Amartya. "Democracy and Its Global Roots." *New Republic*, October 6, 2003, 28–35.

Sernett, Milton C. *Afro-American Religious History: A Documentary Witness*. Durham, NC: Duke University Press, 1985.

Sherer, Robert Glenn. "Negro Churches in Rhode Island before 1860." *Rhode Island History* 25, no. 1 (1966): 9–25.

Silcox, Henry C. "Delay and Neglect: Negro Public Education in Antebellum Philadelphia." *Pennsylvania Magazine of History and Biography* 97, no. 4 (1973): 444–64.

Sillen, Samuel. *Women against Slavery*. New York: Masses and Mainstream, 1955.

Simmons, William J. *Men of Mark: Eminent, Progressive, and Rising*. Cleveland: Revell, 1887.

Sinha, Manisha. *The Slave's Cause: A History of Abolition*. New Haven, CT: Yale University Press, 2016.

Sizer, Theodore R., ed. *The Age of the Academies*. New York: Columbia University, 1964.

Sklar, Katherine Kish. *Catharine Beecher: A Study in American Domesticity*. New York: Norton, 1976.

Small, Edwin W., and Miriam R. Small. "Prudence Crandall: Champion of Negro Education." *New England Quarterly* 17, no. 14 (1944): 506–29.

Smith, Anna Bustill. "The Bustill Family." *Journal of Negro History* 10, no. 4 (1925): 638–44.

Smith, Arthur Warren. "Early Baptist Missionary Leaders: I. Daniel Sharp." *Baptist Missionary Magazine*, September 1909, 336–38.

Smith, Edward D. *Climbing Jacob's Ladder: The Rise of Black Churches in Eastern American Cities, 1740–1877*. Washington, DC: Smithsonian Institution.

Smith, Jesse Fowler. "Suffield and the Baptists." *Chronicle: A Baptist Historical Quarterly* 13, no. 1 (1950): 5–17.

Smith, Ned B. "A Historian's Notebook." In *Canaan Bicentennial 1761–1961 Program*, 5–29. Canaan, NH: Reporter Press, 1961.

Smyth, Thomas. *The Complete Works of Rev. Thomas Smyth, D.D.* Edited by John William Flinn and Jean Adger Flinn. 10 vols. Columbia, SC: Bryan, 1908–12.

Snow, Edwin M. *Alphabetical Index of the Births, Marriages, and Deaths, Recorded in Providence from 1636 to 1850 Inclusive.* Providence, RI: Rider, 1879.

Sorin, Gerald. *The New York Abolitionists: A Case Study of Political Radicalism.* Westport, CT: Greenwood, 1971.

Speicher, Anna M. *The Religious World of Antislavery Women: Spirituality in the Lives of Five Abolitionist Lecturers.* Syracuse, NY: Syracuse University Press, 2000.

Stanton, Elizabeth Cady. *Eighty Years and More: Reminiscences 1815–1897.* New York: Fisher Unwin, 1898.

A Statement of Facts, Respecting the School for Colored Females, in Canterbury, Ct., Together with a Report of the Late Trial of Miss Prudence Crandall. Brooklyn, CT: Advertiser Press, 1833.

State of Connecticut. *The Code of 1650, being a Compilation of the Earliest Laws and Orders of the General Court of Connecticut: Also, the Constitution, or Civil Compact, Entered into and Adopted by the Towns of Windsor, Hartford, and Wethersfield in 1638–9; to Which Is Added Some Extracts from the Laws and Judicial Proceedings of New-Haven Colony, Commonly Called Blue Laws.* Hartford, CT: S. Andrus, 1822.

State of Connecticut. *The Public Statute Laws of the State of Connecticut: Compiled in Obedience to a Resolve of the General Assembly, Passed May 1838, to Which Is Prefixed the Declaration of Independence, Constitution of the United States, and Constitution of the State of Connecticut. Published by the Authority of the State.* Hartford, CT: John L. Boswell, 1839.

Stattler, Rick. "Finding Guide to the Moses Brown Papers." From notes of Pam Norbeth. Rhode Island Historical Society, 1996. https://www.rihs.org/mssinv/Mss313.htm#unittitle.

Staudenraus, P. J. *The African Colonization Movement, 1816–1865.* New York: Columbia University Press, 1961.

Steinkraus, Warren E. "Martin Luther King's Personalism and Non-Violence." *Journal of the History of Ideas* 34, no. 1 (1973): 97–111.

Sterling, Dorothy, ed. *We Are Your Sisters: Black Women in the Nineteenth Century.* New York: Norton, 1997.

Stevens, Elizabeth C. *Elizabeth Buffum Chace and Lillie Chace Wyman: A Century of Abolitionist, Suffragist, and Workers' Rights Activism.* Jefferson, NC: McFarland, 2003.

Stewart, James Brewer. "The Emergence of Racial Modernity and the Rise of the White North, 1790–1840." *Journal of the Early Republic* 18, no. 2 (1998): 181–217.

Stewart, James Brewer. "The New Haven Negro College and the Meanings of Race in New England, 1776–1870." *New England Quarterly* 76, no. 3 (2003): 323–55.

Stewart, Maria. *Productions of Mrs. Maria W. Stewart, Presented to the First African Baptist Church and Society of the City of Boston*. Boston: Friends of Freedom and Virtue, 1835. Facsimile edition in *Spiritual Narratives*, edited by Sue Houchins. New York: Oxford University Press, 1988.

Strane, Susan. *A Whole-Souled Woman: Prudence Crandall and the Education of Black Women*. New York: Norton, 1990.

Strother, Horatio T. *The Underground Railroad in Connecticut*. Middletown, CT: Wesleyan University Press, 1962.

Stubbert, J. R. *"Set Thee Up Way-Marks": Historical Sermon Delivered in the Second Baptist Church, Suffield, Conn., on the Seventy-Fifth Anniversary of Its History, Sunday, May 23, 1880*. Hartford, CT: Case, Lockwood, and Brainard, 1882.

Sumner, Charles. *Charles Sumner, His Complete Works*. 20 vols. Boston: Lee and Shepard, 1900.

Sweeney, Douglas A. *Nathaniel Taylor, New Haven Theology, and the Legacy of Jonathan Edwards*. New York: Oxford University Press, 2003.

Swerdlow, Amy. "Abolition's Conservative Sisters: The Ladies' New York City Anti-Slavery Societies, 1834–1840." In *The Abolitionist Sisterhood: Women's Political Culture in Antebellum America*, edited by Jean Fagan Yellin and John C. Van Horne, 31–44. Ithaca, NY: Cornell University Press, 1994.

Swift, David E. "Black Presbyterian Attacks on Racism: Samuel Cornish, Theodore Wright, and Their Contemporaries." In *Black Apostles at Home and Abroad: Afro-Americans and the Christian Mission from the Revolution to Reconstruction*, edited by David W. Wills and Richard Newman, 43–84. Boston: Hall, 1982.

Swift, David E. *Black Prophets of Justice: Activist Clergy before the Civil War*. Baton Rouge: Louisiana State University Press, 1989.

Tappan, Lewis. *The Life of Arthur Tappan*. New York: Hurd and Houghton, 1871. Facsimile reprint, Westport, CT: Negro Universities Press, 1970.

Thayer, George B. *Pedal and Path: Across the Continent Awheel and Afoot*. Hartford, CT: Evening Post Association, 1887.

Thomas, Calvin. "James Hulme Canfield." *Columbia University Quarterly* 11, no. 3 (1909): 299–308.

Thomas, George M. *Revivalism and Cultural Change: Christianity, Nation Building, and the Market in the Nineteenth-Century United States*. Chicago: University of Chicago Press, 1989.

Thompson, Mack. *Moses Brown: Reluctant Reformer*. Chapel Hill: University of North Carolina Press, 1962.

Thornbrough, Emma Lou. *T. Thomas Fortune: Militant Journalist*. Chicago: University of Chicago Press, 1972.

Thornton, Kevin Pierce. "Andrew Harris, Vermont's Forgotten Abolitionist." *Vermont History* 83, no. 2 (2015): 119–56.

Tinniswood, Adrian. *Pirates of Barbary: Corsairs, Conquests, and Captivity in the Seventeenth-Century Mediterranean*. New York: Riverhead, 2010.

Tolstoy, Leo. *Tolstoy's Writings on Civil Disobedience and Non-Violence*. New York: Bergman, 1967.

Tomek, Beverly C. *Pennsylvania Hall: A "Legal Lynching" in the Shadow of the Liberty Bell*. New York: Oxford University Press, 2014.

Townsend, Craig D. *Faith in Their Own Color: Black Episcopalians in Antebellum New York City*. New York: Columbia University Press, 2005.

Tripp, Bernell E. "Mary Miles Bibb: Education and Moral Improvement in the *Voice of the Fugitive*." Paper presented at annual meeting of the Association for Education in Journalism and Mass Communication, Kansas City, 1993.

Trotter, James M. *Music and Some Highly Musical People*. Boston: Lee and Shepard, 1880.

Tucker, Barbara M. "Sarah Harris and the Prudence Crandall School." In *African American Connecticut Explored*, edited by Elizabeth J. Normen, with Stacey K. Close, Katherine J. Harris, and William Frank Mitchell, 155–64. Middletown, CT: Wesleyan University Press, 2013.

Turner, Laura D. "Sarah Harris Fayerweather (1812–1878): School Integrationist." In *Notable Black American Women*, book 2, edited by Jessie Carney Smith, 218–21. New York: Gale Research, 1996.

US Census Bureau. *1870 United States Federal Census, Population Schedule*. Microfilm publication M593, 1,761 rolls. Washington, DC: National Archives and Records Administration, n.d. Ancestry.com.

US Census Bureau. *1860 United States Federal Census, Population Schedule*. Microfilm publication M653, 1,438 rolls. Washington, DC: National Archives and Records Administration, n.d. Ancestry.com.

US Census Bureau. *Fifth Census of the United States, 1830*. Microfilm publication M19, 201 rolls. Records of the Bureau of the Census, Record Group 29. National Archives, Washington, DC. Ancestry.com.

US Census Bureau. *Seventh Census of the United States, 1850*. Microfilm publication M432, 1,009 rolls. Records of the Bureau of the Census, Record Group 29. National Archives, Washington, DC. Ancestry.com.

US Census Bureau. *Sixth Census of the United States, 1840*. Microfilm publication M704, 580 rolls. Records of the Bureau of the Census, Record Group 29. National Archives, Washington, DC. Ancestry.com.

US Census Bureau. *Tenth Census of the United States, 1880*. Microfilm publication T9, 1,454 rolls. Records of the Bureau of the Census, Record Group 29. National Archives, Washington, DC. Ancestry.com.

Van Hoosear, D. H. *The Fillow, Philo, and Philleo Genealogy: A Record of the Descendants of John Fillow, a Huguenot Refugee from France*. Albany, NY: Munsell's, 1888.

Walker, David. *David Walker's Appeal in Four Articles; Together with a Preamble, to the Coloured Citizens of the World, but in Particular, and Very Expressly, to Those of the United States of America*. Edited by Sean Wilentz. Rev. ed. New York: Hill and Wang, 1995.

Walker, David. *David Walker's Appeal to the Coloured Citizens of the World*. Edited and with a new introduction and annotations by Peter Hinks. University Park: Pennsylvania University Press, 2000.

Walker, David. *One Continual Cry: David Walker's Appeal to the Colored Citizens of the World, with an Essay on Its Setting and Meaning*. Edited by Herbert Aptheker. New York: Marzani and Munsell, 1965.

Walker, George E. *The Afro-American in New York City 1827–1860*. New York: Garland, 1993.

Walker, Juliet E. K. *The History of Black Business in America: Capitalism, Race, Entrepreneurship*. New York: Macmillan, 1998.

Wallace, William Allen. *The History of Canaan, New Hampshire*. Edited by James Burns Wallace. Concord, NH: Rumford, 1910.

Walsh, Jeannine B. "Prudence Crandall: A Clarification of the Canterbury Tale and Its Heroine." Thesis abstract, Southern Connecticut State College, 1976.

Ward, Samuel Ringgold. *Autobiography of a Fugitive Negro: His Anti-Slavery Labours in the United States, Canada, and England*. London: Snow, 1855. Reprint, New York: Arno, 1968.

Warner, Robert Austin. *New Haven Negroes: A Social History*. 1940. New York: Arno, 1969.

Washington, Margaret. "'I Am Going Straight to Canada': Women Underground Railroad Activists in the Detroit River Border Zone." In *A Fluid Frontier: Slavery, Resistance, and the Underground Railroad in the Detroit River Borderland*, edited by Karolyn Smardz Frost and Veta Smith Tucker, 165–82. Detroit: Wayne State University Press, 2016.

Waters, Kristin. *Maria W. Stewart and the Roots of Black Political Thought*. Jackson: University of Mississippi Press, 2022.

Watson, John F. *Annals of Philadelphia and Pennsylvania, in the Olden Time; being a Collection of Memoirs, Anecdotes, and Incidents of the City and Its Inhabitants and of the Earliest Settlements of the Inland Part of Pennsylvania, from the Days of the Founders*. Philadelphia: Lippincott, 1870.

Weinbaum, Paul O. *Mobs and Demagogues: The New York Response to Collective Violence in the Early Nineteenth Century*. Ann Arbor, MI: UMI Research Press, 1979.

Weiner, Mark S. *Black Trials: Citizenship from the Beginnings of Slavery to the End of Caste*. New York: Vintage, 2004.

Welch, Marvis. *Prudence Crandall: A Biography*. Manchester, CT: Jason, 1983.

Welch, Vicki S. *And They Were Related, Too: A Study of Eleven Generations of One American Family!* Self-published, XLibris, 2006.

Weld, Ralph Foster. *Slavery in Connecticut*. Committee on Historical Publications, Tercentenary Commission of the State of Connecticut. Pamphlet 37. New Haven, CT: Yale University Press, 1935.

Werner, John M. *Reaping the Bloody Harvest: Race Riots in the United States during the Age of Jackson 1824–1849*. New York: Garland, 1986.

Wesley, Charles. "The Negroes of New York in the Emancipation Movement." *Journal of Negro History* 24, no. 1 (1939): 65–103.

White, David O. "The Crandall School and the Degree of Influence by Garrison and the Abolitionists upon It." *Connecticut Historical Society Bulletin* 43, no. 4 (1978): 97–111.

White, David O. "Prudence Crandall Philleo: Letters from Kansas." Unpublished paper, held by Prudence Crandall Museum, Canterbury, Connecticut, 1972.

White, David O. "Prudence Crandall." Unpublished paper, held by Prudence Crandall Museum. Hartford: Connecticut Historical Commission, 1971.

White, Deborah Gray. *Ar'n't I a Woman? Female Slaves in the Plantation South.* New York: Norton, 1985.

Wicks, Elizabeth. *Address Delivered before the African Female Benevolent Society of Troy on Wednesday, February 12, 1834, to Which Is Annexed an Eulogy on the Death of Mrs. Jane Lessing, with an Address by Eliza A. T. Dungy.* Troy: Buckley, 1834. Reprinted in *Pamphlets of Protest: An Anthology of Early African American Protest Literature, 1790–1860,* edited by Richard Newman, Patrick Rael, and Phillip Lapsansky, 114–21. New York: Routledge, 2001.

Williams, Donald E., Jr. *Prudence Crandall's Legacy: The Fight for Equality in the 1830s, Dred Scott, and Brown v. Board of Education.* Middletown, CT: Wesleyan University Press, 2014.

Williams, Donnie. With Wayne Greenhaw. *The Thunder of Angels: The Montgomery Bus Boycott and the People Who Broke the Back of Jim Crow.* Chicago: Hill, 2006.

Williams, George W. *History of the Negro Race in America, 1619 to 1880.* Vol. 2 of 2 vols. New York: G. P. Putnam's Sons, 1883.

Williams, Heather Andrea. *Self-Taught: African American Education in Slavery and Freedom.* Chapel Hill: University of North Carolina Press, 2005.

Williams, Peter (Jr). *A Discourse, Delivered on the Death of Captain Paul Cuffe, before the New York African Institution, in the African Methodist Episcopal Zion Church, October 21, 1817.* New York: Young, 1817. Ebook.

Williams, Peter (Jr). *An Oration on the Abolition of the Slave Trade; Delivered in the African Church, in the City of New-York, January 1, 1808.* New York: Samuel Wood, 1808.

Willson, Joseph. *The Elite of Our People: Joseph Willson's Sketches of Black Upper-Class Life in Antebellum Philadelphia.* Edited by Julie Winch. University Park: Pennsylvania State University Press, 2000.

Wilmoth, Ann Greenwood. "Pittsburgh and the Blacks: A Short History, 1780–1875." PhD diss., Pennsylvania State University, State College, 1975.

Wilson, Clint C., II. *Whither the Black Press: Glorious Part, Uncertain Future.* Self-published, Xlibris, 2014.

Winch, Julie. *A Gentleman of Color: The Life of James Forten.* New York: Oxford University Press, 2002.

Winch, Julie. "The Leaders of Philadelphia's Black Community, 1778–1848." PhD diss., Bryn Mawr College, 1982.

Winch, Julie. "'You Have Talents—Only Cultivate Them': Philadelphia's Black Female Literary Societies and the Abolitionist Crusade." In *Women and Sisters: The Antislavery Feminists in American Culture,* edited by Jean Fagan Yellin, 101–18. New Haven, CT: Yale University Press, 1989.

Winthrop, John. "Reasons to Be Considered for . . . the Intended Plantation in New England." In *The Puritans in America,* edited by Alan Heimert, 70–74.

Cambridge, MA: Harvard University Press, 1985. https://doi.org/10.4159/9780674038493-014.

Woodson, Carter G. "Anthony Benezet." *Journal of Negro History* 2, no. 1 (1917): 47–48.

Woodson, Carter G. *Free Negro Heads of Families in the United States in 1830, Together with a Brief Treatment of the Free Negro.* Washington, DC: Association for the Study of Negro Life and History, 1925.

Woodson, Carter G, ed. *The Mind of the Negro as Reflected in Letters Written during the Crisis, 1800–1860.* Washington, DC: Association for the Study of Negro Life and History, 1926.

Woodson, Carter G, ed. *Negro Orators and Their Orations.* Washington, DC: Associated, 1925.

Woodward, Carl R. "A Profile in Dedication: Sarah Harris and the Fayerweather Family." *New England Galaxy* 25, no. 1 (1973): 3–14.

Wright, Theodore S. "The Progress of the Antislavery Cause." In *Negro Orators and Their Orations*, edited by Carter G. Woodson, 86–92. Washington, DC: Associated, 1925.

Wyatt-Brown, Bertram. *Lewis Tappan and the Evangelical War against Slavery.* Cleveland: Press of Case Western Reserve University, 1969.

Yacovone, Donald. *Samuel Joseph May and the Dilemmas of the Liberal Persuasion, 1797–1871.* Philadelphia: Temple University Press, 1991.

Yannielli, Joseph. "The Logic of the Antislavery Movement." Paper presented October 21, 2015, Wilberforce Institute for the Study of Slavery and Emancipation. *Digital Histories @ Yale.* http://digitalhistories.yctl.org/tag/mendi-mission/.

Yee, Shirley J. *Black Women Abolitionists: A Study in Activism, 1828–1860.* Knoxville: University of Tennessee Press, 1992.

Yellin, Jean Fagan. *Women and Sisters: The Antislavery Feminists in American Culture.* New Haven, CT: Yale University Press, 1989.

Young, R. J. *Antebellum Black Activists: Race, Gender, and Self.* New York: Garland, 1996.

Zaeske, Susan. *Signatures of Citizenship: Petitioning, Antislavery, and Women's Political Identity.* Chapel Hill: University of North Carolina Press, 2003.

Ziegler, Valerie. *The Advocates of Peace in Antebellum America.* Bloomington: Indiana University Press, 1992.

Index

JENNIFER RYCENGA is a professor emerita of comparative religious studies and humanities at San José State University. She is the coeditor of *Frontline Feminisms: Women, War, and Resistance.*

The University of Illinois Press
is a founding member of the
Association of University Presses.

———————————————————

Composed in 10.5/13 Mercury Text
with Avenir display
by Jim Proefrock
at the University of Illinois Press
Manufactured by Sheridan Books, Inc.

University of Illinois Press
1325 South Oak Street
Champaign, IL 61820-6903
www.press.uillinois.edu